Gangster Warlords

El Narco: Inside Mexico's Criminal Insurgency

Gangster Warlords

Drug Dollars, Killing Fields, and the New Politics of Latin America

IOAN GRILLO

BLOOMSBURY PRESS

NEW ᵧ   ᵢNEY

Bloomsbury Press
An imprint of Bloomsbury Publishing Plc

1385 Broadway	50 Bedford Square
New York	London
NY 10018	WC1B 3DP
USA	UK

www.bloomsbury.com

BLOOMSBURY and the Diana logo are trademarks of Bloomsbury Publishing Plc

First published 2016

Excerpt from C-*Train and Thirteen Mexicans* copyright © 2002 by Jimmy Santiago Baca.
Used by permission of Grove/Atlantic, Inc. Any third party use of this material outside of
this publication is prohibited.

Lyrics from "Don't Touch the President" copyright © 2010 by Bunny Wailer.
Used by permission.

Lyrics from "Los Caballeros Templarios" copyright © 2011 by BuKnas de Culiacan.
Used by permission.

ISBN:	HB:	978-1-62040-379-2
	ePub:	978-1-62040-380-8

Library of Congress Cataloging-in-Publication Data has been
applied for.

2 4 6 8 10 9 7 5 3 1

Typeset by RefineCatch Limited, Bungay, Suffolk
Printed and bound in the U.S.A. by Thomson-Shore Inc., Dexter, Michigan

To find out more about our authors and books visit www.bloomsbury.com.
Here you will find extracts, author interviews, details of forthcoming events and
the option to sign up for our newsletters.

Bloomsbury books may be purchased for business or promotional use.
For information on bulk purchases please contact Macmillan Corporate and
Premium Sales Department at specialmarkets@macmillan.com.

Contents

PART I

War?

CHAPTER 1

This book is about the move from the Cold War to a chain of crime wars soaking Latin America and the Caribbean in blood. But it starts in the United States. Specifically, in a Barnes and Noble bookshop in a mall in El Paso, Texas.

I am sitting in the bookshop café, nursing my third cup of coffee and flicking through a pile of new books. As you do with new books, I am eyeing the photos, skimming the intros, and just feeling and smelling the paper. I am also waiting for a drug trafficker who has spent four decades delivering the products of Mexican gangsters to all corners of the United States.

The man I am waiting for is no criminal warlord controlling a fiefdom in Latin America. He's a white New Yorker with a university education. That is why I want to start the book here. Latin American journalists complain the U.S. side of the equation is never examined. Who are the partners of the cartels wreaking havoc south of the Rio Grande, they ask. Where is the American *narco*? Here, I found one.

A curious twist of fate led me to this meeting. A fellow Brit was cycling through the southwest United States on an extended holiday. Texas was nice, but he fancied something edgier, so he slipped over the border to Chihuahua, Mexico. Unwittingly, he entered one of the most violent spheres in the Mexican drug war, venturing into small towns to the west of Ciudad Juárez, at the time the world's most murderous city. He didn't do too badly, hanging out in cantinas and raising glasses with shady locals. Until gangsters held him in a house, threatened to cut his head off, and got him to call his wife in England and plead for a ransom payment.

Attacks on wealthy foreigners in Mexico are actually very rare, but there have been sporadic cases, some of them deadly. In this case, the thugs had jumped at an opportunity that fell in their lap. Thankfully, they released the Brit on receipt of the cash, and he made it home unscathed. He kept in contact with one of the people he had met on the border, an older man called Robert. While Robert knew the kidnappers, he apparently wasn't involved. He is the man I am going to meet now, one of the gangsters' U.S. connections.

The British cyclist had put us in touch, and I talked to Robert over e-mail and then phone to arrange the get-together. He lives on the Mexican side of the border in one of the Chihuahuan towns. But I told him I didn't want to go there after the kidnapping and suggested we meet in El Paso, a stone's throw from Juárez but one of the safest cities in the United States. In a Barnes and Noble bookshop. Who would hold you up in a Barnes and Noble?

As I finish my beverage, I spy Robert strolling toward me. He probably spotted me first. He is in his sixties, in jeans and a baseball cap, with sunworn skin and a raspy voice. I get yet more coffee, and we chat. He's good company. Soon we decide we want something stronger and move on to a cowboy-themed bar in the mall where they serve local brews in ridiculous-size glasses. I hear Robert's tale as we sip from the flagons.

It goes back to 1968, when the United States was in the midst of the hippie movement and fighting its hottest Cold War battle in Vietnam; when dictatorships ruled most of Latin America, and a recently martyred Che Guevara inspired guerrillas across the continent. Robert is from upstate New York, but in 1968 he went to university in New Mexico. Here he had the fate of landing a roommate from El Paso who had a cousin in Ciudad Juárez. His roommate told him he could buy marijuana for forty dollars a kilo from his cousin. This lit a fuse in Robert's mind; he knew that back home in New York, this amount sold for three hundred dollars.

The basic business of importing is buying for a dollar and selling for two. But with drugs, Robert realized, he could buy for a dollar and sell for more than seven. And he didn't even need to advertise. This was after the summer of love, and American youngsters were desperate for ganja from wherever they could get it, feeding a mushrooming industry south of the border.

"I was young, I was broke, and I was hungry," Robert says. "Then marijuana came like a blessing . . . We scraped our money together for the first load. When it came through, we bought another. Then another."

It is hard for most of us to fathom a business with a markup of 650 percent. You put in fifteen hundred bucks and you get back more than ten grand. You put in ten and get back seventy-five. And in two more deals you can be a multimillionaire. Narco finances turn economics inside out.

As Robert made regular drives back east with his car trunk stuffed with ganja, he could go through school without even having loans. "I was living like a rich kid, driving a nice car, living in a big place," he says.

When he graduated, he had a business to go into. He traveled to Chihuahua to buy bulk loads of marijuana and partied in Juárez discos with rising drug lords. He spread out his commerce to new horizons. He traveled to Mississippi and Alabama, where he sold to the Dixie Mafia, a network of villains in the Appalachian states. He went to San Francisco to sell to students on the lawns of Berkeley. He bought houses and nightclubs with suitcases of cash.

However, Robert's drug-dealing dream hit a wall in the late seventies when he got nabbed by agents from the Drug Enforcement Administration. The DEA did what it calls a "buy and bust." An undercover agent pretended to be a dealer and asked for three hundred pounds of grass from Robert's partner. After police nabbed the partner in his car, they stormed Robert's luxury house, arrested him in his swimming trunks, and grabbed sacks of weed from the kitchen and garage.

This is the flip side of narco economics. Robert splurged on lawyers, got his assets seized, and served close to a decade in federal prison. Yet after he got out, he went back into the trade, moving ganja and a little cocaine with a new generation of Mexican traffickers. This time, he kept a lower profile, shifting smaller amounts to stay off the radar. He carried on past middle age, through marriages and divorces, booms and busts, through the end of the Cold War and the opening of democracy across the Americas. By the time he hit his sixties, he suffered from chronic asthma and heart disease. And he was still smuggling weed.

When Robert started trafficking drugs, his Mexican colleagues were a handful of growers and smugglers earning chump change. They needed Americans like him to get into the market. But over the decades, the narco trafficking networks grew into an industry that is worth tens of billions of dollars and stretches from Mexico into the Caribbean to Colombia to Brazil. Mexican gangsters transformed into cartels and established their own people stateside, often their family members. Two of their biggest distributors were the Chicago-born twin sons of a Durango heroin king. While Robert had been a big shot back in the day, he fell to the position of a small-time smuggler.

South of the border, the cartels spent their billions building armies of assassins who carry out massacres comparable to those in war zones and outgun police. They have diversified from drugs to a portfolio of crimes including extortion, kidnapping, theft of crude oil, and even wildcat mining. And they have grown to control the governments of entire cities and states in Latin America.

"Back in the old days, it was nothing like this," Robert says. "They were just smugglers. Now they prey on their communities. They have become too powerful. And many of the young guys working for them are crazy fucking killers who are high on crystal meth. You can't deal with these people."

I ask Robert if he feels guilty about pumping these organizations with cash year after year. They could never have gotten so big without working with Americans.

He looks into his glass for a while and sighs. "It is just business," he says. "They should have legalized many of these drugs a long time ago."

Some months after I interview him, Robert is arrested again, driving over the border with a trunk full of ganja. He is sixty-eight. He spends four months in prison, pleads guilty, and is given supervised release on time served and medical grounds. He tells the judge his trafficking career is over.

Flip from El Paso over the Rio Grande and fourteen hundred miles south onto a hillside in southern Mexico. I am in the mountains in the state of Guerrero, close to where traffickers grow marijuana and produce heroin. The fate of these hills is locked with that of smugglers in Texas and drug users across America by the pretty green and pink plants here. It's the domain of a cartel called Guerreros Unidos, or Warriors United, a small but deadly splinter of an older trafficking network. The hill is beautiful, thick with pine trees and bright orange flowers. Strange crickets jump on the earth, and exquisite butterflies arc through the air.

The smell of death is overwhelming. It's like walking into a butcher's shop stuffed with decaying meat; putrid, yet somehow a little sweet. While I would describe the smell as sickening, it's not noxious. It's a movie cliché that people throw up when they see or smell corpses. That doesn't happen in real life. Corpses don't make you physically nauseous. The sickness is deep down, more an emotional repulsion. It's the smell and sight of our own mortality.

The stench of rotting human flesh is all over this hill from a series of pits where police and soldiers are pulling out corpses. They are dank, maggot-ridden holes that the victims probably dug themselves. The corpses are charred, mutilated, decomposed.

In Mexico, they call this a *narcofosa*, or drug trafficking grave. But many of the victims here are neither drug traffickers nor police officers, nor in any way connected to the world of narcotics. They are shopkeepers, laborers, students who somehow ran afoul of the Warriors' criminal empire. The troops dig up thirty corpses on this site, near the town of Iguala. And it's just one of a series of narcofosas dotting these hills.

Residents in close-by shacks describe in hushed voices how the Warriors brought their victims here. They would come at night in convoys of pickups, openly holding Kalashnikov rifles to their terrified hostages. Often they were with police officers. The Warriors were alleged to control most of the Iguala police force as well as the town's mayor and his wife.[1]

Some of the corpses have been here for months, but no one came searching—until an atrocity that made world headlines. On September 26, 2014, Iguala's police and their colleagues, the Warrior gunmen, attacked student teachers, killing three and abducting forty-three.

The global media finally learned where Iguala was. How could forty-three students disappear off the face of the earth? It sounded like Boko Haram in Nigeria kidnapping schoolchildren, but this was right next to the United States. Thousands of troops poured in, uncovering mass graves like the one that I am standing in. But they still couldn't find the students.

After more than a month, they followed the trail to a garbage dump ten miles away. Mexico's attorney general said the Warriors murdered the forty-three there, burning their corpses on a huge bonfire with wood, tires, and diesel and throwing the remains into the nearby river San Juan.[2] Police found charred bones in a bag, which was allegedly in the river, and sent them to a laboratory in Austria. It confirmed that the DNA in a bone fragment matched that of one of the disappeared.

However, family members and many journalists refused to believe the government's account. Mexican prosecutors have a history of cover-ups that have left widespread distrust. An independent report by experts also rejected many of the official conclusions. The families demanded police keep searching for the other forty-two students and further investigate the web of corruption that led to this atrocity.

Mexico seemed to have gotten numb to murder. Between 2007 and 2014, drug cartels and the security forces fighting them had killed more than eighty-three thousand people, according to a count by Mexico's government intelligence agency.[3] Some claimed it was many more. I covered massacres where nearby residents seemed eerily detached. When an individual goes through a traumatic experience, the gut reaction is to block it out. Communities do the same. People became weary of killers, cartels, and carnage. Victims become statistics.

Iguala changed that. The fact that the victims were students, the blatant police involvement, the inept government response—all shook the heart of Mexican society. Maybe the moment had just come. At the end of 2014, people took to the streets in hundreds of thousands to protest narco corruption and violence. The faces of the disappeared students filled posters on Mexico City walls and were held up in solidarity from Argentina to Austria to Australia. They were humans, not numbers.

The attacks and protests shattered an illusion called Mexico's Moment. It was a mirage conjured up by the team of President Enrique Peña Nieto and bought by some American pundits and media. It said that drug cartel violence wasn't really that bad, that we could sweep it aside and talk about an expanding Mexican middle class, spring break in Cancún, and iPad sales.

Iguala put violence back on the front page. It highlighted the problems that had been building up for years—of cartels that have become an alternate power controlling mayors and governors, of their tenuous links to federal security forces, of the international community failing to change a disastrous drug policy. It made many realize that the problems will not go away if we ignore them but only if we confront them and change things.

In a painful irony, the disappeared students in Iguala had planned to attend a march commemorating a massacre of students in Mexico in 1968. This takes us back to the height of the Cold War, the era of dictatorships and Guevara guerrillas (and when Robert first bought weed in Juárez). As Mexico was about to open the Olympics that year, soldiers shot dead at least forty-four people at a protest in Tlatelolco square in Mexico City.[4] The Iguala attack on students created an agonizing equation:

46 years after soldiers killed
44 protesters,
46 students were murdered or disappeared

* * *

Despite this dark similarity, the atrocities reflect the different worlds of the Cold War in the twentieth century and the crime wars in the twenty-first. The Tlatelolco massacre was almost certainly orchestrated from the top. The one-party government of the Institutional Revolutionary Party, or PRI, dubbed the Perfect Dictatorship, was worried students would disrupt the first ever Olympics in Latin America.[5] It massacred protesters to scare them off the streets. This was in line with authoritarian regimes across the continent in the era, fighting descent with bullets.

In contrast, Iguala reflected the brave and twisted new world of narco power. Mexico now has a multiparty democracy, and the supposed leftist opposition governed Iguala. But the real power was this mysterious cartel, smuggling drugs, controlling politicians, making alliances with security forces. It is a dark force of shady interests that we struggle to even see.

Whereas the motive for repressing protesters in the 1960s is clear, the Iguala attacks left many stupefied as to why a drug cartel would target students. The trainee teachers are known for disruptive protests and had commandeered buses from the local bus terminal. Were gangsters attacking students as a form of terror, working with corrupt authorities to clamp down on protests? Or did the students unwittingly take a bus in which the cartel had stashed a heroin shipment? Or in their paranoia, did the gunmen think the students worked with a rival cartel. Or were the corrupt police defending a public event of their narco mayor and his wife? Whatever the mechanics, the specter is of a town controlled by gangsters responding to a public order incident with mass murder.

As hundreds of thousands marched on the streets against the terror, protesters called Iguala a state crime, putting it alongside the massacres of dictators. It was a provocative point. There was no proof that President Peña Nieto was involved in the attack. But city police officers, who are agents of the state, were on the frontline of it. Journalists also raised questions about what soldiers and federal police were doing during the shooting.[6] In other cases, federal agents have been convicted of working with drug traffickers in Mexico. It sparks a debate about the responsibility of government when chunks of state apparatus are captured by cartels.

While the Cold War divided the world into camps, it had a certain moral clarity for all sides. People saw themselves in struggles of good against evil. Those who died protesting an authoritarian regime, whether it be right wing or Stalinist, could see it as a fight for freedom. But most murders in Latin America's new crime wars leave no such satisfaction. People seem to die for nothing.

The bloodshed in Mexico has grabbed the world's attention as it runs right up to the Rio Grande (and occasionally into the United States). Mexican politicians retort there is similar violence across the region. They are wrong to use this as an excuse. But they are right that fighting between shady criminal gunmen and trigger-happy troops rages in many corners of the Americas.

In the *favelas* of Brazil, the crime "commandos" are in close urban combat with police and rivals, a conflict that has killed even more than in Mexico—and which U.S. Navy SEALs go to train in.[7] Honduras became the most murderous country outside a declared war zone as Mara gangs displace thousands, some who flee to the United States as refugees. The ghettos of Kingston, Jamaica, are the killing fields of posses, along with one of the most homicidal police forces in the world.

Why are the Americas awash in blood at the dawn of the twenty-first century? How, after the United States declared Cold War victories in the region, did it unravel so fast? And why are American politicians so mum about these battles that have killed more than many traditional war zones?

The fact that these crime militias have cropped up simultaneously in different countries is no coincidence but shows a regional trend, a product of historical circumstances. And while these conflicts are in separate countries, drugs, guns, and gangsters float between them. It is a chain of crime wars slicing through the continent.

This bloodshed is not in the poorest, least developed region of the world. It takes place in industrializing societies with a growing middle class. Latin American and Caribbean countries continue to modernize, building gleaming shopping malls, cinema multiplexes, and designer gyms, private schools and world-class universities. Millions of visitors sun themselves in top-notch resorts on the countries' golden beaches. This convinces some surprised visitors that the countries are on a quick path to the First World. There is real growth taking place.

At the same time, sprawling slums are home to ultraviolent gangs with links to politicians and businessmen. The parallel universes of crime-ridden ghettos and leafy middle-class neighborhoods live side by side, sometimes meeting and clashing.

In this changing landscape, a new generation of kingpins has emerged along with their own cult followings and guerrilla hit squads. These super villains from Mexico to Jamaica to Brazil to Colombia are no longer just drug traffickers, but a weird hybrid of criminal CEO, gangster rock star, and paramilitary general. They fill the popular imagination as demonic antiheroes. Not only do they feature in underground songs in the drug world—they are re-created in telenovelas, movies, and even video games simulating their new warfare.

And what they do affects us all. Over the last two decades, these crime families and their friends in politics and business have taken over much of the world's trade in narcotics, guns, and humans as well as delved into oil, gold, cars, and kidnapping. Their networks stretch throughout the United States into Europe, Asia, and Australia. And their chain of goods and services arrives at all our doorsteps.

In this book, I attempt to make better sense of these hybrid criminal organizations by tracking a path through the new battlefields of the Americas. Traveling across the continent, I focus on four crime families: the Red Commando in Brazil, the Shower Posse in Jamaica, the Mara Salvatrucha in Central America, and the Knights Templar in Mexico. They are puzzling postmodern networks that mix gangs, mafias, death squads, religious cults, and urban guerrillas.

When you see these groups in action, you can identify clear parallels in how they operate. Similar systems of spies watch who comes into villages in Michoacán, Mexico, and favelas in Rio de Janeiro. Gangs clear neighborhoods to create defensive buffer zones in both San Pedro Sula, Honduras, and the garrisons of Kingston, Jamaica. Gangsters hold their own trials in the suburbs of São Paulo, as they do in the Mexican mountains. These parallels paint a clearer model of what these groups are and how they operate. The invisible crime system takes some form.

Gangster militias are both products of violent societies and contributors to their increasing bloodiness. Between 2000 and 2010, murder rates rose 11 percent in Latin America and the Caribbean, while they fell in most of the world.[8] Eight of the ten countries with the highest homicide rates are now in the region, as are forty-three of the world's fifty most violent cities.[9] With so few murders being solved, it's impossible to say exactly how many died at the hands of cartels and commandos. But organized crime has a big presence in all the countries with the highest rates.

When you tally up the total body count, the numbers are staggering. Between the dawn of the new millennium and 2010, more than a million people across Latin America and the Caribbean were murdered.[10] It's a cocaine-fueled holocaust.

Politicians are confounded about how to handle this gangster power and bloodshed. Governments from Mexico City to Brasília send out troops with shoot-to-kill policies while denying they are fighting low-intensity wars. After shocking attacks on police in São Paulo, officers are alleged to have gone on a revenge killing spree and murdered almost as many people in ten days as Brazil's military dictatorship did in two decades.[11] In some cases, politicians are in league with the gangsters and are part of the problem. But politicians aren't the sole cause of this mess. Others may not be allied with narco kingpins but genuinely struggle to find a policy that works. Some governments have experimented with new ideas, such as organizing gang truces, as in El Salvador, or offering disarmament deals, as in Colombia—with varying degrees of success.

Washington has no coherent strategy. The United States continues to spend billions on a global war on drugs, while there is little enthusiasm at home for the fight. It bankrolls armies across Latin America, from Mexico to Honduras to Colombia—and U.S. courts give asylum to refugees fleeing those same soldiers. Diplomats cozy up to their Latin American counterparts by saying they only face generic gang problems, but then Pentagon officials rock the boat by screaming that Mexico is losing control to cartels. Faced with such contradictions, politicians often take refuge in the default option: ignoring it.

But this is no longer a problem that politicians can afford to ignore. The gangster economy affects people now: from the gas in your car, to the gold in your jewelry, to your tax dollars (or euros, or pounds) financing the war on drugs. The bloodshed may be concentrated outside U.S. borders, but all the major groups move money and merchandise throughout the United States and have operatives lurking in its cities. Some have attacked U.S. agents abroad. Others have carried out murders on U.S. soil.

The web of the four crime families in this book stretches across the hemisphere, leading to all kinds of unlikely places. It spins off to lime prices in New York bars, British secret agents, World Cup soccer stars, bids to hold the Olympic Games, questions over the start of the London riots. In the summer of 2014, it was linked to sixty-seven thousand unaccompanied children arriving at the U.S. southern border, causing what President Barack Obama called a humanitarian crisis. While not all had run from bullets, some showed clear evidence they would be murdered if they went home. Less publicized was that tens of thousands of adults from the region were arriving on the southern border asking for political asylum. Some people ask why it matters if neighboring countries fall to pieces. This is one of the reasons.

CHAPTER 2

Just south of the Rio Grande, a path marks a line of death drawn by one of the most brutal bands of murderers the Americas have ever known. The criminal army known as the Zetas has butchered victims across much of Mexico as well as in Texas and Guatemala. But the sites of their five worst massacres lie along a stretch of three hundred miles roughly following the curve of the U.S.-Mexico border. One end of this line sits forty miles from Eagle Pass, Texas, a peaceful sleepy town that was the first U.S. settlement on the river. The other swaddles a series of lagoons that flow into the Gulf of Mexico. The sites are in farmhouses, fields, and on city streets.

I retrace this line of death over three days traveling with veteran border journalist Juan Alberto Cedillo in his beat-up Volkswagen. I wrote news reports on most of the massacres soon after they happened, but I want to get a better sense of the geography of this terror. I also want to document as much as I can about the sites while they can still be identified. Four of them have no plaques to remember the horrors and their victims. Many here, especially those in power, don't want to be reminded of the carnage that has taken place in one of the most developed regions in Latin America. They want to forget.

The most western site is by a small town called Allende in arid countryside dotted with cattle ranches. The grayish land is flat and plain, the town relatively prosperous from border trade and beef. In February 2014, police and soldiers trekked through barren fields here to dig up a ranch where the Zetas had dissolved bodies in acid inside metal barrels. The Zetas called it "a kitchen."[1] When we visit, I find there are still scattered plastic cans that contained the industrial acids used for this melting of flesh.

Police were searching for hundreds of people who had gone missing from the area. But they couldn't work out exactly how many had died on this macabre ranch as they only found bones or stubborn chunks of tissue that had survived the toxic mix. Excavating the farmhouses and digging up other nearby ranches, they gathered about five hundred body parts, from skulls to bits of toes, and shipped them to a laboratory in Mexico City where they are still stored.

In trying to comprehend this violence, I have interviewed paid assassins, from teenagers to seasoned middle-aged murderers. Tracing their life stories, I can explain how they are pulled into the ranks of organized crime, trained to kill, and gradually take more and more lives. They have told me how they separate themselves from the act of murder by seeing it as a job, by bottling guilt deep inside. But seeing slaughter on this scale still leaves me incredulous as to how a cartel could commit such an atrocity. It is not a crime scene, but a death camp.

We follow this geography of horror into the sprawling city of Monterrey, Mexico, home to global beer and cement companies. In the heart of the town sits the charred remains of a casino that the Zetas set afire in 2011 while it was full of people playing bingo and slot machines. Fifty-two customers and employees suffocated or burned to death. The victims included wealthy locals, and this is the one site that families managed to get authorities to make a memorial for; an obelisk with Venetian blue tiles was finally inaugurated in August 2014 on the third anniversary of the tragedy. "For those who pass these waters, stop the violence in our society and wash the tears of those who suffer from it," reads the message.

Another twenty miles to the east, we drive through Cadereyta Jiménez, home to one of Mexico's biggest oil refineries. On a road into the town in 2012, the Zetas dumped forty-nine decapitated corpses that they had also chopped hands and feet off of. The logistics alone of holding, butchering, and transporting so many victims are hard to fathom. Two years later, only eight were identified. It's hard to trace people who have no faces or fingerprints.

Families from across Mexico trawl these sites, and nearby morgues, to see if their loved ones are among the victims. The Mexican government revealed in 2014 that more than twenty-three thousand people had disappeared in the country in seven years, with the missing concentrated in drug trafficking hot spots. One mother in Monterrey described to me how she watched her eighteen-year-old son, a philosophy student, be marched away by a group of thugs with Kalashnikovs. After three years of searching she has still not found him, or his body. Her face was a mask of grief. This lack of closure devastates people psychologically.[2]

The road southeast takes us to the site of the last two massacres, near San Fernando, Tamaulipas, a farming town that has become synonymous with Zeta violence. Frustrated by being so associated with bloodshed, San Fernando's mayor is desperate for other things to be remembered by. In April 2014, he organized local fishermen and chefs to make the world's biggest shrimp cocktail, a titanic soup that was recorded in the Guinness Book of Records at more than a metric ton. When I visit the town hall, I am shown videos of cooks pouring shrimp from an endless line of plastic containers into a monumental cup that looks like something from *Land of the Giants*.

San Fernando has deep horrors to run from. In 2011, soldiers unearthed 193 corpses in fields on the outskirts of town. The Zetas had pulled many of the victims out of cars and busses during a murder spree that lasted months. Most had their skulls smashed or had been stabbed rather than shot. It is reported the Zetas made some victims fight each other in gladiatorial style combats, using hammers and knives to slay each other.[3]

Finally, down a long dirt road lies a barn where the Zetas gunned down seventy-two people in 2010. It might have been the biggest massacre of unarmed civilians in one moment in Mexico since General Pancho Villa killed almost all the men of a mining town in 1915.[4]

The barn victims were undocumented immigrants heading to the United States in search of a better life. Hailing from Honduras, El Salvador, Guatemala, Ecuador, and Brazil, they had traveled thousands of miles, crossing jungles and mountains, and finally hoped to see Texas by nightfall. One woman was heavily pregnant. The Zetas blindfolded them, bound their hands, and lay them on the ground. Then they lined up and fired hundreds of bullets into them.

To get to the barn we drive down fifteen miles of dirt road through fields of dark red sorghum, a crop used as animal feed, which stretches out like a bloodstained carpet. The barn has been left derelict, its bullet-ridden doors hanging off their hinges. As we approach, two enormous and beautiful white owls flutter out and arch into the sky. I remember how many cultures link owls with death.

The fields are abandoned, weeds growing where the corpses lay. You could drive past and never know what happened here.

*   *   *

My mental vision of war was first shaped by my grandfather. He was drafted into the British army when he was eighteen and spent the end of the First World War wading through trenches in France, resisting the final German advance and pushing the Wehrmacht into an armistice. Six decades later, when I was a toddler, he mimed to me how he would thrust forward with his bayonet.

This war of a century ago bears little resemblance to the violence in the Americas today; obviously it was on a far greater scale than these crime wars. But I like to compare it for one reason. It reminds us that Europeans can be just as barbaric in committing murder and atrocities. Some look for cultural reasons to explain the severity of violence by groups such as the Zetas. They ask whether there is a deep fascination with death in the Mexican psyche; or whether Jamaica has one of the world's worst murder rates because it's a country of former slaves who have anger in their blood. But history tells us that every culture is capable of horrific violence. We are all barbarians. I prefer to search for structural and political causes that lead people to shed blood.

My second vivid image of conflict came in the 1980s during the last freeze of the Cold War. Still a child, I was petrified there would be a nuclear attack that would turn Britain into a post-apocalyptic wasteland. I watched movies that simulated atomic war with its buildup, bombing, and aftermath and had recurring nightmares of mushroom clouds exploding over southern England.

In some ways, this side of the Cold War was the polar opposite of the violence in the ranches of northeast Mexico or the favelas of Brazil. It was a threat of monumental proportions, but it was one that was far away and never realized. In Latin America, the threat is smaller, local, and very real. However, there is a similarity. The Cold War was an endemic conflict that lasted almost half a century. Likewise, some of the crime wars in Latin America have already lasted decades and drag on with no clear end in sight.

I saw a third vision of conflict as a teenager when I visited friends in Belfast, Northern Ireland, in the last years of fighting between the Irish Republican Army, Protestant paramilitaries, and British security forces. This physically resembled the new conflicts in Latin America more. Soldiers and militarized police patrolled the streets and conducted checkpoints. Catholic and Protestant armed groups were clandestine forces operating deep inside their communities. Attacks included ambushes and car bombs.

However, the level of death in the Americas is much greater. The Troubles of Northern Ireland claimed thirty-five hundred lives over three decades. Mexico's cartel clash claimed more than sixteen thousand lives in 2011 alone; Ciudad Juárez, which has a smaller population than Northern Ireland, suffered more than three thousand murders in a single year.

So should we call these crime battles in the Americas actual wars?

Journalists writing on the bloodshed make the comparison all the time. Police and soldiers also often describe them in martial terms as they work out battle tactics to fight militias such as the Zetas. And residents of embattled communities frequently refer to war, albeit one they cannot clearly define.

However, politicians are more cautious about using the word. Occasionally, they find it convenient to use martial language to rally troops and the public to an offensive. More often, they dismiss any implication that they are at war, because this would be disastrous for their countries' images and tourist and investment dollars. Consequently, Latin America's crime wars are not legally recognized as armed conflicts.

Does it even matter what we call them? A mass grave with 193 bodies is a horrific crime however you frame it. A different choice of words won't bring victims back from the dead. It won't turn back time so a mother won't have to see her son dragged away while she is powerless against men with rifles.

But the choice of words has implications. If there were a declared armed conflict in Mexico, then its government would have to abide by international conflict treaties. Both Mexico's leaders and its cartel bosses could be judged by the International Criminal Court. (Some lawyers have campaigned for this.) Declaring war zones would turn U.S. policy on its head. It could not just hide its support for Latin America's armies in anti-drug efforts but would be identified with conflicts being watched by the Hague. Judges would have to change their criteria for deciding if people fleeing them qualify as refugees.

I have grappled with such questions in reporting on Latin America's bloodshed since 2001. Searching for the answers, I have found a growing group of thinkers trying to make sense of the violence. They come from a broad range of backgrounds and work in different milieus, and they include human rights lawyers, military strategists, and academics from anthropologists to political scientists. While their aims differ, they are united in seeking to understand this tragedy, and all their thinking can help construct a model in which we can better comprehend the wanton murder and find solutions to it.

The fighting by cartels and commandos, these thinkers show, is a new type of armed conflict that is not quite a civil war but is more than criminal violence. It is a gray bloody space in between whose rules are still being written. Criminal militias use light infantry weapons, including rocket-propelled grenades, belt-driven machine guns, fragmentation grenades, and automatic rifles. But they lack the guerrillas' driving aim of conquering a country. The conflicts don't have clear start dates, and it is a struggle to end them. Yet they claim more victims than the thousand battlefield deaths said to define a civil war.[5]

Political scientist Ben Lessing calls them "criminal conflicts" and observes that they are "supplanting revolutionary insurgency as the hemisphere's dominant form of conflict."[6] Others just call them "crime wars," summing up the merging of delinquency and war.

Robert Bunker is an external researcher for the U.S. Army War College trying to make sense of this slaughter.[7] The son of a soldier, he grew up reading the *Marine Corps Gazette* before becoming an academic specializing in national security. Latin America's crime wars provide him a new and baffling puzzle.

"We have this blurring of crime and war. And it doesn't fit either nice model for us. It is crime and war mixed together. It doesn't fit the modern paradigm. And this is why it's driving everybody bananas. It doesn't fit how the world is supposed to be. So our thinking has not caught up and our institutions and laws have not caught up."

It is impractical to apply treaties such as the Geneva Conventions to these crime wars. They were written for a different age, aimed chiefly at warring nation states. But we do need to establish limits on the crime wars as we search for peace. In Ciudad Juárez, Mexico, the newspaper *El Diario de Juárez* made this point following the murder of a twenty-one-year-old photographer on his lunch break. In a front-page editorial entitled "What do you want from us?" *El Diario* addressed the cartels directly:

> Even war has rules. In any outbreak of violence protocols or guarantees exist for the groups in conflict, in order to safeguard the integrity of the journalists who cover it. This is why we reiterate, gentlemen of the various narco-trafficking organizations, that you explain what it is you want from us so we don't have to pay tribute with the lives of our colleagues.

*   *   *

Inside this mix of crime and war, gangster gunmen are often more effective in achieving their aims than are larger government forces in achieving
theirs. Like traditional warlords, gangsters control fiefs through both fear
and authentic support from some residents. They are strong in villages or
ghettos where governments are weak. These are no longer the shantytowns
of the 1970s, where people immigrated with the hope of heading somewhere better, but slums where many youth are born and die with little
aspiration but to have gangster glory.

One alarming development is the extent to which gangsters control
their own justice systems. From Mexican mountains to Jamaican ghettos,
crime bosses try those accused of robbing or raping and sentence them to
beatings, exile, or death. It's jungle law. But many residents find it more
effective than any justice the police and courts offer.

Wielding such power, gangster warlords threaten the fundamental
nature of the state, not by trying to completely take it over but by capturing parts of it and weakening it. They chip into the state's monopoly on
violence—or, more precisely, the monopoly on waging war and carrying
out justice. When the state loses this it becomes less able to impose its will
on many issues, including the most basic, such as collecting taxes and
policing protests. People lose faith in the government, as happened in the
Mexican state of Guerrero after the Iguala massacre. Some form vigilante
militias to defend themselves. Others burn town halls. If governments
lose more control in this way, it could have devastating consequences.

CHAPTER 3

They remind me of the Dirty Dozen. Except there are more than twelve of these guys. And they look more badass.

In the classic 1967 war movie, the Allies recruit twelve scarred convicts for a mission to parachute behind enemy lines and kill Nazis. The Allied command figures these murderers are the best men to murder murderers.

In 2014, the Mexican government made a similar calculation: It decided that gangsters were the best people to take out gangsters. In the Pacific state of Michoacán—one of the most gangster-ridden states of all—it formed an elite squadron with the job of hunting down leaders of the bizarrely named Knights Templar cartel. The unit was nominally part of a Rural State Force created that year to deputize vigilantes fighting the traffickers. But full-on mob assassins also jumped in. Many hailed from a gang known as Los Viagras in the market town of Apatzingán, a hub of drug traffickers. Others came from mountain villages amid marijuana and opium fields.

I find about fifty members of the squadron milling around a parking lot at the entrance to Apatzingán. They are comparing weapons and getting ready for a mission to storm through villages seeking out Knights Templar leader Servando Gómez, alias La Tuta. They are seriously tooled up. Supposedly, the Rural Force are only allowed to carry government-issued AR-15 rifles. But who cares? They have everything up to huge G3 machine guns, which the Mexican army uses.

They refer to their weapons by farmyard names, which is fitting because Michoacán is a fertile agricultural state. They call fifty-caliber bullets *jabalitos*, or "little boars." Their beloved Kalashnikovs are goats' horns. To turn the AK-47 into a really lethal machine, they use circular clips with a hundred bullets. When you spray a hundred caps in ten seconds you have a pretty good chance of hitting your target, and anybody close by. They call the circular clips *huevos*, or "eggs." A lot of them carry grenade launchers, mostly fixed to their rifles. They call the grenades *papas*, or "potatoes." They tape grenades and ammo clips round their waists and across their chests, giving them the look of authentic desperados.

The gangsters also show me their personalized sidearms. The pistols are decorated in diamonds and other stones with classic narco designs. One of them has "El Jefe"—"The Boss"—engraved into his pistol.

They are itching to get into a gunfight. As the fifty men show off their weapons and get themselves psyched up for their op, testosterone flows in bucketloads. One of them asks me how much prostitutes cost in my country, and there is a roar of laughter. One guy is almost two meters tall, bearing a G3 in his right hand. He waves to a slim teenager carrying his ammo. "This is my *chica*." He smiles. "How do you say that in English? This is my 'bitch.'"

The guy with the Jefe pistol asks if I take "ice," the name they use for crystal meth. The Michoacán mob churns out meth by the ton, providing for tweakers from Kentucky to California. "El Jefe" remarks how pure the local ice is. DEA agents have told me that they agree. They say that Michoacán meth is the purest they have ever found.

I take photos of the guys with their weapons. They do battle poses. The two-meter-tall guy tells me not to take his picture. I say that is fine. Another man in his late forties appears from nowhere and points his finger at me. He accuses me of being a DEA agent.

"He is DEA. Why is he taking photos?"

I reaffirm that I am a journalist and I try to shake his hand. He refuses. "The DEA busted my brother in Texas," he growls. "The agent was posing as a journalist." The atmosphere changes in a flash. I tell him that I am not even American. I'm British. I point out a website that features my work. El Jefe finds it on his smartphone. My accuser relaxes a little and turns to me.

"If I see you again, I am going to put a bullet in your head." He taps his forehead with his finger and points at me. To make sure the message gets across, he adds, "I'll throw a *papa* [grenade] at you."

I do my best to smile.

* * *

Back in the 1970s, hit men from Mexico to Brazil used to be assassins who killed quietly in the black of night. Now they have transformed into commandos with light infantry weapons, even shoulder-held rocket launchers. The Zetas build their own tanks, which look like something from the fantasy road wars of *Mad Max*. They pour into towns in convoys of thirty pickups to massacre terrified residents. And they attack soldiers in ambushes, opening fire with fifty-caliber rifles. In many cases, they use the same battle tactics as Latin America's old guerilla armies.

The leftist guerrilla was an emblematic symbol of Latin America in the twentieth century, personified in the iconic photos of Che Guevara. In the new millennium, guerrillas have disappeared from most of the continent. The growth of democracy has allowed former radicals to become politicians, even presidents. The idea of establishing Marxist dictatorships has been discredited. Some of the remaining guerrillas, like those in Colombia, have become major cocaine traffickers.

But where the beret-wearing freedom fighters have subsided, cartel armies have risen. Tragically, the cartel *sicario* with a Kalashnikov is a more dominant symbol of the new Americas. Many young people idolize Chapo Guzmán more than Che Guevara.

Like guerrillas, drug cartels are deeply rooted inside communities. As Mao Tse-tung famously said, "The guerrilla must move amongst the people as a fish swims in the sea." Gangster militias also draw their strength from villages and barrios. As in counter-insurgency campaigns, governments get frustrated confronting an enemy they can't see and unleash soldiers to torture and murder civilians, trying to take away the sea from the fish.

But this comparison with insurgents does not mean that gangster gunmen will act in all ways like traditional guerillas or should be treated in the same way. Many Latin Americans see insurgents as the honorable fighters who liberated their land from the tyrants of the Spanish Empire while they view cartel hit men as demons. A traditional insurgent believes in their vision of a greater good, whether inspired by Marxism, Islam, or nationalism. The gangsters are chiefly motivated by just one god—mammon—the green of dollars bills. The strategic objectives of the bloodshed also differ. Guerrillas usually try to topple governments and take power. Cartel gunmen often attack security forces to pressure governments to back off.

A central objective of the gangster gunmen is to control their fiefs. If the government threatens them, they may launch insurgent-style attacks.

To back these up, they often claim to be fighting for the poor. But in other cases they cut deals with governments, or directly control them. They can help the powerful fight their enemies and give them a share of their spoils, working like a paramilitary.

Conflict has transformed around the world since the Cold War. Warlords have left mounds of corpses in Africa from Liberia to Uganda. While they differ from the gangsters of the Americas in many ways, they also use ragtag armies with barbaric tactics alongside new technology. And they also base their power on the control of fiefdoms.

Militant Islamists are a very different—and much bigger—threat than the gangsters of the Americas. The Islamic State showed it can control territory the size of a country. But you can't help but find common ground. In 2012, when the Taliban beheaded seventeen people at a wedding in Afghanistan, shocking the world, the Zetas left the bodies of forty-nine headless victims in Mexico. When the Syrian regime first wanted to demonstrate the horrors that Islamic rebels were committing, it couldn't find any footage, so it showed video that turned out to be by Mexican cartels. (It soon had plenty of its own to show.) Islamic radicals and gangster militias both recruit poor lost teenagers and train them to be murderers; they both fight with small cells and ambushes. And in both cases, Washington is flummoxed on how to deal with them.

A Mexican cartoonist summed up the common ground following the 2015 attack on French magazine *Charlie Hebdo*. His cartoon showed a picture of a masked man with an AK. "Ahhhhh. It's an Islamic terrorist," says one voice. "*Tranquila, tranquila,*" says another. "It's just a hit man from the Gulf Cartel."

Military historians recognize the growth of asymmetric warfare and governments' difficulties in dealing with it. The strongest theories on it come from *The Transformation of War* by Martin van Creveld, well ahead of its time when it was published in 1991: "Large-scale, conventional war—war as understood by today's principal military powers—may indeed be at its last gasp; however, war itself, war as such, is alive and kicking and about to enter a new epoch."[1]

Gangster warfare has ravaged the Americas, paradoxically, when many nations appeared to be getting freer and wealthier. The Cold War finished (with the U.S. declaring victory). Dictatorships collapsed, giving birth to young democracies. Borders opened up to free trade, governments liberalized their economies, and Francis Fukuyama declared "The End of History."

But as we look back on the last two decades, we can identify clear causes of the new conflicts. The collapse of military dictatorships and guerrilla armies left stockpiles of weapons and soldiers searching for a new payroll. Emerging democracies are plagued by weakness and corruption. A key element is the failure to build working justice systems. International policy focused on markets and elections but missed this third crucial element in making functional democracies: the rule of law. The omission has cost many lives.

The deregulation of economies created some winners while leaving swathes of the world's slums and countrysides in poverty. Meanwhile, a global black market in contraband, human trafficking, and guns has expanded exponentially.

Narcotics are the biggest black market earner of all. Estimated to be worth more than three hundred billion dollars a year, the global industry has pumped huge resources into criminal empires decade after decade.[2] It has had a cumulative effect, heating up the region to a boiling point. The brutal logic of the underworld is that the most terrifying gangsters get the lion's share of the profits, leading to the ultimate predators such as the Zetas.

However, the violence rages on during a historic turning point in the drug debate. Four U.S. states and Washington, D.C., have legalized marijuana along with the entire country of Uruguay. Politicians across the continent have come out of the closet to criticize the war on drugs. Actors and musicians line up to join the cause of drug policy reform.

Yet while the debate has transformed, the old policies largely stumble on. The U.S. spends billions on DEA agents in sixty countries and bankrolls armies to burn crops from the Andes to Afghanistan. Most narcotics remain illegal and keep providing massive profits to those violent enough to claim them.

The next task is to move from a change in the debate to a change in the reality on the ground.

As I look at the Red Commando, Shower Posse, Mara Salvatrucha, and Knights Templar, I profile certain gangster bosses. Their power and wealth vary; some are wanted billionaires, others chiefs of single ghettos.

They differ in how violent (and in some cases evil) they are. Some have codes to protect innocents. Others carry out war crimes. But they are united in controlling fiefdoms and fighting this new type of conflict.

The characters and groups I have chosen don't represent an A to Z of gangster warlords and cartels. There are way too many criminals across the Americas who share these traits. Some of the biggest dogs, such as Joaquín "Chapo" Guzmán, are not extensively profiled, although of course he traffics his way into the text. But the characters and organizations I chose are emblematic and represent different styles. I look at the class-based ghetto warfare of the Red Commando in Brazil, the political power of the don in Jamaica, the immigrant street gang of the Mara in Central America, and the religious cult and guerrilla tactics of the Knights Templar in Michoacán. I am interested in how these gangsters wield power, how they wage war, how they operate as political and fighting forces. I am interested in what drives the insane level of violence, and what can be done to stop it.

In the case of the Knights Templar, the megalomaniac Nazario Moreno oversaw a highly pyramidal structure. In contrast, the Mara Salvatrucha is a federation of "cliques," where power lies largely with local leaders. Thinkers have long debated whether individuals or social forces are more influential. Good contemporary historians look at both and how they interact to shape our world.

Drug traffickers and hit men are tough to interview. Sometimes they can be aggressive. Other times they want to use publicity for their own purposes. Often they genuinely want to share their life stories and are looking for ways out or repentance. A seasoned killer in Jamaica wanted advice on his creative writing. A Brazilian gang boss showed me his poetry.

Most were trained to be killers when they were teenagers and are in a sense both victims and victimizers. Yet perhaps they don't deserve forgiveness. They have committed horrendous crimes, from murdering and kidnapping to trafficking women.

For those of us trying to understand this mess, the villains' stories offer vital visions into their crime world. But their cohorts often view their talking as akin to snitching and the interviewees run a genuine risk of being murdered. Dozens of gangsters in Latin America have talked to the press by name and been killed in retribution, sometimes within hours of their interview being aired. The gangsters I talk to detail crimes they have not been convicted for, including dozens of homicides, some on U.S. soil. In some cases, they agreed that I can publish their names. In others, they asked for me to leave out surnames or use aliases. I could not refuse these requests; journalism is not worth people getting killed for.

Latin America and the Caribbean are home to 588 million people divided by language, race, and social class: It is not one place, but many. A paradox of the crime wars is how extreme violence goes side by side with everyday life. While parts of Mexico and Brazil suffer crazy murder rates, others are very peaceful. The resorts of Cancún are safer than most American cities. Yucatán State has the same murder rate as Belgium, Mexico City as Boston. Even in the most violent areas, people keep on with the grind, feeding their families, getting kids to school, partying away the evenings. There needs to be more engagement with these communities, not further isolation from them.

Crime wars cut through politics in strange ways. Drug policy reformists vary from leftists, who say the poor suffer most, to libertarians who want the market to reign. Refugee claims are sucked into a polarized immigration debate. Human rights defenders expose soldiers killing civilians while police chiefs scream about the spread of gang power.

But despite these differences, the issues are largely non-ideological. It is a morally blurred conflict without any clear side to be on. Liberals, conservatives, and socialists all agree that sky-high murder rates are terrible for society. All agree that a functioning justice system is needed to protect people. It is a crisis we have to work together to overcome.

The last decade in the Americas has shown how bad organized crime can get. It is not just the gangs themselves who are the problem, but their model, which could emerge in other countries and continents. How we as a society deal with this challenge could determine whether these gangster warlords are a blip in history or will get even deeper into our communities and lives.

PART II

The Red: Brazil

They sprang from the fierce embrace of victor and vanquished. They were created in a turbulent, adventurous society, settled upon a fertile land. By way of amplifying their ancestral attributes, they had a rude schooling in force and courage.

—EUCLIDES DA CUNHA, *REBELLION IN THE BACKLANDS*, 1902

They don't live too big over there. Ghettos are the same all over the world. They stink.

—JIM KELLY AS WILLIAMS IN *ENTER THE DRAGON*, 1973

CHAPTER 4

"*Cocaína*," the bony teenager calls out, standing on a dirt street behind a table that displays baggies of white powder with price tags. Besides the cocaine are packets of compressed marijuana and rocks of crack. A steady stream of customers pay for the goodies with crumpled reais bills. There are bags for four dollars, eight dollars, sixteen dollars; all budgets and tastes catered to here.

A dozen yards away, two guys drive up on a motorcycle. The one on the back has an AR-15 assault rifle with a grenade launcher strapped to his shoulder. He makes no effort to hide the weapon. This is their territory. Police only come into this favela in heavily armed convoys, which normally gives enough time for the dealers to run—or shoot at them.

I've seen cocaine being sold from British pubs to New York corners to Mexican red-light districts. But I've never seen it flogged quite as openly as here, a favela known as Antares on the outskirts of Rio de Janeiro, Brazil's glamorous and bloody second city. In the favela, they call these bustling drug points *bocas*, or "mouths." It's a curious name. I wonder if it refers to the mouth that feeds drug users' needs—or the mouth that feeds the favela with money.

There are several other bocas around the favela, and dealers even offer their wares through a fence onto a platform of a train station; middle-class customers can arrive by rail and buy cocaine without venturing into the favela and rubbing shoulders with the poor and dangerous.

As I hover round the boca table, a group of excited teenagers shout out prices and lift up bags of herbs and powder. I explain that I'm a journalist from England, and an older guy who is running the drug shop introduces himself as Lucas. He's a gregarious twenty-eight-year-old wearing sports clothes and eighties-style bling. I find Rio's residents—known as cariocas—to be among the most friendly and charismatic people in the world, and the drug dealers are no exception.

It's just before the 2014 World Cup, so I talk about soccer, the international language that can help you pass the time with anyone from barbers to taxi drivers … to coke dealers. Lucas lights up at soccer talk and runs off to get his cell phone. He shows me his phone's wallpaper, a photo in which he has his arm round one of the players on the Brazilian national team. I don't want to embarrass the soccer star by naming him, but I'll say that he's got an astounding right foot and played in a European Champions League final.

"This is my friend." Lucas flashes with pride. "He grew up close to here."

This first time I go into Antares, it's a sweltering Tuesday afternoon. I'm with an American journalist named Joe Carter who has spent a decade in Brazil working intensively in these slums and has inevitably had to deal with drug dealers like these. Joe is showing me what he describes as one of the most hard-core, and surreal, favelas. Antares is a long way out, an hour by car from Copacabana Beach and its G-stringed bikinis. Unlike many favelas that climb the side of Rio's mountains, it's on flat arid land beside train tracks. Poverty colors all that is here: the unpaved streets, the birds pecking at piles of garbage, the tin roofs, the children kicking up dirt as they run, the weary faces of the old.

Antares is the territory of Rio's oldest and biggest drug gang, called the Comando Vermelho, or Red Commando.[1] The commando's presence is obvious as soon as we drive down the entrance road. Groups of young men guard all the paths in and out, talking into radios. Again, they make no effort to hide themselves, sitting lazily in the sun with their guns and walkie-talkies. The control of the commando—and absence of the state—is naked.

The lookouts are mostly watching for police, who sporadically come into Antares to make arrests, which often end in raging firefights. They are also on alert for gunmen from the two neighboring favelas, who they are at war with. The favela on one side is controlled by their hated rivals the Third Commando, traffickers who broke away from the Reds in the early nineties.[2] The favela on the other side is controlled by shady gunmen known as militias, made up of former police and others on a bloody mission to rid the city of drug gangs. The teenagers and young men holding the guns here have lived through this war their entire lives; it's all they know, they've no idea what peace looks like.

The Antares gunmen call all their enemies—the police, militias, and Third Commando—by the collective name *alemães*, or Germans. When I hear this, it makes me chuckle. Growing up in England, the enemies in our games of soldiers were Germans, but I'm amazed that Brazilians in this real battle use the same term.

I first hear an explanation that it's because Brazil actually fought in World War II, sending an expeditionary force to join the allies in the Mediterranean theater. Brazilians are proud of this campaign, and a towering metallic sculpture to 467 dead servicemen adorns Rio's Flamengo Park.

But somebody else tells me that explanation is rubbish. The real reason, he says, is that German immigrants who came to Rio often joined the police, and the name stuck. *Alemãe* conjures up an image of a tall white uniformed repressor.

A pasty white Brit like myself also grabs attention here, so when we get into Antares's main street we check in with the head of the residents' association to explain we are journalists. I try to be open about what I do. Back in 2001, the Brazilian investigative journalist Tim Lopes filmed gangs in a favela with a hidden camera. He had also filed another report that preceded a police crackdown. The gangsters discovered him, tied him to a tree, and conducted a "trial" in which they found him guilty. They burned his eyes with cigarettes, used a samurai sword to cut off his arms and legs while he was still alive, put his body in a tire with gasoline and set him on fire. They call this murder technique the *microonda*, or "microwave oven."

However, when I tell the association president we have come to document the blatant criminality, he is remarkably relaxed and gets a young guy on a motorcycle taxi to show us round. Most of these favela residents' associations, I later find out, are effectively controlled by the commando. Gangsters approve the president and use the association office as a base. In return, the commando will pump money through the association to provide for public works, building sewage systems and laying concrete on streets.

The gangsters get especial popularity by paying for free street parties, known as *bailes funk*, or funk dances. The kids at the drug mouth tell us there is one on Friday night from midnight till dawn. "You have to check it out," Lucas says.

*   *   *

When we drive back to Antares late Friday, police have set up checkpoints on the main roads toward the favela. You have to go through the scrutiny of the police officers, then a stretch of no-man's-land, and then the scrutiny of the commando guards. When we go in, the police shine a flashlight at us then wave us through; but when we come out at dawn, they stop the car and search us thoroughly, looking for drugs. Why else would we have gone into Antares, they ask, if we weren't off to get high?

The drug shops are certainly doing good business that night. The favela is buzzing. We arrive just before midnight, and they are only just setting up the funk dance, but the streets are already crowded. The bocas claim a steady line of customers, and I see a woman snorting a line of cocaine off a car hood. There are more guns about than in the day, ragged teenagers and young men standing on corners with their assault rifles, chatting, sipping from plastic cups of beer.

I look around for Lucas but don't see him when another man approaches and asks who we are. He's also decked out in sports clothes but with a harder, more aggressive look than Lucas. I shake his hand and explain again I'm a British journalist interested in checking out the party.

He nods vigorously. "It's nice that foreigners like you come down here. Enjoy yourselves. Nobody is going to mess with you."

The message is implicit: Our security is guaranteed by the Red Commando. The teenagers with rifles are criminals, drug dealers, murderers. But they are the authority here. Nobody is going to mug us because that would bring attention that would be bad for business. Inside the favela, the commando gunmen are the police.

The dance finally starts around one A.M., and residents crowd into a muddy clearing in the heart of the favela, what would be a town plaza if it were paved. There's close to a thousand people, from children to grandparents, in front of a wall of speakers thirty feet high and sixty feet wide.

These parties are known as funk dances because they started back in the 1970s with American funk records. But over the decades, the music has mutated beyond recognition. In the eighties, Brazilians who went to Miami brought back records from a subgenre of hip-hop called Miami bass. It's characterized by funk rhythms re-created on synths and drum machines, which women (and sometimes men) shake their "booties" to. Home computers in the 1990s allowed Brazilians to make their own recordings, creating the unique favela funk sound.

Brazilian funk has simple electronic beats juxtaposed with singing or rapping in a distinct local style. Sometimes the vocalists talk about gangs and guns. More often they talk about sex, very explicitly. Brazil is famous (or infamous) for its liberal attitudes toward sex and showing off women's toned asses in carnival parades and game shows. This open sexuality is especially visible in the slums; favela funk involves booty shaking that would put Miami to shame.

Sure enough, in the Antares dance, lines of women in tight shorts and bikini tops thrust their backsides to the beat. The music overpowers the speakers, coming through distorted and deafening. But no one seems to care. Young and old party. A graying man dances with a plastic beer glass in hand with a trio of middle-aged women. Boys not yet teen-agers practice their dance moves and burst into laughter. A woman pushes a pram with a baby somehow asleep through the fierce din. This is the time when everyone forgets about their problems, the lack of money to feed the kids, the father in prison, the brother who died in a crackle of gunfire.

As the boogying gets more furious and passionate, the commando gunmen drift onto the dance floor. They move their bodies while holding their rifles in front of them. A funk song comes on with lyrics supporting the drug traffickers. The gunmen form a line and raise their rifles in the air, shouting along with the chorus: "Red Commando! Red Commando! Red Commando!"

The Friday night action in Antares is a truly surreal scene. Yet it's only an extreme example of the way that criminal militias have become so domin-ant in ghettos across the Americas. Mexican, Central American, and Caribbean gangsters also organize their own street parties where people dance to songs of their glory. And lookouts watching for enemy gunmen—though normally more hidden—are a frighteningly common feature of the continent's urban sprawls.

Of course, many poor neighborhoods across the region don't have anything like this criminal presence. But Antares is no freak occurrence. In the state of Rio alone, it's likely more than a million people live in neighborhoods where the Red Commando or rival armed groups of traf-fickers or militias hold sway.[3] While I watch gunmen dance with their rifles in Antares, similar scenes take place in favelas across Rio's slopes and plains.

To understand how gangs became so powerful, we have to take a closer look at the environment itself: the ghettos of Latin America and the

Caribbean. In Brazil, they're called *favelas*; in Colombia, *comunas*; in Jamaica, garrisons; in Mexico, *barrios* or *ciudades perdidas* (lost cities). People also call them slums, shantytowns, and makeshift sprawls. Others complain these names are alienating and say we should think of something more positive.

But whatever we call them, ghettos are a reality of the Americas. They are physical spaces with hard boundaries, entrances and exits that take you into a world that suffers marginalization and contrasts to the society outside. Inside they can be overwhelming, the lives and problems of thousands on top of each other and entwined. And they can be exciting, the explosive growth of young people with an insatiable energy. They are the source of cutting-edge culture that sets trends in global music and fashion; the scene of raging gun battles; the home to children who have become seasoned murderers; and the setting for people showing warmth, compassion, and perseverance. Day after day.

If we are going to make any sense of organized crime in the Americas, we have to come here.

That's not to say that the poor are the cause of crime wars. Rich businessmen often pull strings and many gangs could not operate without complicit politicians. The chain of money and services linked to organized crime leads to all our doorsteps.

But ghettos are a fundamental building block of the crime world, a fertile soil where cartels and commandos grow, a source of young bloods wanting to prove themselves, a battleground where wars are fought.

The ghettos of each country and city across the Americas have their own stories. But most were born in a similar way: people arriving from the countryside or leaving decaying inner cities and squatting land. This land is often on dangerous terrain: slopes of hills that crumble in mudslides, riverbanks that flood in the rainy season, swampy earth where sinkholes swallow entire blocks.

When migrants first squatted land, they built homes of any material they could, especially corrugated iron, plastic sheets, and cardboard boxes. These were the shantytowns the world knew of the Americas in the 1960s and 1970s, with the word "shanty" referring to the makeshift homes. They are referenced in news reports, movies, and songs of the era; Desmond Dekker's ska classic "007 (Shanty Town)" was an international hit in 1967. However, the ghettos have morphed as residents rebuilt their homes with breeze-blocks, wood, and cement. Most of the neighborhoods today are not technically shantytowns but aging concrete sprawls covered by tangles of electric cables where power is often taken free from the grids. And most in the millennial ghetto generation are no country migrants but those born there.

In the 1960s, two American anthropologists traipsed round Latin American shantytowns engaged in a fierce intellectual debate. In one corner, Oscar Lewis described them as slums of squalor and hopelessness. The ghettos contained an inherent culture of poverty that was reproduced generation after generation, he argued. They lacked class consciousness and the ability to work collectively, which meant they would not improve their lot.

In the opposite corner, William Mangin wrote that shantytowns showed signs of hope and initiative, of people organizing to better themselves. Mangin said residents built homes that had some value, acquiring a little wealth, a path that could bring them into the system. Focusing his study on Peru, he wrote a landmark piece in the *Scientific American*.

> Although poor, they do not live the life of squalor and hopelessness characteristic of the 'culture of poverty' depicted by Oscar Lewis; although bold and defiant in their seizure of land, they are not a revolutionary lumpenproletariat ... The squatters have produced their own answer to the difficult problems of housing and community organization that governments have been unable to solve.[4]

Emotionally, I prefer Mangin's argument. But almost five decades on, history has shown they both missed an important development. Unlike what Lewis said, the ghettos have given birth to powerful organizations that have recruited thousands into their ranks, provide a certain social control, and even pave streets. But unlike Mangin's hopes, these organizations are criminal empires that have not brought residents into the system but hurtled them into a violent collision with it.

In Brazil, this clash between government and favelas often takes a racial tone. You can't get far talking about commandos and crime without bumping into the race question. And like everywhere in the world, it's a sensitive issue.

Brazil likes to view itself as a rainbow nation with little prejudice. This notion was crystalized back in 1933 in a book by a young sociologist, Gilberto Freyre, called *The Masters and the Slaves*. He discusses how sleeping across race lines in Brazil (especially white men with black women) created a uniquely mixed-race society, different from anywhere in Europe or the United States.

These 1930s views can sound innocent or patronizing. But they also show a forward-looking optimism, the search for a better ideal, a sense of post-racial nation. The year 1933 was also when Brazil launched its first professional soccer leagues, in which black and mixed-race players flooded into the game, creating the nation's iconic winning style.[5] More recently, the arguments were updated in a 2006 Brazilian bestseller, *We Are Not Racists*. It reiterates that the vast majority of Brazilians have a mixed heritage.

Others reject this idea as a farce that hides a highly prejudicial system. They point out that favelas are dominated by people of more African ancestry. Some even view crime as poor black people getting their own back on the whiter middle class. Paulo Lins, who wrote the book *City of God*, made this point at a seminar of Latin American writers and journalists that I gate-crashed.

> The police is a force of repression. They go into favelas and they kill innocent people and say they are drug traffickers. Rio is a completely racist city. It's a thing people don't like to talk about, but if you are black then you don't get mugged. The other day, some robbers went into a fancy party and stole everybody's wallets. They robbed a hundred people. However, there were two black people there and they let them off.

Like in the United States, Brazil's racial divide has its roots in slavery. The Portuguese Empire shipped millions of enslaved Africans to toil on sugar and coffee plantations and chop Brazil's precious wood. There is much dispute over the exact numbers of the Atlantic slave trade. But the most respected estimates come from a database compiled at Emory University in Atlanta, which counts all available records of slave ships. It finds that slavers shipped an astounding 4.86 million Africans to Brazil.[6] This is ten times more than the 450,000 slaves that arrived on U.S. plantations; Brazil had the biggest African slave population on the planet.

Brazil's independence from Portugal in 1822 did not create a progressive free republic. Instead, power moved into the hands of a Brazilian emperor presiding over his South American realm. Slavery continued unabashed, outliving abolition in the British Empire and the U.S. Emancipation Proclamation. When Brazil finally abolished slavery in 1888, it was the last country in the Western world to do so.

Leaving the plantations, many freedmen headed to Rio, then Brazil's capital, and claimed their turf by squatting on the surrounding hills. However, while the favelas show a more Afro Brazil, they are not exclusively so. They include others of Brazil's multiracial fusion of Europeans, indigenous, and X amount of combinations. The commando gunmen guarding Antares may be generally darker skinned than the bathers on Ipanema Beach, but they still show a spectrum of shades and features.

The name *favela* itself claims a curious origin, one that also speaks to the violent foundations of Brazil. In the nineteenth century, *favela* referred to a spiny plant that grew hundreds of miles from Rio, in the Bahia region. Here, a preacher known as Anthony the Counselor founded a colony of landless peasants and freed slaves in an arid valley sprinkled with favela plants. The Counselor was a fire and brimstone type who predicted water turning to blood and stars falling from the heavens.

The Brazilian government, now free of an emperor and going through a modernizing phase, determined to crush the Counselor and his band, viewing them as superstitious outlaws. It 1896, it unleashed the War of Canudos to bring them to heel. The war descended into a grueling campaign in which the starry-eyed rebels beat back waves of troops. Finally, the Brazilian army used cannons and dynamite to massacre the rebels, killing some fifteen thousand in 1897.

The soldiers who carried out the slaughter marched back to Rio where they had been promised land as payment. But the government repudiated its debt and left them homeless, forcing the veterans to settle on a hill beside the city. This is the big irony of the tale: after crushing one group of squatters, the soldiers were forced to become squatters themselves. The slum built by these battle-scarred veterans became known as the Morro da Favela, or Favela Hill. It's murky whether this was because the soldiers had brought back favela plants and they took root there, or just because

they had been among the favela plants for so long that they were associated with them. Either way, the name stuck as the slums expanded along
miles of Rio's dazzling slopes.

For much of the twentieth century, successive Brazilian governments
provided nothing for favelas: no sewage works, paved streets, or security.
Many slum residents were also barred from voting by a literacy requirement. The communities grew outside the system, scrambling to provide
for themselves. In recent decades, there has finally been an effort to give
favela dwellers deeds and urban services, but it has been a slow and tricky
process.

Brazil's 2010 census found a third of favela households still had no
sewage collection or septic tanks. It counted a total of 11.4 million
Brazilians living in favelas.[7] That's more than the populations of many
countries. But it should also be kept in perspective. Brazil is the fifth
largest nation in the world, with two hundred million people. Favela
residents only make up 6 percent.

However, in Rio de Janeiro State, home of the original favela, slum
dwellers are more than 12 percent, making up two million of the sixteen
million people. The favelas begin a stone's throw from Copacabana Beach
and slope up the hills that spiral through the spectacular-looking city to
the jungles behind. Steep narrow streets thread round them in labyrinthine patterns. Overhanging trees allow cheeky marmoset monkeys to
spring into their alleys.

In the early 2000s, Chicago academic Ben Lessing wandered into these
favelas. He had come to Rio to study environmental regulations. But
seeing this crazy urban habitat made him switch direction and begin his
work on crime wars.

"Immediately when I got to Rio, I saw the absurdity of the situation
there. You had this archipelago of favelas right in the heart of the metropolis, sometimes in the wealthiest neighborhoods. You had a significant
portion of the population, maybe about a million people, living under the
dominion of armed groups. It was very clear from the first time that I
went into a favela that the drug traffickers held the monopoly on armed
violence. To people living there, this wasn't abnormal. It was just the way
things were."[8]

As I watch the young gangsters raise their rifles to the pounding electro
beats, I wonder how this alternative gangster government became so

strong here. A central theme running through the crime wars of Latin America is that of inequality and class struggle. The region is home to some of the most unequal societies in the world, and many gangsters claim this is what drives them. But even within this environment, the Red Commando is an extreme example of a crime syndicate embedded in a community, with a rhetoric tinged with class struggle and leftist politics, starting with the name.

How was the Red Commando born?

CHAPTER 5

All gangs have their creation story. Accounts, tales, and myths trickle round the streets about who was there on day one, how they got together, what they vowed. The creation story of the Red Commando is especially alluring.

I hear varying versions from gang members, community activists, and police officers. But they all concur on a central detail: the Red Commando was born back in the heady days of the Cold War and Brazil's military dictatorship, which ruled from 1964 to 1985. It came about when ghetto criminals were locked up with leftist guerrillas who fought the dictatorship.

The guerrillas—who were mostly middle-class intellectuals— wanted to be granted political prisoner status and held away from other inmates. But the dictatorship's generals thought otherwise. They feared that awarding the leftists a political status would legitimize their insurgency. They also wanted to teach the uppity rebels a lesson. They put them in the most high-security prison—on an island—with the most hard-core bank robbers and gunslingers from the favelas. The ghetto villains, they believed, would soon rape and beat the politicos into submission.

But the opposite happened.

The political prisoners "educated" the bank robbers with their revolutionary ideas. And together they formed a united group mixing the cell structure and politics of the guerrillas with the violence and street connections of the gangsters. The Red Commando's unique political influence from the guerrillas gave it its name and quasi-socialist discourse.

From a few dozen inmates in a wing it spread like a virus through the prison system, spilling onto the streets as members were released or escaped. Dozens of adherents became hundreds, became thousands.

It's a fascinating creation story. But I want to dig further into how this alliance between guerillas and gangsters led to fights in Rio's favelas that would claim tens of thousands of lives. And there is one man, I discover, who is best placed to fill in the details, a man who was there when the alliance was forged and has survived decades of bloodshed to tell the tale. I need to talk to "the brain" of the Red Commando, the man they call the Teacher.[1]

CHAPTER 6

For a man who has spent most of his life in prison, and suffered beatings to an inch of his life, electric shocks, starvation, and every other method of torture known to Brazilian police and jailers, William da Silva Lima appears remarkably unfazed. He has a look that says "You won't break me" as he sits with his back straight, owlish eyes staring like laser beams. It's a bit like Paul Newman in *Cool Hand Luke*. Times a thousand.

Despite being known as the Teacher, William left school at twelve. But as he talks to me, he shows that he's both knowledgeable and sharply focused. He has the ability to swiftly answer questions on complicated issues with a clear and firm position. This ability, it strikes me, can make bosses in these crime organizations. It's not only who can hit the hardest. It's who can lead. The Red Commando has no single kingpin but a copula of bosses, and the Teacher survived on this top rung for decades.

William was first incarcerated when he was seventeen and has been in the penal system most of his life. He's now seventy-one. His specialty crime (and love, it seems) is robbing banks. He once escaped from a prison island and was robbing banks within days of achieving his freedom, carrying on for ten months until police officers nabbed him again.

He doesn't come across as a regular tough guy, being short and slim and having the habit of spontaneously reciting poetry. But he carries an intimidating air. A prison guard almost killed him by opening up his head with a metal baton, an injury that left William with a degenerative nerve disease. William describes how the guard was mysteriously murdered, and smiles broadly. He has a distinctive grin, lighting up his nerve-damaged face and penetrating eyes. He also talks about guards getting burned with gasoline and rival prisoners being "executed."

With the degenerative disease almost crippling him, authorities finally allowed William conditional release on the grounds of his medical condition, age, and time served. Even so, he wears an electric bracelet round his leg. He looks too old and frail to stick up banks, but police want to make sure.

William clearly sees himself as a social bandit. He comes from the ghetto side of the Red Commando—what they call "proletarian prisoners"—but says he was politicized even before he was locked up with leftist guerrillas. He views the world in black and white terms, in which the system—the police, politicians, businessmen, the rich—is the enemy. The poor struggle, and the Red Commando is the spear of that struggle. He shrugs off atrocities by his clan with phrases he repeats several times to me. "The Red Commando is the resistance. It doesn't negotiate with police."

In line with seeing himself as a resistance fighter, he wrote his own account of his tribulations, which was printed by a local press. It's called *Four Hundred Against One*, after the number of police who surrounded and shot dead one of his cohorts.[1] The cover has a picture depicting favelas in one corner with kids bearing pistols; a prison in the other corner with a giant skull; and him standing at the bottom alongside the word *Liberdade*—or Freedom. This is one of the three words of the Red Commando slogan he tells me: "Peace, Justice, and Liberty."

A Brazilian director made a movie about the Red Commando and also called it *Four Hundred Against One*.[2] The film, which has been a smash on the Internet, is an action-packed watch with lots of gangsters with Afros and flares in blazing gunfights alongside some seriously funky music. It also has some interesting real footage of shoot-outs. (As always, the actor is better looking than the true-life personality.)

While the name of his Red Commando colors the walls of favelas, William now lives outside the slums in the middle-class Copacabana area. It's a nice street although his apartment and furnishings are modest.

His wife, Simone, is some two decades younger, a woman with a kind and pretty face from Brazil's Afro center of Salvador. She provides legal services to inmates, and they met when he was in prison, carrying on their relationship though years of incarceration, escapes and recaptures, and several children. (He escaped to see two of them born.) She is sharp-witted and will contradict him on certain points, being more critical of the commando. They make a nice couple. An old photo shows them kissing through prison bars, their eyes closed in the embrace.

I am introduced to William by a Brazilian journalist who was critical of the dictatorship, making him one of the better guys in the Teacher's eyes. The journalist hugs William and tells him it is fine to tell his story. He is still hesitant at first. But once he finds his rhythm he doesn't stop talking. He recounts extensive details of his childhood, and several times when I ask about the Red Commando he lifts his hand and says, "I'll get to that later." And he gives that distinctive broad grin.

After hours, he gets into the gritty details, and during two long visits to his home I hear the blood-soaked tale of how the Red Commando became such a power in the world's fifth largest nation. His story begins in the 1940s, when Brazil was just half a century out of slavery and empire.

CHAPTER 7

William was born a thousand miles from Rio in the northeastern state of Pernambuco. His father hailed from a family of sugarcane workers of Portuguese descent; his mother was part Amazonian Indian. His mixed heritage gave him high cheekbones and light skin. It was August 1942, and the Brazilian navy had just sailed into World War II. His father bequeathed him the English name William in the spirit of the war alliance with the United States.

His parents broke up when he was two years old, and he stayed with his father and grandparents. His mother would visit and take him out for sorbet. He remembers her as kind and beautiful. One day when he was five years old, she took him for his treat and didn't return him, running off to her native village in an indigenous area.

"I was really happy in her village. It was deep in nature. You could drink the clean water. There were beautiful trees you could climb up. But it didn't last."

After five months, his father and uncle arrived with two military policemen and a man from the justice department waving a court order for his custody. His mother screamed and held him, but the policemen pulled her away and beat her. This is one of William's most vivid childhood memories.

"The policemen hit her again and again in front of me. I'll never forget that image. From that day on, I hated policemen."

He lived with his father and grandparents, starting school when he was seven. His father became the driver for the manager of the sugar mill and would often be on the road. William spent most of his time with his grandfather, who cut cane in the seething hot fields, the job African slaves had done for centuries. His grandfather was warm like his mother and showed a fighting spirit. He taught William how to stand up for himself.

"He would talk about the struggle for better conditions. He took me to meetings with sugarcane workers in the square. I loved hearing the workers talk about their fight. I became politicized."

One day, police broke up a meeting of sugarcane workers, causing a scuffle. An officer on horseback ran over William's grandfather. He was badly injured and for the next year, William would run back from school to care for him. He never recovered and passed away of his injuries and age.

William hated the police even more.

Following the death, William moved across the country to São Paulo, where his father found a new wife and a job as a bus driver. William liked this bustling city attracting immigrants from all over the globe: Italy, Japan, Lebanon. He made good friends and loved to play soccer from dawn until dusk. But his homelife went from bad to worse as he fought bitterly with his father and stepmother.

He finished primary school at twelve and got a job as a delivery boy for a laboratory. He often fled arguments at home by sleeping in the Praça da Sé square by the elegant cathedral; he loved the street life but often lacked enough to eat.

At fifteen, he got a job collecting rent for a landlord. It paid better than the lab, but he was still struggling to put food in his mouth, and his father never helped. So he planned his first robbery.

"The landlord was a rude pig of a man. I would go on trips to collect rent with him, and he would make me wait on the street while he slept with prostitutes. I had no qualms about stealing from him."

William pilfered checks from the landlord and got two of his friends to cash them. The furious landlord ordered the police to drag William to the bank. But the clerk said he wasn't the person who had collected the money.

"They couldn't do anything. I lost my job, but I got away with the crime."

William flashes an especially broad grin when he tells me this story. Fifty-six years later this robbery still gives him satisfaction. He is one of those thieves who gets pleasure out of the act of stealing itself; he wants to beat the system. Later when he robbed banks, he loved to shoot the pictures of bank managers off the wall.

He made a good haul out of the stolen checks, buying kneepads for the beautiful game and eating in a restaurant that he had previously walked past longingly. He even invested in materials to make stuffed toys and sell them in the market. But his business didn't last, and he was soon out on the streets picking pockets.

"It was a good time full of dreams of independence," he writes in his memoir. "This strong desire for independence is perhaps what led me to a place behind bars."[1]

William's young criminality comes across as innocent compared to the gangbangers of today. He smiles proudly at how he deftly pinched wallets from businessmen in their 1950s overcoats. The new generation of teenagers talk about firefights and cutting off heads.

But William still got himself locked up. Police finally nabbed him for picking pockets when he was seventeen, and he had his first taste of incarceration. After four days, his father signed a paper promising to take care of him but then left him angrily on the street. William went back to thieving, drifting from São Paulo to Rio de Janeiro.

Brazil's seaside city was in its glamorous days of carnivals and bossa nova made famous by the 1960s hit "The Girl from Ipanema." William was a young hood in this mix, picking pockets, mugging, and robbing houses. It didn't take too long for him to get arrested again, this time for burglary. He had just turned nineteen so was no longer a minor, and a judge gave him five years, plunging him into the jungle of Brazil's prisons.

From the outside, scarred-up tattooed prisoners look terrifying. But from the inside, they are often the ones who are frightened. Being a prisoner is one of the weakest positions you can be in as a human, your basic decisions out of your hands, at the mercy of guards and inmates. Prison is a necessary evil to protect society. But all prisons are hard; and Brazilian prisons are hellish.

Brazil is a progressive society in many ways. But if you take Dostoyevsky's adage that "the degree of civilization in a society can be judged by entering its prisons," then Brazil comes across as barbaric. Its jails suffer bitter overcrowding in dilapidated buildings and extreme violence, including decapitations, and the constant threat of male rape.[2]

Bad prisons are a feature of most Latin American countries. Too much violent crime translates to too many violent prisoners, alongside poor budgets to deal with them. As Brazil is such a big country, it has one of the biggest prison populations on the planet, with more than half a million inmates; the penitentiary system is a world in itself. This means it has the region's highest overall number of violent offenders, and these end up concentrated in certain notorious penitentiaries. One of them is Bangu in Rio. This is where William was sent as a slight nineteen-year-old.

When William arrived he found prisoners divided and powerless. The main reason he would later form the commando was to put order among the inmates. But when he first came in, he had no gang to back him up. Prisoners slapped him, and he hit back. He may have been small, but he had nerves. "I am not a violent person," he says. "But I don't like being hurt."

One warden earned the nickname "Hit You While Weeping," because he loved to beat prisoners while they cried. (It might surprise us, but tough guys do cry. And jails are full of tears.) One day when Hit You While Weeping was thumping him, William snapped and struck back. As a punishment, he got his first taste of the solitary confinement cells.

"Do you know what they are like? Can you imagine what it's like to live in them?" he writes.

At first, I couldn't eat anything as water only came every twelve hours, and urine and shit accumulated in such quantity that it destroyed your appetite . . .

Looking at yourself in the mirror, shaving, distinguishing smells and colors, all this disappears after a while and you replace it with other things to survive. One of them was to hold your right hand up high, and keep it clean, so you can use it for eating, and you keep the left hand for all the other tasks. It is a question of hygiene . . .

The first nights, I didn't sleep, as I was walking from right to left, singing to hasten the dawn and the coffee. If the warden was one of the vicious ones there would be no food just a volley of blows. There is nothing left but for you to die, retch, or become completely mad!

The beatings are not too serious though, because between two strokes of the nightstick, the back relaxes.[3]

CHAPTER 8

In 1964, during William's first long prison stretch, an event took place that would drastically change the young robber's life: The army launched its coup.

Governing South America's largest country, Brazil's military dictatorship became a reference point for Latin American dictatorships of the era, influencing other regimes, such as those that took power in Argentina and Chile. The generals invented what they called a "Doctrine of National Security" justifying their rule. It wasn't that sophisticated; if they felt the nation was in enough trouble from inflation, strikes, and unrest, they argued they could kick out the elected government and take over. Chile's Commander in Chief Augusto Pinochet and Argentina's General Leopoldo Galtieri ate up this thinking.

The generals made their move in an era when the U.S. government was particularly worried (or paranoid?) about the spread of communism. This fear was put on steroids by the October 1962 Cuban missile crisis. The following month, the CIA released a report entitled "Castro's Subversive Capabilities in Latin America." The moth-bitten document with SECRET stamped on it has now been declassified. It names almost every country in the region as a potential target of Cuban and Soviet infiltration. But it singles out Brazil. "Brazil, where communists have penetrated the government and military to some limited extent, the tide of nationalist and anti-US feeling is strong, and depressed socio-economic conditions and inefficient government administration provide Castro many opportunities."[1]

The infiltrated government it referred to was led by President João Goulart, a Catholic farm boy from southern Brazil who took office in

1961. Goulart was known popularly as Jango, in the Brazilian spirit of referring to politicians informally like soccer players. (Lula, Dilma alongside Pele, Ronaldo.) There is still debate about how radical Jango was. His proponents say he was a center leftist like those who would rule Brazil four decades later. His adversaries claim he was a Castro in sheep's clothing.

Jango launched a massive literacy campaign, which was sorely needed in Brazil, if reminiscent of a program in Havana. And he made powerful enemies. To alleviate millions of landless peasants, he expropriated large nonproductive plots, angering old plantation families. Foreign corporations were enraged by a tax reform that hit companies with headquarters abroad. He also spearheaded a campaign for a nuclear-free Latin America, presenting the U.N. General Assembly with a draft resolution.[2] The Pentagon saw this as a threat to its defenses.

The Brazilian generals moved against Jango in March 1964. Documents declassified in 2004 confirm allegations that the U.S. backed the coup. The U.S. ambassador of the moment, Lincoln Gordon, wrote in a cable that the CIA was "giving covert support for street rallies ... and encouragement (of) democratic and anti-communist sentiment in Congress, armed forces, friendly labor and student groups, church, and business."[3]

But the real juice is a recorded phone conversation between Ambassador Gordon and President Lyndon Johnson at his Texas ranch. The audio in the National Security Archive allows us to hear the entire conversation, listening to plotting from the heart of power.

In the briefing, Gordon tells the president how U.S. Navy ships are sailing from Aruba to the Brazilian coast to back up the generals. The U.S. commander in chief grunts his approval. "I think we ought to take every step that we can, be prepared to do everything that we need to do," Johnson says. "I'd get right on top of it and stick my neck out a little."[4]

These Cold War politics aren't worth getting too worked up about now. It is a debate of the last century, its physical and ideological battles largely history. The American government and secret services did what they believed was right to stop the spread of authoritarian communism, and in the process supported violent dictators and sustained wars. The cold warriors claim the final result—the Soviet Union collapsing—vindicated their efforts. Others argue blood was spilled in vain and the advent of democracy delayed.

But whether it was right or wrong, we need to look at how the Cold War played out in Latin America to understand crime families like the Red Commando. The gangster militias took life during these ideological conflicts, often under dictatorships, before becoming more deadly and uncontrollable in the era of democracy. We need to understand this move from Cold War to crime wars.

Following the coup, a first wave of political prisoners flooded the jails. These were not the leftist guerrillas, who would arrive later, but a mix of trade unionists, soldiers, and sailors sympathetic to ousted President Jango.

The political prisoners' talk of struggle and repression touched a nerve for William, and he became close to them. He was drawn to how they read, and borrowed books, starting a long love affair with literature. He adored the Brazilian writer Euclides da Cunha and his famous story of the War of Canudos, *Rebellion in the Backlands*. In the book, Cunha expresses sympathy for the wild-eyed rebels and paints the modern republic as being as barbaric as those it crushed. These ideas added to William's vision of a world divided into a repressive system, and a struggling, if faulted, underclass fighting for freedom.

A love of reading is a trait shared by criminal bosses across the Americas. Another Brazilian capo known as Marcola is said to have read three thousand books in prison, while the Mexican drug lord Nazario "The Maddest One" Moreno was a keen reader and writer (of his own bible). Other kingpins have a higher level of education than many in their armies of assassins. Jamaican crime lord Dudus Coke was studious in high school and said to be studying for a law degree at the time of his arrest. The capos generally come from bad areas, but they become the better educated within those areas. Some form of education, it seems, can be a trait that helps these kingpins rise.

When William was released from prison, he decided to move up in the world; he went from robbing wallets to robbing banks.

I wanted to live better as fast as possible. I had finished with stealing wallets, doing little thefts, mugging passersby. I left prison and decided to go to banks, armed with a gun to find the money that I needed. I would never get it through a normal job, that of a slave. Of course there were risks, but I was ready to take them. Prison had made me a professional criminal.[5]

Psychologists would call William a habitual criminal. It's hard to argue against that case. But he doesn't fit into the psychological profiles made of these repeat offenders. He's not of low intelligence, he is sociable and charismatic, and he doesn't appear naturally violent.

But he was a natural rebel. I wonder if he was looking for revenge for his mother and grandfather whom he saw beaten by police. Or had he become so used to prison he craved to be behind bars, another phenomenon recognized by psychologists? Or did he love the adrenaline of running in with a gun and asking for the loot?

Whatever his motive, it was a good time to be robbing banks in Brazil. Between 1968 and 1973, Brazil enjoyed its economic miracle, with growth of up to 14 percent a year. Rio was the financial heartland, before the big banks moved to São Paulo, and there were sacks of money to pilfer. William was one of the most reckless stickup artists stealing them.

This economic boom didn't improve everyone's lives. A small group of businessmen favored by the dictatorship got the lion's share. So while the country was getting richer it was also becoming more unequal. This spurred opposition, and paradoxically, as the economy grew, so did armed rebellion.

By the late sixties, Brazil's guerrillas became a significant force fighting the military regime. They were encouraged by the era's global revolts: in Prague, rebels stood in front of Soviet tanks; in Berkeley, rebels protested Vietnam; and in Brazil, rebels shot at soldiers.

Like in many insurgencies, several guerrilla groups formed and splintered, creating an alphabet soup of cells with interchanging members. The largest was the Revolutionary Movement 8th October, known as MR8. Members of the Brazilian Communist Party founded it, citing the day that Che Guevara was captured in Bolivia in 1967. As the name suggests, they were inspired by Guevara and his Cuban revolution.

However, while Cuban rebels defeated the weak Batista regime and took power, Brazilian insurgents were never able to fight open warfare against the generals. Most Brazilian opposition remained peaceful, and only a few thousand took up guns. They became a classic urban guerrilla outfit. They couldn't control territory like Cuban rebels, but moved around clandestine safe houses and launched sporadic attacks.

The guerrillas hailed overwhelmingly from the ranks of students and intellectuals. Their most famous member was code name Estela, who was none other than Brazil's current president Dilma Rousseff. Another, Franklin de Sousa Martins, would go on to become a press officer for President Lula. And another, Fernando Gabeira, would join the Green Party, win a seat in parliament, and run for mayor of Rio.

Gabeira gained notoriety for two actions. The first was being photographed on Ipanema Beach wearing a purple women's G-string. The picture gave him a lot of cred with young voters when he ran for mayor. This is a revolutionary, Brazilian style. The second was kidnapping the U.S. ambassador in MR8's most notorious operation in 1969.

The kidnapping of Ambassador Charles Burke Elbrick was one of the biggest Cold War attacks on U.S. officials in Latin America. It later got made into the Oscar-nominated Brazilian film *Four Days in September*. Elbrick was a sixty-one-year-old foreign-service veteran who had served in Poland during World War II, followed by Yugoslavia, where he dealt with Tito. He was in Brazil fifty-seven days when he was nabbed.

His wife, Elvira, recounts the abduction in detail.[6] She describes how they were delighted to leave communist Eastern Europe for South America, looking forward to carnivals and Copacabana. Two months in, Elvira was getting ready for a charity event selling Levi's jeans and cupcakes, when her secretary said that her husband had been kidnapped.

"What! We just had lunch together," I said. "When?" And she said, "About three minutes after he entered his limousine to go back to his office."

He was caught on a side street, intercepted by a Volkswagen, and they dragged the chauffeur out of the limousine and tore out the telephone, put a tarpaulin on Burke in the back of the car ... Then they went on and on and on for quite a long time—close to two hours—and later Burke told me that he had read enough of Agatha Christie and Alfred Hitchcock to know that sometimes by hearing you could judge where you were going.

Elbrick realized they were driving into the mountains. The MR8 guerrillas dragged him out to a ranch where Gabeira was waiting, sat him on a stool, and gave him a book of Ho Chi Minh to read. Then they questioned him all night.

> He felt they were going to shoot him on the spot. He didn't know what they were going to do, so he resisted which he shouldn't have done. That's when they beat him terribly on the head. So he was all night long being quizzed about nothing that he could answer. He knew nothing about the country . . .
>
> But they began to treat him all right really and then he could communicate. He said, "Why do you rely on violence with an innocent victim like myself knowing nothing about your country, or your politics? I've just arrived here and violence doesn't pay." And they said, "Well, because the government won't listen to us."

President Richard Nixon had sent Elbrick to Brazil. But according to Elvira, Nixon left him out in the cold, refusing to intervene. Luckily, the Brazilian regime itself negotiated a settlement, handing over political prisoners, and Elbrick was released after four days.

Elbrick suffered seventy-five stitches in his head and underwent ten operations over the following decade. Two years after his treatment was finished, he died of pneumonia, age seventy-five. Following his death, Elvira managed to catch up with Nixon at a funeral.

> I said, "Do you happen to recall a man by the name of Burke Elbrick?" And he said, "Oh, yes. I appointed him as ambassador to Brazil."
>
> And I said, "Do you remember that he was kidnapped down there and that you were his Judas and his Pontius Pilate?" And I said, "Goodbye, Mr. Watergate," and walked away.

While Nixon left his ambassador in the lurch, the U.S. government supported Brazil's military dictatorship as it killed and tortured. The Brazilian military junta was a long way from a Stalin or Hitler regime that murdered millions. But it was a repressive dictatorship. A truth commission determined that during its rule, police and soldiers murdered or forcibly disappeared up to five hundred people. They tortured and imprisoned many more, and thousands went into exile.

A declassified U.S. State Department memo describes this torture in graphic detail. The torturers, it explains, used classic Brazilian techniques such as electric shocks from cattle prods and the *pau de arara*, in which prisoners hang by their arms and legs from a metal bar. The memo also depicts new techniques that its author finds interesting as they inflict maximum pain while leaving minimum marks.

> If the suspect does not confess, and if it is believed that he is withhold-ing valuable information, he is subjected to increasingly painful phys-ical and mental duress until he confesses. He is placed nude in a small dark room with a metal floor through which an electrical current is pulsated. The shock felt by the individual, though reportedly light in intensity, is constant and eventually becomes almost impossible to withstand. The suspect is usually kept in this room for several hours. He may then be transferred to several other "special effects" rooms in which devices are used to instill fear and physical discomfort. Extreme mental and physical fatigue sometimes results, especially if the person undergoes such treatment for two or three days. All during this time, he is not allowed food or water.[7]

Among those who suffered this agony was the young Dilma, alias Estela. She was arrested at age twenty-two and jailed for three years. When she later became president, she recalled the torture of her youth. "The interrogation started, generally with electric shocks, growing in intensity, and then there were sessions of *pau de arara*," she remembered. "My jaw was dislocated. That still causes me problems until today." These wounds, she said, "are a part of me."[8]

The torture and murder campaign damaged Brazilian guerilla groups but didn't destroy them. Militants kept launching attacks that would kill close to a hundred police officers, soldiers, and civilians. To finance these strikes, the guerrillas turned, like the ghetto criminals, to robbing banks. Financial institutions in Rio were hammered from all sides.

During the height of the insurgency, William was caught holding up a Rio bank branch and officers suspected him (mistakenly) of being a guerrilla operative. Police handed him over to an army base where for four days he suffered electric shocks and beatings while his interrog-ators demanded to know which cell of guerrillas he belonged to. They also gave him truth drugs, but he would hold them under his tongue and spit them out. In the end, when he was hanging up by his arms and legs, battered and bruised, he yelled, "I belong to the organization of joint smokers!"

The memory of telling his interrogators this line causes him to smile particularly wide now—but I don't know what kind of pain it gave him back then.

"What about the Red Commando?" I ask William for about the fifth time. He raises his hand. "I am just getting to that."

CHAPTER 9

The name Red Commando first appears in government reports and newspaper stories in 1979. William confirms it was baptized that year, but says the organization was brewing for about five years before, as political prisoners mixed with criminals in this turbulent period. He sees it as a natural, organic thing. "I didn't found the Red Commando," he says. "It was born. It was born of oppression."[1]

Political prisoners forged links with inmates in various jails. But the biggest fusion was made on the Ilha Grande prison island, Brazil's own Alcatraz. William was sent there after he led a prison riot.

Following his arrest for bank robbery, William was held in the Helio Gomes transit jail where he waited for a prison placement. As a holding pen, Helio Gomes was especially violent, inmates stuffed together, seasoned killers alongside green teenagers. William saw men cut up and raped in front of him. He was determined to escape.

He plotted his jailbreak with a dozen cohorts. They smuggled in a saw, chisel, and hammer and dug a hole from their cell to a corridor. Their plan was to climb out the tunnel when guards changed shifts, overpower them, dress in their uniforms, and head over the roof.

When he describes this to me, it sounds like such a harebrained scheme I wonder how they dreamed it could succeed. But it got quite far. They made it through their tunnel right as guards were switching shifts and took nine hostages. And they succeeded in disguising themselves in the uniforms and getting through the cellblock. But then it (predictably) fell apart.

"A guard recognized us, so we had to set him on fire with gasoline. We got to the roof and police snipers were shooting us, so we used our hostages to make a shield. Luckily the story of the riot got out on the radio. Otherwise the police would have killed us all."

They nearly killed them anyway. Hundreds of officers surrounded the rioters and moved in with gunshots and blows. William was shot in the hand and beaten, and spent a month in hospital before they shipped him to Ilha Grande.

Like on all prison islands, natural defenses stop inmates from escaping Ilha Grande. It sits in seething heat, surrounded by rough sea and covered by inhospitable jungle. But the most vicious animals were in the gray cell-blocks and dirt yards—convicted killers and the guards keeping them in line.

When William arrived on the island with others from the Helio Gomes jailbreak, angry officers forced them to walk a gauntlet while they took revenge blows. They beat one prisoner so badly he needed artificial resuscitation.

They named William as a ringleader and sent him to a wing of a 120 prisoners, considered among the most dangerous in Brazil. Ninety were common criminals and thirty were leftist guerillas. The inmates called this wing "The Pit."

Looking back, it's easy to see the foolish mistake of sticking desperado bank robbers like William in a pen with leftist guerrillas. But it's easy to judge with hindsight. In the rocky days of the seventies it was hard to imagine this motley crew of convicts would create a movement that would cause Brazil problems three decades later. And pressure came from high up not to recognize the status of political prisoners.

The fusion of prisoners was not straightforward either. It might sound like a joyous moment of cross-class solidarity. But there was friction between the university-educated children of middle-class Brazilians and robbers from the villages and favelas.

"The political prisoners fought to differentiate themselves from the rest of the inmates, an attitude that we considered to be elitist," William writes. "In our eyes, their desire to single themselves out from the other detainees was an expression of the hegemony of the middle class."[2]

But in response to a brutal prison regime, the alliance gradually solidified. Guards entered the Pit during day or night to beat prisoners. They were trying to crush their resistance by keeping them on edge. To defend themselves, the prisoners invented a technique of bunching together with whoever was being beaten, creating a scrum to shield them.

As William recounts this moment, his face looks intensely happy. It was a defining moment for him. After years of suffering hidings from police, soldiers, and prison guards, he witnessed a way to stop it, through solidarity. I am reminded of the Italian peasant cooperatives that declared that while one twig can be broken, a bundle of twigs will stand firm. (Italian fascists later stole the concept.)

As they drew together, the Pit prisoners created rules for their wing. The first challenge was to ban fighting and murder among themselves. Any grudges had to be settled on the outside. Rape was forbidden. Theft was forbidden.

Influenced by the political prisoners, they shared and rationed food. While authorities provided basic provisions, prisoners relied on what relatives sent from the mainland. Dividing it up, William found, they could eat better more often. (Like the parable of the feeding of the five thousand.)

The Pit prisoners then found a surprising chance to challenge guards legally. Two inmates working on the outside perimeter made a dash to the bushes to try and escape. The guards dragged them back and beat them to death.

The murder was in full sight of the prisoners, but it was outside their bars, so they were powerless to help the victims. However, the political prisoners prepared a legal complaint and everyone in the Pit signed on as witnesses. William was amazed that several warders were punished. He saw their movement could challenge the system.

Prison authorities also recognized this threat of politicized criminals. To try and diffuse it, they moved the leaders to other jails, transferring William to mainland Rio State in 1976. But rather than stopping the newfound organization, they spread it.

Inmates in Rio's prisons were just waiting to be organized, William says. With tens of thousands of convicts crowded into shit-infested, decaying buildings, brutality had got out of control. William points to a young father inside for marijuana who was being repeatedly raped. In another case, he saw a man murdered over a piece of bread. They needed structure to stop them from behaving like animals. William and other Pit veterans got prisoners to accept rules that put a basic order in their lives and offered the weak a defense against predators.

This is a driving force behind prison gangs in Latin America. Inmates organize to survive. This includes arranging basic things such as sleeping spaces. In some prisons, they even have to share space for conjugal visits. Without rules, they face the threat of their spouses being raped.

But guards saw prisoners organizing as a menace and tried to break them up. William and a friend called Nelson Nogueira dos Santos led prisoners to scrum together against beatings as they had on the island. The guards took Nelson to another cell and battered him. Nelson started a hunger strike and William and the others followed suit.

A hunger strike was an interesting technique for inmates to choose. The criminals were increasingly following the global tactics of political prisoners from that era. However, the guards refused to budge, and Nelson died of starvation after forty-eight days. The rest abandoned the effort. The hunger strike was broken, but it echoed through the prison system.

In one jail, twelve prisoners took the director hostage and demanded safe passage to Mexico. Police stormed in and shot all the inmates dead, along with the director himself. In another case, one of William's friends tried to escape and was surrounded by guards. He managed to stab an officer to death before they slew him. "He made it one all, instead of one nil," William says, comparing the double killing to a soccer score.

The deaths alarmed prison wardens, so they reversed course and moved the leaders, including William, back to Ilha Grande. They figured it was better to have the disease concentrated in the Pit. But it was hard to contain it even there. Other inmates on the island began following the Pit prisoners. The organization spread into the general population.

Not all the prisoners liked the new rules. A gang of robbers butted up against the political upstarts and murdered two of the Pit prisoners. The Pit prisoners responded by capturing six members of the gang. They judged them and found them guilty. And they bludgeoned and stabbed them to death.

Murdering six men is a savage act. But Pit prisoners saw it as a fight for survival and the only way to shield themselves from more attacks. It is striking they "judged" the prisoners, one of the first "trials" of the commando's alternative justice system, which would spread through prison wings and ghettos.

"The repercussions were huge throughout the entire penal system," William writes. "In a short time the code of the old Pit was extended to all prisons: death to anyone who attacked or raped a comrade."[3]

When the prison director wrote up his report on the "executions," he needed to give the Pit prisoners a name. He wanted to show his superiors there was a conspiracy. It's also simply hard to describe these actions without a name. Thus he called them the "Red Commando" in his report. Ironically, it was a prison director who baptized them.

Authorities giving criminal groups names that stick is common. It's likely Mexico's notorious Guadalajara Cartel was named by DEA agents in their dispatches to Washington. Again they needed to give the conspiracy a name and wanted to grab attention.

The Brazilian media picked up on the director's report and the mysterious communist crime group became a national story. If inmates across Rio State hadn't heard of this collective of prisoners before, then they had now.

At first, the Pit prisoners resented the name that had been invented by a prisoner director.

"We had been thoroughly demonized," William writes. "Words are not neutral. We had become a 'commando,' which in military language signifies an active center that must be destroyed by its opponents. And as if that was not enough, we were also 'red,' an adjective which has always aroused murderous reflexes among the police and the military."[4]

However, as the name spread through prisons and streets gathering mystique, William and the others eventually warmed to it.

"We said, 'Well we're reds aren't we.' And we began to use it with pride."

The growth of the Red Commando made the Brazilian dictatorship realize that locking up political prisoners with gangsters did more harm than good. And in that same year, they passed an amnesty law, granting political prisoners freedom despite being in guerrilla groups, shooting soldiers, and robbing banks.

The Red Commando was not the only reason for the 1979 amnesty. The military regime appointed a new president in General João Baptista Figueiredo, who declared he wanted to steer Brazil back to democracy. He allowed more freedom of the press and promised free elections (which took another decade to come about). The country was also in economic turmoil after oil prices shot up, and some generals thought it better to let civilians handle the mess.

The amnesty allowed thousands of exiles to return. Gabeira, who had kidnapped the U.S. ambassador, came back from Sweden where he had been living. The regime pardoned his crimes and this was when he posed on the beach in a women's G-string. It was an era of reconciliation.

The amnesty had a flip side that was even more controversial. As well as pardoning the leftist militants, it also pardoned police, soldiers, and prison guards of their murders, angering human rights defenders. Whatever they had done, everybody was given a clean slate.

Everybody, that is, except for William and other common criminals in the Red Commando.

William looks irate when he talks about this. The political prisoners they had been fighting side by side with could walk out of jail free and climb in politics or the media. But William and others stayed in the filthy prisons. William is particularly miffed as he was convicted under the dictatorship's same laws.

Of course, it is hard to justify releasing convicts who had robbed banks for personal gain. But William sees his crimes as political in a broader sense, and himself as a robber because he was born poor. This echoes a self-justification made by gangsters across the Americas.

To William, it stank of betrayal. However, he wasn't going to be second best to middle-class leftists. If the regime wouldn't free him, he would find his own way out. On January 2, 1980, William escaped from Ilha Grande. In doing so, he took the Red Commando from the cellblock to the ghetto.

CHAPTER 10

William took advantage of the amnesty turmoil and New Year celebrations to make his move. He smuggled in a revolver, arranged to work on the outside perimeter, and tore off into the jungle.

Even away from the prison building, it was tough to escape the torturous island. Many inmates who tried had been hunted down by guards or had starved to death in the wild. But fortune shined on William when he found students who had come on a speedboat for a New Year's camping trip.

He swung out his gun to commandeer their boat. But there was no bloodbath. In the spirit of Brazilian sociality, William made friends with the campers and went off to another island where they passed the night drinking whiskey. When the campers left, one of them lent William clothes, and he arrived on the mainland wearing shorts and Hawaiian sandals.

Walking into town, William called up friends, who promptly arrived with guns and announced they were planning a bank job. William wanted in.

Over his next months on the run, William went on the most spectacular bank-robbing spree of his career. With his contacts from the growing Red Commando, he got intelligence on stashes, firearms to go in blasting, and outlaws to back him up. Among them was another seasoned commando stickup artist called José "Zé Bigode" Saldanha, or Joe Mustache. (He wore a handlebar mustache.)

"We would go in and shout, 'This is the Red Commando, get down!' " remembers William, joy shining through his eyes. "Then we would shoot down photos of politicians and throw firebombs at police."

Following the fusion with the guerrillas, the Red Commando claimed its robberies made a political statement. Brazilian journalist Carlos Amorim writes how they expressed themselves in their newfound revolutionary terms: "The vocabulary of crime found new words. Robberies were 'expropriations,' or 'taking back.' A gang became a 'collective,' and was baptized with a name like 'liberation group.' "[1]

William made—or expropriated—a lot of money in these robberies. But now seeing himself as a resistance fighter, he didn't keep the money for himself, instead spreading it through the Red Commando's web. Some cash went back into prisons to support comrades behind bars. This set a tradition in the commando that carries on today. Those on the outside pay the hoods in jail, providing members with a kind of insurance scheme.

They also gave money to a guerrilla group that had been involved in the formation of the Red Commando, William says. Despite the amnesty law, some guerrillas still operated until the dictatorship ended. William complains a lot of money disappeared into the hands of guerilla leaders who later became politicians.

"Who knows what they did with the money?" William sighs lightly, his anger seeming to have dissipated over the decades.

William also turned his loot into charity. He took to ground in favelas in northern Rio such as one called Serrinha, where he had prison buddies. It was a good place to evade the police, getting lost in the labyrinth of alleys. In his newfound neighborhood, William bought concrete to pave the street and paid for the sewage system. This began the tradition of the commando financing community schemes—or buying the support of residents not to snitch.

While criminals had given handouts in the slums before, the commando was novel in its sprawling network and sense of mission. The Reds' spectacular bank robberies made front pages, adding to their mystique. Young hoods lined up to join.

As membership mushroomed, Red Commando leaders decided they had to teach the young gunslingers the values they had learned on the prison island. So they wrote a pamphlet with twelve points and passed it round. Police later found a copy from a captured bank robber and nicknamed it "The Manual of the Good Bandit."[2]

The journalist Amorim points out that it was in a similar format to a pamphlet used by a guerrilla cell whose members had been involved in the commando. But in many ways, the manual is apolitical. Some of its commandments try to instill limits on violence. Number five is to "Respect woman, children and the vulnerable."

Others are tips on how to be an effective criminal, such as number three, which says to "Always have a gun that is clean and with bullets."

Another command, number two, repeats an adage of wisdom of seasoned criminals by simply saying, "Don't trust anybody."

Such rules don't constitute an ideology. But they are a code of values. And that is perhaps the best way to describe the Red Commando; it's an honor code to regulate criminals within a community.

Rules can also attract members. If an organization has a pamphlet, however banal, it spreads word of the group, makes it more "official." Many teenagers with a lack of direction are drawn to something that gives a sense of inclusion and purpose.

William's glorious freedom of dancing at favela parties and robbing banks was short-lived. After the spree of heists, bank owners put pressure on police to round up the gang leaders. The Red Commando was also a victim of its own success, William moans, as every holdup was blamed on them, even ones that they didn't do. And police officers claimed any two-bit criminal they arrested was a Red Commando member.

The heat put William on top of the wanted list, his photo drilled into the minds of police officers. He was safe in the favela, where he could hide and people wouldn't inform. But he made the mistake of going downtown. Police recognized him and nabbed him after ten months on the lam.

Other commando bosses met a bloodier fate, with police gunning to take them out for good. A leader called Nanai escaped Ilha Grande to a waiting car on the coast. A police helicopter followed him and alerted officers who shot him dead at the wheel of a black Volkswagen Bug.

A few months later, William's bank-robbing buddy Joe Mustache was cornered in a block of apartments. Four hundred police surrounded him, but Mustache kept his ground and fired from the windows like the finale of *Butch Cassidy and the Sundance Kid*. The standoff lasted hours, allowing reporters to broadcast the siege live on the radio. Four hundred policemen versus one desperado. Saldanha was reported to shout out the window, "Calm down, my friends, let's talk about this!"

Before a police marksman shot him dead.

As William marched back into prison, inmates cheered and banged the walls to greet him. The spree of robberies had made him infamous. And while he was outside, the commando had recruited members throughout the prison system. Now, he was no lonely villain but a leader of a growing gang. And as he had paid money from the outside, he would be cared for while he was banged up.

Still William was determined to win his freedom. In 1983, he and other Red Commando prisoners made another escape attempt through a tunnel. They managed to get outside, only to be recaptured by angry military police. William was forced to lie down and a guard smashed him over the head with a crushing blow.

> Stretched out on the ground, I didn't see the blow coming and didn't have time to make a defensive gesture. Later I woke coughing up blood, my head filled with infernal pain. At the hospital where they sent me they explained that I had nearly died and it was a miracle I was not paralyzed.[3]

He still suffers from the injury today.

Some believe bad and good things arrive in our lives together, like clouds with silver linings. In William's case, his injury coincided with his love for Simone. He tells the story in romantic language.

Simone came to the prison as a support worker and helped with his many legal cases. William was impressed by her bravery entering the jail of leering hardened criminals. He made their meetings last as long as he could, as he told her his life story, his fears, and his hopes. He quickly fell head over heels and wanted to declare his love for her but was terrified she would refuse. Eventually, on what was supposed to be their last meeting, she beat him to it.

> Simone spoke calmly. She had been touched by our first meeting in August. Having heard so many lies about me she had expected to be faced with a powerful boss figure and had seen instead a simple, vulnerable person wearing shorts and espadrilles with no desire to impress and apparently without any special power. A gentle person. She had

immediately felt sympathy and indeed tenderness for me. Who was I really? What was I feeling? She was absolutely devastated at having to leave. She wanted to tell me that she was in love with me.

It was written in the stars.[4]

Brazilian politics were also going through a loved-up period as the generals put a civilian in power in 1985, ending the military dictatorship. In the democratic spirit, the guerrillas rose inside legal political parties and broke off remaining links with the Red Commando.

But the commando continued to grow, spreading to almost every prison in Rio State and many favelas. Jailing its leaders such as William did not stop them giving orders to those outside. Latin American nations struggle with the problem of gangs ruling the streets from behind bars. Penitentiaries provide venues where leaders can meet and communicate. They are places where up-and-coming thugs get a chance to know the top guys and win their favor. Those on the street obey the orders of those in prison and pay their dues, because they know they could end up jailed themselves.

Brazil has tried moving leaders to far-off jails and isolating them. But it is hard to cut off gang leaders completely as the law allows them to talk with counselors or family members who convey messages. Furthermore, Brazil's prison directors often bow to the pressure of the Red Commando to give them certain liberties, allowing leaders to share cells. If the commando doesn't get its demands, it can orchestrate attacks on police and start prison riots.

Despite the problems it causes, the commando also creates a certain order in the jail, often reducing violence and providing an alternate authority that guards can deal with.

"Negotiating with the commando is the only way that the guards can operate," says Simone after her three decades of working in jails. "Like in any society above a certain size, you need organizations. The prison authorities give the inmates nothing. They leave it up to the commando to create order."

This creates another paradox of Latin America's crime wars. Prisons are meant to stop gangsters from committing crimes. But they became their headquarters.

CHAPTER 11

The growing legion of Red Commando gunmen meant more salaries to pay. But as the eighties progressed, banks in Brazil, and across the world, installed sophisticated security such as cameras and time-locked vault doors. Moves to credit cards and electronic money also meant fewer bills to pilfer. The golden days of bank robbing—especially by urban guerrillas in flared trousers—were over.

However, the Red Commando found a new business, one that could finance its expansion for the next generation. They made their fortune with the drug known as blow, snow, yayo, Charlie, Chang, perico, parrot, c-dust, or, more commonly, cocaine.

In the Antares favela, I see the Red Commando's lucrative product on display, the white powder packaged into transparent baggies. The funk partiers sprinkle the dust into lines and snort it up their noses to get the coke high: a buzz of energy, the feeling of elation, the urge to dance hard to the beat, the ability to have prolonged sex. In New York, a gram can cost a hundred dollars, and in Europe, it sells for over 150 euros. But here, close to the Andes where it comes from, it's cheap and cheerful at about fifteen bucks a gram.

Some Antares residents choose the even cheaper form of crack rocks at two dollars a hit. Crack is made by cooking up cocaine with baking powder and is smoked in a glass pipe, or more often in a beer can with holes pricked through. It gives a more intense version of the coke high, an extra rush of elation, and is way more addictive.

The history of the "wonder drug" has been well documented. German scientists first isolated cocaine from the coca leaves of the Andes in the

1850s. It boomed in the United States in the 1970s when it powered the disco explosion from Miami to New York. Colombians produced most of this cocaine, flying it straight over the Caribbean to Florida. These were the days when *Time* named it the all-American drug and Woody Allen sneezed into a tin of cocaine to cinematic guffaws in *Annie Hall*. While audiences were in stitches, the coke dollars created the first drug trafficking billionaires in Pablo Escobar and his cronies in the Medellín Cartel.

From the 1980s, cocaine became increasingly popular over the pond in Europe. Ravers in London, Madrid, and Rome all wanted some of the action they saw in *Miami Vice*. A major route for this Atlantic-bound cocaine is naturally Brazil; Colombia and the other coca-producing countries of Peru and Bolivia all share land borders with the South American giant. Once in Brazil, traffickers take cocaine on the many commercial ships to Portugal and Spain, or to Africa and over the Mediterranean into Europe.

Colombian traffickers worked with Brazilian crooks to move the powder through their country. As the Red Commando controls Rio, one of Brazil's biggest ports, it was quick to get a piece. The Red Commando hoods began as paid couriers, moving produce and guarding it in stash houses. But soon they became traffickers themselves.

As well as moving drugs to Europe, the Red Commando capitalized on the local market. Simone has one story about how the cocaine heading east leaked onto Rio's streets.

"In the early eighties, you started realizing that drugs were moving through the city, going on these boats to Africa and Europe. Then one summer, a Chilean ship was searched by police and the traffickers threw these crates of tomato cans that had drugs in them into the sea.

"The cans washed up on the beach. They were these big red tins and people opened them up and found all these drugs inside. Suddenly everyone was taking the chemicals. It was known as the summer of the cans."

It's a cute story. But U.S. and Brazilian drug agents describe another way that might have been more important to cocaine spilling onto Brazil's streets. Colombian traffickers often paid their couriers with cocaine instead of money. This made both parties happy. For the trafficker it is cheaper, while the courier makes extra cash selling the drugs locally.

For example, a kilo brick of cocaine costs about two thousand dollars in Colombia. But on the streets of Brazil, it can be broken down into grams and sold for fifteen thousand. It is easier for a trafficker to pay someone with a brick and allow them to make the markup themselves. When the trafficker gets his drugs to the United States, a brick can be broken down to fetch more than a hundred thousand dollars, and in Europe it can make double that.

Such is the wonder of cocaine economics. Its prices shoot up at such a ridiculous rate along the chain that everybody wants a part of it, especially the ones with the biggest guns. The result is that trafficking routes for cocaine, such as those through Brazil and Mexico, leave behind millions of users in their wake.

The Brazilian cocaine market boomed. The party powder found a river of customers in the nation of two hundred million, blending in with Brazil's festive lifestyle just as it did with the American disco scene. Brazilians shook to samba and funk on the coke high.

Brazil is now likely the second biggest consumer of cocaine in the world after the United States. The United Nations estimated 1.4 percent of Brazilians had used the powder or rock in the last year, close to the 1.5 percent of Americans believed to use it.[1] In its aspiration to reach the first world, Brazil is becoming a true consumer nation—in both car and cocaine sales.

The U.N. estimated that there were 2.8 million Brazilian cocaine users, smoking or snorting their way through ninety-two tons of blow every year. That translates to more than a billion dollars annually going to gangs such as the Red Commando. And Brazilians also spend on marijuana and other drugs.

It was a fate of history that Brazil's cocaine market exploded when the Red Commando was in place in the favelas. The money financed the commando's sellers and soldiers to spread further across Rio State, and then to cells, allies, and rivals across Brazil. The commando opened bocas like the ones in Antares in hundreds of favelas, creating thousands of employees.

In line with its revolutionary rhetoric, the Red Commando justified selling coke by saying it was a vice of wealthy Brazilians that gave the poor an income.

"The middle class went to the favela and they wanted drugs. So the Red Commando provided it for them," William says.

However, the vice spread to favela dwellers, with dealers sniffing as they sold it. Many slum residents also developed a taste for rocks, sparking a crack wave in Brazil today that is reminiscent of the U.S.

crack epidemic in the eighties. A government survey found that Brazil has now usurped the United States as the biggest crack-using country in the world, with at least 370,000 people burning their lives away through pipes.[2]

The Antares favela has a spot under the train bridge where hard-core addicts hang out. They call it a *crackolândia*, or a "crackland." I go there to find two dozen smokers lying about in filthy clothes, drawing on pipes, with numb expressions on their faces. The Red Commando might put on lively parties, but this is another side of what it brings here.

Cocaine sales in Brazil, Europe, and the United States all added to the fortunes of Pablo Escobar and his fellow Colombian crime kings. *Forbes* said Escobar was personally worth three billion dollars, with some other media outlets putting his wealth in eleven digits.[3] I am suspicious of pinning exact numbers on their treasure as no one really knows the precise wealth of these traffickers, probably not even the kingpins themselves. But judging from the amount of cocaine users and money paid for it, it is fair to estimate he was a multibillionaire.

Escobar's story is immortalized in a mammoth Spanish-language TV series with 113 episodes that is a hit across Latin America. The drug lord built an entire neighborhood in Medellín, financed an army of killers to shoot police, and brought down an airliner, killing 110 people, including two Americans.[4] His murder spree made him enemies everywhere, leading to a manhunt involving the Colombian police and army, rival traffickers, the DEA, Pentagon, and CIA. When Colombian special forces finally killed Escobar in 1993, they posed smiling with the body of the world's greatest outlaw.

However, Escobar's death hardly dented the cocaine trade, with a host of other players taking over. Rival traffickers such as the Cali Cartel and later Norte del Valle Cartel got a piece as did right-wing paramilitaries. But one of the biggest winners was the Revolutionary Armed Forces of Colombia, or FARC, the leftist guerrilla army.

The FARC formed back in 1964, uniting armed peasants into an insurgent force that vaguely followed the Cuban model. The guerrillas were a minor threat until the eighties when in their seventh conference they approved the motion to traffic in cocaine to fund their revolution.[5] It was an effective fit. A guerrilla army provides a strong organization to traffic drugs, and cocaine money buys guns, uniforms, and food for more guerrillas. They grew, especially following Escobar's downfall, taking over important coca producing regions.

After Escobar, Mexican cartels also took a bigger share of the cocaine trade to the United States and Brazilian traffickers of the trade to Europe. Among them were smugglers in the Red Commando.

Escobar left his shadow over criminals across the continent. Some see the heights he rose to, while others note his superstar profile led to his death. However, when I ask William about the Colombian drug lord, his face crunches up.

"Pablo Escobar was a traitor. He ordered hits on kids. He used police as security," William says.

I wonder if Escobar ever double-crossed the Red Commando. But Simone chips in with another explanation for William's ire.

"They are jealous in Brazil, because Pablo Escobar reached a level that none of them got to." She smiles. "You talk about traffickers here. But he had billions and billions of dollars."

William cuts in again. "He was a mercenary. He was right wing. He was a traitor." I ask William what he thinks of the FARC guerrillas, and his tone switches 180 degrees.

"They had some good ideas," William says. "They sold cocaine to the United States."

It is interesting to hear William's sympathy for the FARC. In many ways, the Red Commando and the FARC traveled opposite journeys. The Red Commando was a gang of criminals who became politicized; the FARC was a political force that got into drug trafficking. But I see the similarity. They both claim to represent the poor, fight police, and sell cocaine.

William's sympathy for the FARC also reflects the Red Commando's business interests; the two groups became increasingly close in moving cocaine and guns. The FARC controlled large coca-producing areas and built their own labs to turn the green leaves into cocaine bricks. However, the guerrillas didn't themselves smuggle the cocaine into Europe or the United States, instead finding traffickers they could sell to or trade with.

The Red Commando was a perfect partner, sharing the idea of being a poor man's army. Furthermore, the commando built a web to traffic guns, which it could trade with the FARC for the white powder. The Reds bought many of their weapons in small South American nations such as Paraguay, Bolivia, and Surinam where corrupt soldiers stole them from national armies. That is why the gunmen I see dancing in the favelas are armed with military-grade rifles and grenade launchers.

The alliance pumped cocaine profits back into the FARC, swelling the ranks of the guerrillas. By the turn of the millennium, the white windfall allowed the FARC to command seventeen thousand troops, blow up Colombian soldiers, and carry out mass kidnappings—which made them even more money.

This fusion of insurgent attacks and cocaine trafficking made American agents ring the alarm bells of "narco terrorism." The phrase was probably coined in neighboring Peru in the early eighties when President Fernando Belaúnde Terry warned of the Shining Path guerrillas working with coca growers.[6] But U.S. agents really took it up to refer to the FARC, which became a focus of worry amid the War on Terror. The term brings together the DEA, responsible for the narco part of the phrase, with the CIA, responsible for the terrorist part. The agencies combined forces with their web of narc informants and spy planes to go after the Colombian guerrillas. And this drew them into chasing the Red Commando.

The Red Commando point man to deal with the FARC was Luiz Fernando da Costa, alias Fernandinho Beira-Mar, or Seaside Freddy. Born in a Rio favela in 1967, Seaside joined the army at eighteen, before police arrested him for robbing jewelry stores and selling drugs. In prison, he got to know Red Commando leaders including William and gained their respect. "He is a good man," William tells me. "A good friend."

Seaside was also a violent, jealous man. Brazilian police tapped a phone call in which he ordered the murder of a guy who dated his former girlfriend. He told his thugs to cut off the man's hands, feet, and ears with a chain saw before shooting him, according to the transcript.

Escaping prison in 1997, Seaside moved around Surinam, Bolivia, and Paraguay, buying guns for the commando. U.S. agents following the FARC then spotted him in Colombia in 2001, in a town called Barranco Minas. Over three months, Seaside delivered 2,400 handguns and 543 rifles to the guerrillas in exchange for cocaine, according to informants cited in U.S. court documents.[7] Seaside was working with the head of the guerrillas' sixteenth front, a commander called Tomás Molina.

The Rio security minister flew to Washington to discuss the case with American and Colombian agents. They launched Operation Black Cat to get the Red Commando trafficker.

It wasn't an easy takedown. Colombian forces struck Barranco Minas and shot Seaside three times, but he got away in a Cessna plane. Again, the Colombian military tracked him and shot his aircraft down. Still, Seaside wasn't giving up. While hundreds of soldiers hunted him, he fled through 150 miles of jungle toward the Venezuelan border. But before he could make it over the line, soldiers descended upon him. Wounded and exhausted, Seaside was captured without a shot, and Colombia extradited him to Brazil.

However, Seaside's arrest didn't stop the cocaine flow. New commando bosses filled his shoes, going back to Colombia and turning to Peru, which has stepped up its cocaine production to cater for the booming markets. The United Nations estimated that Peru churned out 340 tons of cocaine in 2013, compared to 309 tons in Colombia. While Brazilian jails hit record overcrowding, the cocaine pipeline keeps flowing, keeping the baggies of powder full from tables in the Antares favela to nightclubs in London.

CHAPTER 12

Cocaine profits boosted the Red Commando to a size that William had never imagined. But the white gold that spurred its growth drove it into conflict. Traffickers ordered the death of anyone caught stealing from drug shops and stash houses. And midlevel commanders fought over money, leading to splinter groups.

The biggest break off became the Third Commando. The name was first used in the early 1990s, although some of the Third's traffickers were drifting away before. The Third Commando created an identical structure to the Reds, with operatives running drug shops under the command of favela bosses. However, they distinguished themselves by taking the moral high ground of saying they wouldn't sell crack—a claim that several traffickers I talk to confirm as being sincere.

In the late nineties, another commando calling itself the Amigos dos Amigos, or Friends of Friends, also emerged, making it an even more complicated battlefield. The splinters meant the Red Commando not only fought police but also other favela armies, who all recruited thousands of soldiers. In some favelas, former police officers and others formed militias to hit back against the drug dealers—and forced residents to pay protection for this service. The rival commandos and militias battled back and forth over territory, creating a patchwork of shifting turf across the ghettos of Rio State.

The fighting made Brazil's murder rate skyrocket. In 1980, there were thirteen thousand homicides in Brazil; by 1992, this rose to twenty-eight thousand. By 2003, there were fifty-one thousand murders. It is one of the most extreme spikes of violence in the continent. In Rio State alone, fifty-two thousand people were killed in a decade.

*　*　*

The violence exploded just as Brazil was trying to demilitarize. The guer-rilla uprising was over, the Cold War finished, civil liberties written into new laws. Yet, instead of peace, Brazilian security forces found themselves up against more guns than ever.

One of those policing this bloodbath is Rodrigo Oliveira, commander of an elite Rio police unit called the Coordenadoria de Recursos Especiais (CORE). He joined the force in 1994 and has served twenty years, shoot-ing it out with drug traffickers in the worst favelas.

Walking through the police base to meet him, I see his squad's vehicles resemble tanks with shooting holes and thick armor that has been pock-marked by bullets. The CORE is a bit like a SWAT team in the United States. Except it has seen far more action. Its logo is a skull with a knife through it and its officers are built like wrestlers with muscles bulging out of their necks. Many practice Brazilians' own strand of jujitsu and are fans of Ultimate Fighting Championship. They are seriously combat hardened.

Commander Oliveira seems remarkably happy for somebody with such a high-risk job. After we talk for ten minutes, he reveals that he has a bullet embedded in the back of his head from a shootout with traffickers. The bullet hit him when he was called in to help two officers who were cornered in a house under fire. A colleague hauled Oliveira out, saving his life. It was the day of Oliveira's son's first birthday.

"The bullet stuck in my head and the doctors couldn't get it out." Oliveira points to the back of his braincase. "I was in the hospital for two days, and one week later I was back at work. There is a reason for that. If you stop, you are going to be afraid the next time. You can't stop."

The son of a Rio tax lawyer, Oliveira said he always dreamed of being a police officer. However, he joined the army first, where he spent four years. Paradoxically, he saw no combat in the army, but he has been in hundreds, perhaps thousands, of firefights in his two decades in the police.

"I have lost count. Every day we go into the favelas we are under fire. Nowadays the guys from the army come here to train with us. Instead of police training with the military, it is the military training with the police. Right now we have U.S. Navy SEALs here learning our tactics. We have a very particular laboratory."

The U.S. special forces are interested in Rio's police officers because they are some of the most experienced in the world at a certain type of combat: fighting urban war at super close quarters. The narrow favela streets often force CORE officers to abandon their armored vehicles. They move in pairs, covering each other and linking to the following pair in a chain, a tactic that is heavily drilled. A constant challenge is to be on higher ground than the commando gunmen. To avoid being outflanked, officers work out routes through the labyrinthine slums and rely on helicopters flying overhead.

Even the helicopters are vulnerable. In 2009, Red Commando gunmen in a favela known as Morro dos Macacos, or Monkey Hill, fired at a police chopper, shooting the driver in the leg. He crashed the helicopter into a soccer field, where it exploded, killing two officers.

This intensity of favela combat has captured the attention of soldiers around the world. It has even become the setting of a video game set in conflict zones. *Call of Duty: Modern Warfare 2* re-creates a favela in graphic detail, with the alleys and staircases coming alive for joystick warriors. The gangsters in the game are called the Brazilian Militia—and look suspiciously like the Red Commando. Their symbol is a blood-red hand. The fights of Brazil's traffickers and police are replayed in bedrooms from Tokyo to Toronto.

For Oliveira and his colleagues, it's no video game. They not only face the high-caliber firearms stolen from South American armies. Traffickers also use homemade explosives that are perilously unpredictable. A specialized CORE bomb unit diffuses these IEDs. Its officers often get fingers or limbs blown off.

"The guys from the bomb squad all have problems with their hands and with their bodies." Oliveira shakes his head. "It's like a ghost train. They don't speak very well and they don't listen very well. You don't have to be crazy to work there. But it helps."

The joke shields pain over a steady loss of colleagues. In 2014 alone, 306 officers in Rio were shot, eighty-seven of whom died. One death that particularly hurt Oliveira was that of the colleague who saved his life. Gunmen fired at him while he was riding in a helicopter, leaving him dead in the seat.

"It was terrible. I couldn't do for him what he did for me. He was just twenty-eight years old."

Oliveira says the killing makes him feel anger toward the Red Commando and its founders such as William.

"I just want to shoot them." His face hardens. "It is an option for them. They choose and I make my choice."

Many in the force feel such hatred. They refer to the criminals as *vagabundos*, or vagabonds, a defined enemy, just as the commando gunmen call the police "Germans." The hate of the *other* drives both sides.

Human rights defenders argue that it is the officers who are too trigger-happy. Brazil's police kill about two thousand people every year for allegedly attacking them or resisting arrest, according to Amnesty International. One Rio officer was recently charged for an extrajudicial killing, and it was revealed he had been in shootouts in which sixty-two civilians were killed.

Oliveira says that civilian deaths are tragic, but blames the commandos for operating inside densely populated neighborhoods.

"We are in a war. The drug gangs compete in an arms race and bring weapons of war into the city. The population is in the middle of this combat. It is a war that won't finish, because the drug dealers are in the middle of the communities."

Such trials and tribulations are re-created in the painfully realistic *Tropa de Elite* movies about Rio cops. Police complained about the films showing officers shoving plastic bags over suspects' heads and shooting like crazy in Red Commando favelas. But they perhaps missed the nuance; the cops are painted as flawed heroes, risking their lives while many in society hate them. In one scene, a black policeman speaks out in a law class and tells the cop-hating students, "You don't know how many children enter drug trafficking and die. In your [middle-class] neighborhoods, you don't see these type of things. You're misinformed." The second *Elite Squad* film was the highest grossing Brazilian movie of all time.[1]

I ask Oliveira what he thinks about the Red Commando's claim to fight for the poor. He sighs and scolds the military dictatorship for locking up bank robbers with guerrillas.

"This is what you get when you mix political prisoners with common prisoners," Oliveira laments. "The common prisoners start having an ideology, and they learn how to organize."

However, he denies that the community really loves the Red Commando. "Maybe only five percent like these guys. The other ninety-five percent don't like them. But they are scared to oppose them."

While the gangs have thousands of affiliates in Rio State, Oliveira points out that they are still a tiny minority among two million favela dwellers.

Back with William, I ask if this war is really a good thing. Tens of thousands have died. Has this made anyone freer?

William, as always, answers slowly and firmly. He blames the police for perpetrating the violence. "Who brings the guns into the favelas?" he asks. "It's the officers making money out of this. They want the war to continue."

Some police officers have indeed been convicted of gunrunning, although commando traffickers such as Seaside Freddy also smuggled weapons. When I point this out to William, he reaffirms his phrase of defiance. "The Red Commando is the resistance." William sees it as a sign of strength and dignity that the commando has resisted the security forces for three decades and that there is still no sign of police destroying it.

CHAPTER 13

William voices the politicized vision of the Red Commando's founders. But I wonder how much the gun-toting youth on the street today share his quasi-socialist perspective. The drug dealers shout the name Red Commando to electro beats, but how much do they know about urban guerrillas and military dictatorships? I want to find out how revolutionary the Red Commando really is behind the slogans.

At the Antares drug shop, I talk to Lucas, the young manager, who showed me his photo with the Brazilian soccer star. He tells me he has just finished his shift, and we go to a small bar-restaurant and chat while we sip Coca-Cola out of plastic cups. After working in Mexico, where cartels are aggressive to anyone discussing their business, I am surprised how openly he talks about the crime world here, using the name of the Red Commando without hushing his voice.

Lucas is exhausted. I ask him how long he worked, and he tells me he does twenty-four shifts on and off. In each shift, he will move thousands of dollars, but he only makes a small percentage.

The Red Commando has developed a hierarchical model, he explains. The head honchos are the copula of gangster chiefs in the penitentiaries. They decide who will be the boss of each favela, known as a *dono*. Lucas is then one of several *gerentes de boca*—or "drug mouth bosses." Defending the turf are the *soldados*, or "soldiers," flashing the big guns in the parties. On the bottom rung, the skinny kids who waved drugs at me are called "vapors." The name is because they should vanish into thin air if the cops come—although they are a loud bunch.

"This work might look easy, but it is tiring and stressful," Lucas says. "You have to keep alert, watch the money all the time, watch the drugs, watch the customers, watch the sellers. That is why I look so old. I am only twenty-eight, but I look like I am in my thirties."

Actually, I don't think Lucas looks so bad for his age. He has a slim, athletic build in his designer T-shirt and gold medallion. I ask if he plays sports, and he nods his head vigorously. He hasn't always been a drug dealer, he tells me. He played professional soccer, keeping goal, for much of his adult life.

At first, I think he might be boasting. But I discover there are thousands of professional players recruited in neighborhoods like these to kick balls in minor leagues for pitiful wages. Brazil has a whopping five hundred professional soccer clubs with twenty-three thousand players, way more than anywhere else in the world. It also exports more than a thousand players a year to clubs around the globe, with a handful going to top teams in Spain, England, and Italy.

This dream of playing professional soccer fills the hearts of many favela kids. But I hear it can be a burden as much as a boost. Some don't bother to study as they think they are going to be the next Ronaldinho or Neymar. Instead, they end up like Lucas, selling blow.

I ask Lucas why he left the game as goalkeepers can play till they are forty. He looks sad. He explains that he had a fight with a player on a rival team. The player was a member of the shady militia that operates in the neighboring enemy favela.

"He said he was going to kill me and steal my organs. I had to go back to the Red Commando. They are the only ones who can protect me."

Lucas was born in Antares and has no roots outside. Favelas used to be places that people emigrated to searching for something better. Now they are places people are born and die in, too often violently. His father worked for a time at a public waterworks but then himself got into drug dealing as the trade grew in the eighties. Lucas was one of his father's fifteen children with various women.

Despite the risks of the Red Commando, Lucas enlisted when he was twelve, leaving school after sixth grade to hit the streets.

"I wanted fame at that time," Lucas says. "I was never scared. I am not frightened of gunfights. I love the adrenaline."

This is typical. Many of the new generation sign up before they are teenagers. A report on the young gunslingers by Luke Dowdney, called

Children of the Drug Trade, refers to them as "child soldiers." It is a valid description.[1]

Lucas soon saw plenty of blood. He had a good friend who became a crack addict and stole some money. The commando ordered him to return the cash, but he failed to pay up.

"I tried to help him, but I couldn't," Lucas tells me. "They covered him with gasoline and burned him alive."

When Lucas was fourteen, he tasted intense combat when traffickers from Antares were called to support the Red's position in another favela against the Third Commando. His first job was to hand ammunition clips to a commando soldier using a machine gun, but as the battle went on for several days he took up a gun himself. "I earned respect for the way I could fight. I became a soldier."

Since his bloody initiation, Lucas has been in more gun battles than he can remember. He shows a bullet wound on his leg. He was wearing a bulletproof vest, saving his life. He proudly describes spraying bullets at police when they come into the favela.

I ask Lucas if he feels guilty about police who have died at the hand of the commando. He shakes his head forcefully.

"The police are shit. You let the police in your door and they kill you. They kill kids. They kill anybody."

This strong stance against police fits in with the founders' thinking. Lucas, like William, hates what he sees as a repressive state. Lucas also defends the Red Commando's social projects such as paying for a rudimentary sewer system in Antares. He adds that the commando will pay for medicine if people are sick and for funerals when they die.

"The city doesn't do anything for us," Lucas says. "So we have to do it ourselves."

Furthermore, the commando doesn't shake down businesses or rob people in the neighborhood, Lucas says. Instead, they provide a certain security. They are a like a mini oil state; they don't charge tax but provide services, asking only for loyalty in return.

But when I ask Lucas about political movements and ideology his face turns blank. He keeps selling drugs to support his wife and six-year-old daughter, he tells me, but he wants a way out.

"I have to find a proper job. I know I can do it. If you stay in the commando, the only options are to end up in jail or in the cemetery."

* * *

Like most of the commando youth, Lucas reads little. But he loves music and can recite songs word for word about the Red Commando, its battles and its gangsters. Sitting in the café, he sings me a verse about the cocaine king Seaside Freddy.

I wonder how the singers are motivated to write these lyrics, and how much they reflect any sense of the political roots. To find out, I track down a vocalist called MC Cheetah, who sings on Red Commando funk records. Cheetah lives closer to the center of Rio, where favelas are built on sharp hills like the villages of southern Italy. He talks to me and croons his verses as we sit on a plateau high up the slopes, the towering statue of Jesus behind us.

Cheetah is in his early thirties, short and slim, wearing a backward baseball cap. He used to perform regularly, but stopped after death threats. As well as singing, he works as a porter. He also spent time selling drugs as a vapor and confesses to firing at police.

Growing up in a favela, Cheetah says he would hear the funk parties from when he was a toddler and was drawn to the music. By the time he was a teenager, he was a regular at clubs, including some where the youths would have punch-ups to the songs, known as fight dances. My ears prick up. When I was a teenager I used to go to punk rock slam dances and get the occasional black eye. It was a way to let off steam, forget whatever adolescent stress we thought was bothering us. He describes having a similar motive; but it sounds like it was a whole different level of thumping.

In the Rio fight dances, mobs form on each side and clash in the middle in a melee of kicks, punches, elbows, and head butts. It is just for fun, not what the favela kids consider real violence (i.e., killing people). But some of the fight dancers are beaten black and blue and a nurse is often on site to bandage them up.

"It was our five minutes of happiness," Cheetah says. "One time, I got smacked so hard that I had to eat soup for three weeks. But I didn't care. The music brought it out in me. I was pumped full of adrenaline."

Cheetah performs his songs for me. His style is between rapping and singing, a kind of melodic chant. The melody is interesting to my ears, different from music in either English or Spanish. The Brazilian sound has its unique fusion of African and Portuguese influences.

Cheetah's songs are explicitly about the Red Commando and gang life. It's the most hard-core version of the music, called *funk proibidão*—or "banned funk." Police can actually arrest singers who perform this music for association with organized crime, although they rarely do.

I ask why he sings about crime and drugs. Does he think it's good? Does he feel there is a cause?

"It is not that it's good," he says. "It is just us. This is my family, my friends, my brothers, the people I have grown up with, the people I have laughed and joked with, picked up women with and fought side by side with."

He has several cousins and many friends in the commando. Police killed one cousin when they stormed the favela. Police also killed a friend, taking him into an alley and shooting him in the face. In anger, he writes lyrics about shooting police.

However, his most successful song was against the Third Commando. He sings it to me a cappella over the sounds of the street. In the recording, it is over the beat of a soulful 1970s Brazilian crooner called Tim Maia and its melody is melancholic. But there is nothing sweet about the lyrics of his song, entitled "The Third Commando is Worthless."

> *This is for the soldiers,*
> *The Third Commando is worthless,*
> *If the Third Commando comes up here,*
> *We are going to give it to them,*
> *With our AK-47s, with G3s and .762s.*
> *The whole week, my boy Alexo is selling drugs,*
> *So that you can smile, and the Third Commando can cry,*
> *When we grab them,*
> *We just want to kill them,*
> *Cut them,*
> *And dice them up,*

(He says at that point there is normally a spray of gunfire—)

> *We are sincere,*
> *We don't give any money (to politicians or cops),*
> *If you fuck up,*
> *You are going to the cemetery,*
> *I just want to see if they try to come here,*

In the life of crime,
I show no weakness to anybody
Here comes the Red Commando! The Red Commando! The Red Commando!

The song was a hit with Red Commando operatives across the city. But it didn't make Cheetah any friends in the Third Commando. They discovered which favela he lived in and got on the frequency of the traffickers' walkie-talkies to threaten him.

"They said, 'We are going to invade your favela and we are going to kill you.'"

Cheetah hoped it was a bluff. But then, true to their word, Third Commando thugs launched an assault on a funk dance he was at. During the ensuing gun battle, Cheetah escaped.

"My son was born soon after that, and I decided not to risk performing. It is safer that way, but I miss the buzz of singing and people shouting along and firing guns to the music."

I don't hear much of William's revolutionary rhetoric in Lucas or Cheetah. However, I do hear a hatred for the police and a sense of belonging. This latter factor is key. One reason that young people join commandos and cartels is to be part of something. The crime family offers security in a dangerous environment, as in Lucas's case, and provides a home for people who don't feel included in the wider society.

But Lucas and Cheetah are on the lower rungs of the commando. I need to speak to the midlevel operators who move between the leaders such as William and those on the street to understand how they think. I need to speak to the favela donos.

American journalist Joe Carter trails the streets looking for a favela boss who will talk to us. In his work filming in favelas, he has been forced to deal with gangsters to smooth out any problems with residents. The gangsters are the de facto authority for neighbor disputes as well as drug dealing.

He manages to get us a sit-down with a commando operative in his late thirties with a reputation for violence. I'm told he has eight tattoos of skulls on his body—one for each police officer he has killed. (The commando use skulls to portray the police, just like the CORE officers use the skull to represent themselves.) One time, the police approached the favela, and this dono was seen standing at the entrance in a bullet-proof jacket and metal helmet firing wildly at them with an automatic rifle.

We meet the gangster inside the offices of the favela residents' association. This confirms what I have heard from many people: The commando is the real power behind these neighborhood groups. They choose the director and they funnel money into them to pay for their social schemes.

The favela boss is an imposing figure, with strong African features and a powerful build. I am told he is a worshiper of candomblé, a Brazilian folk religion that mixes African and Catholic saints and is favored by many gangsters. I'm also told he is stoned a lot and gets paranoid. I sit down with him and show him a first book I wrote about Mexican cartels, with photos of opium plants and bricks of cocaine. He looks at it and up at me, his eyes flicking nervously. I tell him I am writing a new book and want to talk about his experience in the criminal underworld. He doesn't look happy. He mentions a local gangster who gave an interview and ended up in prison. He won't tell his story.

Back on the trail, we go to another favela where Joe has contacts. Here we find a commando member called Fidel. I find it interesting that he has the same nickname as Latin America's famous revolutionary. He doesn't look much like his namesake though. This favela Fidel is clean-shaven with light black skin and built like a tank, wearing a pair of soccer shorts and sneakers. He is relaxed, sharp, and confident. The thirty-seven-year-old was dono for close to a decade but recently stepped aside to focus on a small business and get the police off his back. He agrees to tell me about running a favela for the commando.

Fidel is a clear authority in his neighborhood, giving orders and nods to various people in cars, on motorcycles, and on foot who come past. He says we can talk in a bar-café, and the owner rushes to give us a good table. We chat while there is a Champions League soccer match on a TV in the background. The English team Chelsea loses while we speak.

Born in the late seventies, Fidel was a toddler when William founded the Red Commando on the prison island. He moved with his family from the state of Minas Gerais to a central Rio favela when the commando was growing. Unlike many wayward kids on his street, he lived with his father, who was a working man. And although Fidel joined the commando at twelve years old, serving as a lookout, he stayed in school until he was seventeen.

This question of gang leaders having a better education than many of the soldiers strikes me again. It's not only who can hit hardest. It's who can think. Fidel can do both.

Completing school, Fidel got a job as a bank teller. This is uncommon among the commando recruits, many of whom have never had formal work. However, Fidel got pulled back into the crime world following a family tragedy. His older brother was a commando gunslinger and was murdered in a beef with some of his friends.

"They betrayed him." Fidel shakes his head. "When they were out dancing at a club, he was sniffing coke and they shot him in the back of the head."

The murder was not sanctioned by the commando leadership, so Red gunmen went after the killers. Fidel helped them; he had to avenge the murder of his brother. The commando took care of the offenders in its usual way. But the revenge killing became a rare crime that police investigated and Fidel's name came up. He was convicted as an accessory and spent eight years in Rio's worst prisons.

Inside jail, Fidel moved closer into the Red Commando for protection. While prison was a savage place, the Reds shielded Fidel from problems. "If people even looked at us bad, they could be killed," he says.

As a smart and charismatic youth, Fidel won favor with the Red leadership. Among those who supported him was William, whom he shared a cell with.

"William is a great man, one of the biggest bank robbers in Brazil." Fidel taps his head with his index finger. "He's smart. He taught me a lot."

Fidel joined the Red Commando in prison riots, once taking fourteen guards as hostages. It was all part of the constant push and shove between the commando and prison authorities, which sporadically explodes into violence.

He describes how the jailed Red Commando bosses would meet to decide certain issues, such as starting a riot. They would also give their blessing to new favela bosses or sanction the invasion of a turf. The power with this leadership is less about who is a formal boss, Fidel says, and more about who is most influential through convincing arguments.

"Some people can talk and others can't. If someone is making sense, if they are right, then people will listen to them and follow them."

When Fidel was released, the commando leadership asked him to take over as dono of his favela because the boss running it was tyrannical and corrupt. "He was treating people badly, beating up residents and making them suffer. And there was money missing from the accounts. I had to put some order in the favela."

With the commando leadership behind him, Fidel took over in a bloodless coup, the old boss running for his life. He claims his control was firm but just. He wouldn't punish residents in his neighborhood unless they committed a heinous crime, such as rape. But after he ruled there was no going back.

"Someone has to do a lot of shit to get himself killed. But once I have warned you, then I am not going to give you a second chance." I ask Fidel how he actually knows if people are guilty. He describes how they conduct trials, listening to witnesses, and then he makes a call. Sometimes, the accused will confess to the crime, he says, and that will give them a better chance of getting off with exile instead of death. In certain cases, Fidel would confer with the bosses in prison before passing judgment.

It is not a justice system that would be approved by the United Nations Commissioner for Human Rights. But it is effective at reducing some crimes in communities where the rule of law fails to reach.

Brazilian academics refer to this alternative justice system as *parallel power*. André Fernandes, a journalist who heads a favela news network, says it is at the heart of the commando's control. "The fact that the commando is the arbitrator of life and death makes them the absolute power in these communities," he says.

This role of judge and jury is one of the many jobs that the head of a favela has to do. Fidel also oversaw thirty drug mouths, moving tens of thousands of dollars every day. His banking experience gave him ideas on how to wash the money through small businesses and front accounts. He had to appoint the mouth bosses, keep them in line, and stop them from stealing. And he had to oversee the soldiers. He was CEO, military commander, and arbitrator—a minor warlord, or gangster chieftain.

During his command, he led the invasion of a neighboring favela controlled by the Third Commando. He said residents urged him to come as the Third treated them so badly. "If anyone just looked at them then they would make them kiss the ground until the sun rises. People welcomed us in."

He planned the invasion carefully and the Reds stormed the favela in the early morning when the Third gunmen were idle. They killed eight of them and the rest fled. The Reds secured the territory.

Fidel says he has finally decided to step aside to concentrate on a legitimate business, buying and selling cars. He is healthy and focused, and unlike many gangsters, he doesn't use drugs, which helped him save his loot. He owns several of his own cars and could afford to get out of the favela, but says he prefers to be close to his people. He left his position as favela boss after showing the books were straight and he owed no money.

The fact the Red Commando allows its operatives to step back shows it is more benevolent than most crime organizations in Latin America. For many cartels and gangs, the only way out is death.

I ask Fidel if there was anything he regretted in his time leading the favela. He doesn't mention the violence. He sees it as something that was thrust upon him, rather than something he should feel guilty about. It is a sad fact that many of these gangsters simply don't see killing as wrong. This normalization of murder is one of the biggest obstacles to stopping the homicide epidemic in the Americas.

However, Fidel says he regrets selling crack.

"Crack destroys lives. If I knew what it was like, I would never have brought it here. Once people try it, they get hooked, and then they would sell their own mother." Fidel throws his hands up. "It is the weak who get addicted to drugs. Strong people can resist it."

Fidel is one of the strong ones.

Unlike the lower-ranking thugs, Fidel understands well the mix with urban guerrillas that helped found the Red Commando. He has a lot of respect for William's ideas and sees the organization as an important form of resistance. But he is a pragmatist rather than a dreamer. He has made the commando work for him, instead of hoping for a revolution. I ask him how the violence can stop and he shakes his head.

"The violence is part of life. It's part of humanity. People are dying but then other people are being born. It doesn't make the world end. The fighting is not going to stop now. Maybe in two hundred years it will."

When I look back at the interview later, I reread Fidel's last answer, trying to make sense of what he is saying. It strikes me as a profound point from this favela chieftain, a reflection on the nature of humanity and violence. When I cover this bloodshed, I try and search for ways to stop it; I feel I have to, to justify seeking out murderers and misery. I imagine there has to be an end somewhere, even if that solution is evasive. But Fidel's observation is more realistic, if cynical; the violence will go on whatever we do.

For Fidel, the commando is a way to have pride, a code of behavior. But he is not interested in trying to defeat the government. His thinking is shared by many donos across Rio. They fight police when they come into their favelas, but don't push outside. The result is a sustained stalemate with the police in much of the state, a low-intensity war playing out year after year without altering the bigger picture.

But while Rio remained in deadlock, two hundred and fifty miles away in São Paulo, a commando took William's dream of criminal guerrilla warfare to new heights, striking at the heart of Brazil's economic powerhouse.

CHAPTER 14

When the Brazilian government moved commando leaders to distant jails, it had a side effect: They set up new chapters wherever they went. Just as the Reds had multiplied through Rio state prisons, they spread through the national system, from Brazil's northern coast to the Amazon jungles. In some cases, new cells kept close to the bosses in Rio. In others, they formed separate commandos with a loose affiliation.

The biggest prize was São Paulo. The heaving metropolis competes with Mexico City as the largest urban area in the Western Hemisphere with some twenty million people. It's ranked in the world's twenty most economically powerful cities with a booming stock exchange and auto, textile, and pharmaceutical industries. Its downtown has the biggest skyline in South America, and vast ethnic neighborhoods, including the largest Italian and Japanese communities outside their homelands. São Paulo State, which houses the city, has forty-three million people, more than most countries on the continent. It also has 2.7 million residents in favelas and 215,000 prisoners in 160 overcrowded jails.

In this megalopolis rose a crime group that was inspired by the Red Commando but that has posed an even bigger threat. The PCC, or Primeiro Comando da Capital (First Commando of the Capital), emerged after the worst of many Brazilian prison massacres—the slaughter of 111 inmates in Carandiru jail in 1992. After a hard-fought case, judges ruled that policemen had shot inmates in their cells after they surrendered.

The next year, in 1993, a group of inmates in the nearby Taubaté prison founded the PCC. According to the gang's creation story, they made their pact during a soccer game. William says one of these founders was a friend of his, a man who had been in prison in Rio and seen the power of the Reds.

"He took the seed of the Red Commando and planted it in São Paulo." William flashes with pride. "They took the rebellion to their city."

Another prisoner who founded the PCC and became its most vocal leader has a strikingly similar profile to William, and by coincidence is his namesake (almost). Marcos Willians Herbas Camacho, known as Marcola, also came from a broken home, was arrested as a teenage pickpocket, became a bank robber, served years in prison, and escaped repeatedly. And like William, he is a keen reader, telling a parliamentary committee in 2006 that he likes Nietzsche, Victor Hugo, and Voltaire.

His rhetoric is also similar to William's. He responded to questions from the parliamentary committee with a discourse reflecting the same mix of class struggle and social banditry.

"Our idealism is that of solidarity, of the prisoner knowing that there is great injustice in the penitentiary system," Marcola told the committee. "Since we're children we get used to living with misery and violence. In any slum there are daily murders. Violence is natural for the prisoner. That's why the prisoners' organizations oppose that violent nature. What do they do? They forbid the inmates to take certain attitudes that would be normal to them, but that invade the other guy's space. Do you understand that?"[1]

The PCC took the Red Commando's slogan of "Liberty, Justice, and Peace." Furthermore, it wrote a statute, similar to the Red's "Manual of the Good Bandit" if a little more sophisticated. The PCC's statute has sixteen points and refers to itself as a Party—with a capital P. (It's sometimes called the Party of Crime.) The statute is full of talk of resistance, such as point number 16, in which it enshrines its allegiance to the Rio mob.

"In alliance with the Red Commando, we will revolutionize the country from inside the prisons and our armed wing will be of Terror," it says in the statute, which has been found on various prisoners. "United we will conquer."[2]

Like in Rio, the PCC spread into favelas. But in São Paulo, the commando took a different form. Its gangsters don't flash rifles and brazenly sell dope off tables, but operate more clandestinely, selling drugs inside safe houses or by delivery and keeping guns hidden. However, they still control residents' associations, operate alternative trials, and sell narcotics by the bucketload.

Everton Luiz Zanella is a top organized crime prosecutor in São Paulo with the life-risking job of making cases against the mob. He recently brought racketeering charges against dozens of its cellblock leaders, resulting in extended sentences. Meeting in his headquarters, the lean attorney concedes that despite his efforts, the PCC keeps growing.

"The PCC not only keeps getting bigger here in São Paulo. It is also expanding in other Brazilian states and even in neighboring countries like Paraguay and Bolivia," Zanella tells me. "It's not only a problem here, it's an international problem."

The PCC is so strong in São Paulo because it has no major rival. Marcola and his cohorts have managed to stop splinters from breaking off or adversaries from moving in. As the PCC lacks enemy gunmen, an odd thing has happened: While it has grown, the homicide rate in São Paulo has gone down, from more than fifteen thousand murders in 2001 to fifty-six hundred by 2011.

This is a paradox of Latin America's crime wars. Having a single strong mafia means less violence than if there were several weaker groups. This lack of opposition, however, makes the PCC a more forbidding opponent for the government. It has murdered hundreds of police officers, prison guards, and judges. But two major attacks stand out for making the government tremble, the first in 2006 and the second in 2012.

When Paulistas (the residents of São Paulo) went to bed on the night of May 11, 2006, it appeared to be a Thursday like any other, the drawing to a close of a week in the hectic megalopolis. But in the early hours of Friday morning, gunmen—fifteen cars of them—appeared outside a São Paulo police base, spraying it with bullets and hurling grenades and firebombs. In other parts of the city, smaller stations came under fire. Police sent backup, only for cars to be pinned down in ambushes.

News of the attacks spread through the city the following day, alongside rumors that gangsters were going to hit downtown. Office managers let people leave early and pull their kids from school, causing marathon traffic jams that paralyzed the city. As cars were snarled in gridlock, gunmen hit several more police bases.

On Saturday morning, São Paulo's governor said the situation was under control. But it had only just started. Attacks spread to government offices, banks, and a shopping center. The gunmen ordered passengers off buses and torched them on the streets. Many stayed in their homes as the violence raged into Sunday, watching live reports of burning buildings and crying family members in hospital wards.

More than seventy prisons across the state erupted into simultaneous riots. Inmates took hostages and climbed on penitentiary roofs waving their fists at camera crews sweeping over in helicopters.

Then just as suddenly, the attacks stopped on Monday morning. Paulistas cautiously held their breath and went back onto the streets to see the carnage, the burned-out banks, the bullet-ridden police stations, the funerals of officers and civilians.

The final figures were staggering. There had been more than five hundred attacks. Eighty-two buses were burned. Eleven banks were heavily damaged. Thirty-three police officers and eight prisons guards were dead, and many more injured, some crippled for life. And more than seventy civilians, including a mix of suspected attackers and innocents caught in the crossfire, had been killed.

The PCC had carried out a bigger offensive than the urban guerrillas of the seventies could ever imagine. It had turned a booming financial center into a war zone in a split second. The logistics alone are remarkable. The PCC showed it could move thousands of operatives to make simultaneous, disciplined attacks over a metropolis of three thousand square miles.

As calm returned, Paulistas all asked the million-dollar question: Why? What was the motive behind the biggest attack on the government in modern Brazil?

I hear three motives to explain the offensive. The first is the most heavily cited in the media. According to this version, the PCC launched the attacks in response to the São Paulo state government ordering the transfer of PCC prisoners, including Marcola, into secure units. The prisoners responded with the "Terror," with a capital T, they warn about in their statute.

The second version is one that some Brazilian journalists mutter privately but they are cautious about printing. According to this account, corrupt police officers had kidnapped Marcola's stepson for ransom. There have been previous cases of Brazilian police officers kidnapping the families of drug traffickers. The traffickers normally pay up. According to the rumors, Marcola did the same this time and handed money to the police. But instead of releasing him, they asked for even more cash. And he ordered the attacks.

The third version is frighteningly banal. The PCC had ordered sixty flat-screen TVs to watch the World Cup, which was to start in under four weeks. But someone in the prison system had hijacked the TVs. The PCC carried out the attacks to get the TVs back.

I ask the organized crime prosecutor Zanella about these theories. He acknowledges hearing all three of them, but says he has no conclusive evidence. Perhaps it was a combination of them all, a cumulative effect of tensions that led to the PCC letting out the dogs.

There are signs that PCC demands were met following the attacks. Some prisoners had their transfers canceled. "The government can use the justification that a transfer would put the prisoner in danger with rival gangs," Zanella says. Media also reported that the plasma TVs found their way to the cellblocks. And there are rumors that Marcola's stepson was released by his abductors. When I ask about this last point, he smiles. "I have heard the story, but there is no official record of this kidnapping."

The Chicago academic Ben Lessing tries to discern what lies behind the violence in crime wars. One driving force, he argues, is what he calls "violent lobbying." This is violence aimed at pressuring officials to change certain policies such as prisoner transfers, troop deployments, or extradition laws. Gangsters murder police, burn banks, and set off car bombs as a form of political pressure to achieve their demands.

"They are saying to officials, 'I am serious and I can inflict a lot of pain on you. So you'd better do what I am asking,'" Lessing says.

This would fit it in with the PCC's motivation here—whether those demands were to stop a transfer to secure units, free a kidnapped kid, or to be able to watch Brazil get knocked out of the World Cup by France (as happened that year).

The São Paulo terror of 2006 made world headlines (for a couple of days). But less reported was the wave of attacks in the week that followed. This time it was not criminals hitting police, but police killing civilians.

Police officers were understandably enraged by the attacks against them. They were also frustrated. It was tough to find the gunmen, hidden in the sprawling metropolis. So police hunted through favelas searching for the culprits.

Officers admit shooting dead 123 criminals in eight days following the attacks. But human rights defenders say it was many more. These activists have gathered evidence of 493 civilians being killed over the period, including those shot dead by police and others murdered by mysterious masked gunmen. The human rights defenders say these triggermen were officers in plain clothes acting as death squads. The police were out for blood, they say, and went on a revenge killing spree.

Debora Santos, a working-class Paulista housewife, describes to me the night that her son Edoson was killed. On the Monday following the PCC attacks, she had Edoson over for dinner. They were talking about the turmoil like everybody across São Paulo, and were shocked by it. Edson had been a difficult youth who had served time in prison for robbery. But she was pleased that he had gone straight, working as a street cleaner, enjoying being a father to his three-year-old son. He left late on his motorcycle. That was the last time she saw him alive.

The next day, his boss called looking for him. She was surprised that he didn't show up to work as he had been vigilant about keeping his hours. "I couldn't believe it. I called everywhere but there was no sign of him. Then I heard on the radio that dozens of people had been killed. We went down to the morgue. And there I saw his corpse."

Debora worked to reconstruct the case. After Edoson had left her house, he had been stopped by police officers at a gas station, witnesses said. The police questioned him about his criminal record and he had replied that he had done his time and was straight now. Leaving the police, he rode on his motorcycle down the street when masked gunmen shot him dead.

Debora was at first too devastated to do anything. "I went into deep depression after my son's killing. I couldn't eat or sleep. Then after forty days, I had a vision in which I saw him. He came to me and said, 'Mama, you have a mission to fight against these murders.'"

She found other families who had lost loved ones in the killing spree. Many had similar stories, of people being questioned by police at checkpoints and attacked shortly afterward. Their suspicion was that police were locating anyone with criminal records and passing their details to waiting death squads.

The number of families grew, becoming known as the Month of May Movement. They gathered evidence but prosecutors said there was still insufficient proof to show police carried out the murders. They carry on their struggle today.

Debora shows me a Father's Day card that her grandson recently wrote.

"I love you Dad. I'll always love you and I wish you could come and see me. I wish you could collect me from school. Sometimes, I feel that you are by my side. Happy Father's Day."

Media covering Latin America have seriously overlooked the story of the "Month of May Murders." If the protesters are right then São Paulo police may have murdered almost as many people in eight days as Brazil's military dictatorship did in twenty years. It is one of the worst massacres in the history of the Americas.

However, the police deny the death squad accusations and claim it was the gangsters themselves who were behind the hits. Many Brazilians have also rallied round the officers, feeling more scared by the specter of the PCC. A handful of policemen were put on trial over some of the shootings. In almost all the cases, juries acquitted the officers, saying they acted in self-defense.

Many people have short memories. The 2006 violence in São Paulo flared up with its great intensity and dissipated just as fast. Mothers like Debora stumble on with the pain of their loss as do the families of slain police officers. But for millions of other Paulistas life simply went back to the grind. This is a strange characteristic of the Latin American crime wars: Intense violence can break out in a flash, and disappear just as fast.

In July 2012, the PCC launched another sinister campaign. This time, it wasn't a weekend of terror but lasted several months. Gunmen ambushed police officers on patrol; murdered them arriving to work; killed them finishing shifts. Police tried to reinforce security but it is hard to defend against assassins who come out of nowhere dressed like millions of others in the crowded streets. Fifty police officers were killed, then seventy, then ninety. By November, the assassins had murdered 109 officers.

Finally, the state's head of public security resigned. And the attacks stopped like clockwork.

I hear accounts that the PCC had a problem with the security head, a former military officer named Antonio Ferreira Pinto, and had been killing police to force his resignation. When they got their demand, the assassinations stopped. It was, in Ben Lessing's terms, a classic case of "violent lobbying."

The prosecutor Zanella confirms he heard this, but it cannot be proven. "They didn't like Pinto because he had come from the military," he says. "Afterwards, the state government put a civilian in the job."

A dangerous pattern has emerged in Brazil. The government is repressive, the commando uses violence, and the government gives concessions. It's a vicious circle.

Right now, the PCC is on the periphery of the city. But what if it pushes downtown and takes a piece of big businesses? What if they move into shakedowns and kidnapping as gangsters in Mexico and Central America have? The specter is of a crime group with a monopoly on its rackets poised on the edge of the biggest economic base in South America.

CHAPTER 15

"I have the honor to announce that the games of the thirty-first Olympiad are awarded to the city of . . ."

OOC President Jacques Rogge fumbled with an Olympic-size envelope in October 2009, as sports fans, mayors, and presidents held their breath. When he finally managed to pull out the card and read the answer, "Rio de Janeiro," the Brazilian delegation led by President Lula exploded. The 2016 Summer Olympics would be in Brazil, the first time ever that South America would hold the games.

President Obama was more serene. The bookies' favorite, Chicago, was beaten out alongside Madrid and Tokyo. South America had trumped Asia, Europe, and the United States.

The Rio win was doubly sweet as it came on the back of Brazil capturing the equally coveted 2014 World Cup. These awards in turn followed sustained growth in Brazil and the discovery of new oil fields, boosting the economy to the seventh largest on the planet. Lula oversaw this boom, steering a party of leftists to run a popular centrist government.

"That's my man right here," President Obama said at a G-20 summit he attended with Lula. "Love this guy. He's the most popular politician on earth. It's because of his good looks."[1]

Lula indeed scored high popularity ratings, leaving office in 2010 with over 80 percent approval. His status allowed him to handpick his successor, Dilma, the former guerrilla. Brazil was on the path to becoming a new superpower, pundits said. *New York Times* correspondent Larry Rohter released a book that year entitled *Brazil on the Rise.*

*   *   *

However, Rio's breathtaking landscape had an embarrassing sore that its rulers didn't want world athletes seeing when they arrived to throw javelins and somersault into swimming pools. In the favelas, Red Commando gunmen waved their Kalashnikovs and touted their drug baggies.

To remedy this, Rio's governor backed a policy called "Pacification," in which police and soldiers would force out commando gunmen and reinsert the power of the state. Favelas would be transformed from the surreal scenes of gangster-governed ghettos to generic urban neighborhoods. Tellingly, the term *pacification* was also used by the U.S. Army to clean insurgents out of villages in Vietnam.

The Rio Pacification program had begun modestly in late 2008—after Brazil had been awarded the World Cup and while bidding for the Olympics was in process. It started with officers setting up what they called a Police Pacifying Unit, or UPP, in one of the tamest slums, Santa Marta. The downtown favela is the scene of the video for Michael Jackson's hit "They Don't Care About Us," in which the star prances around the sloping streets and points an accusing finger at a police officer.

Following the Olympic decision, the government put its weight firmly behind Pacification and expanded it across the urban sprawl. By the eve of the World Cup in 2014, forty UPPs stood in favelas under the eye of the towering Jesus.

Rio's police commanders created a unique model to install UPPs, one which governments across the hemisphere watch. First they announce on television that they are going to enter, giving the date to deliberately allow criminals to flee. Officers then invade in overwhelming force backed by soldiers and marines to set up the UPP base. Rather than leaving, as the police had done for decades, the UPP officers stay round the clock, making sure the commando gunmen don't return to the street.

Without a doubt, the Pacification scheme has transformed certain favelas. Police officers now patrol some streets where commando gunmen ruled for decades. Traffickers may still sell drugs, but they do it more quietly from inside houses rather than in public view.

The scheme has coincided with a little gentrification in which bohemian foreigners and Brazilians buy property around the slums. I find an American screenwriter who has bought a home in a favela and an Italian who has opened a fish restaurant on the edge of one. Most importantly, the Rio State government claims that homicides have hurtled down 65 percent in pacified communities.

Security pundits looked to the Pacification scheme as a model that could be applied to crime-ridden ghettos across the Americas. It has clear merits. The principle that the government, not gangsters, should run these neighborhoods is obviously a good one.

But Pacification has shortcomings. Police commander Oliveira says that while it may have cleaned up the center of Rio for tourists, many favelas in the sprawling city are unaffected. For example, Antares on the outskirts remains as strongly in the grip of the Reds as ever. The police simply do not have the numbers to be in all the favelas all the time.

"You just transfer the problem from one area to another area," Oliveira says. "If I tell a criminal that I am going to his house tomorrow, is he going to stay in his house? Of course not. And that is what has happened. Now the problem has gone from the middle of the city to the periphery."

There is also tension in pacified territories, with police murdering residents they are meant to be saving. Two months before the World Cup, a well-known dancer, Douglas Rafael da Silva, was shot dead in the Pavão Pavãozinho slum, which snakes up from Copacabana Beach. Unlike most of those killed in favelas, Da Silva was a success story who danced on a popular TV show, and his death provoked protests that turned into riots.

I go to the site where Da Silva was killed. He was shot on the roof of a building and fell twenty meters into a nursery. Police claim they were returning fire with drug traffickers and weren't sure whose bullet hit Da Silva. But witnesses I speak to say that police fired at unarmed youths because they were smoking marijuana and hit the dancer.

"Police are totally unprepared for working in this community," says Paulo dos Santos, a neighbor and actor who had worked with Da Silva. "They are the law, but they don't respect it. We don't want these type of cops."

Such rejection of the police is not universal. Leandro Matus, who owns a bicycle shop next to where Da Silva fell, says he still prefers the police to the hoods. "At least there are less gangsters with guns now," Matus says. "I don't trust the police, but they are the lesser of the two evils."

But convincing many residents to accept the police over the commandos is a challenge. Oliveira says the government needs to win support by using carrots, not just sticks. Much more government invest-ment needs to go into social programs for pacification to work, he says.

"The commandos fill the space that should belong to the state," Oliveira says. "The only part of the state that goes inside these areas is the police. Other parts of the state have to go inside the favelas as well. We need investment in education and in health. But it's not happening. It is just police officers. This way, we are not going to win this war."

The government's claim of homicides hurtling down also needs to be scrutinized. It is hard to count murders in a small unit such as a single favela; people from there can kill in other places and bodies could be dumped elsewhere. A broad survey of homicides across the state gives a bigger picture. Analyzing the state murder stats, you find that between 2008 and 2012, the number of homicides indeed went down, although by a more modest 25 percent. However in 2013, they went up by 18 percent.

There are also signs that even if Rio has become somewhat safer, the commandos—and murders—have moved to other Brazilian cities. A decade ago, Maranhão State used to be a backwater known for its Amazon jungle running up to the Atlantic. But in January 2014, Brazilians were shocked by a video of gang members in its biggest prison beheading three inmates. Prison officers leaked the gruesome footage to show the horror they have to deal with. Maranhão has seen a quadrupling of homicides over a decade, as well as bus burning and attacks on police stations reminiscent of the São Paulo violence.

Other provincial cities also suffer a spike in shootings, crack selling, and commandos. Brazil's most murderous cities—which are among the most homicidal in the planet—now include Maceio in the far east, Fortaleza in the north, and the historic João Pessoa.

If you looked at homicides across Brazil like a map of lights, you would see them flashing around the country. The killing zones move, but overall the same amount of light is shining through. After rocketing up in the eighties and nineties, Brazil's homicide rate has remained stable (and high) over the last decade. This is sadly in spite of economic growth and talk of Brazil becoming a superpower. In 2012, there were 51,108 people murdered in the nation. Considering its population of two hundred million, this doesn't make Brazil the highest per capita in killings. But it has the highest total number of homicides among any nation outside a declared war zone. It's a colossal death toll.

I ask William what he thinks about the Pacification scheme and the idea of Brazil rising. I thought he might have sympathy for Lula and Dilma's leftist governments as they included comrades from the guerrilla movement. And it was under Lula's government in 2009 that William was finally authorized to live outside prison, staying in his home with his bracelet on his leg. He is spending the winter of his life in an apartment, not a jail cell.

However, William has no good words for Lula. "He is a traitor. He promised things but then he put his hands everywhere. He wears different clothes, but he is the same as the rest of the rulers. He is a disgrace to Brazil."

William also slams the Pacification scheme. In this, he coincides with the police commander Oliveira, saying the government only cares about sending in force and not providing services.

"The first thing they do when they pacify favelas is to make sure people pay their electricity bills," he says.

But what is the alternative, I ask him. Does he really believe this low-intensity war between the Red Commando and the police can lead to something better? Does he think the movement he created is a good thing?

William sticks to his guns.

"It is a war. The police are the aggressors. The Red Commando is the resistance. It doesn't negotiate with police."

William is clear in his conviction of his life's work; in his final years he has found a peace in himself that he fought for something worthwhile. In his mind, the Red Commando provides a necessary order at the bottom of the society. It gives the criminals a code of honor and pride and puts them on a more level playing field against a repressive system. Society will have to change, he argues, before this changes.

The Red Commando has so far been content to stay on the periphery of Brazilian society, filling the space in the favelas and prisons. It is the most extreme example of a class-conscious crime movement in the Americas. But many other gangsters also use the language of social injustice to explain their actions. Cavernous inequality and failure of the state at the bottom rungs of society are a key part of Latin America's crime wars.

Despite their quasi-political discourse, the Red Commando has only had a limited impact on Brazil's politicians. But in another part of the continent, a gangster used a ghetto base to catapult himself to the heart of power; he even awarded himself the title of the highest official in the land.

It is to this president of Jamaica that we now turn.

PART III

The President: Jamaica

The little pirate dem come here and rob up the resources for the country. Because that is what dem been doing a long bloodbath time . . . I am not a politician but I suffer the consequences.

—PETER TOSH, ONE LOVE PEACE CONCERT, 1978

CHAPTER 16

In the spring of 2010, the beautiful Caribbean island of Jamaica was enjoying a bumper tourist season. More holidaymakers than ever before relished its golden beaches, making it set to have a record two million visits over the year.

Some stayed inside their five-star resorts, sipping rum punch while protected by gun-toting security guards. Others partied to reggae music in the beach clubs of Montego Bay and Negril and smoked the island's celebrated *sensimilla* ganja. Some visited the old plantations to see where for centuries slaves had sweated to churn out the sugar of the British Empire that sweetened tea and cupcakes from Birmingham to Bombay. The most adventurous took trips into the capital, Kingston, to take snaps of the Trench Town slum where the legend Bob Marley grew up and composed melancholic masterpieces such as "No Woman, No Cry."

But as the last days of spring flowed into summer, the island erupted like a volcano. Images of shoot-outs between soldiers and mysterious gunmen in Kingston ghettos shot to the world's top news story. On a tourist plane flying from Montego Bay, the captain told passengers they would have trouble landing in Kingston airport because gangsters were firing close-by with a 50-caliber machine gun. As the bodies piled up, it became clear the "tropical paradise" was suffering its most intense week of unrest since it gained independence from the British Empire in 1962.

The violence was the legacy of a structure of gangsters that had been growing since that independence, known on the island as the "don system." Generation after generation of politicians had used the system, allying with shady gunmen to bring in their votes. Now these gangsters were rich from drug profits and had grown into a monster the politicians could no longer control. The fighting centered around the most infamous ever of these dons: Christopher Michael Coke, known more commonly as Dudus, or the President.

Jamaica doesn't officially have a president. When it became independent, it transferred power to an elected parliament and prime minister, while keeping the faraway British Queen Elizabeth II as its symbolic monarch. But in the ghettos of West Kingston, many said Dudus was the real ruler of the island, his title, President, making him bigger than the P.M.

Dudus had run the Caribbean's largest drug trafficking organization, known as the Shower Posse, for almost two decades with little hassle from Jamaican police. His presidential status seemed to be sanctified when the United States issued an extradition warrant for him for smuggling marijuana, cocaine, and guns, and the Jamaican government refused to act on it. Prime Minister Bruce Golding said it was because the Americans used illegal wiretaps. In West Kingston, they joked that the prime minister did what the president ordered.

The failure to arrest a notorious crime king pushed Jamaica into political crisis. The opposition called for Golding's resignation while the United States refused visas for prominent Jamaicans and delayed sending a new ambassador. After eight months of rising pressure, the prime minister finally caved in and on May 17 gave a televised speech promising to detain Dudus.

The ghetto came to its president's defense. Residents of West Kingston slums took to the streets saying they would shield the Prezi. "Jesus die for us. We will die for Dudus," said one banner held by a woman on the Spanish Town Road. "Dudus is the way. We will die fighting," said another.

The government took them at their word; it sent out the Jamaican constabulary, one of the most homicidal police forces in the world. But even they weren't able to storm Dudus's stronghold, a ghetto called Tivoli Gardens.

The President's loyalists blockaded the entrances to Tivoli with towering barricades. The fortifications were built with barrels of concrete, sacks of sand and stone, and burned-out cars and trucks. Former Jamaican soldiers turned mercenaries reinforced defenses with razors, electrified wires, and homemade explosives that used bottles of cooking gas and mobile detonators. Behind the barricades, hundreds of gunmen took to rooftops with assault rifles and machine guns.

The police surrounded Tivoli, creating an uneasy siege that made residents struggle to get supplies. But the President showed he was not alone. Gunmen from other ghettos rose up and attacked police stations with bullets and firebombs. Two officers died in an ambush. The security forces were being challenged from behind.

More ghettos joined Dudus, even some that had not traditionally supported him. In a fevered moment, the gangsters felt they could defeat the police. Dudus seemed invincible.

The shaken Jamaican government declared a state of emergency and ordered out the military. Soldiers took to the streets in full-on Humvees, tanks, and helicopters.

"We are going to hunt them down as they ought to be hunted down and bring the full brunt of the law on them," Jamaican Minister of National Security Dwight Nelson avowed.

Gun battles exploded on the edge of the Tivoli barricades. Even for soldiers, it was a struggle facing gunfire from rooftops and windows. Shooting rattled on and a soldier fell dead, while nineteen more were injured. A local news crew was pinned down under gunfire. Towers of smoke rose from burning buildings.

When the soldiers and police finally broke through the barricades, they went on a killing spree. While some gunmen still fired sniper shots, most of Dudus's army saw they were overwhelmed and ran to ground. But for troops steaming through the tower blocks and slum streets, it was a free-fire zone. While bullets riddled the sides of buildings, terrified residents hid in their homes, often lacking food and water. The injured struggled to get through the melee to hospitals. A local morgue was overwhelmed with bodies. Corpses lay on the street being eaten by dogs.[1]

After three days of unrest, the Jamaican government announced that the President's ghetto army had been crushed. In the incursion, seventy-three civilians had been killed, it conceded. Human rights defenders and a former prime minister claimed there were many more deaths and most victims were innocent civilians. The security forces had also rounded up more than a thousand alleged gunmen and piled them into the national soccer stadium because there was no space in the police cells. Fourteen police stations had been attacked, two of them burned to the ground.

But the object of the manhunt, Dudus himself, had escaped. The security forces were flummoxed as to how he had slipped through the siege lines. He also avoided a mysterious U.S. spy plane spotted flying over

Tivoli. People asked if he had invisibility powers along with his biblical status as ruler.

Some on the street viewed his escape as an act of cowardice, the supreme general abandoning his troops.

"The man tek off like a puss when him hear the first bum drop," one of his gunmen told a local newspaper, which is to say, "Dudus had run like a cat when he heard the first artillery fire."[2]

The journalist Gary Spaulding elaborates, in the vibrant prose of Jamaican journalism, that the President had sacrificed his subjects of Tivoli like "lambs to the slaughter."

> Like a mighty rushing wind, a curious brand of religious fervor descended on western Kingston only days before the torment of Hell intruded.
>
> Some Tivoli residents had proclaimed with great religious intensity that they were prepared to suffer the ultimate sacrifice for their benefactor and community hero . . .
>
> They hollered for reprieve when they were abandoned on the sacrificial altar.
>
> In a curious paradox to the crucifixion story, it was not one man who had paid dearly for the sins of all.[3]

Dudus stayed invisible the following weeks. Police combed the island, with likely support from American agents, but the President seemed to have disappeared in a puff of smoke. The failure to capture him amid growing anger over the Tivoli massacre heaped more pressure on Golding's government.

Then after a month, Dudus appeared in anticlimactic if slightly humorous circumstances. Police arrested him at a routine roadblock into Kingston. He was in a car with a well-known evangelical reverend. And he was dressed as a woman, with a curly black wig and round spectacles. At least for Dudus, his mug shot showed him with the black wig and not the pink one he also had in the car.

A comedy TV show dug the knife in, airing a sketch with a pretend Dudus in drag being stopped at the checkpoint. "This is the church sister Prezi," the mock reverend says, pointing to the wigged gangster. "I mean Precious, Precious." Jamaican novelist Kei Miller wrote that "Bad man nuh dress like girl," quoting a famed reggae song. Miller observed that there is actually a history of cross-dressing gangsters in Jamaica, and concluded, "That bad man dress however de rass him want to dress. And that's exactly what makes them de real bad men."[4]

Dudus's supporters said that he used drag as he feared Jamaican police would murder him. Dudus lived with the memory of his father, himself a major drug trafficker, perishing in a mysterious fire in a police cell back in 1992.

When he was caught, Dudus claimed he was heading to the U.S. Embassy to hand himself in. Once arrested, he immediately waived his right to oppose extradition and traveled swiftly to the United States, where he was relatively safe from angry Jamaican police.

Dudus survived but his reign was over. And the Jamaican president found his new home in a New York City jail cell.

When the Kingston unrest exploded, I was covering Mexico's own worst wave of violence since its revolutionary wars. Watching Jamaica go up in flames, the link was obvious. Mexico was not alone in battling a curious new threat.

However, few have explored the links between Jamaica's bloodshed and the wider narco wars of the region. A key reason is that most Jamaicans don't see themselves as part of Latin America. They speak English and patois rather a Latin tongue and consider themselves culturally closer to Africa. They have forged strong links with the mother continent, where Jamaican leaders tour and Jamaican singers command vast audiences. Mexico, Colombia, and Brazil offer less kinship.

However, the Afro Caribbean nations grapple with many of the same problems as the Latin countries they share the hemisphere with. All are former colonies of European empires struggling to build political and judicial institutions since independence. All have big populations of dispossessed alongside corrupt European and American influenced elites. And all have become major drug trafficking routes.

There are physical as well as comparative links between Jamaican and Latin crime families. As the U.S. piles resources on its southern border, Mexican and Colombian cartels switch back to the Caribbean to move cocaine, returning to the old pirate sea where smugglers have moved contraband for centuries. The cartels work with local crime syndicates such as the Shower Posse. It is a sad truth that gangsters are among the best entrepreneurs at crossing physical and cultural borders to take advantage of markets; Mexican and Colombian cartels are more aggressive than most legitimate businesses from their countries at tapping the potential of the Caribbean and Central America.

In understanding the crime world, the Caribbean is especially interesting for the ties between drug traffickers and politicians. Gangsters conspire with officials across the continent. But Jamaica and other islands show extreme examples of how kingpins and politicians work together.

One of the few thinkers to explore these connections between the Caribbean and hemispheric drug trade is Daurius Figueira, a criminologist from Trinidad and Tobago. Figueira long wrote about the traditional Caribbean issues such as race, but became interested in organized crime as he saw its daunting presence on the islands.

"Having experienced the appearance of a drug culture, I became interested in what is the nature of the business in the Caribbean … We have always been a transit zone for Latin American transnational drug traffickers. But in the literature the requisite attention has not been paid to the Caribbean as a major illicit transition zone both to the United States and to Europe and now to West Africa.

"You have this archipelago of small island states that provide impunity to these transnational organizations. And because of the operations of these cartels we have now developed indigenous Caribbean traffickers who wield considerable power and influence."[5]

To make sense of the new crime order in the Americas, I realize, it is crucial to travel to the ganja-and-gun-filled ghettos of the Afro Caribbean.

CHAPTER 17

As I figure out logistics for going to Jamaica, I wonder if my plan to talk to Shower Posse gangsters about their fallen president is too ambitious. In Mexico, I spent years covering the crime beat before I got interviews with cartel gunslingers. Now I try to figure out how I can sweep onto the island and do it.

My first stop is a fellow Brit who spent several months in a Kingston ghetto. He's a Londoner who used to sell ganja south of the River Thames and went to Kingston with a British-Jamaican friend to soak in the Caribbean atmosphere. When I inquire over a beer about talking to Jamaican drug traffickers he doesn't look positive.

"Any time I asked about how things worked in the crime world, they froze up," he tells me. "I had a lot of trouble there. They asked me all the time what the fuck I was doing in the ghetto and why I wasn't on the beach with the rest of the tourists. If you go there asking about criminals, you might as well be Old Bill [police]. Good luck with it."

It isn't a good signal. But I ask him if at least he enjoyed the island with its famed rum and dance hall parties.

"I was watching my back all the time. My friend could help me sometimes, but he couldn't be with me every minute of the day. In the end, he said to me, 'Sorry, but the guys here just don't like you.' They were talking about how some tourist had been kidnapped and the kidnappers got a good payoff. I left because I thought they were going to target me."

He makes it sound dangerous as well as difficult. But I try other avenues. Luck comes when I find a fellow journalist who made a documentary about Jamaican gangs with a Kingston film producer called Colin Smikle. The name grabs my attention as it is an anagram of the Irish revolutionary Michael Collins (almost).

I call Colin on his Jamaican cell via an Internet line and get poor reception. He tells me he can sit me down with the Shower Posse. Or at least I think he does. The line is crackly and Colin has a strong Jamaican accent. I get my ticket to Kingston.

When I arrive in Kingston at night, I'm apprehensive that Colin won't deliver. These contacts often come up short. I'm even more nervy the next morning when he shows up late to the hotel and we have a long breakfast. It turns out it's his birthday, which is November 5, the day in England when we burn effigies of Guy Fawkes, the Catholic dissenter who tried to blow up parliament in 1605. Colin tells me he identifies with our British antihero.

"I really would love to blow up parliament here in Jamaica. Seriously, I am not just saying it, I would really do it. Politicians here are the cause of all our problems."

I am starting to like Colin. But I'm getting worried I'm veering off from meeting gangsters to unveiling a new gunpowder plot. However, after we finish breakfast, he puts my anxiety to rest. He drives me straight into Tivoli Gardens to meet Dudus's family.

Jamaican homes are known as "yards" because many are built in cordoned off sections of courtyards. I go to the yard of Dudus's family on his mother's side. Dudus was the illegitimate child of a renowned gangster known as Jim Brown, and he lived with his mother in Tivoli, while Jim Brown had a home outside the ghetto with his wife and other children. There is also a rumor that Dudus was not the real blood child of Jim Brown. However, this has never been proven and Dudus has the don registered as his father on his birth certificate.

The family home includes a series of bungalows in a fenced-off area. Dudus's mother passed away after he was imprisoned. However, the yard is full of various family members, including Dudus's twin aunts and several cousins. Two dozen goats wander round the yard and on the roofs of the houses. Many residents of the Kingston ghettos, I find out, keep goats in their homes, using them for milk and meat. They let them wander alone down to the market to eat the remains of vegetables, and they somehow know how to wander back. Stealing another man's goat while they wander is as big a sin as anyone can commit here, and has been the motive for murders.

I sit in a plastic chair in the open yard and Colin introduces me. He seems incredibly at ease with Coke's family as he explains I want to "reason" with them (the Jamaican word for talking), saying that I want to hear the truth about Dudus.

The twin aunts are in their fifties but look older, the victims of a degenerative medical condition that runs in the family. The most talkative is called Twinny. Aunt Twinny eyes me suspiciously. Dudus's cousins in their late teens and twenties are more relaxed. All want to explain that Dudus was a benefactor, a Robin Hood, a man of God. They call him "Mikey" with affection.

"Mikey a loving person. He a peaceful man," Aunt Twinny says. "The politician not look out for people but Mikey look out for people. He do nuff [enough] good things here. He get treats for kids: pizza, ice cream, school uniform, shoes, Reebok, Nike."

A young female cousin called Keriesha chips in: "The politician run the country. But man here cyan [can't] go to no politician. So them go to Mikey. Anyone with a problem them go to Mikey. Him a caretaker for the community."

I ask what they think about him being in a U.S. prison for trafficking drugs, and U.S. agents testifying that he and his enforcers carried out wanton murder. Aunt Twinny screws up her face and shakes her head.

"Dem lies. Him a peaceful man, him always reading Bible. When him here you in peace, you can sleep with your door open. Now everyone on their own. You cyan sleep in peace."

The meeting with Dudus's family is the entrance to a surreal trip into the Kingston ghettos and Shower Posse that Colin takes me on. He introduces me to hired guns, smugglers, corner dealers, crack cooks, and pimps. He is a force of nature. Every ghetto we drive into, he pulls up and immediately asks for the local enforcers by name. He seems to know everybody and everybody seems to respect and like him. He has a phenomenal memory for names, connections, and stories.

Colin grew up on these streets, moving around as a kid to know many different ghettos. He also has a sprawling family, which connects him in all directions. One of his cousins, he reveals, was a Shower Posse hit man, a brutal murderer who once beat a man to death with his bare hands. (The cousin was later himself murdered. He who lives by the gun . . .)

In contrast, Colin was an athlete, which took him out of the slum to know the better parts of Kingston. It has kept him in good shape into middle age. He later got into working as a location producer on films and

TV in Jamaica's small but creative industry. His specialty is as a point man for filming in the ghetto.

Like myself, Colin loves to talk, and we ramble on for long hours about the history of Jamaican violence, what drives it, how the communities have been scarred. Colin sympathizes with the ideas of Marcus Garvey, the Jamaican who became a father of black nationalism in the United States and across the Americas in the 1920s. Garvey is a hero in Jamaica, his face on coins, name on streets, and statue shading parks.

However, Colin is cynical about Jamaica's current politicians of all stripes. He puts the blame squarely on these politicos for using ghetto gunmen as pawns in their power games and turning the streets into killing zones. The political parties divided the ghettos up, he explains, by creating what were called garrison communities.

I had heard Jamaica's ghettos described as garrisons before but hadn't given the name much thought. But Colin explains what it means: They are literally fortified communities. Many of the entrances are permanently blocked with barricades so there is only one way in and one way out, and the gangs watch clearly who passes through it. Other streets are jammed by temporary obstructions of garbage cans and metal posts that gangsters use to run impromptu checkpoints. Colin points to children practicing putting up street blockades with tires, rocks, or whatever they can find.

The garrison, he explains, is a political creation forged following Jamaica's independence. Back in the 1960s, the young nation's politicians worked with ghetto strongmen to bring in the ballots. They created the garrisons as turfs where they could control the voting and stop the opposing side coming to canvass.

As a result, the parties secure ridiculously high votes in garrisons—98 percent in some areas. In return, politicians hand out building contracts and other benefits to their loyal communities, often channeling that money through the dons.

Within this structure, the dons become a link between politicians and their ghetto constituents. Like Dudus's cousin said, the residents can't get to see their Member of Parliament, but they might get to see a don like Dudus.

All the garrisons and dons are clearly aligned to one of Jamaica's two main parties. The People's National Party, or PNP, is considered more left wing, and its followers are often referred to as socialists. The Jamaican Labor Party, or JLP, is considered more conservative, despite its name. Its followers are referred to as laborites. Tivoli Gardens is a hard-core laborite area. Garrisons known as Spangler and Tel Aviv are PNP areas.

The laborites use green as their color while the PNP uses orange. This creates the bizarre comparison with Northern Ireland, which is split between green Catholics and orange Protestants. In Jamaica, they take this color-coding to extremes. Laborite garrison loyalists will drink Heineken beer in its green cans while PNP fanatics will never touch it and prefer Red Stripe. It sounds hilarious. But in some places, slurping on the wrong beer can get you shot.

In Jamaica, they call this divide political tribalism. In 1997, the Jamaican parliament created a National Committee on Political Tribalism to write a report on the issue. The paper lays bare the problem that plagues the island. As it states:

> Political tribalism was a type of politics known to the ancient Greeks and Romans. It is political because the tribal grouping is not ethnic but based upon politics. In a tribe, members of the group and persons within the tribal confines must obsequiously obey and observe the rules and rituals of a tribe or suffer the consequences for disobedience and dissent. Thus, political tribalism is the antithesis of our constitutional democracy, with its freedom of association and the incidental right of the citizen at will to join or support the party of choice.
>
> Political tribalism, the use of violence in political activities, the creation of political garrisons were not a natural outgrowth of a political process, but rather they were nurtured and nourished as strategic initiatives to secure or retain political power.[1]

This war between political tribes reached its peak in the bloody 1980 election—as the Cold War turned hot in the Americas. The tribal conflict was debated in ideological terms, the PNP socialists siding with Cuba and the laborites with the United States. This was before the gangs became major international drug traffickers and battled over narco profits.

Back in 1980, mobs with guns, clubs, and machetes from one garrison would swarm into an opposing garrison. The borders between communities became dangerous frontlines. As the violence raged, gangs attacked the homes on these frontlines with firebombs and turfed out the families to create buffer zones of deserted streets. It is easier to defend your territory if no one is living in the blocks right next to it and you can quickly identify an enemy approaching. Many of these buffer zones are now crumbled and overgrown, creating physical divisions between rival garrisons. I walk through these no-man's-lands where trees and bushes cover the fallen remains of homes, the haunted scenes of old bloodshed. Violence shapes spaces.

The fortification and buffer zones make the garrisons highly defined areas. In Mexico, you can often move between middle-class, lower-middle-class, and slum areas that are on top of and all over each other. But in Jamaica, you know clearly when you are entering and when you are leaving a garrison. It is a marked territory.

Residents baptize garrisons with their own creative names. You have the Concrete Jungle, Southside, Spanglers, Rema. Others are named after tough places around the globe including Gaza, Tel Aviv, Zimbabwe, and Belfast. Often the name of the local gang and the garrison are interchangeable; the Tel Aviv gang claims dominion of the Tel Aviv garrison. It's hard to know which one came first.

Garrisons are embattled communities. But in a twisted way this makes them strong communities. People grow up fighting together. Everybody knows everybody else. And every young man in a garrison is a potential recruit for the don's field army. Or as Colin puts it, "Every ghetto youth is a soldier."

In many ways, the entire community is criminalized. When police come in, they enter in force. The police face heavily armed ghettos, and in response they are extremely trigger-happy. This is similar to Brazil, but considering the population levels, the Jamaican police are way more homicidal. In 2014, they killed an average of one person a day in the nation of three million. Cops commit one of four homicides in Jamaica. (In the United States, it is estimated to be about one in twenty. In England, it's about one in five hundred, and a single police killing can provoke major riots.)

The fact that Jamaican garrisons are so tight-knit and criminalized makes it easy to connect with gangsters. In Mexican towns, the cartel is a clandestine force. But in the garrisons, the gangsters are on the streets, on the corners, in the rum shops.

It also helps that many people are smoking weed. It's a cliché. But it's true. I have never seen people smoke so much. On some days, Colin and

I drive round in the early morning and people are getting wasted. At night, they burn and burn. Rather than passing round joints, they smoke their individual mini spliffs. They sell it dirt cheap, a small bag for a dollar. It's mostly a local strain called Lamb's Bread (also referred to as Lamb's Breath) or what they call "high grade," more potent strains developed in Amsterdam or California.

Amid the smoke-filled yards, the patois is thick and colorful. While I had heard it before, I didn't appreciate how strong it could be. The language is said to have developed in the seventeenth century when slaves mixed West African dialects with English. As a Jamaican patois version of the Lord's prayer says,

> *Wi Faada we iina evn,*
> *Mek piipl av nof rispek fi yu an yu niem.*[2]

(Our father we in a heaven,
Make people have enough respect for you and your name)

People will often use a toned-down version of patois, especially when speaking to a foreigner. Another form of speech is known as Jamaican English, which uses the accent and some elements of patois but is closer to British or American English. Meanwhile, Jamaican newsreaders speak much like BBC presenters. The difference between these forms of speech is considered a continuum, with every variation in between.

Back in my early twenties, I lived in south London and was involved in a music scene called "jungle," a mix of electronic and reggae forged in London's cultural melting pot. Like many British kids at those raves, we threw in Jamaican words we had picked up thirdhand from the streets of London and reggae records. *We went round our friend's yards, got mashed up and asked for big ups on the pirate radio.*

In Kingston's garrisons, it was endearing for me to hear old people use what was cutting-edge slang in England. But then it dawned on me they invented it and we were the followers. And I realized that if you throw patois about in Jamaica as a foreigner you can sound like a patronizing son of a bitch. It's an extremely culturally charged form of speech.

I saw many other origins of terms in British youth culture. The "Concrete Jungle" I had heard in countless songs is an actual neighborhood here. The word "gully," meaning "tough" in London slang, refers to rough garrisons with drains running through them. Songs and rhymes to advertise dances on London pirate radio stations are based on those of Jamaican radio.

However, I was surprised how one-way the influence is. I asked Jamaicans about British music and they seemed to care little for it, even by the artists of Jamaican descent. Jamaica of course has its own phenomenal music scene. But people also listen to American music. Hip-hop and soul are predictably popular on the island. But I was surprised to hear people tell me they like country and western.

"Country music?" I ask one of Dudus's cousins called Donavon, having to double take when he says it. "What do you mean?"

"You know, by white people." Donavon smiles. "Like from the Westerns."

Westerns were extremely popular in Jamaica, inspiring older gunslingers to baptize themselves with names such as Butch Cassidy. The cowboy flicks also inspired the term *posse* for gang.

Crime aside, I find the people of West Kingston to be warm and open, as in the ghettos from Brazil to Mexico. Like many other outsiders who have trekked into these areas, I'm touched by the people's generosity of spirit; their ability to forget about the cultural or socioeconomic gulf; and their openness to talk as human being to human being, showing spontaneous friendship from the heart.

CHAPTER 18

Tivoli Gardens' history of violence physically shapes the garrison. At the entrance, you can still see the remains of barricades from the 2010 incursion to get Dudus, barrels and concrete slabs that soldiers struggled to move away. Bullet holes from where troops let loose with their rifles still pick away at Tivoli buildings, making them look like blocks of nibbled cheese.

These bullet holes are thickest in the heart of the garrison, which is filled with a series of apartment buildings. The structures look much like the council tower blocks in London (which they were based on) or what are called projects in the United States.

Round the corner from these apartments, a building displays a vast cross, a memorial to Tivoli residents shot dead by police. The deaths were not actually from the final battle to catch Dudus, but from two previous police raids into the President's turf.

"Lest We Forget. In Memoriam of Those Who Died," it says above the towering crucifix.

Below is a list with the names and ages of fallen residents. Many are teenagers and young men, age nineteen, twenty-two, thirty-two. But others are older residents who cops shot down, even an eighty-one-year-old called Trew Seymour. And there are tragically the names of slain children, including a six-year-old called Cruise Green. Tivoli residents are reminded of police brutality every time they walk on the main street.

While showing the police as the enemy, the walls tell passersby of the local heroes, dons and their soldiers, with expansive murals to fallen gangsters. One wall on a central street carries an enormous image of Dudus's father, known by his nickname, Jim Brown, along with the title "Don of Dons." Jim Brown is depicted over a funeral wreath; he wears a backward cap and has his hand raised, showing off gleaming rings. He has a wise, impassive look, the kind of image one sees in paintings of nation founders. Police have painted over many gangster murals, but for some reason they have left this one.

Next to the painting of Jim Brown is the mural of one of Dudus's gunmen shot in the line of duty. Mario, alias "Sovady," killed in 2009 at age twenty-one, is depicted with a tough-looking sneer. He is painted in front of the Jamaican flag with white doves flying past his face. FALLEN SOLDIER, it says above him. GONE BUT NOT FORGOTTEN.

Interestingly, there is no painting of Dudus himself. I am not sure if the gangsters have to die before they get their mural. But while not on the walls, Dudus's name is on the lips of residents. Despite the newspapers saying he had betrayed his people when he fled Tivoli, many residents I speak to still see him as their president and wish that he would come back.

"Man Dudus done good. He the big man," says a young man in the Tivoli tower blocks as I film with a video camera. "Since 2010 them take him away from we, like removing God from heaven, Dudus the President."

Colin hooks me up with a long and colorful cast of gangsters in Tivoli. Some are veteran hustlers who spent time "juggling" (selling drugs) in hard-core American and British neighborhoods from the Bronx to London to Manchester. "I used to live Moss Side," says one corner vet, enthusiastic when I say I am from England. "Nuff IRA man there."

(Moss Side is a rough part of Manchester with big Irish and Afro Caribbean communities. There have been links between black and Irish gangsters, perhaps explaining his reference to the Irish Republican Army.)

Other Tivoli hoods I meet are young hungry gunslingers, often referred to as *shottas*, which is perhaps a mutation of the word "shooters." One shotta I meet is just fifteen and has already notched up several kills—or, as they say, has several *duppies*. The word *duppie* means "ghosts" or "spirits." Someone who has a lot of duppies has murdered many; he is claiming ownership of their souls.

One day as it beats down with rain, we go into a tower block and Colin introduces me to some of the top boys running Tivoli since Dudus was taken away. We talk on the steps, filled with their ganja smoke as the raindrops thump on the building. In this inner sanctum of Tivoli, they are happy showing off their 9 mm and Desert Eagle pistols as we chat.

Simon, a stocky twenty-seven-year-old, is a lieutenant who keeps control of drug selling points on the corners and oversees a band of gunmen lurking around.

"We come like the police. We serve and protect," he says, sitting on the steps. "If there is house break-in. We gonna kill them."

Since Dudus was arrested, Simon explains, several of the President's deputies have been vying for control of the Shower Posse, yet no one has established their firm leadership. The lack of authority creates tensions that periodically spill into violence.

"Nuff man dying now. This a big problem. We have to put order again."

To get a better sense of how the reign of Dudus was established here in West Kingston, I seek out a veteran gangster, someone who was there when it all started. For this deeper perspective, Colin introduces me to Kami, a seasoned Shower Posse enforcer who knows the history. He is what they refer to in the garrison as an *elder*. But then again, so is anyone who has made it past the age of about thirty-five.

In his early fifties, Kami is a hardened killer who has sent more *duppies* to the sky than he wants to count. After spending years as a trusted assassin for the Shower Posse, he went on to command squads of Dudus's soldiers. He's earned his stripes among the posse and has been able to take a step back in the last couple of years, only going on jobs if a seasoned hand is needed. Meanwhile, Kami's son has followed in his footsteps as a feared Shower Posse enforcer, hungrily claiming duppies and earning respect among the young bloods such as Simon. His son's reputation helps secure Kami's own position. It's a family affair.

I spend a day riding around Tivoli with Kami, and on a second night I visit his yard, which is in a garrison called Southside, a couple of miles along the waterfront from Tivoli. The Southside garrison was also part of Dudus's ghetto empire, which stretched through all laborite strongholds of Kingston, via either direct control or alliance.

Kami speaks to me in English with an American accent as he spent many years in the United States where he served as a Shower Posse enforcer in its mainland operations. He was what they call a *yardie*, a Jamaican gunman overseas. He'll still switch from American English to patois but doesn't mix them.

Sporting long dreadlocks, or cords of hair knotted together, Kami considers himself a Rasta. The Rastafari movement was born in Jamaica in the 1930s, mixing the teachings of Marcus Garvey with a veneration of Emperor Haile Selassie of Ethiopia and the dream of returning to Mother Africa. Kami says his beliefs put him in good standing with Dudus.

"The Prezi has a lot of respect for Rastas," Kami says. "He likes the faith."

The tens of thousands of Rastas living in Jamaica today vary in their beliefs. Some are strict in their prayer and vegetarianism and live in communes in the hills. Kami mixes Rastafarianism with being a posse triggerman. But that is no different from many gangland killers across the world, who consider themselves Catholic, evangelical Christian, Muslim, or of other religions.

In contrast, Kami's father was a Hindu, the descendant of Indians who arrived in Jamaica in the mid-nineteenth century. After the British parliament declared Jamaica's slaves free in 1838, many abandoned the sugarcane fields, so indentured Indian workers filled this labor gap. Most "East Indians" stayed to form their own businesses. The Indians are also credited with bringing marijuana to the island.

Jamaica today is a majority Afro country, with 91 percent classifying themselves as black. However, many Afro-Jamaicans have ancestors from other ethnicities. Aside from the British colonists who stayed on, there was immigration from China and the Middle East. Kami's features show a mix of his Indian father and an Afro mother.

I ask Kami how many brothers and sisters he has. His answer astonishes me.

"Forty-four."

"Forty-four?" I repeat, trying to figure out if we are talking about the same thing.

"Yes. Sixteen brothers and twenty-eight sisters."

Such prodigious procreation is hailed by some in Jamaica. The bass player for Bob Marley is known as Aston "Family Man" Barrett as he fathered forty-one children. I also hear of a local legend known as Charley Mattress said to have fathered over fifty. (He owned a mattress factory, as well as spending a lot of time on them.) I even find a report in the Jamaican newspaper, the *Gleaner*, which interviewed one of Mattress's children, who said she had fifty-six siblings and had spent her life looking after them.[1]

Such enormous families can give Jamaicans blood links in all directions, sometimes connecting politicians and gangsters. Many also have a family member who is a famous reggae artist. Kami himself is the cousin of one of the most successful dance hall singers, who recorded a song with American rap legend Biggie Smalls.

Kami also has a large family of his own, with twelve children from several baby mothers. He currently has a beautiful girlfriend in her early twenties and a newborn baby. As we sit in their home, Kami tugs on ganja spliffs with the frequency of a chain smoker, the yard buzzing with friends and family while speakers on the street blast dance hall reggae music.

Spending time with Kami, I can't stop liking the guy, despite him being a cold-blooded murderer. He is open and chatty and carries little violence in his body language. He tells me how he likes creative writing and shows me some pieces. One is an idea for a comic strip. It's a world with mice and cats and dogs, where the mice are women, the cats are moneylenders, and the dogs are fighters. Its protagonist is a dog who smokes a lot of weed and is always in debt with the cats. It's actually pretty funny.

Besides talking about ganja-puffing canines, Kami is a wealth of information about Dudus, the Shower Posse, and the development of organized crime in Jamaica. His own life and criminal career follow the twists and turns of the don system that created Dudus, from the political wars to the global trafficking to the building of the Presidential Click—Dudus's personal faction within the Shower. It starts back in the mid-twentieth century, when Jamaica first cut the shackles of Her Majesty's government in London.

CHAPTER 19

When Kami was born in Southside in 1959, it was no ghetto. In contrast, it was an affluent part of Kingston, a waterfront area in the twilight years of the British Empire. "This was a nice neighborhood." Kami shrugs. "Ships from all round the world would come to the harbor. Sailors would be buying and selling goods so you could find anything you wanted."

Jamaica was generally a more peaceful place back then. In 1962, the year it gained independence, there were just sixty-three murders reported on the island. In 1980, as the political wars raged, there were 889. In 2009, at the height of Dudus's rule, the body count hit 1,682.[1]

This is a shocking explosion of death; the number of killings has gone up more than 2,500 percent in a period of time when the population hasn't even doubled. The fact that there used to be such a low murder rate proves that wanton killing is no natural state of affairs. Jamaicans can live peacefully. However, certain structural factors drive mass murder. At the heart of these is the don system that trains and directs assassins.

When Kami was growing up, it didn't take him long to find the crime world; his father was a smuggler taking boatloads of marijuana to the United States. Farmers grow ganja in abundance in Jamaica, so it is dirt-cheap and fetches a big markup stateside. Kami's father supplied marijuana to the smokers of the beatnik generation. In the early sixties, it was easy to smuggle on the shipping path from Jamaica to Florida, before the war on drugs. The Shower Posse would later transform this drug route from a stream to a tidal wave.

With his father wealthy from marijuana smuggling, Kami enjoyed a good living standard, eating well and attending school. However, the streets outside got steadily rougher, as waves of migrants from the countryside settled on the waterfront in sprawling shantytowns. Among them was a slum dominated by Rastas known as Back-O-Wall on the site of what is now Tivoli Gardens.

Back-O-Wall was in such desperate poverty that it had just two bathrooms to serve over five thousand people.[2] A government report described it as "a dehumanizing, dirt poor, labyrinthine squatter settlement of dirt-floor, zinc and board or wattle-and-daub shanties and hovels, criss-crossed by a maze of narrow earthen footpaths; densely populated; bereft of plumbing and electricity."[3]

It was to these utterly squalid conditions that politicians came to buy their supporters and organize them into garrisons.

Two politicians dominated Jamaica in the late twentieth century: the charismatic socialist Michael Manley on the PNP side and the articulate conservative Edward Seaga on the laborite side. The two are contrasting figures physically as well as ideologically and make good sparring partners for cartoonists. Manley is overflowing with words, smiley, preachy, handsome, bulky, comfortable in casual dress in the tropical sun. Seaga is serious, precise, straight-faced, slim, dressed in well-pressed shirts tucked into his pants however hot it is. It is Seaga who is credited with inventing the garrison, and many paint him as the villain of the story. However, Manley's supporters also carried out their own share of political murders and followed suit with their own garrisons.

Seaga—pronounced *see-ah-gah*—is a curious character. Born in 1930, he is a light-skinned Jamaican of Lebanese and Scottish ancestry. He was vocally pro-capitalist and pro-American, anti-communist and anti-Cuban. However, he managed to gain cult support in certain Jamaican ghettos, challenging the PNP socialists for the votes of the poor black majority. Kami himself is a lifelong supporter of Seaga, and has met him several times.

"Eddie Seaga is our man. He is very intelligent, very cultured," Kami says, using the affectionate "Eddie." "He loves music. You know he used to run a record label?"

Seaga's musical accomplishments are quite something, I discover. In 1955, after graduating from Harvard, he was one of the first entrepreneurs to record Afro-Jamaican bands. His West India Records Limited went on to become one of the most successful labels in the Caribbean, with prominent calypso and ska artists launching Jamaica's phenomenal music industry.

Seaga's fascination with Afro-Jamaican culture can also be seen in academic papers he wrote on religious sects and faith healers. He studied Jamaican Revivalism, a movement that mixes Baptist-style worship with West African dance and drums. Seaga recorded masses in the Back-O-Wall ghetto in which people murmur as they dispel evil spirits.[4]

Moving into politics, Seaga became the Member of Parliament for the rough West Kingston district in 1962, a seat he would hold for forty-three consecutive years. His research helped him find ways to reach his poor black constituents. In 1964, he personally arranged to repatriate Marcus Garvey's body from London to Jamaica, giving the people the bread of their national hero. The next year, he married a brown and beautiful Miss Jamaica, providing him with needed macho credentials.

Along with symbolic gestures, Seaga built a base of patronage. Becoming the Minister of Welfare and Development (or as Rastas said, the Minister of Warfare and Devilment), Seaga ripped the Back-O-Wall slum to smithereens in 1966. Many Rasta residents opposed their eviction, standing in front of the bulldozers. Seaga sent in baton-waving police. Tearing away all trace of Back-O-Wall, he renamed the neighborhood Tivoli Gardens and built the London-style high-rises at its center. The selected tenants who got keys to the new apartments voted for him in overwhelming numbers for decades. Tivoli was dubbed "the mother of all garrisons," a model of a politically loyalist ghetto that was followed across the island.[5]

Seaga was quick to see his supporters as a fighting force. When he spoke in central Kingston and PNP cohorts heckled him, he retorted in anger: "If they think they are bad, I can bring the crowds of West Kingston. We can deal with you, in any way, at any time. It will be fire for fire. Blood for blood."[6]

The laborite hold on Tivoli relied on local thugs making sure no PNP activists came to preach their socialism. By the early 1970s, a chief laborite enforcer emerged in the garrison called Claudius "Claudie" Massop. I ask Kami when people began to refer to Massop and other gangsters as dons. He smiles.

"It was about the time that the *Godfather* movie came out. Everybody in Jamaica just loved it. It's a film that you can watch a million times and learn something new from each time."

In the 1972 movie, the Godfather is of course Don Corleone. The title spread though Jamaican garrisons, and the don system went national.

The influence of this movie strikes me. It seems superficial, something that shouldn't be taken too seriously, cartoon characters based on gangster flicks. But the dons had real guns, real power, and drove a real high level of bloodshed.

Kami became one of their triggermen shedding this claret. As a teen-ager, he was doing well at school. But he needed to stand up for himself on the increasingly tough streets. When he was fifteen, he bought his first pistol from a Greek sailor off a visiting ship. By that time, Southside had become a laborite garrison allied to Tivoli. It was an especially violent area as it had frontlines to PNP socialist ghettos on several sides. Kami joined the gunmen defending these borders. They formed into a group called the Skull Gang.

"We were laborite a hundred percent. I hated the PNP. If they dared come here to try and give out leaflets or look for votes, they were dead. If they even came close to our streets we shot at them."

In the sense that the gunmen fought to defend their neighborhood, it was classic gang mentality, guarding a turf from rivals. They also wanted to safeguard their families. If a mob came in, it could firebomb homes and machete residents. In Jamaica, these neighborhood gangs are also known as corner defense crews.

However, these gangs had political affiliations. And there was money involved. Kami describes how his don carried wads of cash and would spread it around the soldiers. It began casually, some cash here and there, but then became more formalized with money paid out every week. A soldier's salary wasn't a great deal, but it provided a steady income for unemployed ghetto youth.

Kami presumed the cash was funneled from politicians. However, while Jamaica's parliamentary inquiry and almost all politicians acknow-ledge the don system, the financing has never been thoroughly documented.

It is also widely alleged that political parties provided firearms to their loyalists, but again there is little solid proof to show that. Either way, Kami says the don had his hands on plenty of guns and ammunition for his troops, and the battles with rival garrisons became more intense.

"We had crazy gunfights, block to block. This was when I first killed people. I didn't feel bad about it because they were firing at me. I wasn't up close executing them or anything. It was a fair fight."

I ask Kami if he was trained to shoot. He shakes his head. The gunmen teach themselves, learn through experience, he says.

"You might practice firing at cans or bottles. But you really learn on the street. When the fight breaks out, you see who has got the nerve to shoot and who hasn't. There are a lot of kids here who just naturally have that killer instinct."

One of these thugs with a killer instinct was Lester Lloyd Coke, a bulky roughneck over in Tivoli Gardens. Kami met Coke through a mutual friend, Vivian Blake, who he used to play cricket with. Blake and Coke would later go on to form the Shower Posse together.

Being big and broad, Coke was known as "Jim Brown" after the American football player who starred in *The Dirty Dozen*, which was a big hit in Jamaica. Jim Brown was several years older than Kami and already had several children. One of them, born in 1969, was Christopher Michael Coke, alias Dudus, the future President.

The street fighting heated up steadily during the seventies as Prime Minister Manley launched Jamaica's great experiment in democratic socialism. Manley was born into politics, the son of PNP founder Norman Manley who governed Jamaica when it gained independence from Britain. The family is of mixed race, known in Jamaica as mulatto, a group associated with privilege over the majority of Afros in the Caribbean. However, Manley preached that the elite had to be shaken up for an egalitarian society to be born. As Manley explained to U.S. TV host Gil Noble:

> There are tremendous social pressures in Jamaica. Like almost all countries that had a long colonial experience, Jamaica is a product of that experience, and reflected at the time of independence sharp class divisions, a very small and highly privileged elite.... The attempt to build an egalitarian society begins with the dismantling of the citadels of privilege.[7]

While an intellectual, educated at the London School of Economics, Manley used populist gestures to win poor black voters. He flew to Ethiopia to visit Emperor Haile Selassie, an icon for many Jamaicans. Selassie gave him a staff of ebony with an ivory handle; Manley held up the staff on his 1972 campaign trail, and it became known as the "Rod of Correction." The rod gained him Rasta support, inspiring a reggae record and promoting the myth that Manley was a reincarnation of Joshua, freeing the enslaved.

"We've come too far, we're not turning back now," Manley chanted at a campaign rally, as he banged on the orator stand like it was a drum. "We have a mission now, and I say to you, my friends, together we are going to march forward under God's heaven, building democratic socialism."[8]

Winning power, Manley turned his ideas into social change with far-reaching reforms. He taxed the wealthy and redistributed land; introduced a minimum wage and free schooling to tertiary level; empowered unions and took royalties from American and Canadian companies mining Jamaica's bauxite, a mineral used in the car industry. Manley's leadership inspired. But the radical reforms also divided. Ghetto supporters rallied around him and pledged to fight for his cause. Wealthy plantation owners and businessmen accused him of being a raging communist. Manley retorted that if they didn't like it, there were five flights a day to Miami. Thousands took up the offer and fled.

Tension increased as Manley got friendly with Castro in Cuba, 230 miles over the Caribbean. In 1975, Cuba sent troops to Angola to fight the U.S.-backed army of South Africa. Secretary of State Henry Kissinger flew to Jamaica to ask Manley to condemn Cuba's involvement. Manley was loath to help apartheid South Africa. He told Kissinger to shove it.

"Now there are certain people in the world who ask why are we taking this risk to anger the United States of America and the answer is this," he chanted in a speech following the meeting. "We are not angering the United States of America. They are angering themselves."[9]

"We have that friendship with Cuba as part of a world alliance of third world nations who are fighting for justice for poor people," he said in another speech.[10]

As Manley veered to the left, the fighting in Jamaica's ghettos became increasingly ideological. PNP gunmen claimed they were defending Jamaica's revolution. Seaga told his laborites they were fighting a communist plot that would drag Jamaica into the abyss. The blood-soaked garrisons had turned into a minor Cold War battleground.

As corpses piled up, mutual accusations sharpened. Seaga claimed Manley was a puppet of Havana. Manley countered that laborite thugs were supported by a CIA campaign to destabilize Jamaica.

"Here is how destabilization works," Manley told a rally. "The secret group that is trying to mash up the country will go in among the youth and find one that looks like a leader ... and sell the idea of starting a bitch of a street fight."[11]

This accusation that the CIA backed the laborite shock troops has far-reaching implications. This was the force that would become the Shower Posse, commit wanton murder across the United States, and lead to Dudus's Presidential Click. However, the charge is tough to prove.

The gist of the accusation is that the CIA carried out a "destabilization campaign" similar to those well documented in Guatemala in 1954 and Chile in 1973 to get rid of leftist rulers. According to this theory, the agency cooked up media stories trashing the Jamaican government, bolstered the opposition, and armed political gunmen. Laborite thugs unleashed violence that hurt Manley and helped the opposition voting machine.

Two former CIA agents came out supporting the claims. However, both had left the agency by the height of the Jamaican violence and become vocal critics of U.S. foreign policy on a range of issues. Philip Agee had left the CIA back in 1969. He went to Jamaica in 1976 and released the names of the nine alleged CIA agents he said were in the office working on the operation. (Agee later had a barrage of accusations thrown at him from being a double agent to an alcoholic womanizer. He had his U.S. passport revoked and died in Cuba.)

The other agent, John Stockwell, worked in the CIA until 1976, heading the agency's Angola operation. After leaving, he visited Jamaica and said he saw definite evidence of a campaign.

"(There was) every indication of a massive CIA operation going to destabilize the government and make the economy scream," Stockwell said in a 1982 TV interview. "It was not published in the *New York Times* and the *Washington Post* and the big television networks didn't do studies on it, primarily because even if the journalists of the big organs knew what was happening and might have wanted to, because of the secrecy, they couldn't get the truth of what the United States was doing."[12]

Seaga fervently denies the CIA armed his supporters. It is likely the matter will only be settled if and when the CIA releases its files on it. But it is notable that many in Jamaica to this day are convinced that the CIA was involved.

Likewise, there is much talk of crates of Cuban guns arriving, without hard evidence that Havana provided military help to Manley. However, it is proven that a handful of Jamaican militants did travel independently to Cuba and underwent guerrilla training. In his colorful portrait of Jamaica,

The Dead Yard, Ian Thomson interviews one of the veterans who flew to Havana.

"He went into woods, he waged mock war and, armed with M16s, Uzis and SLRs, crawled on his belly across semi-swampland," Thomson writes. The trainee guerrilla then "accidentally almost killed one of the instructors with a grenade."[13]

Back in Southside, Kami says he wasn't sure where all the guns were coming from. But they certainly had plenty of weapons by the late 1970s.

"The guns got bigger. We weren't just playing with pistols anymore. We had submachine guns and automatic rifles. Some people even got their hands on plastic explosives."

Tivoli lies on the docks where smugglers can bring in weapons on ships while drugs are smuggled out. The docks are one reason that Tivoli is such an important garrison; whoever dominates the Kingston waterfront controls a major trafficking corridor.

Decades after this tumultuous period, Kami is still vehemently partisan. He spits venom at the mention of Manley.

"That hypocritical son of a bitch. I would love to have killed him."

In fact, Kami says that he and his fellow triggermen really did try to shoot at Manley one time, but police guarding him saw them off. This sounds so crazy, I ask Kami to repeat it. He reiterates that he really tried to assassinate the prime minister. Looking up archive newspapers, I find that Manley indeed got pinned down by gunfire on several occasions, including in Spanish Town in 1980.

Kami hates Manley so much because he blames him for the so-called Green Bay massacre in 1978, when soldiers murdered five Southside youths. Kami had grown up with some of the victims so he was particularly outraged. The pro-PNP soldiers were trying to get laborite gunmen such as himself, Kami says, but the victims were not involved in the political war.

"They were good youth who died that day. That was an evil treacherous thing the soldiers did."

The massacre was one of the most cold-blooded of Jamaica's political violence. A man lured the victims to the Green Bay army shooting range on the pretext of guard work. When they arrived, the troops opened fire on them.[14] Various soldiers were charged, but after a delayed trial, a jury acquitted them.

The soldiers may have been rogue elements rather than carrying out a hit sanctioned by the prime minister. But whoever gave the order, many laborites hated the Manley government more than ever.

The Green Bay massacre also produced a curious side effect: The political gunslingers came together in a peace treaty. In a sudden moment of realization that poor blacks were murdering poor blacks in the power games of light-skinned politicians, the gangsters agreed to put down their guns. Key in the peace movement was the Tivoli don Claudie Massop.

In the months following Green Bay, the political street fights virtually ceased. Taking advantage of this harmonious moment, Massop and others decided the truce could be enhanced by a music event, and organized the One Love Peace Concert. It was an extraordinary meeting of politics, gangsters, and music, only possible in Jamaica. Headlining the event was none other than the legend himself, Bob Marley.

During this turbulent period, the Trench Town singer was at his most prolific. But like most Jamaicans, he couldn't escape the violence. In 1976, gunmen stormed into Marley's uptown house and shot him in the chest and arm. They also shot his wife, Rita, manager, and a friend. All survived following hospital treatment.

Police never found the culprits of the Marley shooting, and the motive remains murky. The common explanation is that the gunmen were laborite thugs angered by Marley playing at an event organized by Prime Minister Manley, which was seen as a virtual election rally. Some writers speculate that Jim Brown, Dudus's father, was even among the shooters. However, others say the whole thing was over a personal quarrel.

Whatever the cause, it made Marley leave for self-imposed exile in London, where he recorded his landmark *Exodus* album. The Tivoli don Massop then personally flew to England to convince Marley to return to his homeland for the peace gig in April 1978.

By all accounts, One Love was one of the most astonishing concerts in musical history. It filled the National Stadium, with tens of thousands divided into sections marked "togetherness," "love," and "peace." It took place exactly twelve years after a visit to Jamaica by Ethiopian Emperor Haile Selassie. It began under a burning afternoon sun and finished during a full moon seen through clouds of ganja smoke. And the most prolific stars in the history of reggae played their finest performances.[15]

As the concert heated up, singer Peter Tosh came on stage and launched into a tirade against politicians for driving the violence. Known for a more angry stance than his former band mate Marley, Tosh roused the crowd as Prime Minister Manley and laborite Seaga watched nervously from the side.

"The little pirate dem come here and rob up the resources for the country. Because that is what dem been doing a long bloodbath time," Tosh said in his booming, reverberating voice. "Eliminate all the shitstem that makes black poor people live in confusion. Cos hungry people are angry people. I am not a politician but I suffer the consequences."[16]

It was incendiary rhetoric. However, when Bob Marley stepped up, he switched from attacking the political leaders to inviting them on stage. As his band played a marathon version of his hit "Jammin," he addressed Jamaica's two political warmongers.

"Mr. Michael Manley and Mr. Edward Seaga. I just want to shake hands and show the people that we're gonna make it right, we're gonna unite ... The moon is right over my head, and I give my love instead."

As the crowd roared, Manley and Seaga stepped forward, and Marley joined their hands together. The result is a photo of Manley on the left, Marley in the middle, Seaga on the right, their arms raised and hands linked. It is an iconic image of music trumping war.

But when you look at the photo for a while you see betraying details. Both Manley and Seaga are looking away with awkward expressions. If you watch a video of it, you see that after the picture, they pull away from each other hurriedly. They may have been up for a photo op. But they weren't ready to bury their political war in peace and love.

Among the thronging crowds, Kami also says that he was suspicious the peace would not last.

"It was really weird. We had been fighting these guys a couple of months ago and then they were in the concert with us. I was amazed that no trouble started. It was a nice moment. It showed us how things could be in a better world. But this was Jamaica and you knew that shit would go down sooner or later."

The shit went down in early 1979 when police gunned down Tivoli don Massop, who brokered the peace treaty. The officers pursued him in a taxi, pulled him out, and shot him with more than forty bullets. Mourners carried Massop's coffin through the slum streets and fifteen thousand from Tivoli, Southside, and other ghettos wept at his funeral. Then bullets rained.

The murder of a gang boss who fought for peace sparked the inevitable conspiracy theories. Did police kill him because they prefer gangs to be fighting? people muttered. Or was it all part of the destabilization?

Whatever may have driven the officers on that fateful day, the street war returned with a vengeance. In Jamaica's 1980 election year, raging street battles and mob attacks caused record homicides. In a horrific incident, political gunmen set fire to an old people's home, a blaze that killed 153 elderly women. (A tragedy commemorated in the reggae song "Eventide Fire a Disaster.")

Amid the slaughter, Manley lost the election. Under his rule, Jamaica appeared ungovernable. But it wasn't just violence that finished his experiment in democratic socialism. The exodus of the rich to Miami sucked wealth from the economy, and Manley's closeness to Castro cost millions in U.S. aid. Shortages of flour, rice, and oil sparked runaway inflation and strikes.

Promising a return to the growth of the 1960s, Seaga won a landslide victory. The representative of West Kingston, architect of the garrison, and idol of the laborite street fighters was at last in power. Taking office in the same year as Ronald Reagan he aligned himself with his ideological buddy, visiting the White House and getting Reagan's blessing for his plans to bring American investment back to Jamaica.

Some of Seaga's constituents in West Kingston also eyed the business prospects of the United States. But rather than offering bananas and bauxite, they saw the potential for marijuana and crack cocaine. In carving out these markets, the scarred gunslingers of Jamaica's political wars unleashed themselves on America's crack-laden streets of the eighties.

CHAPTER 20

Kami entered America like a thunderbolt. He was in the United States less than twenty-four hours when he gunned down two men on a New York street corner.

He got the call to come to New York as Jamaica's electoral war raged in 1980. Kami had just turned twenty-one and was proving himself a capable killer in this political violence. The message came that his friend Vivian Blake was in New York and needed muscle.

"It sounded like a good idea to go to America and make some cash. And the way bodies were dropping in Jamaica, I knew that I would die sooner or later if I didn't get away."

Kami had known Blake for years and trusted him. Like Kami, Blake hailed from the rough streets of West Kingston but had a decent education, winning a scholarship to a private high school.

"Vivian was a really bright kid. He always had ideas about making money. He was really organized. From when he was young, he was going over to the United States, and he was making bucks. It was good to be associated with him."

Blake earned his fortune with three products: marijuana, cocaine, and guns. He bought marijuana from Jamaican farmers, took it to the West Kingston waterfront, and transported it to Florida and New York, from where it spread across the United States. The smugglers hid the weed in commercial ships, among bananas, tobacco, or minerals; they took it on small fishing boats or speedboats; and they hid it on planes among passengers or even air stewardesses.

Smuggling guns back from the United States was even easier. The gangsters bought firearms in states with liberal laws such as Texas using straw buyers—U.S. citizens paid to go in the shop. They hid the guns on the same commercial ships or fishing boats heading back to the island, taking them into the docks they controlled in West Kingston.

Cocaine was just arriving in Jamaica in 1980 and it would be key to the posse's expansion. When Colombians first shifted big volumes of cocaine in the 1970s, they simply flew it in light aircraft straight from Colombia's coast to Florida. But police cracked down on such blatant trafficking by the eighties. So Colombians switched to the Caribbean islands from where they could bounce the disco powder into America on small boats. Jamaica is halfway between Colombia and Florida so it is a perfect stop-off point. And as Jamaican smugglers had already carved out trafficking routes for marijuana, it was simply an extra product to throw on board.

I ask Kami if it was easy for him to get into the United States. He smiles.

"I didn't even need a passport back then. I just had a false Green Card. It was sent over to me. Vivian had his people somewhere sorting them out." (The posses are specialists in false documents.)

It was Kami's first trip outside the country. He flew into JFK airport at night and got a taxi to a house in Harlem that he had been told to report to. He arrived to find Blake wasn't there. However, there were other guys he knew from Kingston.

The Jamaicans in the Harlem house were raging about a beef with some Latin Kings, a long established street gang in New York and Chicago. The Latin Kings had shot one of the Jamaicans for selling drugs on their turf. The Jamaicans were arguing about how they should respond.

Kami volunteered to step in.

"I said, 'Look, I am new here. Nobody knows my face. I can get close and they won't know what has hit them.'"

After more discussion, they agreed to let Kami go in for the kill. The next afternoon he went out with a pistol to where the Latin Kings hung out slinging drugs, up on 225th Street and Broadway. He hid the gun in his jacket and walked toward them.

"First I walked past them slowly, checking out their positions. I was biding my time. But one of them said, 'Hey, he looks like one of those Jamaicans.' So I had to make my move. I pulled out my gun and blasted. I took out the first two I saw and the rest ran. If they hadn't, I would have killed more."

*   *   *

Such brazen murder characterized the yardies' entrance to America. Kami and others had just come from the street wars of Kingston and were accustomed to killing without hesitation. They fought like they had nothing to lose. Gangbangers in the United States were taken by surprise.

They often used submachine guns and automatic rifles, spraying their enemies with gunfire. This was how the name "Shower Posse" came about, the fact that they showered their rivals with bullets. Kami said they coined it in late 1980.

"It was Vivian's idea. He said that we needed a name to set ourselves up in New York. We wanted to show people that we were here."

The label worked, with Shower Posse becoming a powerful brand that instilled fear across America and back home in Jamaica. Members often refer it as just "The Show," pronouncing an *owe* sound.

As well as smuggling drugs into the United States, the Shower Posse aggressively took over street corners. This distinguishes them from Colombian and Mexican cartels, who concentrate on wholesale, moving tons of drugs for billions of dollars. The cartels mostly sell their narcotics to middlemen and don't care who ends up serving them on the corner, where there is maximum exposure.

In some ways, the Jamaicans eyed a smaller dream than the Mexicans and Colombians. However, the posses also saw the big markup in profits in street sales. For example, cocaine sells for about thirty thousand dollars for a kilo brick in the United States, according to DEA agents. But when it is cut into grams and sold on the street, it can fetch more than a hundred thousand dollars. Whoever controls the corners makes this.

As well as smuggling their own drugs, the Shower would steal narcotics from other people, Kami says. They prowled for information on where cocaine was stashed or a load was coming in. And they stormed in, showering bullets.

"We were kind of unorthodox that way. Most people handed over the drugs once they had a gun to their head. But some of the Spanish [Latinos] didn't give it up that easily. So we had to cut them up."

Kami almost apologizes as he recounts this torture. It is strange how people have these different sides to their character, how they can be friendly and funny on one hand and hack people up with knives on the other. You forget you are talking to a serial murderer.

* * *

Taking over street corners, the Shower Posse found a way to make even more money: crack. The rocks of concentrated cocaine are sold cheap, for about ten dollars a stone as opposed to a hundred dollars for a gram of powder. But crack users get hooked more quickly and come back for more and more.

In his book *Cocaine*, Dominic Streatfeild traces what may have been the first crack use to the Bahamas in the late 1970s.[1] Picking up the c-dust on its way stateside, Bahamians experimented by cooking it with baking soda to create the crack form, he finds out. By the early eighties, the recipe spread across the United States.

Jamaican posses are sometimes labeled as the gangs who brought crack to America. That is likely an exaggeration. Crack is easy to make and various gangs, both American and foreign born, began to cook it. But the Jamaican posses were certainly major players, especially Shower, the biggest posse of them all.

Cooking up crack is not rocket science. But it can be tricky, fiddly work, which some people have a knack for. Among the Shower, specialist crack cooks emerged, honing their techniques. In Kingston, I meet a veteran chef who was part of Shower's American operations. He has two methods to cook crack, he explains: steaming and microwaving. In the steam method, he cooks the cocaine and baking powder in a glass vessel with water over a flame. Some water disappears in the steam, so the rocks are smaller but more concentrated. In the microwave method, no water is lost, so the rocks are bulkier, but not as pure. He says he personally prefers the steam method, which makes the customers get a stronger high so they come back for his quality product. He beams with pride as he describes his drug-making skills.

Kami was better with a gun than in a kitchen. As an enforcer, his job was to collect debts and hit anyone who got in the posse's way. Hard. For his work as a soldier in the United States, the Shower paid him five hundred dollars a week and extra money for certain jobs. He was often ordered to muscle drug dealers and allowed to take whatever stash they had, which could be packages of cocaine, heroin, or marijuana. He would normally hand these drugs to colleagues who ran corners, preferring not to expose himself by standing in the rain selling dope. Kami was no millionaire, but he made more money than he ever could have in Jamaica. And he considered it an easy low-risk life, compared to back home.

"We lived good over in America. We had nice cars, we had cash for what we wanted, we went out to nightclubs and restaurants. And compared to Kingston, you felt safe over there. People didn't want to fuck with us."

With brazen violence and a steady drug supply, the Shower Posse expanded fast. In New York, it set up operations in the Bronx, Harlem, Queens, Brooklyn (including Crown Heights), and New Jersey. More planeloads of eager gunmen arrived from Jamaica, spreading the posse to Toronto, Chicago, Los Angeles. And it kept growing. By the mid 1980s, it was in Baltimore, Kansas City, Houston, Philadelphia, Boston, Denver, Cleveland. Kami believes that by the late eighties, the Shower had more than two thousand operatives across the United States. Federal agents make similar estimates. After several years in New York, Kami himself moved to Atlanta to spread the Shower gospel.

While Blake ran the American side of Shower, Jim Brown took care of the Posse's business in Jamaica. Dudus's father established himself as the new don of Tivoli Gardens, following the police shooting of Claudie Massop, and the short-lived reign of another don who died of a coke overdose. The Shower Posse now brought together the control of a physical turf in Jamaica with an international trafficking operation.

The Posse was helped by the fact that Seaga and the Labor Party held power. The Tivoli gunmen had long identified as laborites and fought on that side of the tribal war. Seaga would later march at the front of Jim Brown's funeral procession and describe him as the protector of the community. And Jim Brown's lawyer was even a Labor Party senator, Tom Tavares-Finson.

However, while the don system survived, it mutated. The Tivoli thugs were no longer just gunmen defending a voting turf. They were now part of a global trafficking web. The drug money made them less reliant on the politicians' handouts. But they kept on with the political racketeering for a new reward: impunity.

Shower Posse garrisons turned out votes for Labor members of parliament, including the PM Seaga. Meanwhile, Jim Brown had good luck with the police and courts. In one case, a bus driver made the mistake of getting into an argument with Jim Brown on the street. When he realized who he was cussing, he fled in horror to the nearest police station. But rather than protecting the bus driver, the police handed him over to Jim Brown and his thugs, who beat him to death outside.

In a second case, in 1984, Jim Brown led a squad of gunmen into the Rema garrison and allegedly killed twelve people. Police arrested Jim Brown over the homicides. But the don was quickly released for lack of evidence. When the judge freed him, his henchmen fired a gun salute outside the courthouse and carried him on their shoulders through the streets.

It is hard to prove the specific acts of corruption. Jamaica—like many countries in the Americas—struggles to punish officials; the system won't investigate itself. Yet Jamaican statesmen talk openly about the gangster politics in general terms. As the parliamentary report on garrisons and dons says:

> In a transactional sense, the Member of Parliament is sure of retaining his territorial support, while the rankings (dons) are able to acquire wealth and local power as well as protection from the forces of law and order.[2]

During this period, Dudus was living his teenage years, the son of this don at the zenith of his wealth and power.

Jim Brown made sure that his children all went to good schools, with Dudus attending the fee-paying Ardenne High outside of Tivoli. I visit Ardenne to find an ordered campus where boys run round in khaki uniforms and girls sport blue and white dresses, like a scene from colonial times. After hunting round the buildings, I find Dudus's old mathematics teacher. He is hesitant to talk at first, but in heckling British journo style, I corner him until he reveals something about teaching math to the President.

"He was a very good student, an excellent mathematician," the teacher tells me, warming up. "He would sit quietly and study. He wasn't arrogant. He didn't seem to use his status to bully other kids or anything. I didn't even know that he was Jim Brown's son for a long time. But he was very smart. Do you know that he was studying a law degree when he was arrested?"

It is hard to verify this law degree, but it is certain that Dudus's education would mark his rule. He was a calculated leader, juggling business, politics, and philanthropy. And while he used violence, he was more controlled than previous dons, and careful about implicating himself.

* * *

Back under Jim Brown, however, the Shower Posse exercised little control over its bloodletting, leaving a growing pile of corpses across the United States. Sometimes, their victims were American gangsters such as the Latin Kings that Kami gunned down. In other cases, the victims were Shower Posse members themselves, who they executed for stealing money or getting out of line. In some cases, the victims were innocent civilians who did nothing more than tread on the toe of a Shower Posse thug at a dance hall club.

The Shower Posse thrived off its bloodthirsty reputation. In Miami in 1984, Shower gunmen shot dead five people, including a pregnant woman, at an apartment said to be a crack house. A witness later testified that Jim Brown himself was a shooter after flying in from Jamaica. The pregnant woman begged for her life before Jim Brown shot her in the head, the witness said. The following year, the posse shot up a reggae dance in the rented Fort Lauderdale Fire Department's Benevolent Association hall. Stray bullets killed a twenty-four-year-old sound engineer.

The Shower also clashed with rival Jamaican posses seeking their fortune in America. Just as Blake and Jim Brown built the Shower empire, gangsters from PNP garrisons went to New York and formed the Spangler Posse. Other Jamaican gangs included the Dunkirk Boys and Tel Aviv. When posses met in America, they brought their Kingston street war with them. In August 1985, the Spangler Posse was having a picnic in a park in Oakland, New Jersey, when the Shower attacked. A shootout left three dead and nineteen injured.

As the posse's victims piled up, police departments struggled with scattered homicide cases from Florida to New Jersey to as far away as Ohio and Colorado. Federal agents working organized crime had good files on the Italian mafia but knew little about these dreadlocked gunslingers from the Caribbean. However, feds gradually cottoned on that murders across the country were connected to a new organized crime conspiracy they needed to take very seriously.

A lead came in 1984 when Jamaican police seized a shipment of weapons on the docks in Kingston and Interpol got their hands on the guns, passing the data to the ATF in the United States.[3] The ATF realized the weapons had been used in homicides in several states and launched a nationwide investigation. As the case sprawled, the FBI and DEA got on board.

The feds unearthed a long trail of blood. By the late 1980s, federal agents said the Jamaican posses were linked to more than fourteen hundred murders across the United States.[4] It is hard to verify this number, which became widely cited in the media, but anywhere close to it would show that the Jamaican gangs were a significant factor in the rise in violence that plagued American cities throughout the decade.

The Shower's gory reputation that gained it territory brought down the wrath of U.S. law enforcement. In the late eighties and early nineties, federal stings with code names such as Rum Punch nabbed hundreds of yardies in dozens of cities. U.S. courts were quick to convict posse members and give them multiple life sentences.

This crackdown would teach the Shower Posse—and other international traffickers—a lesson: in the United States, they couldn't get away with the same level of violence they did in their homelands. In response, gangs from Jamaica to Mexico would establish a modus operandi of keeping a lower profile on U.S. soil, while carrying out wanton murder back in their countries. It's a behavior with painful consequences for Latin America and the Caribbean. But it also shows a certain level of law enforcement can contain these gangsters.

Kami was among those swept up in the crackdown. Luckily for him, police only nailed him with a 9 mm pistol and a small stash of marijuana, not for any of his murders. Unluckily, he was nabbed in Atlanta and transported to a federal prison in Kentucky, where he had little posse backup. He was locked up with poor white prisoners who targeted this half Afro, half Indian Rasta from the Caribbean. He describes how a two-hundred-pound "redneck" started a fight with him on New Year's Eve.

"He was a big guy and I thought he was going to tear my head off. He came right at me. But the fight was over in seconds when I stubbed out a cigarette in his eye. He went into hospital but I think his eye healed in the end and he was able to see again."

Despite this violence, Kami said that American prison wasn't that bad, especially compared to Jamaica.

"In American prison, you get blankets and a bed and meals. In Jamaica, it's not a prison you are in. It's a dungeon. You sleep on cold concrete and after a few months, if you are lucky, you might graduate to sleeping on a newspaper."

* * *

As American police hammered posse members, some flipped and ratted on their leaders, leading to indictments of Vivian Blake and Jim Brown, who both took refuge in Jamaica. However, Jamaica itself stopped being a safe haven for the Shower after 1989, when Seaga lost power and Manley returned to office.

Seaga's policies had helped some, but failed to pull many Jamaicans out of poverty, so they turned back to Manley. However, Manley said he was a changed man in 1989, leaving socialism behind to become a moderate leftist. He promised to keep good relations with the United States and help business, focusing on limited welfare programs and winning voters with his charisma.

It is striking how quickly Jim Brown fell from grace after Seaga lost power. The next year, in 1990, a U.S. court in Florida indicted Jim Brown for the 1984 crack house killings and Jamaican police arrested and held him while he fought extradition. As the legal resources dried up, Jim Brown was due to be extradited to the United States in 1992. But he never made it. A mysterious fire killed him in his cell.

Officially, Jim Brown's death by fire was an accident. But his lawyer (and Jamaican Labor Party politician) Tom Tavares-Finson described what most people thought of that.

> If you believe Jim Brown just burned to death by accident in his jail cell you'll believe in the tooth fairy. The only thing I can tell you for sure is I saw the body, and Jim Brown is dead.[5]

Conspiracy theories raged as usual. It was said that police killed Jim Brown as they were scared of what he would tell Americans about political corruption. Whatever the motives, Jim Brown's death would be a harsh lesson for young Dudus, who was determined not to end up in a Jamaican jail.

Adding to the pressure on Dudus, his half brother Mark Anthony, known as Jah T, was killed at almost exactly the same time. Jah T was leading the Shower Posse while his father was in prison. A mysterious gunman shot him as he rode on his motorcycle. When he died in intensive care, dozens of his henchmen stormed the hospital threatening the doctors for failing to save him.

Dudus, now aged twenty-two, had to step up. He became the new don, while the posse was on the ropes and his family was being slaughtered.

CHAPTER 21

Dudus was crowned king of Tivoli when the Shower Posse was at an all-time low. It was flailing from the U.S. crackdown, the loss of its allies in the Jamaican government, and vicious infighting. Dudus was a college boy and illegitimate son who many West Kingston gangsters thought didn't have the nerve to turn this around.

But defying expectations, Dudus built himself up as the President and took the Shower's garrison gangster rule to new heights. He outlived fifteen more years of PNP government before being strengthened by the Labor Party returning to power under Bruce Golding. It took American agents almost two decades to assemble their evidence against Dudus and they had to fight their diplomatic battle with Golding to bring him in.

However, the U.S. prosecutors eventually built an enormous case against the Prezi through arrests across the United States, extensive DEA probes in the Caribbean, and help from some officers in the Jamaican narcotics division. The case files sit in a New York federal courthouse in lower Manhattan, where I spend days devouring them. Filling a series of boxes, they contain a broad array of evidence and testimony, running from the early nineties to Dudus's sentencing in 2012 and subsequent appeals.

Key to the federal case are several witnesses including hit men and traffickers from inside the Shower Posse, who took the stand in New York in 2011 and 2012. The prosecution also used its taped conversations of Dudus talking by telephone in Jamaica, sometimes to his cohorts in New York. This evidence paints a detailed picture of the President's empire.

During the hearings, the hit men not only described how Dudus trafficked cocaine, marijuana, and guns. They also gave graphic accounts of how he ran his fiefdom in West Kingston, including his extortion and vote rigging. The prosecutors didn't need to go into such detail to prove the conspiracy charges. But perhaps they did it to hammer the nail in the coffin; or maybe they wanted to send a message to Jamaica that they were watching. As a result, the New York trial presided by Judge Robert Patterson is probably the most detailed description of the new type of criminal power in the Americas ever heard in a U.S. courtroom.

The witnesses were themselves drug traffickers and killers, and they made plea bargains in return for their testimony. This is an age-old problem in racketeering cases; lawyers say the witnesses are lying criminal rats trying to save their own skin. But despite stabs by Dudus's defense, their statements were devastating for the President. Especially strong was the testimony of hit man Jermaine Cohen, alias Cowboy, who said he had seen Dudus personally take a chain saw to a hostage. In a recess after he described that, a woman in the New York courtroom went up to Cohen and said he and his family would die.

Jamaican journalists have also made important discoveries about Dudus's path to glory, adding telling details. One account is written in the locally published *Jamaica's First President*, by K. C. Samuels, which narrates the passage to power in vivid color.

"The road that led to *The Presidency*," Samuels writes, "was one littered with violence and intimidation; disputes, disagreements, shouting matches, stabbings, choppings/hackings, shootings, fire-bombed houses, rapes, tortures, robberies, extortions, murders and overall mayhem."[1]

Dudus cultured a different image from his father, the bulky, brash Jim Brown. While Jim Brown would fly into a rage and hit first, ask questions later, Dudus had a reputation for being controlled and calculated. Kami, who returned to Jamaica following his stint in the Kentucky prison and worked for Dudus, describes him as being reserved, often in deep thought.

"He would speak slowly and clearly, not shouting or swearing. But he has a real charisma. People hang onto his words. He just has something special."

Dudus also contrasts physically with his father. While Jim Brown was built like a quarterback, Dudus is just five feet four. His nickname, Dudus—pronounced with a *u* like *bud*—is said to come from his penchant to wear African-style shirts like a Jamaican politician called

Dudley Thomson. A Pan Africanist, Thomson strengthened links with the mother continent and was an advocate of slave reparations.

But despite his quiet intellectual demeanor and African shirts, Dudus quickly gained a reputation for brutality. He had to. The Shower was under imminent threat, its last two leaders murdered. He had to regain control, and that was cemented in blood.

But there is a notable twist to the President's violence. The court witnesses described murders they say Dudus ordered in Jamaica and times when he was personally involved. But U.S. prosecutors did not charge the President with any homicides on American soil, instead nailing him on conspiracy to traffic drugs and guns. It appears that Dudus had learned from his father's mistakes and realized it was best to taker a lower profile in the United States. He didn't go to Miami to shoot pregnant women in crack houses like his dad did. He stayed on the island and ordered his U.S. affiliates to move their narcotics without mayhem.

In Jamaica, it was a different story. One of his gunmen describes in a written testimony how when Dudus took power, he assembled his most loyal soldiers to go on the warpath. First, Dudus went round the homes of various Shower veterans, older men who had served with his father, pointing guns at them and firing bullets over their heads until they swore loyalty to him. The college boy was showing he was no weakling.

Next, Dudus avenged the death of his half brother Jah T. According to the witness, a traitor from inside the posse was behind the murder. As he testified:

> Dudus told me that he believed that Ludlow Wilson aka "Blood," another member of the Shower Posse, was responsible for Jah-T's death . . .
>
> In my presence, Dudus instructed a member of the Organization to locate Blood, who was at a dance that evening in close proximity to Tivoli Gardens. After learning that Blood was leaving the dance, Dudus sent at least two people to Blood's residence, which was close to the Lizard Town area of Tivoli Gardens . . .
>
> Shortly thereafter, I heard gunshots. A short while later, the individuals Dudus had sent to Blood's residence returned to the Top Ten area, holding handguns, and one of them reported that he had "dealt with the boy," referring to Blood.
>
> Then, also in my presence, Dudus directed a boy of about sixteen years of age to obtain a cart (a flatbed on wheels) from nearby

Coronation Market, to put Blood's body on the cart and leave the body near the railway line that runs past Tivoli Gardens high school, in an area called "Industrial Terrace." This was an area that was often used by the Organization to dispose of bodies.[2]

The witness then describes how Dudus ordered a multiple homicide on the site where his brother had been shot. This was particularly cold-blooded, as the President ordered the gunmen to murder anyone they could find to make a point.

Dudus gathered approximately four Shottas and sent a high-level Shower Posse member to obtain a number of rifles from the Lizard Town and Java areas. Dudus then directed the Shottas to go to Maxfield Avenue and "shoot up the Avenue," which means to kill as many people as they could.

Dudus said that the Shottas must do that in retaliation for Jah-T's death. The Shottas left thereafter and returned within an hour. They reported that they had "dealt with it." I later learned that four or five people were shot on Maxfield Avenue by the Shottas that evening, including two females.

Such ferocity can appear irrational, a senseless attack on people on a street. But there is a method to the massacres. Dudus's violence sent different messages to different people. Businessmen saw that they had to deal with the President or face the consequences. West Kingston's veteran gangsters saw that Dudus could handle power. And a new generation of thugs wanted to follow him.

Among the recruits was Jermaine Cohen, the son of a pot maker in Denham Town, a garrison bordering Tivoli. Known as Cowboy, Cohen would later become the U.S. prosecution's star witness against Dudus.

Cowboy testifies that Dudus ran his own "jail" in Tivoli, a cell made of cement slabs where he held his "prisoners." Many residents knew about this jail, so it was a public reminder to stay in line. People who had the misfortune of being taken there would later be seen bruised or mutilated. Cowboy describes using a baseball bat to beat up prisoners in the cell.

Other inmates were never seen again. Cowboy says he would use a hose and bucket to wash guts from the concrete slabs.

One time, Dudus's thugs dragged a crack dealer known as Tall Man to the jail. Dudus was punishing him over missing money. In the highlight

of the New York case, Cowboy told the prosecutor how Dudus took a
chain saw to his prisoner.

> A. (Cowboy) They go in the jail, tie him up in the jail, tie up Tall Man
>   in the jail.
> Q. (Prosecutor) After that what happened?
> A. Dudus get the saw, the power saw.
>   . . .
> Q. Where did Dudus go with the power saw?
> A. In the jail, sir.
> Q. What did you hear after he went in the jail?
> A. Rrrrrrrrrrrrrrrrrrrrrrrrrrrrrr.
> Q. Did you hear anything else?
> A. I hear one screaming, one scream, I don't hear anything more, sir.
> Q. After that occurred, did you go into the jail?
> A. Yes, sir, go in the jail, sir.
> Q. What did you see in the jail?
> A. I see human remains.
> Q. Describe what it was like in the jail at that time?
> A. Lot of blood, lot of feces, human feces, and hands and foots cut off
>   and head cut off.
> Q. What was the smell like?
> A. Smell really awful, sir.
> Q. What did Dudus look like?
> A. Dudus got blood on his hands and on his sneakers.

Cowboy goes on to describe several more savage murders by Dudus and
his henchmen. In one case, he tells how a mentally ill Tivoli resident
called Andrew made the fatal mistake of stealing a motorcycle belonging
to Dudus. Police arrested Andrew and took him into regular prison.
But Dudus's men bailed him out and took him to the Tivoli concrete
slab jail.

When Andrew's mother and aunt found out, they rushed to Dudus to
beg forgiveness. They said that Andrew was mentally ill and they would
pay for any damages. Dudus said he would take care of it and they left.

In the evening, Dudus went into the jail with a hatchet to a crying
Andrew. When Cowboy went in half an hour later, he found Andrew's
severed corpse.

"His body looked like a cow beef chopped up," Cowboy said.

In one sense, Dudus's bloodshed was typical of gangsters around the world: gaining power through fear. But the President's violence was unusually public. The concrete slab jail was in a place that many would pass. Another witness who testified, a student, described going into Tivoli and seeing thugs place a corpse in the market in full view. Shoppers and stallholders were afraid to move it or call the police, she says. She concludes that Dudus had ordered the corpse to be put there as a form of intimidation.

What's more, Dudus not only punished people who crossed him, but also those who broke rules that he imposed. He banned rape, a serious problem in Jamaica's garrisons. He also banned stealing from residents, whom he considered under his protection.

While some people who broke these rules could be taken to the "jail" and beaten or killed, Dudus's soldiers also held minor offenders inside a chicken coop. The wires forced them to crouch in painful positions for several hours. It was next to a street in public view, so it humiliated its victims. Those in the chicken coop were often women who had robbed or fought with neighbors.

Dudus also disciplined his own thugs. Kami described to me how Dudus made him the commander of a squad of soldiers. Residents accused some of these men of committing rape, so Dudus ordered Kami to punish them. Kami says he took the accused soldiers into a yard and tied them up. Then he got residents to beat up the offenders with bats.

"Some of the people who came to carry out the beating were the brothers of the girls who had been raped. They were angry so they smacked the soldiers really hard. The soldiers were beaten up bad. But they were not killed. It was a way to keep the men in line."

Such punishments did reduce certain "anti-social" crime, by all accounts. Residents I speak to say that in Tivoli under Dudus you had less fear of anyone breaking into your house or mugging you. This all built up Dudus's status as ruler. He clearly took away the government's monopoly on administering justice. The fact that residents referred to the concrete hell as a "jail" made it appear more official. Adding to the government comparison, Dudus's right-hand man and accountant was known as the

Minister of Finance. And witnesses described the posse shaking down businesses as collecting "tax." To top it all, the Shower Posse's structure in its entirety is often referred to as "the system"—part of the island's don system.

Cowboy uses the term *system* throughout his testimony. When he was first given a gun by Dudus, he says it made him "bond to the system." He talks about "rules of the system," how the enemies are "outside the system" and how the system extends to the United States, England, and Canada.

Cowboy was eventually cast out of the system. One day he got into an argument with Dudus's aunt Twinny. Reading Cowboy's statement, I realize that this is the same Twinny that I met in Dudus's family home. Twinny spat at Cowboy, he says, and he responded by punching her in the face. When Dudus found out, he tried to have Cowboy murdered, provoking a shoot-out. After more fighting and running, Cowboy fled to the United States, where he would sell crack and marijuana, get caught, and turn witness.

Jamaican criminologist Anthony Harriott is one of the foremost academics on the island's organized crime. I ask him to explain the Shower Posse under Dudus to me. He takes my notebook and draws a small circle, surrounded by a medium-sized circle, surrounded by a big circle. In the inner circle, he writes PC, short for Presidential Click. This is the core of Dudus's empire in Tivoli Gardens itself. In the middle circle, he writes the names of the other ghettos that pledge allegiance to Dudus, including Denham Town, Southside, Rose Town, and others. This is the President's broader empire in Jamaica. In the third circle, he writes the names of cities around the world where the Shower operates: London, New York, Toronto. "This is the larger international network," Harriot says. "The Shower encompasses all three circles."

To survive in the United States, Dudus adapted the Shower's modus operandi. The stateside dealers no longer announced themselves as Shower and they avoided outrageous incidents such as spraying gunfire into nightclubs. Instead, they operated as semi-autonomous cells with little knowledge of what other cells might be doing. But as the prosecution's case shows, they had a clear line of contact back to Jamaica, including direct phone calls with Dudus.

In many aspects, cells became like franchises. They would buy drugs supplied by the Shower and pay regular tributes back to Jamaica. The payments were not just in cash, but Shower operatives abroad were also expected to send other goods, including clothes, sneakers, TVs, and game consoles. The stateside dealers then had much independence as to how they could run their own business, serving up marijuana and crack on American streets. This cell-like structure is also used by other traffickers into the twenty-first century, particularly Mexican cartels.

The cells continued to buy guns through U.S. straw buyers and send them home. In a tapped phone call, Dudus discussed a shipment of eight firearms. The posse hid the guns and bullets in commercial goods including refrigerators, deep freezes, and soap boxes. A witness describes Dudus testing the weapons. He says that the President particularly liked a carbine M-16, a Heckler & Koch assault rifle that fires 7.62 caliber rounds, and a Desert Eagle semi-automatic pistol.

Dudus also adapted his smuggling techniques. To get through tighter airport security, he recruited an army of female mules who took cocaine packages inside their vaginas. The New York court heard from a witness how the smugglers stuffed the cocaine into condoms and gave them to the girls in an apartment.

> Once we escorted the females up to the Apartment, each female would be given a package of the wrapped cocaine and instructed to insert it in her vagina to make sure that it fit. The exterior of the cylinder would be lubricated with jelly or Vaseline for that purpose. If the cocaine did not fit, it would be hammered or beaten at the Apartment and the female was instructed to try to insert it again. Dudus, myself, and other senior members of the Organization were present at various times during this process.

The technique could only move small amounts at a time, with three to four hundred grams in each package. So Dudus made sure plenty of mules traveled to keep supply up. Moving lots of small packages meant that if a mule was busted it would be less costly. Furthermore, a single plane could have many mules on board, and customs agents would never catch them all. If they caught one, agents would be busy while others waltzed through.

Many of the mules were small-scale commercial importers, known as "higglers," who had visas to go to the United States to buy their goods. A lot were happy for their drug money. But the U.S. prosecution also showed evidence that the Shower forced girls to carry narcotics. A mother from Tivoli wrote a letter saying that her daughter refused to carry cocaine, and in vengeance Shower Posse gunmen raped her and shot her in the vagina.

The President's ban on rape apparently had exceptions.

Dudus also smuggled cocaine in another direction: on the several daily planes to London and Manchester. As a former colony, Jamaicans could visit the United Kingdom without a visa. And in Britain, cocaine collected a bigger markup than in the United States.

The rise of Dudus coincided with a surge in British cocaine use. By 2002, Britain's deputy high commissioner in Jamaica Phil Sinkinson claimed that one in ten passengers on flights from Jamaica to the UK were packing drugs.[3] The claim was repeated in a United Nations report that said there could be twenty mules on planes from Kingston to London, overwhelming British customs. This is hard to prove as most smugglers don't get caught. But police certainly viewed the trafficking from Jamaica as a major problem, and in 2003, the British government changed the rules to demand that Jamaicans need visas. It was a harsh blow for a Commonwealth country and along with the drug couriers, many innocent Jamaicans have since been denied a chance to see their families.

British police were also worried about the Jamaican cocaine trade being linked to a spike in shootings in English cities. In London, police launched Operation Trident in 1998, targeting gun crime in Afro Caribbean communities. The operation netted many triggermen and cocaine traffickers, but has come under criticism for using dodgy criminal informants and overly targeting Britain's black community.

One infamous Tivoli gangster who sold crack and did armed robberies in London was Errol Codling, who also happened to be a reggae singer who went by the name Ranking Dread. He was deported back to Jamaica where he reportedly died in prison in 1996, although some rumors say he is alive and back in the UK. A Shower Posse enforcer called Maxwell Bogle was also in London before he went to the United States, where he was arrested and given a fifty-year sentence in 1999.

London detectives also allege links between the Shower Posse and British gangs although hard evidence has not been produced in court. Among those named are the Peckham Boys, a gang of mainly black British youth in southeast London.

A Trident report leaked to a British newspaper also cited the Shower Posse as having links to North London's Star Gang.[4] Trident officers investigating the Star tailed a suspect called Mark Duggan in 2011. When they tried to stop him in a taxi, he made a run and police shot him dead. Duggan's family denied he was involved with drug trafficking and called the killing an execution.

Duggan's shooting sparked England's 2011 riots. They could be compared to unrest in Baltimore or Ferguson but on a bigger scale. First mourners marched peacefully in protest of the police killing. Then youths fought pitched battles with police, looted, and burned buildings, leading to five deaths in Britain's biggest unrest in decades.

The vast majority in the riots had probably never heard of the Shower, and most weren't even in gangs. The unrest hit a nerve with many young people at the bottom of society, in sink estates with failing schools and tensions with police. Riot fever spread to mainly white youths in Manchester and even to provincial towns like Gloucester. But the origins of the riots lie in Trident and its armed units, and the heavy-handed response to the spread of gangs, crack dealing, and gun culture.

CHAPTER 22

As Dudus earned stacks of dollars and sterling, he showed his charitable side. Gangsters have long given to their communities, often to persuade residents not to snitch. But Dudus took this charity to new heights in the scale and frequency of handouts, from parties, to schoolbooks, to medicine, to Christmas presents.

The charity adds to Dudus's construction of himself as the President, looking after his subjects. But perhaps he also genuinely wanted to help his community. This fits in with the educated Dudus, the man who studied quietly in his math class, who respected Rastas, prayed, and wore African-style shirts. Human beings are complicated animals. On one side, Dudus could chainsaw a crack dealer; on the other he could give out books and tell kids to stay in school.

A sign of Dudus's emotional connection to his charity work was in a letter he later wrote to New York Judge Patterson asking for leniency in his sentencing. Obviously, he wanted to do less time behind bars. But it is notable that he spends four pages going into minute detail about the charity projects, which he clearly paid a lot of attention to.

As he pens in the handwritten letter:

Dear Justice Patterson,

Good day to you sir. I am humbly asking if you could be lenient on me during my sentence hearing ... I would like you take these facts into consideration ...

I did a lot of charitable deeds and social services to help members of my community. I was involved in community development where I implemented a lot of social programs that the residents of my community could better their lives, programs that teach them about self empowerment, education and skills.

Dudus mentions his "back to school" handouts of satchels, books, pencils, and uniforms. Tivoli residents describe to me how it worked. Before classes began for the academic year, Dudus's thugs would go to a patio in front of the Tivoli apartment blocks. Kids formed lines according to their age groups, from elementary to high school age, and were given their goodies.

There were similar handouts at Christmas, with the posse dishing out shiny plastic toys from the United States. A young Tivoli man tells me how Dudus also liked to wander round the garrison, spontaneously bestowing gifts, and describes him as an angel from heaven.

"Nuff time I want lunch money, him there. More time you have hunger, him take it away. Christmas time, a him again. Birthday, a him again. Back to school, a him again."

When I listen back to a recording of this interview, the words that strike me most are "you have hunger, him take it away." Many of us don't know the aches of hunger. But for these ghetto youth it is a painful reality, one that haunts like a beast. The man who expels that hunger can win loyalty for life. This explains why protesters marched against the extradition of the President, with banners such as "Jesus die for us. We die for Dudus."

In his letter, Dudus also describes how he funded formal community works, founding the Tivoli school, the Western Institute of Technology, which gives out qualifications valid across the Caribbean. He stresses he backed a youth club, in which children play sport and do voluntary work such as combing the hair and cutting the nails of aging grandmothers. And Dudus describes setting up a Parent Association Committee, which has homework classes and makes sure kids under sixteen are off the street by eight.

Again this shows the contradictions of the President. While he recruited some youth as gunmen, he got others to comb the hair of grannies. But residents I talk to hold up his argument that he cared about children. In the letter to the judge, he emphasizes how he is a parent himself and asks for leniency to be with his son.

I got a son who is eight years old, he has been traumatized because of what I am going through. I was told that he is constantly asking for his

Daddy and when he is going to see me again and he cries all the time since I am gone.

Dudus also financed big events in Tivoli that drew outsiders from all over Jamaica. Using his soldiers, he guaranteed those coming in wouldn't get robbed, adding to his mystique as a ruler; he might take life away, but he could keep you safe if he so chose.

The shows included a weekly reggae dance called Passa Passa and open-air boxing bouts, in which contenders fought in a makeshift ring. The boxing was a real slugfest, with anybody able to enter, and fighters of different weights going at each other. The BBC's Jamaica correspondent Nick Davis described to me covering one of these bouts.

"The Thursday night fights were a big deal, like the buzz occasion. With the Passa Passa dances and the boxing, West Kingston had become quite glam for uptown people and it was safe. They could go and revel in that ghetto life for a night. And to be fair, those downtown dances are great fun, they are vibrant, they are what Jamaica is all about.

"Thursday night fights were for all comers to go in there. They would seal off the street and put some tires with concrete and poles to mark the ring. People had their boxing gloves and it was like, 'Who do you want to go up against?'

"So people would do betting on that grandma against that grandma or that huge fellow who was like the reigning champion and everybody would be saying, 'Oh yes. Knock him out.'"

Meanwhile, the Passa Passa nights won fame as one of the top dance events on the island, attracting throngs of revelers to party on the street till dawn. The music was mainly dance hall, an offshoot of reggae that dominates Jamaican clubs. Dance hall deejays chant fast in distinctive melodies over pounding electronic beats. The sexuality of the dancing makes both Miami bass and favela funk look mild, with women at Jamaican dance hall nights competing on how they can shake their back-sides while wrapping their legs behind their backs and standing on their heads (no exaggeration).

Dance hall has been at the cutting edge of dance music globally. It blasts in discos from Germany to Australia and its sounds have influenced songs in many other genres. American pop star Miley Cyrus did a watered-down version of Jamaican dancing, known as twerking, two decades after they were doing it in Kingston.

However, critics moan dance hall is a symptom, or a cause, of the island's violent youth. The music promotes misogynistic and gangster values, they complain. Some dance hall songs will give "shout-outs" to posses and triggermen. This contrasts with reggae in the time of Bob Marley with its socially conscious lyrics.

I personally think music doesn't have an enormous impact on behavior and other factors are more important. People become paid gunmen because of harsh realities such as poverty, impunity, family members inside the crime world, and the gang on the corner recruiting, rather than music on the stereo. Many people round the world listen to gangster music and don't choose that lifestyle.

However, Caribbean gangsters do get their name and fame spread through records. And Dudus became the most sung about don in Jamaican music. The President courted Jamaica's top musicians with two massive annual events: Champions in Action in August and Jamboree in December. Many of Jamaica's top artists played there, international stars such as Beenie Man, Bounty Killer, and Movado.

Dudus organized the parties through a formal company that he founded along with his "Minister of Finance." In his love for spreading his title, he called the company "Presidential Click" after his faction inside the Shower. Presidential Click had offices in Tivoli painted up with the name, announcing its rule formally.

As Dudus became a personal friend of many stars, he got name-checked in song after song, with dozens of hot artists blending the words *Prezi* or *Dudus* into their verses. Even over in London, an MC called Skepta released a track called "Badman in Tivoli" about the don.

However, it was the old-time reggae crooner Bunny Wailer who sang the most iconic Dudus song. Bunny Wailer is the stepbrother and former bandmate of Bob Marley, and *Newsweek* named him one of the three most important world music artists of all time. When the United States first called for Dudus's extradition in 2009, Bunny Wailer recorded a song called "Don't Touch the President" defending the kingpin. As the lyrics say:

Don't touch the President, in the residence,
For we confident, say him innocent.
Don't touch the Robin Hood, in the neighborhood,
For him take the bad, and turn it into good . . .

Sometimes out of evil, come good.
Can't you see the progress, in the neighborhood?[1]

It is easy to dismiss such lyrics as bravado. But Bunny Wailer, who never met or befriended Dudus, may actually have believed, like many on the street, that Dudus did good things. For decades, politicians had failed to provide schoolbooks and youth clubs. Here was a drug trafficker doing it. It is interesting how he sings, "Him take the bad [drug money], and turn it into good [charity]." So that "Sometimes out of evil, come good."

One of the biggest stars at Dudus's actual parties was the deejay Vybz Kartel, reported to be a friend of the President. I try to interview Vybz to find out why he sang in support of a drug trafficker. However, Vybz is himself in prison on murder charges and when I turn up at the jail, the guards won't let me in to talk to him.

However, a famed female singer called Ce'Cile agrees to speak to me. Ce'Cile played at one of the Tivoli dances and sings on a track called "Which Dudus," in defense of the don. Mixing reggae with American soul, the diva Ce'Cile crooned about the threat to extradite Dudus before he was captured.

I meet Ce'Cile in a Kingston music studio where legendary reggae stars have recorded. I have seen her in music videos, scantily dressed and dancing sensually to thumping beats. In person, she is truly beautiful in a natural way as well as friendly and articulate. Ce'Cile is an interesting artist, who has had global success with a mix of styles; she has recorded poppy songs that have been hits in the United States, folky reggae tracks that are popular in Germany, and dance hall slammers for the Jamaican crowd. It's telling that Dudus has such international artists singing his praises, not just anonymous ghetto voices.

She tells me to my surprise that while she has played at the Tivoli dance, she is from a middle-class background in a small town. She says she sang at Dudus's event as a young artist and was frightened.

"Then, I was scared shitless. I didn't really get to enjoy the atmosphere and enjoy the people. You hear so much about Tivoli, you are scared. I am a young girl from the country, come on. But looking back, the atmosphere is really wonderful."

Ce'Cile doesn't generally sing about gangsters. Many of her tunes are romantic pop ballads. In some songs, she takes what she calls a "pro-girl" stance, challenging macho dance hall artists. This earned her a "bad girl" reputation. In one track, she sings how Jamaican deejays, who often boast about their sexual exploits, are probably terrible in bed. In another, she questions why there is a Jamaican slur on performing oral sex on women, which many on the island consider homosexual. She sings that men should do it more often. I'm a little embarrassed to ask her about this song. She's not embarrassed to answer.

"It's this girl versus boy kind of vibe. I knew that I would have the ladies with this one. I was booed a lot by the guys when I was on stage but the girls made so much noise, it didn't resonate. The ladies loved it. I talked about this thing that they claim you are not supposed to talk about in Jamaica. It is ridiculous, this macho thing. I wasn't brought up ghetto, so I could say these things."

When I bring up the Dudus song, she puts it down to her rebelliousness.

"I just sang it in the name of bad girlness," she says. "Am I sorry I did it? No ... I only heard stories from what people say. If they are hungry, he gives them food. He protected the community ... I only heard good things, I never heard anything bad."

Like Bunny Wailer, Ce'Cile also says she doesn't know Dudus personally and denies deeper connections to the Tivoli mafia. However, by spreading his name through song she added bricks to the building of the President's personality cult.

Jamaica is a country defined by its music. It's at the heart of the nation, the way Brazil is defined by its football, or Mexico by its cuisine. Artists such as Bunny Wailer and Vybz Kartel have a far bigger reach than the favela funk singers in Brazil. When they sang his name, the cult of the President touched all corners of the Caribbean and reggae listeners around the globe.

CHAPTER 23

The word "warlord" sounds like an ancient term, describing Genghis Khan or Hannibal. But it turns out it's relatively modern. Ralph Waldo Emerson probably coined it in an 1856 collection of essays called *English Traits*. He uses it to illustrate the transformation of English aristocrats from violent feudal lords and buccaneers to statesmen and merchants.

"Piracy and war gave place to trade, politics and letters; the war-lord to the law-lord."[1]

This use of the term indicates knights who won riches and controlled fiefs with the sword in days before the modern state was born.

The term was later, and more famously, used to describe regional rulers in China in the early twentieth century, especially by the British journalist Bertram Lenox Simpson in his 1926 work *Why China Sees Red*. These Chinese warlords controlled areas through force after the collapse of central government in 1916. They wielded power through their individual leadership, along with their militias.

In the late twentieth century, the term made a big resurgence to describe militia leaders in Africa and parts of Asia, like Afghanistan. Journalist Aidan Hartley says he was at the forefront of its comeback, first using it when reporting in Somalia for *Reuters* in 1991. Covering gun-toting strongmen, he says journalists were stuck for language to describe them.

Onto this stage walked a new breed of men who presumed to be the legitimate leaders of a nation. But war, not peace, was all they could offer. Peace was their worst nightmare. Correspondents of our generation had grown up in the Cold War. Nothing like Somalia had ever happened before and at first we had no idea what to call the frightening new strongmen. One day Jonathan and I were talking about the British 1970s sci-fi

TV series "Dr Who," which featured beings known as "timelords" and "warlocks." For some reason we found this inspiring. Somalia was a sci-fi set that had gone back in time. We decided to christen the militia leaders "warlords" and the name was taken up by everybody in the news business. They were ruthless murderers and their terrifying reputation was only enforced by the childish gangster names they awarded themselves.[2]

The word spread quickly to other conflict zones because after the Cold War so many armed groups emerged who were hard to describe. They were not leftist revolutionaries who would have been called guerillas, nor Islamic militants, who governments often labeled terrorists. But they commanded serious firepower that they used to become the de facto rulers of territories. Sometimes, they worked alongside central governments; other times, they fought against them.

Over in Latin America, journalists had used the terms *drug lords* and *cartels* since the 1980s. But for one particular gangster, many media outlets applied the term *warlord*: Dudus Coke.

"Troops and police storming the downtown stronghold of the warlord Christopher 'Dudus' Coke," said the *Independent* newspaper. "The alleged drug warlord was still at large despite the assault on his stronghold," said the *Guardian*. "A block-by-block manhunt for a crime warlord," said the *New York Post*.

There is an obvious reason why journalists made the mental connection between the warlord term applied in Africa and this drug trafficker in the Americas: images of Tivoli gunmen firing at soldiers and those of African militias didn't look that different. Any racial stereotyping is obviously bad for reaching a better understanding of these issues. However, there are valid reasons to compare the criminal power of Dudus with that of warlords on the mother continent.

Jamaican and foreign newspapers also recognized the Shower Posse gunmen as being a "militia" rather than just gangbangers. "The security forces say Coke's militia was very well-organized and mounted stout defense," wrote Karyl Walker in the *Jamaican Observer*. "Coke commanded a private militia and his supporters burned down two police stations," wrote Horace Helps for *Reuters*.

In the following years, journalists slipped the warlord term into stories about other battlegrounds of the Americas, including Mexico and Brazil. "Lazcano's Zetas have been the boldest of warlords," wrote Dane Schiller in the *Houston Chronicle* in 2012. "One of Rio's most dangerous favelas is owned by the church but overrun by drug warlords," the *Daily Mail* said in 2013. "Drug Warlord 'Chapo' Captured in Mexico," said *Time* in 2014.

"Warlord" is not a perfect term. Academics struggle to define the parameters of contemporary "warlordism." Writers also use the word retrospectively to describe anyone from medieval mercenary captains to tenth-century Vietnamese strongmen. Some apply "warlord" to warring presidents. It is a broad expression.

But comparing gangster kingpins of the Americas with warlords who have emerged round the world since the Cold War is useful; it helps us get closer to what these figures have become rather than saying they are simply drug traffickers. It is also instructive to view many of the gunmen in Jamaica, Brazil, or Mexico as militias, rather than just gangbangers. It helps us understand how they are capable of confronting police and soldiers; how they have caused the flight of hundreds of thousands of refugees and carried out massacres comparable to civil wars. It sheds light on the mechanics of how the Zetas or Shower Posse control a fief, sometimes working with the government, sometimes fighting it, like the warlords of Africa do. It gives more depth and perspective.

However, I use *gangster warlord* with the prefix to better place the weird hybrid of Dudus or Heriberto Lazcano, the head of the Zetas. They are still gangsters running rackets while they command militias to rule their fiefs. Meanwhile, their control of territory is not as absolute as the warlords of China in their time. The gangster militias guard the borders of their domains, kill enemy gunmen who enter, collect extortion "taxes," conduct trials, strong-arm politicians, and carry out social work. But the government still provides electricity and runs the schools and other services. The gangster warlords control selective aspects of the turf.

Dudus's rule of his Tivoli fief is an interesting case study. He collected his "tax" from small businessmen, such as market vendors. A witness told the New York court that taxi drivers paid five hundred Jamaican dollars (about five U.S. dollars) twice a week, with collections on Tuesdays and Thursdays. This may not sound like a huge amount of money. But with a Jamaican minimum wage of about fifty dollars a week, it is a significant hit on earnings, and if you extort enough people the money adds up. Furthermore, the act of collecting money is a way to psychologically dominate people. It reinforces the don's power.

Dudus also tapped into another racket associated with modern warlords: winning government contracts. With his Minister of Finance, the President carried out construction projects through a company he formed, called "Incomparable Enterprises Limited." Despite Dudus being openly listed as a director, government ministries awarded it works such as repairs to high-rises and roads. By 2010, Incomparable had received more than one hundred million Jamaican dollars, or about one million U.S. dollars, government records show.[3]

Giving out construction jobs was a considerable source of power in the community. Furthermore, Dudus used his companies to put his gunmen on the payroll. Back in the New York court, Cowboy described how he was given a job and only occasionally showed up. As the prosecution asked:

Q. Would you have to work very hard?

A. No, sir.

Q. And why not?

A. Job controlled by the system.

Q. What was it that permitted you to show up, not work very hard, not be a generally good employee?

A. Sir . . . We bad men. So the jobs got the bad man list. So you can go to the job any time you feel like.

Q. Would it be fair, when you say the bad man list, would it be fair that means it was clear that you were a soldier?

A. Yes, sir.

These government contracts flooded in after the Jamaican Labor Party regained power in 2007 under Prime Minister Golding, the MP for Dudus's constituency. To help the labor party regain power, Dudus oversaw the old racket of controlling the voting base. On the stand, Cowboy testified about this electoral coercion. It is notable that Dudus's defense objected to the line of questioning, saying they were trying Coke on drug conspiracy, not vote rigging; but the judge allowed it, adding to the detailed portrait of Dudus's criminal-political power.

Q: Did the system require community members to vote for a certain party?

A. Yes, sir.

Q. What party was that?

A. JLP.

Q. What was your understanding what would happen if someone in the community voted differently?

A. They get beaten sir.

What's more, there are accounts that Dudus helped the JLP get votes in areas beyond his own garrisons. K. C. Samuels writes that the President had gained such power he swayed ghettos across the nation.

> Dudus could influence what went on in zones not even familiar to him physically—that was no military secret—this was common knowledge on the streets. Then to top all that, Dudus also had the admiration and minds of the common man from all over Jamaica. Everyone had heard of his exploits, he was both feared and revered ... (Somewhere on his way to the throne, Dudus became the symbol of every inner-city youth's victory over a system designed to keep them submerged).[4]

Samuels goes on to say that Dudus pulled such weight, he may have influenced the Labor Party's electoral strategy and the candidates it picked. Labor Party Prime Minister Golding angrily rejected the suggestion that he worked with Dudus in various statements. Nevertheless, when he was later hauled before a parliamentary inquiry, he conceded that he met with Dudus several times after he was elected to represent West Kingston in 2005.

"He was a benefactor," Golding said of the President. "He was typical of what is called dons, wielding a considerable amount of influence and being held in significant esteem by a large number of persons particularly in inner city communities and constituencies."[5]

So Dudus's control extended to drugs, guns, extortion, building, jobs, music, youth clubs, and elections. He had influence in underworld circles from London to New York to Toronto. He was a president with a system, a minister of finance, a jail, generals and soldiers. After almost two decades in power, the gangster warlord appeared invincible. But while seemingly impervious in his stronghold in Tivoli, protected by his shottas and with a friendly Labor government, there was one power he did not dominate: the long arm of law enforcement of the United States.

CHAPTER 24

When Dudus first became don, police didn't know what he looked like. Even while his name was legendary on the streets, nobody in law enforcement could find a photo of him. His invisibility was helped by the fact that he was a small man surrounded by big guys, so you literally couldn't see him. Peter Bunting, who later became Jamaica's Minister of National Security, described to me how Dudus arrived with his protective mob one time when he was watching a soccer game at the national stadium.

"I was at the stadium and I heard a stir and a big group moving in and people were saying, 'It's Dudus.' But you couldn't pick out Dudus in the group because he was a short guy in the middle, with a crowd of guys around him, and he was nondescript."

Finally, in the mid-1990s, police picked up Dudus with a small wrap of marijuana and took him to the station. The detention, Bunting says, was really an excuse to get his photograph and fingerprints. This became one of the only pictures that police and media would have until the 2010 turmoil.

Following the marijuana arrest, Dudus was extremely careful about his security. For fifteen years, he operated under a PNP government, giving him less political protection, and he was afraid that police could arrest or kill him, as they had taken down his father. To defend the President, Cowboy describes how a network of shottas watched for police and moved Dudus round different safe houses, sometimes in the middle of the night. He stayed in various homes in Tivoli as well as a palatial mansion outside the ghetto.

It helped Dudus that police struggled to enter the Tivoli garrison. If any patrol cars ventured inside they risked gunmen firing at them from hidden points in the tower blocks or alleyways. Police almost always entered in massive force, which sparked shoot-outs and massacres every couple of years. The most ferocious of these battles erupted in 2001 when troops stormed Tivoli in search of guns used to assassinate the head of a rival gang. The incursion led to a prolonged firefight, which claimed the lives of a police officer, a soldier, and twenty-five Tivoli residents, including children.

Despite the rare incursions, Tivoli residents could enjoy most of their days without police officers looking after them—or breathing down their necks. Instead, the Shower Posse was the one to "serve and protect." People could smoke marijuana on the street and get free electricity, and they generally didn't have to worry about being robbed as long as they paid their "tax" to the Prezi. But if they ran afoul of the Shower, it was best to run for their lives.

Under the PNP government, Jamaican police officers did try and build up charges against Dudus, Bunting says. But their problem was that they could not get any witnesses; people were either too loyal or too scared; anyone who testified against Dudus in Jamaica risked imminent death. Dudus was also a sophisticated operator, careful not to leave his fingerprints at the crime scene, Bunting says.

"Dudus was a little more business savvy than your typical don. He had gone to a traditional high school. He had modern up-to-date computer systems and cameras to run his organization. He seemed to be able to maintain links into legitimate businesses, and various commercial ventures. He was more of a businessman."

Starved of a witness or smoking gun, Jamaican police turned to a tool beloved by American detectives: the wire.

The details on the phone taps that nailed Dudus later came out in the New York court case amid fierce legal debate. Evidence shows that while Jamaican officers physically tapped the President's lines, the operation was orchestrated from DEA headquarters in Washington, D.C., with a little help from British secret agents.

The DEA had been building up its case against Dudus with arrests and phone taps in the United States. However, it lacked evidence to link the crack and marijuana selling on American streets to the President. To get this proof, the DEA teamed up with the Jamaican Narcotics Division and signed two secret memorandums of understanding (MOUs) in 2004.

The MOUs laid out what they called Operation Anthem to tap the President. They authorized wires on Dudus's cell phones and landlines operated by Cable and Wireless and Digicel. To sweeten the deal, the United States gave Jamaican police $3.2 million dollars. In return, American agents would be hearing Dudus's calls from their Washington offices.

Also in this plot were British agents from the Secret Intelligence Service, commonly known as MI6. Fittingly, Ian Fleming wrote all his novels about fictional MI6 agent James Bond in Jamaica, and the agency appears to have a soft spot for the island, with its name appearing on the MOUs. British intelligence was also concerned about Shower trafficking to British cities.

To keep Anthem under wraps, many in the Jamaican government, and indeed the U.S. and British governments, didn't know about it. While they began tapping calls in 2004, a Jamaican judge didn't sign a document authorizing the wire until 2007. It is also murky when the U.S. State Department learned of the deal. Dudus's defense lawyer Stephen Rosen used this to try and throw the taps out. "We have the illegality of the DEA trying to usurp the authority of the State Department and sign this document," he told the court.

It shows the perseverance of U.S. agents that they took five grueling years of running the Anthem wire before they released their indictment. By that time, they had recorded thousands of phone conversations of the President and his cohorts. (Dudus's defense lawyer said they tapped an incredible fifty thousand calls.)

Besides the wire, a major break came in 2009 when American police arrested Cowboy. The hit man had fled to America after he punched Dudus's Aunt Twinny; on the run, he sold drugs from Massachusetts to Arizona. U.S. prosecutors slapped him with firearms, marijuana, and crack charges. With the prospect of life behind bars, the DEA leaned on him to "flip," or testify, against his old boss. The President was already mad at Cowboy, and the American agents offered protective custody.

With their witnesses and phone taps, prosecutors unsealed the Grand Jury indictment on August 29, 2009. As it says in *The United States of America v. Christopher Michael Coke, aka "Michael Christopher Coke," aka "President," aka "Presi," aka "Shortman," aka "Duddus"*:

The members of COKE's organization, known as the "Shower Posse," and also as "Presidential Click," (the "Organization") reside in Tivoli

Gardens, other areas of Jamaica, and in other countries, including the
United States. From at least in or about 1994, members of the
Organization have been involved in drug trafficking in the New York
area, Kingston, Jamaica and elsewhere. The Organization members
have sold narcotics, including marijuana and crack cocaine, at COKE's
direction and on his behalf. They have then sent the proceeds of the
drug sales to COKE in Jamaica, in the form of cash and/or goods.
Organization members rely on COKE to assist them in their drug
businesses here in the United States and in other countries.

The same day, the State Department sent the indictment to Jamaica
with diplomatic note 296 requesting that the government of Prime
Minister Golding arrest President Dudus and extradite him.

When Golding returned the Labor Party to power in 2007, Jamaican
politics had become largely devoid of ideology. Both parties supported
the free market while claiming to help the poor and both valued working
with the United States. Golding won with a promise of change, blaming
the PNP for crime and sluggish growth. But he didn't so much attack the
PNP's ideas, as attack them as individuals, calling them corrupt.

"If you are not changing course, it means that a few will continue to
plunder poor people's money because we will have to continue to live
with their rampant corruption that has characterized this government,"
Golding told a campaign rally. "But Jamaica has to change course. I have a
team that is committed to changing that course, and I am the driver." (He
says that last phrase extra slow, with emphasis on "driver.")[1]

A bespectacled economist, Golding had grown up in politics, the son
of a Member of Parliament. He took the helm of the Labor Party after
Seaga retired in 2005. Like Seaga, he was MP for West Kingston, home of
Dudus and the Shower. To show himself worthy of representing the
garrisons, he stood with Tivoli residents when police stormed the ghetto
that year. When officers charged, he held his ground and shouted at the
superintendent leading the operation. Around this time, Golding held his
meetings with Dudus.

Two years later, when Golding became prime minister, Kingston was
one of the most homicidal cities in the world. Golding blamed the murder
epidemic on the eighteen years of PNP rule and promised to lock up the
"badmen." But while police arrested hundreds of gunslingers, Dudus not

only enjoyed his freedom but expanded his empire, winning his slew of government contracts.

After the extradition order came in August 2009, the country waited for Dudus to be finally arrested. But summer turned to fall turned to winter, and the President still operated openly. In a December session of Jamaica's parliament, the opposition demanded to know why Dudus was at large. Golding replied there were legal questions over the extradition, including the validity of the wire taps.

"The request did not comply with internal laws," Golding said in the chamber. "It is not a matter as to whether the (justice) minister is inclined to authorize the extradition. It is a question of whether the minister would be authorizing something that she knows to be in violation of the law."[2]

Opposition MPs asked whether Golding had met with Dudus about the case. This sparked a shouting match across the floor and a denial from Golding.

As the government continued to stall into the New Year, the United States turned up the pressure. In February, a Jamaican minister arrived at Kingston airport to travel to Los Angeles, only to find his visa canceled. A week later, the U.S. State Department issued a damning report on Jamaica.

"Delays in proceeding with the significant extradition request for a major alleged narcotics and firearms trafficker who is reported to have ties to the ruling Jamaica Labor Party, and subsequent delays in other extradition requests, have called into question Kingston's commitment to law enforcement cooperation with the US," it said.[3]

The straw that broke the camel's back was the so-called Manatt-Dudus scandal. The PNP bench broke the story in Parliament in March 2010. Even for a country used to political-gangster links, it was shocking.

Golding's government, it emerged, was not only stalling on the Dudus arrest in Jamaica; his Labor Party had hired top U.S. lobbying firm Manatt, Phelps and Phillips to petition Washington to back off on the extradition. Manatt, whose staff includes a former White House chief of staff and senior congressmen, were to charge four hundred thousand dollars for the effort. The laborites had already paid almost fifty thousand dollars.

What's more, there were questions over where this money came from. In a later inquiry, investigators asked Golding if Dudus himself footed the bill. Golding denied that but could not give a source of the funds.

"The society was on the brink of becoming a narco state," says Bunting, who was shadow security minister at the time. "The Jamaican government, or the party in power, was lobbying the U.S. administration to not enforce an extradition request for a notorious criminal kingpin. There just came a point when we couldn't swallow that as a country."

As damning evidence piled up, Golding capitulated. The warrant was issued to arrest the President and Jamaica held its breath.

CHAPTER 25

When the 2010 Kingston unrest flared up, the BBC's Nick Davis found himself in the resort city of Montego Bay. It was the Sunday of a long weekend and he had gone to a friend's party; it's the curse of journalists to have to run out of festivities to cover breaking news. He jumped on a plane to Kingston, but his flight got delayed.

"The captain came over the speaker and said, 'Listen. We may have to turn back as we are getting reports of a heavy-duty armament near the airport.' It was a military grade fifty cal that was in the hands of people aligned to Tivoli Gardens. They had seen drones or aircraft flying over and decided to take potshots at them."

Over the following days, airlines canceled planes from the United States, Canada, and Britain to Jamaica, possibly on instructions from the Jamaican armed forces. However, Davis's flight eventually got clearance to land, with no bullets coming their way. As Davis got a taxi and raced home to get his equipment, he ran into more trouble.

"There was a car driving directly at us on the same side of the road. We realized that we could see police in shooting positions, and gunmen were firing across the road directly at us. As they say in America, 'We flipped the bitch,' or did a backward U-turn, and got the hell out of Dodge."

One of the gunmen confronting the police in Kingston was Kami, the veteran Shower Posse enforcer from Southside. The President ordered every gun on the street, he said. From teenage shottas to seasoned killers, all came out for the ultimate fight.

"We gathered in Southside. There was about fifty of us from the garrison. I had a Glock. Other people had all different guns, AK-47s, Desert Eagles, Uzis.

"All the ghettoes were arming up. Everybody was ready to fight for Dudus. But it wasn't just about him. It was a fight against the system that has never really helped us.

"Groups of ladies were blocking off the roads. They were like the first line of defense because the police would be more hesitant to shoot at them. We organized to take the police from behind. We did well and pinned down a bunch of officers. We thought for a moment we could actually win this thing. But that was just crazy.

"The soldiers came out and it was a different story. The real problem was that we ran out of ammo. This wasn't like the gunfights that we were used to. This went on for days.

"Then they started firing mortars and shit at us. We couldn't keep up. When they broke into Tivoli, it was big massacre. A lot of my friends died."

When soldiers fired these mortar rounds, they were being watched—or assisted—by a U.S. spy plane flying overhead. A local photographer caught pictures of the white P3 Orion circling Kingston. This is likely what the Shower gunmen were firing at with the fifty cal, causing the delay on the plane.

Journalist Mattathias Schwartz of the *New Yorker* filed a Freedom of Information request that confirmed the spook jet was in the air that day. U.S. embassy officials reveal in e-mails that the plane had been approved at least four days before the unrest erupted.[1]

On board, operators shot video with super zoom lenses of the action on the streets, Schwartz discovered. That film could reveal much about whether soldiers fired mortars into housing complexes and carried out extrajudicial executions, which residents of Tivoli claim. But the video has never been released. It lies somewhere in the annals of the U.S. security apparatus.

Bunting, who later became the Minister of Public Security, was watching the action with his fellow politicians. He describes how shocked they were when gunmen went on the offensive against police stations. It was a final wake-up call to how dangerous the don situation had got, he tells me.

"It is like they were challenging the state. They were trying to signal, 'Look if you think this is bad, try and attack Tivoli and see what is going to happen.'"

The military reaction has been fiercely debated since. Soldiers used artillery and fired thousands of rounds leading to the seventy-three deaths. Many Jamaican politicians from both political parties defend the troops, saying the challenge justified the force. Bunting is among them.

"The military have confirmed they fired mortar rounds into an open field, primarily as a kind of shock and awe tactic. A large quantity of gunmen fled because they had never encountered this type of weaponry."

I ask him if soldiers messed up when they broke through the barricades and got inside Tivoli. Only one soldier died alongside seventy-three civilians, I point out. He still defends their actions.

"It was really a nightmare scenario. They had to storm a residential area with up to four hundred armed men but they probably made the best of it. As well as the soldier who died, nineteen soldiers were shot and injured. They got rushed away by CASEVACS (casualty evacuation), which saved their lives.

"And they are a highly trained force. This will be our elite, the equivalent of our special forces. Because of the body armor, you don't expect the same level of casualties as you expect against an irregular army that is not going to be as well trained, not going to be as disciplined, not going have the same backup."

On the other side, Tivoli residents describe a hell on earth as soldiers swept through. Any man or boy was a target, they say. Many of the victims were not Shower gunmen but laborers, janitors, students. The soldiers marched victims into corridors of the tower blocks and executed them in cold blood, they say. The army fired the mortars directly into residential areas.

Public Defender Earl Witter, an independent commissioner appointed by the Jamaican parliament, visited Tivoli shortly after the firing stopped and also described a scene of carnage.

Tivoli Gardens bore classic features of a war zone. There were burnt-out houses and apartments and unmistakable signs of the explosion of incendiary devices, described by residents as "bombs." There were many blood-spattered interior concrete walls and floors and aluminum windows shot out or riddled with bullet holes indicating inward heavy weapon fire. Exterior walls of buildings also bore physical indicia of high-powered weapon fire. Frightened and traumatized residents (children, women and aging men but mainly women) cowered in fear.[2]

Parliament assigned the Public Defender to write an extensive report, which was finally released in April 2013. It said the evidence suggested "that there was indeed excessive or undue resort to lethal force by those (security) forces." It also hiked the death toll to seventy-six civilians, with a further five missing. The report noted accusations of extrajudicial executions in forty-three of the cases.

Witter called for an inquiry similar to that conducted by the British government over its "Bloody Sunday" massacre in Northern Ireland, which led to a public apology for soldiers killing civilians. Witter's report finishes with an "epilogue" talking about the wider problems around the Tivoli siege. Citing Bob Marley, Gandhi, and Martin Luther King, it uses poetic language, surprising for a parliamentary report, if fascinating.

> Love bespeaks respect—the great yearning of the hapless horde of Black urban poor. It is they who bore the brunt of atrocities said to have been committed during the State of Emergency; they who, in their unrequited yearnings, turned to "Dudus" as "godfather." They need purposeful and legitimate help to help themselves; to be empowered to help others and thereby help to secure the nation's future.
>
> The alleged perpetrators—rank and file police and foot soldiers—spring from the same ethnic and social class. They have been recruited from that class for over one hundred years. The deviants amongst those Forces are not, (because they do not consider themselves) restrained by the Constitution, the law or rules of engagement. They constitute another minority whose elements continually embarrass and shame their conscientious colleagues by their misconduct. They are a minority who need to be reined in. They need to be converted to the transformative call of One Love.[3]

The Tivoli massacre exemplifies dilemmas at the heart of the crime wars. In theory, the security forces stormed the garrison to search for a suspect. But they clearly saw their mission as regaining territory that had fallen outside the control of the state. All residents became enemy combatants to the marauding troops.

The evidence suggests that many innocent people were killed on those days. But does the blame lie with individual soldiers or the government who ordered them to storm a crowded ghetto? Looking back, it seems inevitable that sending in troops, knowing their history, would lead to a bloodbath. Yet, the Shower Posse represented an extraordinary criminal threat that clearly challenged the state and that society could not ignore.

Dudus's political racketeering also illustrates a central feature of organized crime power in the Americas. The political connections of the Shower in Jamaica are relatively transparent. But gangs and governments across the hemisphere nurture exactly the same type of relations, albeit in a more hidden way. An area to watch closely is the practice of controlling voting bases as done in Jamaica. There is evidence that gangsters are doing the same thing in parts of Mexico, El Salvador, Honduras, and Brazil. Selling votes could be a significant racket in the years to come. It creates the specter of more governments beholden to the dark interests of those that place them in power.

At Dudus's trial in New York, his lawyers fought hard to disqualify the phone taps and protected witnesses.

"I don't know these witnesses," Dudus told the court. "They seem to know more about me than I know about me."

When the judge ruled they would be allowed to stand, the President pleaded guilty. Still, he appealed for leniency, citing how he handed out schoolbooks and took care of the elderly.

"I'm not going to stand in this court and tell you I'm a saint, that I've never done anything wrong in my life," Dudus told the judge before sentencing. "But these negative things that they are talking about me does not describe the true person that I really am ... I'm a good person. I've done a lot of good deeds to help a lot of persons in my community."

Judge Patterson conceded the President had done some worthy charity work. But he said it didn't make up for his crimes. He gave Dudus twenty-three years, the maximum for the trafficking charges.

While he was in prison, Dudus's mother became sick, losing a leg and going blind. Sitting in his cell, the President penned a letter to her, which he wrote on a pink card, sprinkled with glitter and accented by a ribbon.

I need you to keep on staying strong and to continue to pray for me, I'm staying strong for you and the rest of the family and I'm also praying for all of you. I don't want you to worry yourself too much about me, just keep on praying and the Almighty God will take care of us and grant us the desires of our hearts and the requests of our lips . . .

I know how much you love and care for me and that you miss me very much and that you are really hurting because of what I am going through, but with the help of the Almighty God, everything is going to be all right soon. We cannot change the past but we have to look for a brighter future . . .

For the care that you give me from the day I was born until now, by letting you know that I love you world without end. I love you, ma, and miss you very much, you are so special, precious and dear to my heart, and you are always in my . . . thoughts. Love you ma, forever, non-stop.[4]

The letter arrived in Kingston the day after Dudus's mother passed away.

Prime Minister Golding held on to power until November 2011. Just before a new election, he resigned, conceding the Dudus affair had taken its toll. The PNP won a landslide victory against Golding's laborites.

Kami said that many Shower affiliates refused to vote. They saw the Tivoli siege as a betrayal. But they couldn't bear to vote for the hated PNP, so they boycotted the election.

Bunting became security minister under the new PNP. When I interviewed him, he said he hoped the Dudus affair would finally break the relation between politicians and gangsters. "Now, they have to understand the political cost of this alliance is greater than the benefits," he said.

Following the Tivoli incursion, police charged over a hundred Shower members. Bunting says that it was their prosecution that led to the most significant drop in homicides in Jamaica in recent years. The number of murders on the island fell from 1,682 in 2009—when Dudus and his posse were at large—to 1,133 in 2011—when they were behind bars, a reduction of almost a third.

However, in 2013, the murder rate swung up again, with over twelve hundred homicides. Bunting says violence rebounded after new cliques formed in Tivoli and fought among themselves for control of the Shower empire.

I talk to shottas from one of these factions when I sit in the Tivoli apartments hearing the raindrops beat on the roof and watching the gangsters flash their pistols. They moan that without the President's firm hand, the violence could spiral out of control. Simon, the lieutenant, says that "bad men" are raping and killing without being disciplined.

"Tings cyan [Things can't] go on like this." Simon sighs. "Normality, it have to return."

Normality for Simon is having one strong gangster warlord running the area, a state of affairs he has known almost his entire life.

PART IV

He Who Holds the Word: Northern Triangle

Purging his shame for being born,
OD'd, was stabbed and shot,
wanting to believe he was bad.
It was better than falling into darkness
where nothing existed but more darkness.
He wanted to exist even as dirt, no good dirt.

—JIMMY SANTIAGO BACA, "EL GATO"

CHAPTER 26

In the summer of 2014, as President Obama wrestled with the rise of the Islamic State in the Middle East and the outbreak of Ebola in West Africa, he got slapped by a crisis on his doorstep. On the United States' southern border, agents were detaining unaccompanied children without papers in skyrocketing numbers. Border patrol officers threw the kids into immigration centers to be processed. But the sheer volume of children soon overwhelmed the facilities, especially in the Rio Grande valley of Texas, where the largest number surged over the river. In response, Homeland Security bused them to 150 centers across the United States, from New York to small towns in Ohio. It also opened a temporary shelter in the Lackland Air Force Base near San Antonio.

When reporters turned up at Lackland, guards wouldn't let them inside to see how the thousand or so children were living. But a worker leaked a cell phone photo of boys piled on top of each other on a concrete floor, many teenagers, some mere infants, their eyes staring calmly, revealing faces of struggle, resilience. Pasted across the net and flashing up on TV bulletins, it became an iconic image of U.S. border history, like those of Ellis Island in 1890 or the Mariel boatlift from Cuba in 1980.

By the end of the 2014 fiscal year, agents had detained a record 67,339 "unaccompanied alien children." It was a quadrupling of the number since 2011. The highest number came from Honduras, with 18,244 children, a rise of eighteen times in three years.[1] Guatemala and El Salvador followed.

Obama finally released a memorandum conceding there was "an urgent humanitarian situation requiring a unified and coordinated federal response." However, congressmen erupted into heated discussion about what that response should be. Immigration control advocates clamored to change the law to make it easier to kick the kids out. Border agents could send a Mexican child home right away because he was from a neighboring country. But a 2008 law ruled that Central Americans had to be handed to social services and their cases processed through court. With so many arriving, these cases could take years.

In the opposite corner, legislators called for children to be given political asylum. The boys sleeping on the concrete floor of the airbase had fled bloodthirsty gangs who forcibly recruited kids into their street armies and displaced entire neighborhoods, they said. Honduras had become the most murderous country on the planet outside a declared war zone. This was not an immigration crisis, but a refugee crisis. Congressmen tried to pronounce "Mara Salvatrucha," the name of the mysterious gang causing carnage across the region.

Texas Governor Rick Perry waded into the debate by unleashing the National Guard onto the border. A thousand soldiers sat in portable towers watching the gushing Rio Grande. And the children kept coming.

Out on the streets, the debate played out in protests, counter-protests, and lots of shouting. When forty children were taken to a boys' ranch in Oracle, Arizona, protesters tried to block the buses, claiming they were defending the United States from foreign invasion. On the other side of the road, activists held up placards welcoming the children. One cited the phrase from the Statue of Liberty, "Give me your tired, your poor, your huddled masses yearning to breathe free."[2]

In Murrieta, California, protesters successfully turned away three busloads of migrants. The following July 4 weekend, protesters and counter-protesters returned to the town's seething streets, pulling, shoving, and yelling. "Go Home," chanted those battling to stop the children arriving. "Refugees are not illegal," screamed those fighting to welcome them.[3]

The visceral responses reflect how the 2014 unaccompanied child crisis strikes at the heart of America's polarized debate on immigration. But they also get into a question that has been less thrashed out: Should those fleeing the crime wars of Latin America be given political asylum?

The children were clearly not all running from gunshots. They came for a variety of reasons, including wanting to see their parents in the United States and looking for a better life. But in some cases, children showed hard evidence that they risked being murdered if they returned home.

Delegates from the United Nations High Commission for Refugees interviewed 404 children turning up at the southern border. They

The physical war on drugs. A soldier burns opium poppies in northwest Mexico. (Fernando Brito)

Favela. Rocinha, climbing up the hills of Rio de Janeiro, Brazil.

"The Teacher." Red Commando founder William da Silva Lima in his apartment in Rio.
(Ioan Grillo)

"Every ghetto youth is a soldier." A Shower Posse gunman poses in the apartments of the Tivo Gardens garrison in Kingston, Jamaica.
(Ioan Grillo)

Community heroes? A mural in Tivoli Gardens, Kingston, remembers Shower Posse leader Jim Brown and a "fallen soldier."

"Humanitarian crisis" on the border. Migrants, including many children, apprehended crossing the Rio Grande Valley in Texas. (Kirsten Luce)

The war back home. Murder victim in San Pedro Sula, Honduras, the world's most homicidal city for several years running. (Ioan Grillo)

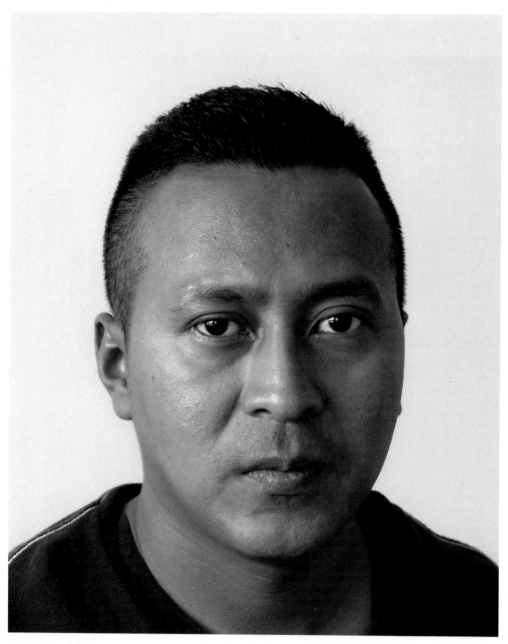

He Who Holds the Word. Marvin Gonzalez, leader of the Mara Salvatrucha in Ilopango, El Salvador, and advocate of the gang treaty.
(Ioan Grillo)

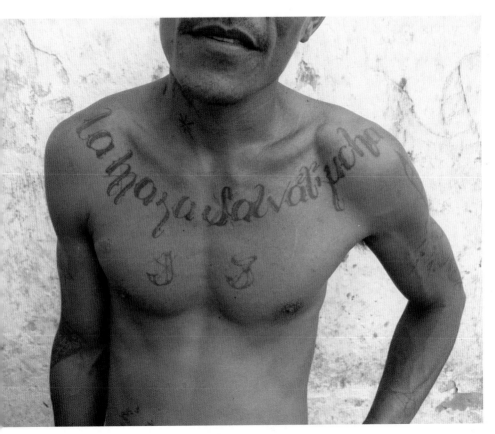

Marked for life. Lagrima, a founding member of the Mara in Honduras, shows his gang tattoos in prison yard.

(Ioan Grillo)

Narco saint. A statuette representing Mexican meth trafficker Nazario "The Maddest One" Moren (Ross McDonnell)

narco tanks. The improvised fighting vehicles of cartels in northeast Mexico. (Juan Alberto Cedillo)

Narco terror. A body hung from a bridge in northwest Mexico.
(Fernando Brito)

Killing fields. Murder victims in northwest Mexico. (Fernando Brito)

Uprising. The *autodefensas*, or self-defense squads, challenge the Knights Templar cartel. (Ross McDonnell)

Citizen's arrest. Vigilantes detain alleged gangsters in southern Mexico.
(Ross McDonnell)

A nation in mourning. Families of disappeared student teachers lead a protest in Mexico City. (Brett Gundlock)

concluded that in 58 percent of the cases, the children could qualify for international protection under the 1951 convention on refugees.[4]

Some immigrant control activists cried they didn't give a rat's ass what the United Nations said. Either way, the child crisis only raised alarm bells about a problem that had been growing steadily for several years. Less publicized was the fact that the number of adults arriving at the southern border and applying for asylum had shot up sevenfold from 5,369 in 2009 to 36,174 in 2013.[5] Seventy percent of these adult applicants were from Mexico, El Salvador, Honduras, and Guatemala.

In most cases, courts reject the claims. Carlos Spector, an immigration lawyer in El Paso, says judges fear unleashing a tidal wave of more applications if they give asylum to Mexicans and Central Americans. To qualify for asylum, applicants also have to prove that the government itself is trying to murder them or that their life is in danger because they belong to a persecuted group. Asylum laws were designed for those fleeing the dictators and ethnic persecution of the twentieth century. But some of the new cases are so strong that judges do approve them.

"People are arriving with such compelling evidence that criminals are working with police or soldiers to try and kill them that judges just can't turn them down," Carlos says. "The facts are irrefutable."

The White House eventually tackled the 2014 child migrant surge from several angles. It asked the Mexican government to detain more Central Americans before they got to the Rio Grande—which they did in massive numbers.[6] It got Honduras to use its own armed forces to hold back unaccompanied children in a so-called Operation Rescue Angels. And it opened offices to process asylum applications from Central America, instead of while the children were living in the United States.

The measures slowed the surge by the end the year. But the White House conceded these were short-term fixes. In closed-door meetings with Central American leaders, officials mulled over how they could stop people fleeing in the long term. How, they asked, had Honduras, El Salvador, and Guatemala become so violent and unstable? And what could be done to stop them collapsing even further?

Honduras, El Salvador, and Guatemala are collectively known as the Northern Triangle of Central America. While triangle refers to the fact they are three countries, their combined shape is more a jagged trapezoid, covered by mountains, volcanoes, and valleys with a choppy Pacific on one side and a mosquito coast of the Caribbean on the other. They are lumped together not only because they are neighbors but because they share similar problems of violence, all suffering from perilous homicide levels. Going south, Nicaragua, Costa Rica, and Panama boast substantially lower murder rates.

The Northern Triangle countries are small and close and their problems spill over each other's borders. If heat gets too much for gangsters in San Salvador, they can drive five hours east to San Pedro Sula, Honduras, or north to Guatemala, and vice versa. The crime networks are also thick heading north into Mexico. The Zetas and Sinaloa cartels operate in Guatemala and Honduras, while rocket-propelled grenades stolen from Central American military caches turn up at Mexican crime scenes. Wars spread.

Central America is divided into seven small countries because after the Spanish Empire collapsed, competing cliques of plantation owners all wanted their own kingdoms. The brief Federal Republic of Central America fell apart in 1840 into a series of banana republics. The very phrase *banana republic* was coined in the 1904 book *Cabbages and Kings* about Honduras, which it parodied as the imaginary Anchuria.

> In the constitution of this small, maritime banana republic was a forgotten section that provided for the maintenance of a navy ... The champagne was bubbling trickily in the veins of the mercurial statesmen.[7]

When the poor majority finally challenged the plantation elites, the region erupted into a series of civil wars in the late twentieth century. By the 1980s, these became the fiercest battlegrounds in the Americas, a place where the Cold War turned red hot. Fighting went way beyond the street battles of Jamaica or the counter-insurgency of Brazil; they were full-on civil wars with aerial bombardments, mass graves, and scorched earth campaigns.

In El Salvador, leftist guerrillas led an insurrection reminiscent of the Vietcong that was surprisingly successful in fighting the U.S-backed dictatorship to a draw. To support their campaign, the guerrillas charged businesses in their territory with a "war tax." The fighting killed seventy thousand and created half a million refugees, many of who went to the United States. In 1989, when Europe celebrated the fall of the Berlin Wall, the Salvadoran guerrillas were in the midst of their biggest offensive.

In Nicaragua, the Sandinistas kicked out the Somoza regime and fought off the U.S.-backed Contras in a war that cost forty thousand lives.

To stop the Contras getting into the cities, the Sandinistas built an intensive police and informant web with its eyes everywhere. This same network is credited with stopping the encroachment of criminal gangs today—giving Nicaragua a lower murder rate.

Guatemala was home to the most deadly conflict of all. After the CIA organized a coup against the leftist President Jacobo Árbenz in 1954, guerrillas dug in for a grueling campaign, winning support in indigenous communities. In the 1980s, generals tried to wipe them out with soldiers and paramilitaries waging a campaign of terror. They decapitated victims in front of villagers and left corpses on public display—techniques that drug cartels later copied.

Honduras was saved from its own civil war by a strong dictatorship and weak opposition. But it was still a battleground. The United States put its biggest force in the region in the Palmerola airbase and used Honduras to train the Contra rebels to fight in neighboring Nicaragua. The Sandinistas responded with an offensive into Honduran territory. Salvadoran rebels also slipped into Honduras to buy supplies and guns.

The White House trained and armed its anti-leftist allies, spending four billion dollars on El Salvador alone. The U.S. involvement put Central America at the center of media attention. Veteran foreign correspondents all have their stories—and sometimes wounds—from the conflicts. Their coverage provided a background track in eighties America, sifting into newscasts on the Iran-Contra scandal, into Oliver Stone's Oscar-nominated movie *Salvador*, into the lyrics of protest songs.

When the wars ended in the 1990s through a serious of peace accords, cold warriors sang victory, while Central Americans were jubilant a new epoch of peace had dawned. And attention to the region vanished. Media bureaus shut down, war correspondents moved onto Yugoslavia and Iraq, U.S. military aid diverted to Kuwait, Somalia. Stories out of the Northern Triangle shrunk from a wave to a trickle.

Until 2014.

As the child migrant crisis erupted on the Rio Grande, TV crews, photographers, and pen-biting reporters rushed back to Central America for the biggest story since the civil wars. They discovered that in some ways, peace had never emerged at all.

CHAPTER 27

The scattered household items give clues to the residents' old lives in the Palmira neighborhood, before they fled in fear of gun-toting gangsters. A decaying poster of the Real Madrid soccer team decorates the cracked wall of a teenager's bedroom. The remains of a hot sauce bottle lie on the floor of a smashed-up kitchen. A pair of women's slip-on shoes sits neatly by a front door that's been kicked off its hinges.

But block after block, no people can be seen.

The hundreds of missing residents of Palmira, in the Honduran city of San Pedro Sula, were ordered to leave by gang members who fight over the turf, explains Captain Cesar Jhonson, of the Honduran National Police as he shows me the abandoned homes. They murdered those who refused.

"There was an old lady living in this house here with her two teenage grandchildren until two months ago." Jhonson points to a bungalow on the corner. "She wouldn't go, so they shot her dead. Nobody knows where the children have gone."

A few miles through the urban jungle, I find one of the families who fled. Forty-five-year-old Miriam Hernandez describes how half a dozen gunmen arrived at her door and gave her twenty-four hours. She frantically grabbed what she could carry and hit the street with her four-year-old grandson. A local charity has lent her a space, and she lives in a corner of floor that she has marked with scarves and towels.

This forced displacement of neighborhoods reminds me of what I saw in Kingston, Jamaica. The posses there pushed out families on the front-lines of rival garrisons, creating buffer zones. Captain Jhonson says the same motive drives gangs in Honduras, forcing this exodus.

Palmira is on the frontline between the Mara Salvatrucha and its rival the Barrio 18, who mark their territory with graffiti sprayed onto the walls in huge letters. Both gangs are on red alert for rival members storming into their turf. It's easier to defend your ground if nobody lives in the immediate blocks; there are no civilian residents in the way so you can quickly spot enemy gunmen.

Soon Palmira could look like the older frontlines of Jamaican ghettos. The houses will crumble and plants will grow over, violence shaping spaces. Unless the flood of refugees is stopped.

Forced displacement is another feature of political and ethnic conflicts that has spilled into Latin America's crime wars. Brazil, Mexico, and Colombia also suffer from the problem. But it has become especially visible in the Northern Triangle. In Honduras, criminal violence has made more than seventeen thousand people flee their homes in recent years, according to refugee monitoring groups.[1] Thousands more have fled from criminals in El Salvador and Guatemala, where gangs also fight over every square inch of towns and cities.

In a nearby police base, Captain Jhonson shows me a map of San Pedro Sula with the territory of the gangs marked out in colors. Blue is for the Mara Salvatrucha and yellow for the Barrio 18. (Hondurans will also refer to members of all gangs as Maras.) Some turf is controlled by other smaller gangs, with names such as the Vatos Locos and Tercerenos. But the MS and 18 command most territory, with their turfs—and war—extending through all the Northern Triangle, into Mexico and into swathes of the United States. The Palmira is one of the bloodiest frontlines of this entire conflict, one of the most brutal neighborhoods, in the most murderous city, in the most murderous country on the planet.

So what does being the most homicidal city outside a declared war zone mean on the ground? On one hand, when you visit San Pedro Sula, you may be struck by how normal it appears. The abandoned homes like those of Palmira are only in a fraction of the city. Most of it looks physically like thousands of towns across Latin America. Electricity works most of the time. Hotels, shops, and restaurants function. Soldiers and heavily armed police drive around but there are no tanks, mortar shells, or aerial bombardments.

This is a curious feature of the crime wars. Extreme violence takes place amid normality. The same was true in Ciudad Juárez and Medellín when they were the most murderous cities on the planet. Markets still function and elections take place even while the homicide levels are off the charts.

But underneath the surface, you find how violence haunts people's lives. Most people in the city know somebody who has been murdered, often a friend or family member. In 2013, there were 1,458 homicides—86 percent of them by the gun—in San Pedro. With a population of 754,000, this means it had a rate of 193 homicides per 100,000.[2] This is more than four times that of the United States' most murderous city that year (Detroit), forty-eight times that of New York, and 175 times that of London.

If a similar rate is sustained over a decade, it means that one in fifty residents of San Pedro will be murdered. Violence disproportionately affects young men, with the murder rate of males aged twenty to twenty-four being four times the average.[3] Certain flashpoints have the lion's share of homicides. So if you are a young male in a bad barrio your chance of being killed over a decade could spin up to one in four.

The killing rate tugs on resources. I visit the San Pedro morgue where the river of corpses is taken. Medical technicians conduct an autopsy on each body, which takes about two hours. It takes longer if the bodies are mutilated or chopped up, as quite a few are. The morgue only has fridge space for twenty-five corpses, so technicians face a constant challenge to complete the autopsies and stop it filling up.

Documenting this bloodshed are a dozen local reporters who cover the crime beat, which they call the *nota roja*, or "red news." I follow round Orlin Castro, who reports red news for a local TV station, covering a five P.M. to five A.M. shift. In his late twenties, Orlin has been on the beat since he was at high school. He is about five foot five with the balls of a giant.

While I travel with Orlin, he is watching his back for some gang-bangers trying to kill him. The gang is angry because he filmed the capture of some of their members. They had tried to bribe their way out, but once he was there with the camera, the police refused the money. In revenge, the gang sprayed Orlin's car with gunfire. Orlin survived with a bullet wound in his chest. He is scared they will hit again, so while he reports the crime beat, he carries a mini Uzi and travels with a friend packing a pistol. As we drive along, he passes me the Uzi, and I hold it awkwardly, hoping I am not going to accidentally shoot us all.

Despite this hit, many other gang members know and like Orlin. They watch his crime segments and he has charisma dripping out of him. He grew up in a rough neighborhood so from his childhood he knows crooks, as well as cops; he seems to know every officer on the San Pedro force.

While I am driving with Orlin, he gets a call that there has been a shooting in the center of San Pedro, and he accelerates to the scene. We arrive to see the corpse of a middle-aged man outside a bar. The assassins, or *sicarios*, drove past on a motorcycle and sprayed him with a Kalashnikov —a common technique here, imported from the Colombians. The AK bullets ripped up the victim's face and left his contorted body in a red puddle. Passersby glance at the spectacle, but are notably calm; it is an everyday occurrence.

We drive with Orlin to the most murderous neighborhood of all, the Rivera Hernandez. A few months earlier, a gang kidnapped a thirteen-year-old girl from outside a school here. They accused her of spying because she came from an area controlled by a rival mob, so they took her to a gang house—what they call a *casa loca*—and killed her. Police arrested them, and residents have made the house a place of mourning, writing orations on the wall.

"You will know the truth, and the truth will set you free," says one oration, citing Saint John.

Such stories of tragedy flow like rivers round the San Pedro streets. The gangs here claim more innocent victims than in Brazil or Jamaica, with many children murdered. Back at the police station, fifty-year-old Jose Guadalupe Estevez describes how a gang member liked his teenage niece, but she refused his advances. In revenge, the gang killed her and her mother.

I had been reporting in Honduras since 2007 and saw it noticeably deteriorate each time I visited. Following a 2009 coup, which provoked a boycott and political violence, the murder rate shot up to its epidemic levels. I went back in 2012 to cover a prison fire that killed an astounding 360 inmates. (It was the world's deadliest prison fire in recorded history.) It struck me how shocked and nervous people had become. But I still struggled to fathom how the gangs here became so brutal.

To try and comprehend the bloodshed, I conducted lengthy interviews with more than twenty gang members in Honduras and neighboring Salvador in 2014 and 2015. Despite their extreme violence, the Mara and 18 members are relatively open to talking to journalists; they are much more accessible than cartel operatives.

Some I talked to are low-level spies, dealers, and triggermen. Others are leaders of cliques that control neighborhoods or entire towns. These leaders are known inside the Mara as El Que Lleva la Palabra, which can be roughly translated as He Who Holds the Word. When I first heard this, I thought it sounded like an indigenous term. I also found it curious that the Maras occupy a geographic space in Central America that the Mayas used to dominate. I wondered if there is a connection. However, as I look into the history of the Mara Salvatrucha, I discover it has little to do with indigenous culture and more to do with killer ants, Charlton Heston, and the heavy metal band Black Sabbath.

CHAPTER 28

To understand the battle tearing apart Honduras you have to trek over the border into El Salvador to see how gangs developed there. And to understand the gangs in Salvador, you have to follow the path of Salvadoran refugees who fled the nation's civil war to the ghettos of Los Angeles. Back during these war years, Salvadoran immigrants in a few L.A. neighborhoods formed cliques, made pacts, and started feuds that would have an impact on the whole of Central America during the decades to come.

My history of Salvadoran gangsters owes much to Juan Martinez, a young anthropologist who has spent years documenting the MS13. Practicing immersive anthropology, Juan spent a year living with Maras in a San Salvador ghetto. He is also from a prolific family, with two brothers, Carlos and Oscar, covering gangs and other issues for the extraordinary online news site *El Faro*. Together with cutting-edge reporters such as José Luis Sanz and Roberto Valencia, *El Faro* is an authority on the Mara issue, breaking story after story. American journalists such as Samuel Logan have also done important research into the gang's bloody origins.

Salvadorans began fleeing for the United States in the 1970s, as the opposition decried fraudulent elections, police fired on protests, and death squads hunted dissidents. The disturbances escalated into war in 1980. That year, a right-wing gunman shot dead Bishop Oscar Romero, who had preached against repression; he was giving communion when the assassin fired down the aisle, and his blood soaked the holy bread. Leftists then formed the Farabundo Martí National Liberation Front to coordinate a guerrilla uprising.

As the insurgents ambushed soldiers, the military waged a scorched earth campaign—trying to take the sea away from the fish. Refugees abandoned the countryside for growing slums of San Salvador or trekked north to California. Many young people fled as both the army and guerrillas recruited child soldiers into their ranks. If you were dragged into the war, you had a good chance of dying, being crippled, or being psychologically traumatized.

Luis Romero was one of these children who fled the war. His story, which he tells me over coffee in San Salvador, is typical of thousands. Luis is one of those naturally funny guys, with a lifelong belly and humorous gait (his nickname is Panza Loca, or Crazy Belly). Even when he describes his toughest times he touches the comical side. His colorful Los Angeles Latino slang adds flavor to his anecdotes.

Hailing from a lower-middle-class family in San Salvador, Luis was fourteen when war broke out in 1980. Soldiers quickly tried to recruit him, pulling him off the bus from school and marching him to the base to shave his hair off.

"They said, 'Are you ready to fight for your country,' and I said, 'I don't know.' And then they gave me a big M16 and said, 'Do you like that?' and I said, 'Yeah.' I was happy. Now I am going to be a soldier. Because the soldiers have a lot of girls, the soldiers have money."

When he didn't return from school, his mother searched frantically. She found him at the base and managed to get him released as he was her only son. Two weeks later, the army nabbed him by a market. With the help of a friend in the army, Luis's mother got him out again. But she knew that if he stayed, he would wind up going to war, so she sent him north to stay with a sister in California.

Luis flew to Mexico City and traveled with an uncle to the border. A coyote—or human smuggler—took them over from Tijuana in the back of a truck. After driving for a couple of hours into California, they stopped.

"The coyote whistled and we jumped out the truck. The first thing I saw was an American girl, a blondie, on a bicycle with an ice lollipop. I got that picture right here in my head. And we could see the big screen of Disneyland. It was that dream of being in the United States. In my mind, the United States was Mickey Mouse, Pluto, and all these Disney people. When I saw Mickey Mouse I was so happy."

This dream quickly turned pear-shaped. He arrived at his aunt's, and they had a party with pork chops to welcome him. But when he said he wanted to go to school like his cousins who were born in the United States, his aunt got angry. She got up at three in the morning to work in a food truck and only scraped by. Luis would have to work too.

"She tell me, in the United States all the wetbacks, she said that, they have got to work."

There weren't great job prospects for a fourteen-year-old without papers. Luis found work in a mechanic's shop for two dollars a day. The mechanic, a Mexican, gave him beer and ganja to smoke. Back in the house, Luis also found his aunt's Colombian boyfriend taking a package of drugs out of the fridge.

"I thought it was spinach or something, and he open it, and said, 'Man, this shit smells good,' and starts rolling a big joint. Then he said, 'You want to taste Peruvian flake?' I said, 'What?' He said *pericazo*, fool [cocaine]. And he get a mirror and he start.

"I get addicted to many things, and I start stealing. And when my aunt catches me, she is mad. She said, 'You get the fuck out the house, you are drunk person, you high on drugs, you stealing. You get the fuck out of here.'"

Luis slept in Lincoln Park and got food from a shelter. The streets were particularly tough for a Salvadoran. The dominant gangs in L.A. were Mexican and African American, and they had fought long and hard for their corners. Salvadorans were a new and small group who all sides bullied. Luis had to learn to take a beating.

Eventually he found a cousin of his mother who would put him up. He got a job delivering Greek food, learning how to pronounce *baklava*, *moussaka*, and *taramasalata*. Making deliveries, he also got recruited by Mexican cocaine dealers, taking packages to customers. He made an extra five dollars a hit and felt rich for an undocumented fifteen-year-old. But he began to snort from the packages before he delivered. The dealers found out and took turns on Luis like he was a punching bag.

"They beat me up badly, and so I was three days with a fever. When I came out, it was Thanksgiving Day. I was sad. I went out to Seven and Shatto Place and got drunk by myself. I thought that nobody likes me.

"Then this girl comes, this beautiful young lady. She is Latina but part Chinese or Korean or something. She asked me if I was okay, and what I was doing. Then she introduced me to the homies."

The girl and her friends formed the Shatto Park Locos clique of the Barrio 18 street gang. Luis's introduction is typical of how kids gravitate to gangs. They aren't looking to be killers. They want friends. Many, like Luis, also need protection, someone to stop bullies beating them to a pulp. Luis remembers his entry with joy, the time when he became part of something. One of the gang members was a Salvadoran called Shaggy, who took him to his apartment, cleaned him up, cut his hair with clippers, and gave him new clothes to wear.

"He give me a big shirt with *tirantes* [braces], a nice pair of shoes, and he let me use his sombrero. He said you look nice right now. They dress me up like Tintan [a Mexican comic]. I was looking so good, man. They was nice with me. The girl, she see me all dressed, and she even make me sex. I took them like my family. They give me money, they call me Pancita Loca."

Still, to become a gang member, he had to go through the initiation. For both the Barrio 18 and Mara Salvatrucha, this means taking a hiding, which they call "jumping in." The 18 do it for a count of eighteen and the MS for thirteen. Either way, it is a bad beating. However, the gang members have strange ways of describing it. They say it is an act of love.

"There was four of them who jumped me in. They were all Salvadoran. They were beating me, and one of them called Tino was shouting, 'One, two, three, four, five, five, five, five, five, five. When they finish, they start hugging me."

This tough love reflects the schizophrenic mix of affection and aggression in street gangs, the switching between victims and victimizers.

Street gangs are different in their nature from drug cartels or mafias. A gang is first a group of friends, an alternate "family," a group for mutual protection. Gangs can vary widely in their form, and some may not even be criminal. Many gangs members are broke and wield little power. Mafias and cartels are formed to defend criminal interests. They move millions or billions of dollars and control politicians.

However, this picture gets blurry. Some street gangs have evolved to manage organized crime syndicates. Collectively, the gangs in Central America have become very powerful and protect major criminal interests. Likewise, cartels have incorporated street gangs into their lower ranks, using them for muscle (and cannon fodder).

The Latino gang system in California is traced back to the early twentieth century, during a big wave of Mexican migration to the Golden State. These first gangs had names such as the White Fence, or *Cerro Blanco*, and Hawaiian Gardens.

In 1921, Mexican migrants founded the Clanton Street gang. (Clanton Street was the old name of Fourteenth Place.) Black and white photos show Clanton members clenching their fists and looking mean in zoot suits.

A few years after the Second World War, a faction of the Clanton who hung around 18th Street and Union Avenue in the Rampart district broke off to become the Barrio 18. This gang stood out by letting non-Mexicans in. Filipinos and others looking for a home joined. When the Salvadoran refugees arrived, many such as Luis also found their place there. Later Hondurans and Guatemalans got in the mix. It was a fruitful tactic. Barrio 18 swelled in members, and in turn, territory.

But while Barrio 18 became a national, and then international, network, it was still built on its cliques. The loyalty of members is first and foremost to their local crew. This is their inner family. An interesting feature is that inside a clique no two members can have the same nickname.

Luis, the Crazy Belly, describes how his Shatto Park Locos clique had about sixty members. There were many Mexicans, about twenty Salvadorans, and other ethnicities including an immigrant from India.

"We called him Capulina, after the Mexican comedian, even though he didn't even know who Capulina is. And he got me to do him a Salvador tattoo, even though he was from India."

I asked what happened to him.

"Some drug dealers killed him. They shot him because he steal some cocaine."

Luis and his clique fought rival gangs. They battled with Hispanics called the Playboys, Maravillas, and Crazy Riders, and with a Filipino crew called the Satanas. They rucked with fists, knives, and bats, and later pistols and Uzis. The L.A. violence gained national attention, reaching more than five hundred gang murders in the city in 1989.[1] But it was nothing compared to the scale of mayhem that would later ravage Central America.

Gangs fought to defend territory. Many sold cocaine and other drugs on the corners, so they were battling over narco real estate. But the gang members also just liked to fight. The rucks meant excitement, adrenaline, and a way to prove themselves.

The anthropologist Juan Martinez sees this as a driving force in gang violence. Members build their reputation inside their gang by their fighting. They elevate themselves as warriors—and you can't be a warrior unless you have someone to battle. In this sense, it can be compared to the violence of rival tribes, who are constantly in conflict to build their warrior status. It becomes endemic, low-intensity fighting that goes nowhere.

While many Salvadorans made their home in Barrio 18, others formed their own gang. Word of the Maras first hit the streets in the late seventies or early eighties. According to Luis, they started from Seventh Street to the Leeward Street area. An *El Faro* investigation says they likely began a couple of blocks south on James M. Wood and West Moreland.[2] Others point a few blocks southwest to the heavily Salvadoran neighborhood of Pico Union. Wherever it was, the founders were a few teenagers hanging on a street corner.

As Martinez explained, the name Mara has nothing to do with Mayas. Bizarrely it comes from a Charlton Heston movie. Back in the 1950s, the film *The Naked Jungle* was a hit in El Salvador with the weird translation of "Cuando Ruge la Marabunta" or "When the Ants Roar." Following this, Salvadorans took the name Mara to mean group of friends, who, like ants, protect each other.

Another odd characteristic is that the first Maras in Los Angeles were rockers, dressing in black T-shirts, long hair, and listening to heavy metal music. In line with this look, they originally called themselves the Mara Stoners. This contrasted with other Hispanic gangs, including Barrio 18, who had what is called a *cholo* style—loose-fitting pants, wifebeaters, and buzzed heads.[3]

The Maras have a sinister hand symbol, which also comes from this rock beginning. Many members followed the metal band Black Sabbath. At this point, the British rockers had Italian American Ronnie James Dio on vocals. During concerts, Dio did his trademark "throwing the horns" with his hand—extending his index and little fingers and holding down the middle fingers with his thumb. He had picked this up from his Italian granny to scare away spirits, but in raucous heavy metal it became a devil sign. The Mara Stoners came out of Black Sabbath concerts waving their own hands in devil signs; they later flipped it upside down, making an "M." In the bizarre world of gangs, a symbol that started at Black Sabbath concerts would become connected to massacres, bus bombs, and a government truce.

Established street gangs first saw the Maras as easy pickings. Not only were they from a new and small ethnic group. They also looked like hippies. Luis cracks up with laughter when he remembers how the Mara Stoners came on the scene.

"Everybody was like what the fuck man, these motherfuckers look like *gabachos* [Americans]. You know, that is a bad trip. So all the gangs start fighting them and killing them. But then in 1984, they start getting bad."

To sound tougher and reinforce their Salvadoran identity, the Stoners re-baptized themselves as the Mara Salvatrucha. People have speculated that Salvatrucha might be a play on the words of Salvadoran and *trucha*, meaning "street smart." Others say it just sounded good.

The Maras swelled in numbers, recruiting refugees who fled the war zone back home. The new arrivals were battle hardened; some had served as child soldiers; others as guerrillas; others had just seen unspeakable horrors, such as soldiers shooting their fathers or raping their mothers with dogs. Escaping that, they weren't going to let shaved-headed thugs scare them. They hit back hacking and decapitating. The Maras made their weapon of choice the machete, which many used at home to cut crops; in L.A., it became their sword.

As Maras left their trail of machete victims, courts threw members into jail. Inside the penitentiary, the gang dynamics change. Prisoners give up trying to fight for their corner cliques and are drawn into bigger forces based on ethnic and regional lines. They have to defend themselves against the Aryan Brotherhood and Black Guerrilla Army wanting to rob, stab, and rape them. Latino prisoners divide into *norteños*, from the northern part of the state, and *sureños*, from the southern part, with the line cutting through Bakersfield, California. The sureños are dominated by a gang called the Mexican Mafia or La Eme.

A dozen inmates at the Deuel Vocational Institution had founded the Mexican Mafia back in 1957 to stand up against African American and white prisoners.[4] Their self-defense soon turned to offense (victims to victimizers . . .) as they took over prison rackets, collecting cell "taxes" and smuggling in drugs.

Mara inmates realized they had to join with La Eme to survive, and the mob was happy to add war-hardened machete wielders to its cellblock armies. The Mexican Mafia uses the number thirteen (M is the thirteenth letter of the alphabet), so as Maras joined up, they became the Mara Salvatrucha 13. This affiliation meant that on the outside the Maras would pay tributes to those in prison, the same gang insurance system used by Brazil's Red Commando. In return, being affiliated with Eme won the Maras respect.

As they gained a formidable reputation, cliques of Maras became friendly with cliques from the Barrio 18, especially those with many Salvadorans. Among them was Luis's Shatto Park Locos.

"They are just a block from us, from Shatto Place. There was a 7-Eleven close to them so they called them the clique of 7-Eleven. We were Salvadorans too, but we jump into Eighteenth Street.

"We are friendly and we teach them how to be cholos, so then they change from this rock style to cholo style. They start using Dickies baggie pants, good shoes. They start getting bald headed."

This Salvadoran solidarity lasted several years. But then it broke into a bitter gang feud.

The roots of this beef are blurry. Author Samuel Logan looks at two street murders sometime in the late 1980s. Meanwhile, anthropologist Juan Martinez, alongside *El Faro* journalists, says it may have all started with a fight at a party in 1989.[5] Some witnesses they spoke to say the ruckus was over a girl. Others say it was a gang member who had flipped from the Mara Salvatrucha into the Barrio 18 without going through the rituals. Either way a fistfight broke out, in which a young Mara was said to beat a ranking Barrio 18 member.

"They couldn't permit that this little gang member had humiliated them. So they returned with an Uzi and shot one of them," Martinez says. "And that is how it started. This started an open war, a total war, with many homicides."

This war helped push L.A. gang deaths to new levels. They went up from 554 in 1989 to a high of 802 in 1992.[6] The fighting between the gangs would also spread way beyond California, to lead to tens of thousands of deaths in Central America. A simple ruck in an L.A. party may have caused one of the most costly gang feuds in world history.

CHAPTER 29

Many criminal organizations can be compared to diseases, but the analogy is used especially often for the Mara Salvatrucha. Police, academics, and even gang members themselves talk about how it is a "virus," how it is "contagious," and how it "mutates." Its biggest contagion was from Los Angeles into the Northern Triangle.

As L.A. gang deaths rocketed, police realized the Maras were a real problem and looked for ways to get rid of them. This became easier from 1992 when the FMLN guerrillas and the Salvadoran government made a peace deal, which they signed in Mexico. The guerrillas and death squad leaders agreed they would put down their guns and fight via the ballot box. U.S. police and prison authorities were delighted. Now it wouldn't be like they were deporting poor young men to a war zone; they were shipping them home to build a peaceful and prosperous nation. Planes left California for Salvador packed with Maras covered in jailhouse tattoos and buff from lifting weights in penitentiary gyms. It appeared to have an immediate impact on violence, with homicides dropping in L.A. from 1993 onwards.[1] A reform of U.S. immigration laws in 1996 then made it even easier to get rid gang members, allowing deportation of foreigners who had committed minor offenses.

The Maras arrived in a shattered country. The economy was in pieces, infrastructure bombed to shreds, and many children were orphaned and half-starved, living in slums on the edge of San Salvador. Furthermore, the peace deal gutted the old repressive security services and replaced them with a new civilian police force that had to start from scratch. Amid this chaos, the planeloads of gang deportees often arrived with no details of their criminal activities and went straight onto the street. They attracted a following.

"The streets were full of children, orphans, directing traffic for coins,"
says the anthropologist Martinez. "To this place, so poor, so depressed,
without education, without health, without money, without anything,
came these guys, bulging with muscles and these splendid tattoos, saying
'Hollywood Crazies' or 'Fulton Loco Salvatruchas,' with tattoos on their
faces and in their eyes, with Dickies and Ben Davies pants, baseball caps
and sneakers. Here many kids hadn't even seen sneakers or baseball caps.
And these guys came from Los Angeles, which seemed like the best place
in the universe. Kids queued up to join them."

The deported gang members with their facial tattoos and Spanglish
had little chance of finding jobs. Many couldn't even find their families or
homes. Instead, they protected themselves by recruiting armies of scrag-
gly orphans to their side. Martinez describes a gang member who arrived
aged thirty to sleep on the street and set up his own clique with fourteen
homeless teenagers. They begged money and turned abandoned buildings into flophouses, or *casas locas*. The begging would gradually turn
into extortion and they would become the power in the neighborhoods.

They also attracted more hardened members. Many soldiers and guerrillas who had been demobilized took to the streets to rob. The politicians
no longer needed these shock troops from the slums. Instead, the Maras
provided them with an organization where they could bring their murdering and torturing skills. In return, they taught the Maras battle tactics,
such as ambushing and sabotaging. These war veterans became the bosses
of many Mara cliques.

Some older Salvadoran gangs, which were really just corner crews,
stood in the way of the new Maras. The Maras responded by annihilating
them, wiping most off the map by the mid-nineties. The MS13 and Barrio
18 then turned on each other, bringing their L.A. war to the Salvadoran
slums.

Viruses can produce different symptoms in different people. If the person
is strong and healthy, he can resist the virus more than if he is malnourished and weak. Likewise, the Maras would have a more virulent effect in
Central America than they had in L.A. In the robust United States, gangs
were largely contained in ghetto areas and the death toll was limited. But
in weakened Central America, they rapidly overwhelmed police. As they
found they could get away with murder in Salvador, the Maras mutated
their violence. They began to make new members commit a murder to

join up. Those who left were given death sentences. And homicide rates rocketed.

The Salvadoran government sent police out with shoot-to-kill policies to the most gang-ridden neighborhoods. But gangsters simply moved, spreading the disease to all corners of the country. Some went into depressed rural areas, creating village gang chapters, a phenomenon rarely seen in the United States.

Not every gang member coming back from the United States wanted to stay in *La Vida Loca*, or gang life. But it was a struggle to get out of it.

Crazy Belly Luis came back in 1992. He wasn't actually deported, but he wanted to see his mother after twelve years away. He found his old Barrio 18 comrades massing in a square called Plaza Libertad while nearby Morazan Square became an MS13 stronghold. As they spread into the neighborhoods, Luis had to watch where he moved in case gang members held him up and found a tattoo they could use as an excuse to kill him. He didn't want to play these gang games anymore but was getting pulled back in. He got together with others like him in a group called Homies Unidos—reformed gang members trying to survive.

"When you get older, people realize, 'I didn't die in the gangs, now I want to live more. I want to go back to school. I want to get a job. I want to look after my children. I want to get *calmado* [to calm down].' But a lot of people don't want to give us a second chance."

As the Salvadoran public became increasingly hostile to gangs, the government launched a crackdown it called Mano Dura (Hard Hand), in which it jailed thousands. But meeting in penitentiaries, Maras from round Salvador only better coordinated their network. And as they consolidated their forces, they pushed over the border into neighboring Honduras.

CHAPTER 30

When I ask Honduran gangbangers when their gangs turned crazy, they all point to a movie they call *Vatos Locos*. This was the Spanish title of a 1993 American film called *Blood In, Blood Out*, a very realistic take on Latino gangsters in Los Angeles. Before the movie came to Honduras, they tell me, the gangbangers used to look like characters from Michael Jackson videos. Literally. They actually modeled themselves on the *Bad* promo. After *Vatos Locos* came out, Honduran gangsters started dressing and acting like L.A. cholos.

I am suspicious of how much impact movies can really have. But every gang member I talk to in Honduras seems to know the film by heart. One of the first major street gangs even called itself Vatos Locos after the movie; it still controls chunks of territory in San Pedro Sula.

I find this depressing. *Blood In, Blood Out* is a finely made film that does its best not to glamorize gangs, but shows their brutality, their capacity to destroy lives, and the rape their members suffer in prison. Its protagonist ends up crippled and facing decades behind bars. But somehow this movie inspired Honduran youth. While fiction about gangsters is based on reality, fantasy can also shape what happens on the ground.

However, I know this movie doesn't explain everything. The Mara Salvatrucha and Barrio 18 causing terror in Honduras have direct links with the cliques in Salvador and Los Angeles. To find out how they were established, I need to talk to the older Honduran Mara leaders. Most are in prison.

I go through the official channels in Honduras trying to get access to the prisons. But people don't return calls, and I almost give up. Finally, the crime journalist Orlin shows me how it is done. I was approaching it the wrong way, he explains. I don't need the government to authorize me to go into the jails. I need permission from the prisoners, the real authority there.

Working with prisoner leaders, we get into two penitentiaries, one in San Pedro and another in the city of Progreso. I had been in prisons in several Latin American countries. But I was still astounded by what I saw. Honduran jails suffer from claustrophobic overcrowding, stinking sewage, and filthy drinking water. But the most surprising thing was how much freedom the prisoners have.

In the San Pedro jail, once you go through the defensive layers of police and soldiers, it is like entering a prisoner-run ghetto. Inmates wander round freely without guards in sight, cooking their own food and running their own shops. Wives and girlfriends pass the whole day among them, some scantily dressed. The prisoners have walkie-talkies and smart phones with sporadic web connections.

The inmates also have dogs. I was amazed when I saw the first prisoner with a mutt on a lead. But there are a dozen in the San Pedro penitentiary. Most are fighting dogs like pit bulls. I watch a prisoner grabbing a young pit bull's jaw and making him snarl and bite hard. Another fully grown pit bull barks at me. I hear they put them into dogfights. I ask what they are called and smile when they tell me. One is named Crimen, or Crime, another Sicaria, or Assassin, another Gringo.

To stop a bloodbath, authorities divide the prisoners in San Pedro into four main wings. One is for the Mara Salvatrucha, another for the Barrio 18, another for non-gang criminals, who they call *paisas*, and another for corrupt police.[1] The paisas are the largest faction with more than two thousand in their wing, and include plenty of paid assassins, drug traffickers, rapists, and kidnappers of their own.

A paid assassin called Chepe used to run the paisa wing and was regarded as a strong boss. Back in 2011, a rival paisa prisoner challenged Chepe's rule so he chopped his head off, walked through the yard holding it up, and tossed it over the wall to the guards. However, some months before I visit, Chepe was released and killed on the street, reportedly by Maras.

This murder has caused bitter tension between the paisas and the Maras who are in the neighboring section. When I go into the jail, this tension is reaching boiling point. The paisa prisoners are painting a huge mural of Chepe, with a saintly gaze. Meanwhile they are on red alert for a fight with the Maras. Many of them crowd by the main gate, keeping watch in case the Maras storm across the yard and besiege their section. And they have guns at the ready.

The firearms are of course the craziest, most surreal thing of all. I long knew that Latin American prisons are full of guns because of all the shooting deaths that occur. But it was still bizarre to see them. The prisoners have pistols, submachine guns, and even grenades. I see two prisoners wearing Uzis on the front of their chests, half hidden by knapsacks. Fights can turn to massacres.

I ask Orlin what is the best thing to do if inmates fire at each other while we are inside. He recommends hiding under a bed.

Prisoners don't kick off during the Friday we are there. But twelve days later, they riot and fire their guns, killing three and injuring forty, including five guards who survive bullet wounds. Police storm cells and seize assault rifles, pistols, tear gas canisters, and bags of bullets. They leave the dogs.[2]

Over in the Progreso jail, I find a former Mara boss who was one of the first MS13 in Honduras. At thirty-five years old he is considered an elder, a Honduran OG. He goes by the name Lagrima, meaning "Tear," and has teardrops tattooed on his face. When I ask him how he got this name, he smiles. "I used to cry a lot."

Lagrima also has gaping Mara Salvatrucha tattoos on his chest and back, and the devil's horn on his right shoulder. He is slim but wiry, in shape from lifting concrete weights in prison. Lagrima is He Who Holds the Word.

In a crowded jail patio, Lagrima explains how the Mara Salvatrucha spread into Honduras from neighboring Salvador. He himself was jumped into the Mara in Salvadoran territory.

Lagrima is from the Choluteca region, home to Honduras's southernmost tip. He grew up in rural poverty, his father working on plantations and scraping to feed his six children.

"There was hunger all the time. That is what I remember from being a kid. It was hard to concentrate at school with pain in my belly. The only hope I had was going to the United States. From when I can remember I dreamed of heading there. Finally, when I got to thirteen I made my move. I left without saying anything to my family and headed to El Norte."

Hondurans emigrated to the United States later than Salvadorans, who themselves emigrated later than Mexicans. But since the 1990s, Hondurans have headed north in huge numbers. Honduras now relies on money that migrants send back for about 20 percent of its gross domestic product—compared to 3 percent in Mexico. It is a huge pulling force, drawing thousands of teenagers northward; migration is a coming of manhood for many youths.

Still, Lagrima's trip was ambitious. He was just thirteen and left with nothing but the clothes on his back. The quickest way north was through Salvador. He trekked and begged his way to the Honduran border, crossed over and arrived at a Salvadoran town called San Miguel. That was as far north as he got. It was 1992, the year that the planes of deportees arrived.

"I was walking through San Miguel and begging change for food. I was hungry but I had known hunger all my life. Then I saw this group of guys on the corner. They had tattoos on their faces and looked really crazy. They called me over. I was scared at first. But they told me not to worry and gave me Coca-Cola and chicken and I was really happy. So I stayed with them. They had a house they slept in so I could stay off the street."

The Maras who Lagrima found were in a clique called the Coronado Little Cycos. Their leaders had been in the United States, and their English phrases, clothes, and stories of Los Angeles neighborhoods all impressed him. Soon he was talking about Coronado, Hollywood, and Leeward like he knew the places. He hung on to their words, and they enjoyed his attention.

"They treated me like a pet. They would have fun shaving my head and dressing me up in their style. They would send me off to buy drinks or get their food. I was happy, because I ate better than I did at home. And I was with these people that were almost American. I thought I was going somewhere."

The missions soon got heavier than going to the shops. The clique told Lagrima that to become a member he would have to kill. They gave him a pistol and ordered him to go into a neighborhood controlled by the Barrio 18. It was a tough test that could easily end in death.

"I was scared but I wanted to be part of the crew. I hid the gun and walked in and there was an Eighteen on the street talking to someone. He had his gang name tattooed right on his face. I was just thirteen years old and still skinny and scruffy and he thought I was just some street kid so I got close. Then I pulled out the gun and shot him point blank, like four times. After I fired, I ran for my life. I ran like I was never going to stop. And when I got back the homies were pleased with me and jumped me in."

As the Mara Salvatrucha mutated in Central America, its initiation beatings also got harder. As well as kicking and punching during the count of thirteen, they would beat initiates with sticks. Some would suffer injuries or even be killed before they began gang life. Once the beating finished, Lagrima was reborn, with his new name and new people.

"You leave your old family behind. The Mara became my family."

Lagrima came of age with the clique, growing older and more murderous as they gained power. He forgot about his dream of going to the United States as he made his life in this Salvadoran city, able to live from shakedown money. His parents never heard from him. When he reached twenty, he was an accomplished killer and extortionist. And he graduated. His boss sent him back to Honduras to set up his own clique. He would become He Who Holds the Word in Choluteca. It was 1999.

Lagrima describes this move into Honduras as a deliberate tactic by the Salvadoran Maras. Around the same time, he says, a Salvadoran gangster called Maldito, or Wicked, also set up cliques in the Honduran capital, Tegucigalpa. The Salvadorans saw the neighboring country as fresh territory that they could sweep into. Scattered cliques of Maras may have emerged in Honduras before this. Gangs of the Vatos Locos, inspired by the movie, were also around. But the Maras really rose in numbers in Honduras from the turn of the millennium.

Both Lagrima and Maldito were from the Coronado Little Cycos, so this has become one of the most common factions (or what they call *programas*) of the Mara Salvatrucha in Honduras. Other Mara factions there include the Normandy and Hollywood Locos.

The basic organization of the Maras is easy to see. The gang is formed by cliques with some thirty to 150 fully fledged members controlling a particular territory—a neighborhood or small town. These core players are referred to as *activos*, or active members. Around them are people who work for the Maras or just hang around with them, whom they call "sympathizers." There are normally hundreds of sympathizers around each clique. They might do lower-level jobs such as spying or delivering drugs or even carrying out murders, but they have not been jumped into the gang. Each clique has its leader, He Who Holds the Word, and his Mano Derecha, or Right Hand.

"It is like the president and vice president," Lagrima explains. "If He Who Holds the Word is out of action for some reason, the Right Hand takes over."

It is more complicated to make sense of how the Mara operates at a national and international level. Lagrima describes how he would meet with other clique leaders in Honduras to decide certain issues by majority decision. But he tells me how he would always have a boss he reported to.

In some aspects, it works like a multilevel marketing scheme. A Mara forms a clique and recruits his operatives. When he lets one of those operatives form his own clique, they are still loyal to him. This generates warlords with their own pyramids inside the greater structure.

Yet there are other factors at play. Members can challenge and dethrone clique leaders. Some Mara bosses become regional leaders, overseeing a number of cliques in cities and states. Most of the veteran leaders are in prisons, and each prison has its own leader, He Who Holds the Word, among Mara inmates. The Mara leaders in the biggest prisons become the most powerful Maras in their countries. However, who holds power between Maras in different countries is murky.

Lagrima recruited about seventy active members into his clique, or seventy "locos" (madmen), as he described them, along with hundreds of hangers-on. I ask him how you control a clique.

"You have to win respect." He taps his head. "And you get this through intelligence. Sometimes you have to beat people or order executions. But you really control people with the mind."

The Maras took the business of extortion that they learned in Salvador to new levels in Honduras. They went from shaking down buses and taxis, to earning from shops, restaurants, and bars, and onto professionals, including lawyers, doctors, and independent journalists. The Maras baptized these shakedowns as *impuesto de guerra* or "war tax," the term that guerrillas had used in the eighties.

Some Mara bosses keep the shakedowns at low enough levels, such as 10 to 20 percent of income, so that businesses can survive and keep paying. But others make people pay such extortionate amounts they are forced to close down, and often run for their lives. It is a strain on anyone running a business in an already struggling country. I find a single mother in her twenties who opened a beauty salon. With the war tax, along with other debts, she shut down and turned in desperation to prostitution to feed her daughter.

Maras also pimp prostitutes, often taking half of what they make. Others have got into loan sharking, giving out small amounts to people who could never qualify with a bank. The interest can be up to an incredible 20 percent a week.

Lagrima describes how he would put their cash into a big metal safe in one of the Casa Locas. He would pay all the clique members a salary and give special bonuses for contract killings. He would then take his own money and kick back cash up the organization, paying for those in prison.

As the Maras expanded, they laundered their money through businesses, owning strip clubs, taxis, buses, and shops directly. And they moved deeper into the biggest earner of all: drugs.

Traffickers have long used Honduras as a trampoline for taking cocaine to the United States. From Colombia, they make short flights to airstrips in the Honduran jungle, or drop bundles off the Mosquito Coast. Sometimes, smugglers bring the cocaine in its paste form and process it in labs inside Honduras. From there, smugglers take it to the Mexican border, or through the Caribbean to the United States or sometimes Europe.

As Honduras is like a big cocaine warehouse, it attracts traffickers from far and wide, including Colombia, Mexico, and Jamaica. There are widespread reports that kingpin Chapo Guzmán came to Honduras, and strong evidence that the Knights Templar bought cocaine there. Furthermore, a police officer I talk to says his informants witnessed Zetas buying weapons in Honduras. Arms including rocket-propelled grenades have been stolen from caches of the Honduran armed forces.[3]

As the Maras grew from a street gang to an organized crime syndicate, they drew closer to these drug traffickers. However, they did not have a straight alliance with any one cartel, but more of a series of business transactions with different traffickers in different parts of the Mara-dominated lands. Their biggest role in Honduras was taking over street drug selling in much of the country.

"We had money and we controlled territory, so it was easy to get into the business," Lagrima says. "We would buy kilos and sell it on the streets in grams, or in rocks of crack. It was good money."

As they worked with drug traffickers, they did other jobs for them. If somebody was in the turf that the traffickers were after, the Maras could take them out—for a fee. Often the narcos would pay them in drugs, perpetrating the drug cycle as they have in Brazil and Mexico.

The Maras also got pulled into the Mexican drug war, working with various sides. In 2004, Maras fought as mercenaries for the Sinaloa Cartel in Nuevo Laredo. The rival Zetas killed five of them and dumped their bodies in a house. A note lay next to the corpses, saying, "Send us more *pendejos* like this for us to kill." (*Pendejo* is a Mexican swear word meaning "pubic hair."[4]) Mexican gangsters were using the Maras as cannon fodder.

Meanwhile in southern Mexico, Maras worked with the Zetas cartel to kidnap migrants from trains, calling their relatives in the U.S. for ransom payments. These kidnappings led to several massacres, such as the killing of seventy-two in San Fernando in 2010. After such brutality against their countrymen, the Maras broke relations with the Zetas, Lagrima says.

"We never really trusted the Zetas and didn't want to be involved in these things. So we banned our people there from working in these kidnappings. We also found out that a lot of the Central Americans helping the Zetas were not even Maras."

As the Maras grew into a more sophisticated crime syndicate, they mutated again. They realized that facial tattoos are a big giveaway and ordered initiates not to put ink on their mugs. While Lagrima stands out with his teardrop tattoos, most new members look like any other Honduran youngsters.

But despite clean faces, the new generation of Honduran Maras became increasingly bloodthirsty. Teenagers murdered at a rate that shocked even veterans such as Lagrima. It became a struggle to control the unruly youths.

"They have lost any kind of values," Lagrima says. "They smoke too much crack and kill all the time. They have made this country too violent."

At the same time that the death toll increased, Lagrima's life changed as he became a father.

"Seeing my son made me think a lot. I don't want him going into the same gang life as me. I don't want him seeing these things."

A turning point came when police arrested Lagrima for murder. He broke away from Mara prisoners and got himself transferred out of their wing. The act is seen as betrayal and he says they have passed a death sentence on him. But he doesn't regret the decision.

"I felt in my heart that I couldn't do this anymore. I don't want to be part of this disease. I want to think about my family. I hope that when I get out of here, I can leave Honduras and make my life somewhere else. There are places that are not like this. There is a world outside gangs."

CHAPTER 31

Searching for the new Mara generation that Lagrima described, I visit a prison for juveniles in San Pedro Sula. When I walk in, I find it is as crazy as the adult lockup.

The youth prison is divided into two sections, one for Maras and the other for non-gang members, or paisas. Courts send Barrio 18 members to another jail to avoid a slaughter. But the Maras are still worried that their rivals could attack the prison. To defend themselves, they have members sitting on the roof watching out for movement in the bushes and nearby streets. It's a bizarre sight, teenage gang members squatting on the rooftop of a supposed penitentiary. They tell me they keep watch round the clock.

These teenage Maras also have their prison leader, He Who Holds the Word. He is a seventeen-year-old called Dani, inside for murder. Dani is only about five foot two, and I have to stoop down to talk to him. But he has the hardest thousand-yard stare I have ever seen. His eyes show the penetrating look of a killer but also reveal the pain of one who has seen too much. I feel that one moment I am looking at a kid, and the next I am looking at a hardened murderer, a power broker, a chieftain.

When I ask him if he fears death, he shakes his head and looks at me incredulously. It strikes me how teenagers who have all their life in front of them don't care about dying; as we get older we fear death more, even though we have less to live for.

I head across town to a drug rehab clinic where I am introduced to another young Mara from this new generation of killers. The skinny twenty-three-year-old has thick scars on his face, earning him the nickname Montana, after Al Pacino's character in *Scarface*. Montana is relaxed and likeable, making jokes and laughing a lot. I spend all afternoon listening to his life story. It makes me shiver inside.

While he is in a rehab in San Pedro, Montana hails from a barrio in the capital, Tegucigalpa, where he grew up and joined the Salvatrucha. His clique was founded in his neighborhood in 2000 by the Salvadoran Maldito.

Montana grew up with both parents, who owned a small restaurant, and he never had money problems to drive him into gang life. But he joined the Maras for another reason. When he was twelve, the Barrio 18 killed his father over an extortion payment. He wanted revenge.

"It was hate that drove me," he says.

But Montana reveals that even before his father's death, his life had gone off the rails. When he was eight years old, an older brother gave him marijuana to smoke. By the time he was eleven, he had tried cocaine. By thirteen, he had smoked crack.

I had thought that drug-taking itself wasn't a big factor driving violence in Latin America. After all, people generally take more drugs in European countries, such as England and Spain, which are much more peaceful. But seeing Montana makes me wonder if smoking weed and snorting coke as a young child could have contributed to how he became a serial murderer who seems to show little regret about his bloodshed.

When I interviewed assassins from Mexican and Colombian cartels, I asked them how many they had killed and they said they had lost count. I thought they might have been avoiding the question. But as I interviewed more cartel members, I began to think they were telling the truth and they really didn't know. In their minds, it is perhaps as clouded as the number of women they have slept with.

In contrast, all the Maras I talk to remember a clear number of kills. It is like a scorecard, cementing their standing within the organization. Montana confesses he has murdered thirty.

He first shed blood when he was thirteen years old. Guns are rife in Honduras and he got his hands on a 9 mm pistol to go mugging—and win the attention of the Mara crew. He held up a man who was about thirty years old, demanding his wallet. When the man refused, he gunned him down.

I ask him if he felt guilty.

"I was paranoid," he replies. "Every time I went out, I thought someone might recognize me from the shooting. But nobody did."

The local Mara boss heard about it and offered Montana a job, which he calls a mission. It came three months later when Montana had turned fourteen. By this time, in 2006, He Who Holds the World was a Honduran who went by the apt moniker Sadist. He told Montana to take out a drug dealer, a middle-aged man who refused to work with the Maras.

"The target had sold drugs for a long time and was stubborn. He had been told, 'You can work for us or you can leave and we might not kill you.' But he wouldn't listen.

"I went round to his house as if I was going to buy some cocaine. There were a lot of people there, including children. There was even a baby in a woman's arms. I pulled out my gun and shot the dealer with five bullets. The magazine had six bullets so I kept one in the chamber in case I needed it. Nobody did anything. I walked out slowly."

I ask him how he felt when he did this, a fourteen-year-old killing a grown man. What was going through his head?

"It felt great," he replies. "I liked it. I felt powerful."

For that murder, the Mara paid him a thousand lempiras, about forty-five dollars. That is how much life is worth in Honduras.

As he killed more, the Maras would hike his pay, giving him several hundred dollars for a hit. Yet he still wasn't a fully fledged Mara member. They raised the bar on what wannabes had to do before they could join. Montana would kill seven before they jumped him in.

While Montana gained his reputation as a killer and smoked crack, he was still going to school. Kids have to share the classroom with such murderers. Teachers are terrified of their students. In both Honduras and Salvador, gang members have killed teachers for telling them off in class or failing them in exams.

For Montana's next mission, he had to discipline a drug dealer who had been smoking what he was meant to be selling. Montana was still fourteen, while the drug dealer was fifteen; it was a child against a child.

"We gave him twenty-four hours to come up with the money for the crack. When we came back, he said he didn't have it. We took him into a house and tied his hands and put him on his knees. He begged for his life. But we couldn't show mercy. We couldn't show weakness."

I ask Montana exactly how he killed him, and he mimes how he stood behind the kid and shot him in the back of the head. I asked him again how he felt after this.

"I felt excellent. You get addicted to killing. You want to kill again just to get that buzz."

Addiction to killing. This is even more frightening than murdering for forty-five dollars. Yet, like cartel hit men, Montana's murder spree was taking part within an institution—albeit a gang. Killing on orders takes away part of the responsibility. Montana considered himself a soldier.

Turning fifteen, Montana got his next chance to slay. A woman had a beauty salon in the neighborhood. She was a pretty twenty-six-year-old who Montana liked—although he realized she was scared of him. The Mara clique had discussed charging her war tax, but decided they would let her off. However, she revealed to Montana that someone was shaking her down. It was a man connected to the Barrio 18. As well as extorting her, the man would abuse her, groping her and forcing her to kiss him.

The extortionist collected on Tuesdays, so Montana hung outside to watch him come. He had learned by this time to plan hits, to work out who might be around and what the escape routes were. On the first occasion, he just watched. The following Tuesday, when the extortionist came again, Montana unloaded five bullets into him.

Montana felt invincible. Yet in his following mission, he messed up. On orders from his boss, Sadist, he shot a target. But despite the fact he hit him with several bullets, the man survived. His gang castigated him for the failure.

"They heated me up as punishment, for letting the guy live."

I ask him what this means and he explains. "They gave me a beating. We have certain rules and you can't break them. One is not going through with a kill. Another is leaving a Mara you are with in trouble. You can't leave any man behind." (Unless he's dead.)

For his next job, Montana killed another drug dealer who was selling on the Maras' turf. He followed him to the market and shot him in the back while he bought vegetables. The stall owners were too terrified to do anything.

When Montana was seventeen, he had completed his seven kills, and the Maras finally jumped him in. They gave him a severe beating with sticks and kicks. And he was reborn with the family.

As a fully fledged member he drew a salary and enjoyed the power a Mara had in the neighborhood. He could also commission others to murder. But with his love for the gun he carried on killing, building up his scorecard. He went from pistols to Kalashnikovs. Corrupt soldiers steal weapons from military caches in Central America, while guns from old arsenals of guerrilla and Contra armies move around the black market. Maras also have grenades and plastic explosives.

Finally, when he was twenty, the police arrested Montana for carrying an illegal firearm. He did six months in prison, the only time he has served for his crimes. But he perhaps suffers psychologically from his killing "addiction." He smoked more and more crack, until he was high every waking hour. One day, he smoked dozens of rocks while also sniffing glue and was taken to hospital almost suffering a hemorrhage. Eventually, he realized he had to go into rehab. Sadist thankfully gave him permission to dry out, realizing Montana could be of more use if he wasn't messed up.

When I speak to Montana, he has been in the rehab shelter for six months, kept active in workshops. After he leaves, he will have to go back to the Mara clique or face their death penalty for desertion.

Evangelical Christians run the clinic, so Montana prays daily and takes part in Bible discussions. I ask Montana if he has taken God into his heart and he nods his head. But I find it hard to believe him. He doesn't appear to show real regret for his killings. Maybe he will at some point in life.

When I ask Montana about the future, he laughs. He lives for the moment. Many in this generation kill cannot even envision the next day.

CHAPTER 32

Back over the border in El Salvador, a new generation of Maras also painted the streets with blood. Faced with this slaughter, some of Salvador's politicians and church leaders backed a controversial mechanism for peace: a truce between the Mara Salvatrucha and Barrio 18.

The Salvadoran gang truce is one of the most important experiments to deal with the crime wars in Latin America. It needs to be analyzed closely to see if it is a model that can work in other places or a tactic that needs to be avoided. But a key problem in understanding the truce is that the government was not open about it. It was organized in secret before the website *El Faro* exposed it. Even after it was outed, the government continued to be evasive about whether it was really supporting the truce and finally backed away completely.

The roots of the peace process lie with the rise to power of the Farabundo Marti National Liberation Front, the party formed by the guerrillas of the civil war. In 2009, it won the election under President Mauricio Funes, ending twenty years of rule by the conservative ARENA. Salvadoran leftists hoped the dreams they had fought for with bullets in the eighties could finally be fulfilled peacefully. But like other leftists taking power in Latin America, they faced the tough realities of a globalized economy and the stubborn persistence of poverty. They were also confronted by rising gang violence; the number of murders in the small Central American nation shot up from 2,207 in 2001 to 3,778 in 2005 to 4,382 in 2009, when Funes was sworn into office.[1]

Salvadorans begged for something to be done about the bloodshed. But nobody seemed to have a solution. Some of the former guerrillas looked at more radical ideas; among them was Raul Mijango, an old insurgent commander who took part in the civil war peace talks. Later, selling propane gas, he suffered extortion and a kidnapping from the Maras and was hungry to find a way out of the mess.

However, a key player in the truce was a general, David Munguia Payes, who Funes named security minister in 2011 amid rising pressure over the violence. Munguia considered taking a more hardline military approach to the Maras. However, he hired the ex-guerrilla Mijango, who he had known since the peace accords, and Mijango persuaded the general that the gangsters could be negotiated with. To help with the truce, they also brought in a military chaplain.

In early 2012, the negotiators met secretly with Mara leaders behind bars. As talks progressed, they put bosses of the Mara Salvatrucha and Barrio 18 together in a room inside the prison. They feared they might murder each other. But after hard stares, a Mara boss known as El Diablo walked up to the 18 boss Viejo Lin and shook his hand. Peace was possible.[2]

To allow the Maras to explain the cease-fire to their soldiers, Munguia moved thirty bosses from high-security prisons to more relaxed jails around El Salvador. This pleased the gang leaders, who liked serving time in less severe prison regimes. But it was extremely hard for the government to sell the idea that it was negotiating with crime bosses to the Salvadoran public. People were bitter over Maras shaking them down and murdering their loved ones. Organizing a truce suggested giving the gangs legitimacy, comparing them to guerrillas with recognized grievances. In the face of this obstacle, the government decided it should keep the deal secret, at least until it had shown a dip in homicides.

"What could I say?" General Munguia later asked *El Faro*. "That I had transferred (the Maras) as an experiment? Ha ha ha. Forget it. They would eat us alive. We needed to have results to show."[3]

Word of the truce went from the jail to the street. One of the gangsters who brought it there was Marvin Gonzalez, a Mara boss from Ilopango, an industrial city on the edge of the capital that is one of the bloodiest battlegrounds. I drive out to Ilopango to track down Marvin. Bizarrely, I manage to interview him in a room inside the town hall, an office for dealing with young people in the community. The government and gang leaders forged such links in the peace process and they remain highly controversial.

Marvin is He Who Holds the Word for Maras in the whole of Ilopango, a city of over a hundred thousand. He doesn't just represent his own clique of 140 gangbangers. He represents another fourteen cliques in the area, with a total of over a thousand members. Short with strong indigenous features, Marvin is markedly different from many gangsters I have met. He is humble and soft-spoken, appearing slightly shy and sometimes evading eye contact. Yet when I listen back to a recording of the interview I realize how sharp he is. Unlike a lot of gangsters, he knows well how to duck inconvenient questions. In other answers, he is very articulate. In his work on the truce, he has developed a political discourse in which he compares the Maras to the guerrillas and the truce to the peace accords.

"In the war, the guerrillas and soldiers came from poor marginalized barrios and they killed each other daily. They were killing among the same people. None of them came from high society. This is similar to us. We live in slums, both the Mara Salvatrucha and the Eighteen. We are killing among poor people. It's a war without sense."

Marvin is also a murderer. He was convicted of homicide when he was eighteen and spent over a decade, most his adult life, in prison. When I meet him, he is thirty-one. He tells me he read a lot inside, especially books on ancient wars. He was behind bars when the truce was made but released soon afterward, and took the orders of a cease-fire to the Maras in his city. I find this timing suspicious, but he insists that his release was coming up anyway.

Born into a poor family that sold vegetables, Marvin describes how the civil war ravaged the slums. In 1989, when he was six years old, a death squad decapitated his uncle, who was in the guerrillas.

"We have known violence since the time of the war. Since we were children, we have witnessed these scenes, scenes that never end, that come every day. There are deaths, bodies thrown out, decapitations. Near to here, people were hung up on a bridge. You get accustomed to it."

When peace came in 1992, Marvin remembers the deported gang-bangers arriving with their Dickies pants and jailhouse tattoos. "The only thing that the United States has sent us in these years is murderers," he says. "They haven't sent us work or any other form of opportunities."

However, when Marvin was recruited into the Maras at fourteen it was by a boss who had spent his whole life in Salvador, serving in the army during the war. He describes him as a cold killer, who only offered the kids guns, not hope.

When he came out of prison, Marvin formed the Ilopango clique leaders into what he calls a "committee" to oversee the peace process. The idea was for the Mara Salvatrucha and Barrio 18 to respect each other's turfs and cease all aggression. Marvin describes how tough it was to persuade bloodthirsty Maras to rest their trigger fingers.

"The truce between gangs was not something easy. People didn't want to stop killing because of pride, because of all they had fought for, because of their barrios, because of their people. You have to sit and have a dialog with your rival, who wanted to kill you, who has killed your family members, killed your friends and neighbors. It was difficult to overcome."

It was especially tough to stop the young gangsters who wanted to prove themselves. In many ways, the truce was an effort by the older Maras to control the generation kill.

"Young people want to show they have courage. But we have to show them that we don't just want people with courage, we want people who can be productive members of the community."

Maras often hit a turning point and curb their violence when they became fathers, like Lagrima in the Honduran prison. Marvin also said that his thinking transformed with parenthood; he has fathered two girls since his release.

"Becoming a father changes your life. Now I have reasons why I want a municipality free of violence. If there are gunshots, where will my daughter play? I don't want her growing up in an environment like we grew up in. I don't want her spending years in jail when she could be at university or learning a trade."

But instead of leaving the gang, Marvin says he wants to make the gang become a force of good. He believes the Mara structure can be used to steer kids on the right path, put them into training and oversee businesses. It is an ambitious goal.

A truce involving tens of thousands of gang members was always going to be hard to keep a secret. But *El Faro* exposed it in just five days, with a story on March 14, 2012. As General Munguia had predicted, the exposure sparked a storm of criticism. Pundits, the conservative opposition, police, and aggrieved citizens slammed the government for negotiating with murderers.

The government stumbled in reaction, with officials giving varying and contradictory explanations. But as they realized the media was staying on the story, they saw that they had to give out better information and brought in former guerrilla press officer Paolo Luers to help run public relations on the truce.

I meet Luers at a bar he owns in San Salvador. He is originally from Germany, coming to Salvador as a journalist to cover the civil war in the eighties and flipping over to join the guerrillas. He worked in their Radio Venceremos, broadcast from Vietcong-style tunnels, and filmed guerrilla propaganda videos in the bush. He has since become a Salvadoran national and given up his German passport. He says he supported the gang truce out of a genuine belief it was saving lives.

"I couldn't let such an intelligent attempt at peace be killed by a storm of criticism," Luers says. "I felt a responsibility to do all I could to make this peace process sustainable."

Like Marvin, he also makes the comparison between the Maras and guerrillas.

"The [gang leaders] are serious people. If they had been born twenty years earlier, they would have been combatants with the guerrillas. I don't have any doubt. And they would have been strong commanders. They got on with the former guerrilla Mijango, and saw that he was not going to betray them. This is because they are similar, in their thinking."

Luers organized press conferences in prisons so gang leaders themselves could talk of their hopes for peace. TV cameras went behind bars to film the surreal spectacle of killers with tattoos on their faces sitting at a table like officials and talking into a cluster of microphones.

The conferences did not stop the criticism. But then something extraordinary happened. The truce started working. Spectacularly.

In its first months, the death toll dived from about fifteen a day to about five a day. On some days, there were no murders—a dramatic news story in a country so accustomed to slaughter. Over the whole of 2012, the death toll dropped 40 percent compared to 2011. It was the biggest dip in violence since the civil war peace accords.

In early 2013, the truce reached its highest point. Building on the cease-fire, Mara leaders such as Marvin worked with city officials to oversee "Violence Free Zones." They held meetings in town halls, in which residents could directly address gangs about local concerns, such as difficulties getting down a certain street because of gangbangers on the corner. In return, the government and businesses promised social work and enterprises to transform the slums.

It seemed the experiment was carving out a new way forward for dealing with Latin America's crime wars. But then things fell apart.

First, the criticism of the truce returned with a vengeance. A central complaint was that while the homicide rate may have gone down, Maras still committed other crimes, especially shaking down businesses. Allowing Mara bosses to sit down with officials only increased their power, critics said. The whole mechanism for the peace process, in which gang bosses such as Marvin formed committees of clique heads, also reinforced the Mara structures. And the gangs used the threat of a return to violence if the process collapsed. Murder rates had become the Maras' currency that they could bargain with.[4]

One of the most fervent critics was Police Commissioner Pedro Gonzalez, head of the anti-gang unit. His hard line is shared by many in Salvador.

"I call gangs a cancer, the new cancer of society," Gonzalez tells me, returning to the disease metaphor. "Every epoch of humans has its problems, and this is a big problem."

When I ask Gonzalez about the truce, he shakes his head.

"It's a farce, a lie. It's very difficult for them to stop committing crimes. It is like if you put a chorizo in front of a dog. It's going to eat it. If a gang member is on the street and he isn't thinking about killing someone, it's because he just killed someone.

"I am not interested in them having a dialogue. If they agree not to kill each other, they get stronger. And if the two sides unite, who will they fight against? The state, and society.

"If you give them money, they use it to buy arms. If you give them a bakery, do you know what they do? They go to the shops, and say you only buy from us or we are going to kill you."

Amid such criticism, a Salvadoran court ruled that General Munguia had to leave his post as security minister; under the 1992 peace accords, military officers could not be in such positions, it said. The truce negotiators said the peace process was being sabotaged. The new security minister, Ricardo Perdomo, backed away from the dialogue when he took office in May 2013. He expressed many of the same concerns that the opposition had about working with gangs.

The final blow came in 2014, when President Funes finished his term and was replaced by Salvador Sanchez Ceren. While Funes had been lukewarm on the truce, Sanchez Ceren lashed out against it, and called for a new offensive against gangs. Authorities transferred leaders back to high-security jails.

Some Mara leaders, like Marvin, desperately try to keep the truce alive. The press officer Luers also continues to support it. But without government backing, without any of the promised social work, and with police hitting Maras hard, most gangsters returned to the gun. The murder rate shot back up. In 2014, there were 3,912 killings, a hike of 57 percent compared to the previous year.

This created another paradox: there was more blood on the streets of Salvador; yet the president suffered less criticism.

The Salvadoran gang truce leaves me with mixed feelings. It is often referred to as the "failed gang truce" because it ultimately broke down. But was it really a failure? It saved perhaps two thousand lives. And it provided hope that another way out of this bloodshed is possible.

El Faro's criticism of the process was not of the idea itself. It was the fact that government was deceptive. As *El Faro's* Oscar Martinez wrote in a *New York Times* editorial: "The president of El Salvador has helped save more than 2,000 lives in the past two years. Now if only he would admit it."[5]

Yet leaders across the hemisphere will likely learn the lesson that a truce is politically toxic. They have seen how hard it was to publicly defend negotiating with murderers. It is easier to let them massacre each other.

While the most publicized, the Salvador truce is not the only gang cease-fire of the Americas. In Medellín, Colombia, in 2010, a former guerrilla and priest backed a truce between two cartel factions. In Ciudad Juárez, Mexico, it is likely the Sinaloa and Juárez cartels agreed to a cease-fire in 2011, which reduced homicides by a stunning 90 percent within two years. If there was any Mexican government backing for the Juárez truce it was a well-kept secret. Governments may see that it is best to be more secretive rather than less.

I ask Douglas Moreno, who was vice security minister during the Salvador truce, if the tactic has a future. From his experience, he says it is something that has to be done by independent actors, such as priests and activists, but it is impractical for a government to back it. When gangsters stop killing each other it is helpful for society. But you cannot give them any concessions, he says.

Moreno also points to gang mediation in the United States that police and social workers have developed over the years. After gang murders in

Los Angeles, social workers will go to the funerals to try and stop revenge hits. Some form of peace mechanism along these lines could be used in Latin America, Moreno says.

The reduction in Salvador's homicides made the rebound all the more painful. A sharp increase in murders creates a feeling of instability, of things spinning out of control. This surge happened in 2014, creating shock waves on the streets. It was the same summer that children from Salvador, Honduras, and Guatemala rushed to the U.S. border in record numbers.

CHAPTER 33

The text message threat is simple and ominous. Seventeen-year-old Jeffrey Pineda in San Pedro Sula, Honduras, has kept it to show to a U.S. judge if he ever makes it over the Rio Grande.

"You mother is very angry with you. Come back now for punishment."

A lanky teenager with a mop of curly hair, Jeffrey had gotten close to a clique of the Barrio 18. I first met his father, who expressed his concern about his kid hanging with the gangbangers, but they dominated his street corner and it was hard to avoid them. After several months with the crew, they gave Jeffrey a mission: to kill his own uncle. He was too terrified to say no, and went with the gun toward the target. When he got close, he chickened out and ran to his father. That was when they sent the message. It is in code. His "mother" means the clique boss; "punishment" could mean death. His father buried the gun in case they need it as evidence. Jeffrey is sitting indoors, terrified to go on the street. They ask me how much chance he would have of getting political asylum in the U.S.

Jeffrey's case might win less sympathy because he had chosen to hang round with the gangsters before they ordered him to murder. Other children fear for their lives because the Maras have targeted them out of the blue; from girls refusing to go out with a gangbanger to a kid just brushing past a boss too closely. But in Jeffrey's case as in the others, their lives are in genuine danger. It is tragic to see these people, who are typical teenagers in other ways, playing with smartphones, nodding their heads to music, terrified for their lives.

Violence is not the only reason for northward migration. I met a thirteen-year-old riding freight trains who said simply, "I want to see my mama." He hadn't seen her in five years; she was too scared of coming home as it could mean she might never get back to the U.S. and would lose her lifeline of income. Some kids run from country poverty. In 2014, coyotes, or human smugglers, also spread the (untrue) rumor that children arriving would be given papers.

But violence is a major factor pushing people north and making them believe such myths and risk their lives jumping freight trains. It is notable that Nicaragua, which is also poor but much less violent, has way less migration.

Many migrant parents in the United States send for their children because they are terrified Maras will either recruit or kill them. I find a coyote who takes people north for sixty-five hundred dollars a shot, giving them two chances. A thirty-year-old man with tattoos on his eyelids, he says has taken children as young as five without their parents. It is hard to comprehend putting a child of that age into the hands of this tattooed coyote and on a path where they could be kidnapped by cartels or disappear in the desert. But this shows how desperate people are.

When the presidents of Honduras, Salvador, and Guatemala met with Obama at the White House, they debated the idea of a "Marshall Plan" to build up Central America, which they dubbed the Alliance for Prosperity. The Northern Triangle countries are poor and small, so even a few hundred million would go a long way in changing them. It is a place where aid could really transform a reality. But it's a hard sell in an indebted United States, already tangled up in various wars.

Before he flew north, I interviewed Honduran president Juan Orlando Hernandez in his presidential palace in Tegucigalpa. A forty-six-year-old conservative, Hernandez made the case, as other Latin American leaders have, that the U.S. has a responsibility to help, because Americans buy drugs.

"I call for the principle of shared responsibility between those who produce [drugs] and those who consume them in the north. In the United States, many officials see the drug problem as basically one of health, as how much it costs to treat an addict and stop them getting involved. But for us it is life and death. That is the difference.

"Never in Central America, particularly in the Northern Triangle and in Honduras, has there been so much loss of life as in this decade. Never. Never in history. And look, disgracefully, this is a not an issue that originates in Honduras."

Hernandez made a fair point. The illegal drug trade is an international problem and we have to find an international solution. This is difficult when politics in every country is invariably local. Gangsters often operate more effectively across borders than governments do.

But Hernandez is only telling part of the story. The Maras do make money from drugs, but a lot of it is from the local market. They also make their money from extortion, prostitution, and loan sharking off their own communities. Over the border in El Salvador, the Maras are hardly involved in the international drug trade, with Salvador having little strategic value for trafficking north.

Still, it is in the United States' strategic interests to stop countries in the neighborhood crumbling to gangsters. With the level of instability in Honduras, it's concerning who could take advantage of the chaos. While fears of Islamic militants working with Maras are overblown, there are genuine risks in allowing the growth of mercenary armies, with networks of gun, drug, and human smuggling stretching through the continent. Building functioning police forces and justice systems in Central America is U.S. homeland security.

Another concern is the new generation of murderous Maras going back to the United States. In a twist of history, the same virus that infected Central America and mutated into a more deadly form is seeping northward again.

The crime reporter Orlin introduces me to a Honduran Mara leader who ran a clique in the United States for eight years; Soñador, or Dreamer, was He Who Holds the Word in Langley Park, Maryland. American police finally caught him with a kilo of cocaine, jailing him and then deporting him back to Honduras. I meet him in a house outside San Pedro Sula. He is a muscular thirty-two-year-old who tells me his story in a blend of English and Spanish.

Born in San Pedro in 1982, Dreamer grew up with a single mother and never knew his father. He jumped into the Mara Salvatrucha when he was eighteen when Maldito, Lagrima, and others spread it across Honduras. He said it was a way to make money and protect his family.

Spending several years in La Vida Loca in San Pedro, he racked up his kills and gained a reputation. Then he headed north. Jumping on freight trains through Mexico, he floated across the Rio Grande in a tire and went through Texas to the east coast.

Dreamer had friends in Maryland, which has been a big destination for Central American migrants since the eighties. Some were Maras. If a

Mara emigrates to the United States, he is required to report to the local crew. Even though most will work as well, they will be on call to do what is required. Dreamer got a job in construction. But his nights and weekends were dedicated to the Mara. With his number of kills, he quickly became the boss of the Langley Park clique.

"The homies up in the United States know how crazy it is in Honduras and what we have been through. They see someone like me, who has done a lot of missions, and I get respect."

It shows a full circle. Back in the 1990s, the deportees from Los Angeles were idols to the malnourished war orphans in Central America. Now the murderous Central Americans are seen as the real thing by American-born gangbangers.

Dreamer said kids lined up to join them. In his Langley Park clique, he had 150 active members and five hundred "sympathizers." They are not only Central Americans.

"We have Puerto Ricans, Dominicans, Colombians, Bolivians, Cubans, even Chinese kids. Lots of people want to join up with us. We have kids all over the schools who are sympathizers."

As U.S. law enforcement is more effective, Maras can't act like they do in Central America. If they carried out anywhere near that level of murder, they would attract unyielding crackdowns. So people are not required to kill to join up.

"We give people other missions, such as taking a package of drugs. They still risk getting sent to jail, but we keep off the radar."

However, the Maras take many of their rackets from Central America to suburban Maryland, such as making businesses pay their war tax. The victims are often Central Americans and other Latinos; sometimes the Maras find out if the owner has family back home they can threaten, showing them photographs. Other times, their words are enough.

"I'll sit down and talk to the guy in English or Spanish or whatever he understands and tell him he has got to pay. Like if it's a liquor store we are going to collect three hundred dollars every Saturday. And most of these people don't argue. But if you do, you know that you are going to get fucked up."

Many of their victims do not have immigration papers so they are scared to go to the police. Latino businesses are not the only targets, however. The Maras also tax businesses in Chinatown, where there are many undocumented workers, Dreamer says.

The Langley Park clique also runs prostitutes. Dreamer describes how they run a delivery service, taking girls to hotels or homes, fifty dollars for fifteen minutes.

"We have all kinds of girls. Dominicans, Colombians. The Colombians are very pretty girls. Sometimes, they might be the girlfriend of a member of the *ganga* [gang]. We split the money with the girls, fifty-fifty."

And as could be expected, the Maras sell drugs. Dreamer said the MS13 buys directly from Mexican mobs, including the Sinaloa, Gulf, and Juárez cartels. As well as selling on corners, they also have members climbing up the food chain, selling kilos to other dealers, Dreamer says.

"There are homies that are making a lot of money from this and moving up. They are getting bigger into the business."

The Mara Salvatrucha fights to defend its turf in Maryland. As well as Langley Park, nearby Takoma Park is MS13 territory. Their old nemesis Barrio 18 is in Silver Spring. They clash and sometimes murder each other, although on a much lower scale than in Central America.

Going into Washington, D.C., and Baltimore, African American gangs such as the Crips still hold sway. A lot has been made of Latino versus black violence, especially in Los Angeles. However, Dreamer and some other Maras I talk say they have no special beef with African Americans.

"Sometimes we might do business with the Crips, like selling them a kilo or something. We have respect for each other. They know that although the Hondurans and Salvadorans might be short, we are quick on the trigger."

The Mara Salvatrucha gained national attention when members stabbed to death a seventeen-year-old pregnant girl, Brenda Paz, in Virginia back in 2003. Born in Honduras, Brenda had hung around with gang members while informing for the police. Since then, federal and state gang units have flagged the Mara Salvatrucha as a priority. The FBI made a series of high profile cases against the gang using racketeering laws designed for the Italian American Mafia. In 2012, the Treasury Department named the MS13 as a Transnational Criminal Organization, the first time it has awarded this title to a U.S. street gang. It is an official recognition of how the Mara Salvatrucha has mutated into a new threat. The act gives federal agents enhanced powers to go after its businesses and money laundering networks.

The efforts have weakened the Maras, but they still operate and murder on U.S. soil. In October 2014, police nabbed Maras waiting outside Garfield High School in Northern Virginia with machetes and a sawn-off shotgun. They were waiting for a student to finish class but somebody informed. Police charged the men with another three murders in Virginia.

The United States is not the only place where the Maras are spreading. Central American migrants have brought the gang to Spain and Italy. As they set up cliques in Barcelona and Milan, they jump in members of other ethnic groups. When Spanish police busted a clique in Barcelona, they found it included a Bulgarian, a Romanian, an Ecuadoran, a Moroccan, and a Spaniard.

These immigrants in turn take the Mara back to their own countries, so the MS turns up in bizarre places. YouTube videos and Facebook pages show the Maras from Morocco to the Philippines to South Africa. They are coming to your neighborhood soon.

The MS13 was born of the U.S. street gang system but has become the most global of any street gang. Its reputation and simple but effective structure helps it spread. And it gels with marginalized youth from different cultures, whether they be the Salvadoran migrants who founded the gang in Los Angeles or Eastern Europeans living in Spain. Vulnerable and displaced, the Mara provides them protection.

The Mara model may be less threatening than vast drug cartels with their wealth and political connections. But the fact that Mara cliques don't depend on big resources also makes them tough to destroy. The gang sets up in towns, villages, cities, whether there is a drug trade or not. It feeds on broken families, poverty, and hopelessness. It makes sense to scattered children in soulless slums who feel loyalty to no government or country, but will pledge their lives to the Mara Salvatrucha.

PART V

The Saint: Mexico

They say that every society has the government that it deserves. While I say that every society and every government have the criminals that they deserve.

—NAZARIO MORENO, *THEY CALL ME "THE MADDEST ONE,"* 2011

CHAPTER 34

Hidden in the smog-ridden north of Mexico City, inside the headquarters of the Ministry of National Defense—or Mexican army HQ—sits one of the most fascinating museums on the planet. The army humbly calls it the Museo de Enervantes, which can be roughly translated as the Museum of Stupefacients. But this boring technical title underplays the incredible collection of artifacts on display, the highlights of what Mexican soldiers have nabbed from drug traffickers.

Some seized narcotics themselves are in the cabinets, but these are the least interesting items. A lot of people already know what marijuana, crystal meth, and heroin look like (although the black cocaine on show is a novelty). The drug lab machinery is more enthralling, including sprawling shiny contraptions to cook meth on an industrial scale. Pieces from trap cars, the vehicles used to smuggle drugs over the border in gas tanks, tires, and false seats, also illustrate the ingenuity of narco engineers. More frightening is the heavy weapons room of captured cartel firepower; you see that narco thugs don't only use belt-driven machine guns and grenades, they even possess shoulder-held rocket launchers, such as the RPG-29, or "Vampire," which can take out tanks.

But the museum's main attraction is undoubtedly a room under the title *narco cultura*. The narco culture cabinets display the ostentatious bling that drug lords buy with their billions of bloodstained bucks. Some pieces are worth high five digits in the stones and metal alone.

Guns are bathed in gold and decorated with gems in the shapes of words and pictures. Some stones form the names of their capo owners, such as a pistol with an engraving of ACF—Amado Carrillo Fuentes, the Lord of the Skies. Others have images of Mexican revolutionaries who the gangsters hail as heroes, including Emiliano Zapata and Pancho Villa.

Others still have names of fashion designers such as the Italian tailor Versace. I find it bemusing that drug lords can praise both revolutionaries and entrepreneurs; they are rebel capitalists.

The narco memorabilia extends to awards that cartel armies give their warriors for bravery. A medallion from the Zetas has a letter Z on one side and picture of gangster soldiers in heroic battle poses on the other. It is the narco equivalent of the Victoria Cross—or Tiffany Cross. Walking on through the hall, you see a cowboy waistcoat, which is really a bullet-proof vest; a cell phone bathed in gold; and a carved wooden chair in the form of the grim reaper. It gets weirder and weirder.

Dominating the end of the narco culture hall is the weirdest item of all: a four-foot high statuette of a saintly warrior clad in medieval armor. It's an impressive piece of art. Its core is a plaster figurine, which is worked over with gold and gems for the coat of mail and fine paint for the skin and goatee beard. The crusader vaunts red Templar crosses on his chest and sleeves and clasps a broadsword. He has that despondent expression of a holy man, wise but sad, as seen on images of Jesus and his saints. He also resembles one of Mexico's most brutal gangster warlords.

Soldiers seized the statuette from cartel thugs who baptized themselves as the Knights Templar, after the order of warrior monks who fought for Christendom between 1119 and 1312. The narco Templars made dozens of similar statuettes and put them in shrines to kneel and pray before. They call them "Santos Nazarios." It is the image of their leader, Nazario Moreno, known as El Chayo, or El Más Loco—the Maddest One.

Troops have also found prayers to Saint Nazario, printed in booklets in the style of regular Catholic prayer books that vendors sell at the stoplights in Mexican cities. As one says:

> Give me holy protection,
> Through Saint Nazario,
> Protector of the poorest,
> Knights of the people,
> Saint Nazario,
> Give us life.

Anthropologists can have a field day dissecting this narco holy image. Saint Nazario mixes Latin America's popular Catholicism with the bling of the drug trade with the rock-star status of crime lords. Personally, when I first see a narcotics trafficker looking like Jesus, it seems hilarious; then I think about it for thirty seconds and realize it's terrifying.

Adding to Nazario's cult status, he wrote his own holy book. Journalists often refer to it as his bible. But *Mis Pensamientos* (*My Thoughts*) doesn't have complete religious stories and parables like the Christian Bible. Instead, it is a collection of musings, similar in structure to Mao Tse-tung's little red book.

As Nazario authored his religious rant, named his cartel after crusading monks, and was venerated like a saint, this dominates coverage about him. In journalese shorthand he is "the head of the bizarrely named Knights Templar who wrote his own bible even as he trafficked tons of crystal meth to the United States."

But these entertaining details overshadow other features of Nazario's empire that are important to understanding what Mexican organized crime has become. Nazario moved from drug trafficking to a portfolio of crimes that made him a major player in the local economy—a gangster capitalist. The Knights Templar took over iron mines, ignoring environmental regulations so they could sell record quantities of metal to hungry Chinese factories. They took extortion to new extremes, making cents of every dollar that moved, even from big business, and attacking those who didn't pay (they burned thirty trucks of a local unit of PepsiCo). And they waded into the avocado, lime, and cattle industries. For Americans, your guacamole on game day, the metal in your kid's remote-controlled car, and the beef in your burger may have passed through the Knights Templars' hands—alongside the meth smoked by your local fiend.

In his home state of Michoacán, the Maddest One got his tentacles into the entire political and judicial apparatus. With mayors, police commanders, and politicians on his payroll, the state apparatus rotted to the core—making it later implode like a putrid tree trunk.

Nazario's rule was so insidious and brutal it ultimately unleashed Mexico's largest vigilante movement to take him down. The so-called *autodefensas*—or self-defense squads—became a significant third force in the Mexican drug war, fighting alongside the government security forces and cartel death squads. The militias unleashed a bloody but bewildering battle. They built a network of barricades that weaved through the state; they took back towns that the government supposedly controlled already; sometimes they fought alongside the Mexican army, sometimes against them. The conflict embarrassed President Peña Nieto and led his government to make a dangerous alliance with the vigilantes.

Migrants in the United States were also key in toppling Nazario. Michoacán émigrés from California to Oregon were so distraught by the terror in their homeland they helped finance the vigilante movement. Some returned home and took up Kalashnikovs. I found immigrants on the frontline who went within weeks from washing dishes in Los Angeles to fighting gun battles against cartel hit men.

And if that isn't enough color for Nazario's crazy tale, the narco saint also died twice. A drug lord of the Maddest One's status has multiple lives.

Nazario first died in December 2010. Mexican federal police claimed they killed him during one of the most ferocious battles of the Mexican drug war: a fight involving two thousand federal officers and about five hundred criminal gunmen. Amid the melee, the officers said they shot Nazario but his gangster henchmen carried his corpse away. His death was confirmed when a grave appeared with his name on it. (Apparently, police didn't want to dig it up and check.)

The president at the time, Felipe Calderón, trumpeted Nazario's demise as a grand victory in his war on cartels. It was especially sweet as Michoacán is Calderón's home state and the place where the president had launched his campaign against organized crime.

After his supposed death, Nazario's followers began venerating him like a saint and statuettes and shrines appeared. Even more bizarrely, people reported seeing his ghost wandering around Michoacán dressed all in white. Under the leadership of this phantom saint, the Knights Templar became more powerful than ever.

By 2014, the sightings of ghost Nazario had become absurdly common; on a single day, I spoke to three people who claimed they had seen him. But I still wasn't sure. I discussed the testimonies with a fellow journalist. Were these sources really seeing him, we asked. Or was this a figment of their collective imagination?

The former turned out to be true. In March 2014, Mexican marines announced that Nazario was still alive. But they also said that they now had killed him. Really.

This bizarre situation reminds me of a quote attributed to Spanish surrealist artist Salvador Dalí. The master supposedly said: "I won't return to Mexico because it is a country that is more surreal than my paintings."[1]

To prove that Nazario was truly in heaven (or hell), the marines released a video of his body. It certainly looks like him. However, while the marines say they killed the Maddest One with two bullets in the chest, this film shows a face that has blatantly been beaten, the eyelids black and nose purple. In the murky world of the Mexican drug war, there is always a second story, and I hear a credible account that explains this bruising. According to this alternative version of events, Nazario wasn't really killed by marines, but he was battered to death by his own bodyguards working with vigilantes. It is of course illegal for vigilantes to murder people (in theory). So the vigilantes handed in the corpse and it was convenient for everyone to say the marines did it. The bodyguards had got so fed up of Nazario's megalomania they turned on him. His final legacy was not of his troops venerating him, but of them hating him.

Nazario's messianic complex illuminates a memoir he wrote. While most drug lords erase details of their lives, Nazario actually self-published this autobiography and distributed it to his followers. It was never on sale, but thousands of copies flowed around Michoacán towns and villages. It was a hot book. If soldiers found people with them, they would often arrest them for being Templar affiliates.

The 101 pages are fittingly titled *They Call Me "The Maddest One."* The book has a front cover with a silhouette of Nazario's face over a deep red background. It is reminiscent of a silhouette image of Che Guevara printed on T-shirts throughout Latin America. As well as styling himself as a messiah, Nazario fancied himself a guerrilla hero.

Maddest One is written in decent grammar, maybe with the help of a writer with a gun to his head (Nazario says he didn't do a day in school). Splattering its pages are amusing sayings such as, "Every nation has the government it deserves and every government has the criminals it deserves." It also provides unusual insight into the life and deranged mind of this gangster warlord.

The memoir needs to be carefully scrutinized, but agents tracking him confirm many of the facts. A Mexican investigator who worked for the federal intelligence service and then a special unit fighting the Knights Templar gave me many rich details on the mob and shared his wealth of files. DEA agents also handed me information on the Maddest One.

Among the American agents who tracked Nazario's mob was Mike Vigil, who spent thirteen years working in Mexico, more than any other DEA agent. He often went undercover posing as a drug trafficker to get into their crazed world. During Vigil's time, a trafficker shot at him from three feet (the bullets missed). Vigil also had the pleasure of turning down the offer of a three-million-dollar bribe from Honduran kingpin Juan Matta Ballesteros—who was later convicted of the kidnapping of DEA agent Enrique "Kike" Camarena.

However, while the agents confirm many names and dates in Nazario's account, they clash with his vision. Nazario portrays himself as a social bandit, subtitling his memoir "Diary of an Idealist." Agents say he was one of the most dangerous serial murderers on the planet with few real ideals at all.

"I think he is a psychopath that wants to romanticize his criminal activities by writing these manifestoes," Vigil says. "The fact of the matter is that he is a drug trafficker, he is a killer, and he represents the worst of Mexican society but has these delusional romantic ideas."

I have lived in Mexico since 2000, so my work on it goes deeper than the other countries covered in this book. I also had great help from Michoacán journalists, including Francisco Castellanos, Leo Gonzalez, Dalia Martinez, Daniel Fernandez, and Jesus Lemus. Lemus may be the reporter who knows most about drug cartels in the world thanks to a quirk of fate; he was jailed for three years alongside top capos. It is a painful story. He had written an exposé of a corrupt politician and in revenge prosecutors filed trumped-up charges against him, accusing him of working for Nazario. Lemus thankfully resisted days of torture and refused to sign a confession and the charges were thrown out after three excruciating years.

My reconstruction of Nazario's life is also helped by many people from his homeland who knew him. The vigilante uprising to topple the Maddest One created a euphoric atmosphere and people were unusually open in revealing details of the crime world. Among those I talked to who knew Nazario were several of his gunmen who later became vigilantes, Apatzingán businessmen Cristobal Alvarez, a woman married to Nazario's cousin, and a lime farmer who Templars tortured while Nazario was present.

The valley he hails from is a tight-knit community with broad inter-linking families. It is a land blighted by poverty, criminality, and beliefs in the supernatural. These features all helped mold the narco saint and his legend from when he was a small child.

CHAPTER 35

Nazario was born on March 8, 1970, in a Michoacán community called Guanajuatillo. It is more a hamlet than a village, a bundle of hovels of tin roofs and dirt floors scattered around wild hilly terrain infested with scorpions and snakes. Even now, it is only approachable down hours of dirt road—through what most insurance companies would label "bandit country."

Michoacán is in central western Mexico, alongside the Pacific Ocean and at the foot of the southern Sierra Madre Mountains. It is spotted with beautiful lakes inspiring its name, which in the indigenous Nahuatl (or Aztec) language means "possessor of fish." Amerindians such as the Purépecha people still have sizeable communities and maintain strong traditions and a level of self-rule. The state was also the destination of many immigrants, including Italians (it has a town called New Italy) and Dutch Germans. This northern European heritage can be found in strong-flavored cheese and tall blondes who could be on Paris runways. Some of these country folk with yellow and red hair are referred to affectionately as *gueros de rancho*—"ranch blondes."

As well as being a historic home of immigrants, Michoacán is a massive source of emigrants to El Norte. There are more people from Michoacán living in the United States than from any other Mexican state; consular programs show 13 percent are from Michoacán, as opposed to just 2 percent from Sinaloa, Chihuahua, or Tamaulipas.[1]

With twenty-two thousand square miles, Michoacán is about the size of West Virginia. To its north, it borders Jalisco, home to Mexico's second city Guadalajara, and to its south the combative state Guerrero, home to some of Mexico's poorest villages. Its position makes it strategically useful for anybody shipping goods (or drugs) north along the Pacific Coast. It is also home to Lázaro Cárdenas, Mexico's busiest port, where ships arrive daily from Asia and across the world.

Tons of minerals from Michoacán's rich earth pour through the port en route to China. The state also produces some of the world's best avocadoes and limes in its fertile valleys. The mining and agricultural wealth can be seen in elegant colonial buildings in the state capital, Morelia. But despite these blessings, Michoacán is one of Mexico's poorer states; money is in the hands of few, and many scrape by as peasant farmers and day laborers.

The poverty in Michoacán and neighboring Guerrero led them to become bastions of a leftist guerrilla movement. Mexico escaped the intensity of Cold War battles in much of Latin America. During the twentieth century, the ruling PRI incorporated much of the left into its own ranks, even while it was the political home of billionaire capitalists. Furthermore, Mexico recognized Cuba so Castro held back from funding rebels in the Aztec nation. However, student protests flared up in the late sixties, culminating in the bloody massacre of demonstrators in the capital's Tlatelolco Square. In the following years, a small guerrilla movement launched a limited insurgency.

The most well-known guerrilla was Lucio Cabañas, a schoolteacher in Guerrero, who headed the Party of the Poor. His band kidnapped the governor before soldiers gunned him down in 1974. Over in Michoacán, there was a prominent guerilla commander in the town Zamora and another in the Purépecha town of Cheran.[2] This guerrilla tradition would be exploited by Nazario, but also be key to the vigilantes fighting the Knights Templar.

Michoacán is also one of Mexico's most religious states. It was at the heart of the Cristero rebellion of the 1920s, in which people took up guns against the revolutionary government that banned masses. Many of the thirty thousand Cristeros who died in the three-year rebellion hailed from Michoacán. Some were beatified by Rome, including fourteen-year-old child soldier José Sánchez del Río. "People are so religious here," a priest called Gregorio Lopez tells me, "because this earth was bathed in the blood of martyrs." Shrines to saints cover even the most humble villages.

Nazario's hamlet is in one of the poorest parts of Michoacán, a seething hot valley known as the Tierra Caliente, or Hot Land. Locals refer to the valley as El Infiernillo, or Little Hell—a name proudly used by a delicious taco joint in its principal market town Apatzingán. According to folklore, the good people of Morelia banished their criminals to the Little Hell to scrape out a living among cacti and lime trees in the scorching heat. However true the tale is, the Hot Land is certainly on the fringes of the law.

Many people have left the Hot Land to seek a living in the United States, creating strong cross-border links (and smuggling routes) to towns from Los Angeles to Atlanta. The Hot Land is a big drug-producing area. Mexican traffickers have grown opium poppies and smuggled opium to the United States since Washington first made it illegal in the 1914 Harrison Act. The earliest traffickers came from Sinaloa State, where Chinese workers brought opium poppies. But the custom of producing drugs spread south down the Sierra Madre, and Michoacán farmers have raised opium since at least the 1940s. They also grow an abundance of marijuana, which they have shipped to the United States since the explosion of American demand in the sixties.

The ganja plantations also feed a bounteous local market. Many in the Hot Land smoke joints of weed casually and openly, when they break from work and when they while their evenings away along with their mescal. This was particularly apparent during the vigilante uprising against Nazario. As vigilantes ran around with Kalashnikovs and grenades, clashing with Templar gunmen and reclaiming towns, many were seriously stoned.

Nazario. The name itself is curious, uncommon in Mexico. It means one from Nazareth, and I wonder if this could have helped give the Maddest One his Jesus complex. Our names sometimes shape us.

Even by the standards of a poor valley in a poor state, Nazario's family was considered pitiable. He was one of twelve brothers and sisters abandoned by their alcoholic abusive father. They were half-starved and ragged.

Nazario naturally dwells on this hardship in his memoir. He also uses it to justify his life of crime. This is common in Mexico's drug trafficking culture. Popular "narco ballads" celebrate the villains, portraying them as poor rebels who have the balls to fight the rich man's system. This echoes the same class rhetoric as the Red Commando in Brazil. As Nazario recalls:

My family and I lived a poverty so cruel and humiliating that we all dressed as bums or in used clothes they sell cheap in the market that weren't in our size. When we ate refried beans with butter it was a luxury and normally we just ate beans in the pan. In my infant mind, I thought the rich ate bread instead of tortillas and Coca-Cola instead of river water. Not one fruit, not one sweet, not anything, just hunger and too much work . . .

A child grows up in such a bad situation, walking alone on the dirt paths of his ranch, bitter, only accompanied by misery, by hopelessness and premature death. Is it only him who is guilty of temporarily choosing the path of violence and illegality? . . . Is the government not guilty for betraying the people and allowing extreme wealth in the hands of a few, and extreme poverty in others?

Nazario's mother, Maria, was alone with twelve children and kept them in line with her fists. Nazario says they called her "the beater" as she smacked them so often. In his memoir, he writes bitterly of these hidings, which seemed to traumatize him. One time he played with a neighbor's horse without permission, and his mother forced him to stand for hours with arms like a cross while everyone passed by, a humiliation that still made his blood boil years afterwards. Later in the book, he says his mother would apologize for the torments when he became a powerful drug lord.

Working as a child laborer in corn and lime fields, Nazario was illiterate until he was ten. He was finally inspired to learn to read by a cult Mexican comic called *El Kaliman*. The adventures of this superhero, he writes, provided him with a refuge from his violent, impoverished reality and he devoured the weekly installments with passion.

In the comic, Kaliman is a mysterious crusader who dresses all in white with a jeweled K on a white turban. His special powers include levitation and telepathy as well as being a martial arts champ. He's also a kind of warrior philosopher who says a wise phrase in each edition. One of Kaliman's most iconic sayings: "There is no force more powerful than the human mind, and whoever dominates it, dominates everything."

In the tradition of superheroes, Kaliman fights for justice and defeats evil. One old comic has him on the cover, muscles bulging out of his tight white suit, his right hand raised in victory. "The light of truth and justice will always overcome," he says.

The details of this Mexican superhero are notable because Kaliman was such a major influence on Nazario. The drug lord too would later dress in white. And his religious rant *Pensamientos* contains many phrases that are startlingly similar to the psychic Kung Fu master's. The Maddest One wanted to be his own superhero.

Nazario also believed he had gained psychic powers like Kaliman. As a boy on the ranch, he claimed to be able to telepathize with animals. As he writes, "I mentally ordered a donkey to come close and he immediately obeyed me . . . These were my childhood pastimes, to become like Kaliman and be able to do good for humanity."

Later, he would claim to control people's minds. It is easy to dismiss this as his delusional megalomania. But several of those who knew him say they were also convinced he could take hold of people's brains. In the Hot Land of Michoacán, many believe in the supernatural. Nazario would create himself as the narco saint because people around him would believe it. In their world, demons, visions, and mind control exist. It would be harder to create the narco saint in a stronghold of atheism and disbelief.

When Nazario was sixteen, he headed to California to seek his fortune. When he recalls this, he emphasizes the negative more than the positive. "Like all poor people without hope, I went to El Norte," he writes. He didn't head to the opportunity of the United States, but escaped the poverty of his homeland. Unlike many migrants looking to become American, he always gravitated back south.

He took a two-day bus ride to Tijuana with an elder brother, before they sneaked over countryside east of the city into what he called "Gringolandia." This was back in 1986, when it was easier to cross than with today's fences and radars.

Staying with a cousin south of San Francisco in Redwood City (which he calls "Red Good City" in classic Spanglish), Nazario briefly worked eleven-hour shifts for a landscape gardener. But he soon gave up hard labor for the world of drug dealing. He was attracted to it, he describes, when he sat in the park and saw a house on the corner serve up a steady stream of customers with marijuana.

I confess that this drug trafficking in plain sight surprised me. It was evident that they made a lot of dollars practically without any risk.

Like all good traffickers, Nazario started at the bottom, selling ganja in the park and guarding stash houses. When an African American and another Mexican dealer tried to bully him off a park corner, he writes, he took their own knife and stabbed them with it, earning his Maddest One reputation. With twelve brothers and sisters he had been fighting all his life.

The Maddest One enrolled briefly in a school in Humboldt County— so he could sell weed on the local reservation. Then, to help his sprouting enterprise, he got himself a three-year work permit so he could go legally back and forth from the United States to his homeland.

With papers, Nazario made his business a cross-border venture. He went back to Michoacán and grew marijuana in the hills to traffic it north. He also brought U.S. cars and drove them south to sell without documents, a classic racket in the Hot Land.

Spending parts of the year between Mexico and the United States is common among people in Michoacán, creating a fluid binational community that links the politics of Hot Land villages constantly to migrant enclaves in Redwood, California; Portland, Oregon; McAllen, Texas.

While in Mexico, Nazario now lived down the dirt roads from his ranch in nearby Apatzingán, which would become the center of his crime empire. Apatzingán boasts a colonial center and is proud to be where Mexico's first constitution was signed. But away from its elegant cathedral and plaza, it's a plain sprawl with 140,000 residents. As the principal city of the Hot Land, it's a meeting point for roughneck farm workers and marijuana growers and has a reputation for being tough and brawly. A nice thing about Apatzingán is that (unlike Mexico City) people don't honk their horns every two minutes. They are worried the driver could pull a gun if they do. Nazario fit in like a deer in the forest.

Cristobal Alvarez, an Apatzingán businessman who later became a vigilante, knew Nazario at this time from the cantinas and dance halls in the town center. He describes him as a *vicioso* (vice-ridden) and violent young man.

> He would always be drunk and stoned and was either chasing girls or starting fights. He liked to intimidate people, to make them scared of him. But he was also smart. He had this incredible memory and would recall people and things exactly. People would follow him.

Alvarez remembers two striking physical details about Nazario. First, the Maddest One was a muscular but short man; he is registered as being just five foot four. Small tough guys are a well-known phenomenon, with actor Joe Pesci making a career playing them. Small men are also among the most notorious megalomaniac rulers, from Hitler to Napoléon. And it's striking how many gangster warlords are short: Jamaican Dudus was only five foot four, while "Chapo" means Shorty, as he is five foot six.

Secondly, Alvarez says Nazario was left-handed. This anomaly of left-handed people using a different side of their brain has long fascinated researchers, who note that leaders in many spheres, including four of the five last U.S. presidents, share this trait (all except George W. Bush). Is it a coincidence or could using the brain in a different way help a gangster become top dog?

In 1989, Nazario's fierce temperament landed him behind bars. He was up to his usual weekend antics, getting plastered and mouthing off, when a young doctor made the mistake of crossing him. According to one account, Nazario liked the doctor's car and ordered him to hand it over, which he refused to do. But the medic may have just stared too long. Whatever it was, the Maddest One whipped out his pistol and shot him. Luckily for the doctor, he survived the bullets.

Nazario served much of the year in prison in the state capital, Morelia. The arresting officers also beat him heavily. He says the punishment did not cow him but made him hungry for revenge.

During this incarceration, police took a mug shot of Nazario. There are few photos of him and this is the most commonly shown. He's trim, young, tough looking, with a thick neck and light brown skin. Knowing the scale of mayhem he will cause, I can look back at the picture and say that I see his psychopathic stare, his frightening aura, the face of a leader but a diabolical one. It's similar to the glare of Charles Manson in a 1966 mug shot before he went on to found the Manson family and unleash its orgy of bloodshed.

But those observations come from the benefit of hindsight. Really, Nazario looks like one more small-town gunslinger just as Manson looked like one more car thief out of juvenile prison.

* * *

So how did the Maddest One turn from a drunken brawler into a self-styled spiritual leader? Two episodes stand out as having a major impact on the young Nazario.

Firstly, four of his brothers were murdered in a series of killings. He writes that he was especially hurt by the slaying of his brother Canchola, in the border city of Reynosa in 1993. Canchola had been a role model for Nazario, sharing his love for comic hero Kaliman and taking him on his first trip to the United States. Nazario was furious as he says Canchola was killed in an argument with his own friends, an act of treachery. The death pushed Nazario to the edge, making him madder than ever.

Secondly, Nazario himself suffered a beating in which he almost died. The fight was over an amateur game of soccer in Apatzingán in 1994. Following an altercation on the pitch, Nazario exploded with rage, swinging at the rival team, only to find himself on the floor getting kicked repeatedly in the head. The boots fractured his skull.

Doctors at the Apatzingán hospital said it was beyond their skills to heal the wound and Nazario was transferred to Mexico City. In the capital, surgeons opened his head and inserted a metal plate to bind his fractured skull together.

The injury made Nazario even more "loco," and he writes that he saw hallucinations and visions. Alvarez said the metal plate would also make Nazario's face bulge when he got angry.

"If he was staring at you, his forehead would be swelling. It was freaky. He was a frightening man."

Nazario was turning into an authentic James Bond villain.

The trauma made Nazario wake up to what a train wreck his life was. Like all good self-redeemers, he touched bottom. And it was at bottom that he met God.

"I realized that I had fallen into the dark and scary maze of fantasy worlds and unsubstantiated pleasures. I admitted to myself that I had become a vulgar alcoholic, physically destroyed, with ghosts in my head."

Nazario based himself in McAllen, Texas, where he smuggled in marijuana. Here he joined Alcoholics Anonymous and worked through his twelve-step program. In giving up the booze, he was drawn to evangelical Christianity and became a fervent believer. He appears to have had an addictive personality, jumping headfirst into things.

The Maddest One first followed Latino preachers before discovering

Christian author John Eldredge. In his book *Wild at Heart*, Eldredge paints a dreamy picture of a muscular Christianity; of a macho man untamed but noble, fighting in a savage but beautiful habitat. Eldredge describes the world as a struggle, in which you "must desire life like water, and yet drink death like wine." It connected with the Maddest One, also sharing his love for nature and his macho worldview.

"A hesitant man is the last thing in the world a woman needs. She needs a lover and a warrior, not a Really Nice Guy," Eldredge writes. "We don't need accountability groups; we need fellow warriors, someone to fight alongside, someone to watch our back."[3]

Eldredge describes aggression as being a healthy part of masculinity.

"Despite what many modern educators would say, this is not a psychological disturbance brought on by violent television or chemical imbalance. Aggression is part of the masculine design; we are hardwired for it."[4]

Many men can read such words and feel less bad about shouting at a car cutting them off. Nazario could feel better about stabbing dealers and shooting doctors. He was hardwired for it.

Copies of Eldredge's books were later found with detained followers of Nazario. In response, Eldredge condemned their use of his work. "It brings me sorrow and anger to know they are doing this and I renounce their use of my words in this way," he said in a statement. "Submission to Jesus is central to the entire message. They seemed to have missed the central point, which gives context to everything else."[5]

Unlike the Catholicism that Nazario grew up with, evangelical preachers often emphasize improving your lot and fulfilling your dreams. This struck a chord with Nazario. Despite all his hang-ups, he developed an incredible self-belief, a conviction he was destined to be somebody.

However, Nazario's dream was to become a brutal gangster warlord. This is the obvious contradiction: how could the Maddest One consider himself a follower of Christ while he sold meth and chopped off heads? It's irrational. But then human beings can be irrational animals.

Those who knew him tell me that Nazario really believed what he preached. In his mind, he was righteous. When he punished people, he felt like he was dishing out Old Testament justice. He took what he wanted from evangelical Christianity and ignored what was inconvenient. You can't blame evangelical writings for Nazario's actions. He twisted them for his own ends.

Nazario also drew inspiration from other curious places. He became a huge fan of the film *Braveheart*, which he would later make his followers watch. The kilted warriors of Scotland fighting the evil English king resonated with his own struggle in the countryside against the Mexico City elite and their *federales*. When vigilantes stormed one of his last homes they found books including *The Art of War*—classic warlord reading. Meanwhile, Nazario would quote Mexican revolutionary Zapata.

It was a contradictory hodgepodge of ideas. But many leaders around the world have managed to gain followers with conflicting and bizarre programs (Jim Jones, Joseph Kony, Pol Pot ...). The pseudo-ideology, Nazario found, was a cement that could bind his criminal empire together.

CHAPTER 36

Cartels are often seen as the basic building block of Mexican drug trafficking. They are gigantic organizations with their names on indictments, and police wall charts showing their pyramidal structures. But some drug agents and academics also look at the wider networks of traffickers in regions of Mexico that cross cartel lines. In different areas, gangster families tend to know and work with each other, intermarry and feud, like extended tribes. Writers on the Italian Mafia don't just break it down into crime families but into criminal systems dominating geographical areas. In Mexico, you can identify similar systems spreading their tentacles into a spattering of gangs and cartels.

The oldest and biggest network is from Sinaloa, the cradle of Mexican drug trafficking. The Sinaloan narco tribe spread out from its Pacific state to more than half of the U.S. border. It gave birth to the Guadalajara Cartel, Tijuana Cartel, Juárez Cartel, and Beltran Leyva Cartel, all run by Sinaloans. Traffickers worked together across the Sinaloan empire, but they also fought. Viciously. One reason that Sinaloan civil wars are so bloody is that personal feuds mix in with turf battles.

Mexico's second gangster system developed in the east by the Gulf of Mexico. Here a network of bootleggers evolved into the Gulf Cartel, dominating border rackets for seven decades and giving birth to the Zetas. The Mexico border has a sparsely populated area from the east of Chihuahua into Coahuila that creates a natural break between the Sinaloan and Gulf gangster systems. The legal business empires in the northeastern states of Coahuila, Nuevo León, and Tamaulipas also have a common regional identity that is separate from the West. The Gulf gangsters rode on the back of this business network, creating front companies and trucking firms to move drugs.

A third weaker gangster system developed to the south in Michoacán and Guerrero. Here, interlocking crime families grew marijuana and opium. But they didn't control any border themselves and had to work with one of the two dominant networks to move their drugs into the United States.

By the end of the twentieth century, the most powerful trafficking family to emerge in Michoacán was the Valencia brothers, based out of the mountain town of Aguililla. Led by Armando Valencia, alias Maradona (he looks vaguely like the Argentine soccer star), they allied with the Sinaloans and trafficked through northwest Mexico.

Competing with the Valencias was Carlos Rosales, who hails from a Guerrero town called La Union, on the border with Michoacán. To move his produce, Rosales allied with the Gulf Cartel and became close to its leader Osiel Cárdenas, alias the Friend Killer (he murdered his friend because he liked his wife).

Rosales recruited Nazario and he is identified as the Maddest One's mentor. Nazario doesn't actually mention Rosales in his memoir; he was probably cautious about giving prosecutors more evidence to use against him. However, both Mexican and American agents say that Rosales was key in elevating Nazario from small-time trafficker to major player.

At this stage, Nazario ran operations inside the United States. With his base in McAllen, just across from the Gulf Cartel stronghold of Reynosa, Nazario moved drugs into Texas.

There are reports that police nabbed Nazario for marijuana in McAllen in 1994 and he did a stint in a Texas prison. Some sources say that his Christian conversion actually happened behind bars. However, I cannot find any record of this arrest in the U.S. court system. If it happened, he could have been detained under a different name. Either way, he managed to win his freedom and continue to grow his drug distribution.

Finally, in 2003, a federal grand jury in McAllen indicted Nazario for trafficking marijuana and crystal meth. Nazario is identified as a leader of a network of smugglers linked to various Texas drug busts.

Nazario's rise coincided with seismic changes in the narco world. The first was an expansion of Mexican cartels at the turn of the millennium as they got rich off cocaine profits. Mexican gangsters had reaped the bounty of marijuana and heroin for decades. Then as U.S. drug agents cracked down on the Caribbean trafficking route in the eighties and nineties,

Colombians turned to the Mexicans to bounce their white powder over their two-thousand-mile border.

The Mexicans began as paid couriers but ate more and more of the pie. By the twenty-first century, drug agents believed Mexicans moved 90 percent of the cocaine into the United States. Furthermore, Mexican traffickers were now buying the drug from Colombians for about two thousand dollars a kilo brick and selling these in the United States for upwards of thirty thousand dollars, the agents say. The lion's share of the profits had emigrated from Colombia to Mexico. Along with the cash came the bloodshed.

The second change was political. Mexico went through a democratic opening and this inadvertently shook the deep political connections of the Mexican drug trade.

In the twentieth century, Mexican trafficking was organized under the one-party rule of the PRI. The PRI created an elaborate system for controlling gangsters: it arrested some and taxed the rest. The traffickers were organized into plazas—or drug trafficking territories—along the lines of police jurisdictions. The plaza bosses paid off cops, who passed the bribes up the system. If a plaza boss got out of line, police could take him down. Money flows up like gas, and power flows down like water.

This corruption system was not static but evolved over the years. It began all the way back in 1915 when the Chinese-Sinaloans first took opium to the United States. The very first U.S. government report into this trade in 1916 alleges Mexican officials were involved.[1] In these early days, drugs were a small-scale business, but by the end of the twentieth century, drug trafficking made billions and accusations were made that the system was organized from the pinnacle of power. Under pressure, Mexican police arrested high-ranking officials, including a governor and even the drug czar.

At the turn of the millennium, this corruption system shattered. Mexico's pro-democracy movement grew along with the opening of political systems across the region after the Cold War. Finally, the PRI lost its grip on the presidency in 2000 to Vicente Fox, a straight-talking former Coca-Cola executive. Mexicans hoped that multi-party democracy would bring them prosperity and freedom. In the euphoric atmosphere, President Fox promised "the mother of all battles against organized crime."

Under Fox, troops rounded up drug lords like never before. In 2003, they seized "Maradona" Valencia in Michoacán and the "Friend Killer" Cárdenas in Tamaulipas, on the border with Texas. The next year, they nabbed Rosales,

Nazario's mentor, who they said was plotting to bust Cárdenas out of prison. Fox's government was ripping up the map of plaza bosses.

However, Fox's mother of all battles wasn't a simple fight of good police against bad traffickers. While federal forces took down some king-pins, gangster Chapo Guzmán escaped from prison and expanded into new realms—backed by some officers on his payroll. Other police sided with his rivals in the Gulf Cartel.

The escape and rise of Chapo has led to an accusation that he was supported from the top, by President Fox and then his successor Felipe Calderón. Traffickers have voiced this charge in their *narco mantas*, blankets with messages they hang from bridges. The war on drugs, they say, was only against selected cartels. Some journalists and academics also support this idea. The most prominent is Anabel Hernández in her work *Los Señores del Narco*.

Los Señores is a phenomenon in itself. The book accusing Mexico's very leaders of being in cahoots with narcos is one of the nation's bestselling nonfiction works. Hernández has not been sued for it. Yet criminal charges have not been filed against the presidents either.

Hernández is from of a generation of strong female Mexican journalists who have taken on the powerful. She was propelled to investigative reporting, she tells me, when her own father was kidnapped and murdered in December 2000 (the same month that Fox took power and Mexico's era of democracy was supposed to start).

"It is difficult for me to say this, but my father was abducted, beaten, put in a car trunk, and tied up in such a way that he suffocated. The case was never solved. The authorities asked for money to continue the invest-igation, which we refused to pay. It's very frustrating. What are you as an individual going to do against a corrupt system? This issue of my father made me change my outlook on life. For me, investigative journalism was a refuge."

Hernández soldiered on, making important exposés. She suffered threats and harassment and lived years under protection from the Mexico City police before going to the United States. She views Mexican corrup-tion as still hierarchical and organized from the top.

"I am convinced that this war on drug trafficking was never real. Its only intention was to protect the Sinaloa cartel and attack others," Hernández tells me. "Fox started his administration with just one thousand dollars in the bank. His companies were all bankrupt. Chapo Guzmán escaped on January 19, 2001. In February, Fox started to spend money, to buy property and remodel his ranch. Where did he get this money? It is completely inexplicable ... He has never been able to sue me because he cannot justify this wealth."

When I interviewed Fox, he firmly denied helping Chapo, as he has done on numerous occasions. "It is an important case, but it is not the hallmark of my government," he said. "One swallow does not make a summer."

Despite the charges, no evidence has directly linked Fox or Calderón to the Sinaloa Cartel. It remains on the record as an accusation without a smoking gun.

Whatever the truth, there is another dynamic I view as central in understanding the Mexican drug war. With the democratic opening, the government became weak and was incapable of imposing its will on drug traffickers.

Democracy did not, as people hoped, make Mexican officials honest. Many were still on the take. But they were not all on the same side anymore. Mexico's multiparty system meant competing cliques of politicians ran different states and towns and their police forces. Fox's center right National Action Party held the federal government. But the PRI still ran most states, including the trafficking heartlands in the north. Meanwhile, the leftist Democratic Revolution Party took power in Michoacán and Guerrero, bastions of the old guerrillas and leftist trade unions.

Drug traffickers might pay off officials in a town or state, but federal officers could be working for their rival. The corruption system became disorganized and turned on itself. Police began competing and actually fighting each other. In 2005, federal officers had a shoot-out with city police in Nuevo Laredo. It was a sign of the violent chaos that would spread across Mexico.

The government lost the ability to be the arbitrator that could control organized crime. Instead, gangsters disputed power themselves under strength of arms. Amid this bloodshed, the mobsters turned from traffickers into warlords. And rather than the police ordering gangsters about, gangsters fought over who could control police forces.

This fighting caused homicides to shoot up at some of the most alarming rates in the Americas. The number of killings by cartels or the security forces assigned to fight them would surge from about fifteen hundred in 2004 to sixty-eight hundred in 2008 to almost seventeen thousand in 2011.[2]

Such a sudden rise in violence grabbed global attention, and hardened war correspondents flew in to cover it. The conflict became known in Spanish as *la narcoguerra*, and in English as Mexico's drug war, or even sometimes as the Mexican Drug War—a named war in uppercase letters. Unlike the fighting in Brazil's favelas or Jamaica's garrisons, it seemed to have a start date, cartel hit squads looked strikingly like paramilitaries, and there was a prolonged military campaign against them. This gets back to the central question: should we define these conflicts as actual wars?

Despite the clear escalation of violence, Mexico's cartel clash still falls into the gray space between crime and war. But it pushes those boundaries. Between 2007 and 2014, the Mexican drug war claimed more than eighty-three thousand lives in a mix of firefights, ambushes, massacres, and "executions." It has also included car bombs, vigilante militias, and thousands of refugees.

However, it is not all about drugs. The cartels fight over fiefs for a range of rackets. The questions of corruption and power are at the heart of the upheaval. Conflicts through the ages have also been about more than what they are named for; the Opium War wasn't all about opium and the Soccer War wasn't all about football.

To describe the conflict in Northern Ireland, we use the term the Troubles—with a capital T—for the violence and unrest from 1968 to 1998. That included a mix of shootings, bombings, riots, and instability. Similarly, the Mexican drug war is a period of massacres, cartel ambushes, military crackdowns, corruption scandals, a systematic attack on journalists, narco blockades, protests, and widespread social unrest. Tragically, its end date is not yet clear.

CHAPTER 37

Nazario took over Michoacán through a serious of shifting alliances and betrayals. He took from one side, turned on them, and then took from the other. I normally favor viewing history as a series of events and reactions rather than something premeditated. But studying the climb to power of Nazario—the man who read *The Art of War*—I actually think he planned it. And it was a cunning plan.

The Maddest One returned from Texas to his homeland around 2004. The U.S. indictment haunted him, and a vacuum had been created in Michaocán by the arrest of the drug lords Valencia and Rosales. He could fill it.

This is a key problem for governments combating drug cartels. Whenever you take down one kingpin, you create a power vacuum, which hungry lieutenants and rivals fight over. Nazario was the hungriest to step into the void and reorganize the Michoacán traffickers into a force stronger than they had ever been before.

First Nazario had to unite the fragments of Rosales's organization and knock out the remnants of the Valencias. To complicate this, he was not Rosales's only lieutenant who wanted to be top dog. Another trafficker called Jose de Jesus "Monkey" Mendez also vied for the honor. To avoid confronting the Monkey, Nazario made a deal with him to divide Michoacán between them. Mendez described this pact several years later in a video confession to the federal police.

"We talked and came to an agreement," says Mendez, who is quite softly spoken, despite his Monkey nickname. "Each one of us had to control his areas. Michoacán is divided in two parts. His side and my side."[1]

Mendez describes how they named a number of lieutenants to oversee the regions of Michoacán for them. Among them were Enrique "Kike"

Plancarte from the city of New Italy, and his uncle, who they all called the Uncle, or El Tio. Another was a rural schoolteacher called Servando Gomez, alias "La Tuta."

Even as he smuggled drugs, La Tuta was still on the Michoacán school board's payroll. He was older, more educated, and more articulate than the other smugglers, and became known as the "Teacher" (Just like William of Brazil's Red Commando). Appealing to Nazario's own pseudo-intellectual discourse, La Tuta gained the Maddest One's trust and became his right-hand man. If Nazario was king, then La Tuta was the king's hand. La Tuta helped shape the cartel's ideology and became a public spokesman, calling up startled TV presenters as they broadcast live. He has a charismatic, friendly rap for TV, the air of a cultivated but down-to-earth tough guy.

Nazario then took advantage of the broader shifts in Mexico's trafficking map. In 2005, the nation's central battle pitted the Sinaloa Cartel of Chapo Guzmán against the Gulf Cartel and their paramilitary wing, the Zetas. Gulf boss "The Friend Killer" Cárdenas had founded the Zetas in 1998, recruiting fourteen former soldiers. He wanted men who could really fight, not just tattooed gangbangers. At the time, nobody noticed it as an earth-shattering event. But it started a trend of militarizing Mexico's drug battles.

The Zetas steadily expanded, recruiting former police and gangbangers that they trained in makeshift camps. As they grew into the thousands they became a semi-autonomous corporation that their masters struggled to control. If the Gulf Cartel was a country, then the Zetas were a state within a state, like the S.S. in Nazi Germany.

After Cárdenas was arrested, the Sinaloa Cartel launched an attack on the Gulf–Zeta stronghold of Nuevo Laredo. Chapo Guzmán had not yet grasped the strength of the paramilitary Zetas and believed he could sweep into the city as he had northwest Mexico. In the first wave, he recruited Maras from Central America. This was when Zetas murdered the five Maras and piled their bodies in a Nuevo Laredo house.

In response, the Sinaloans organized their own paramilitary hit squads. It was at this time, in 2004, that the Mexican drug war really began, with the fighters transforming from gangbangers to heavily armed militias.

Nazario had worked with the Gulf Cartel and Zetas to smuggle drugs into Texas. When he returned to Michoacán, he went back to them to arm and train himself so he could wipe out the remains of the Valencias who had worked with the Sinaloans. This fit in with a wider Zetas tactic at the time. As they held Nuevo Laredo, they went after Sinaloan strongholds across the country. The best form of defense is attack. When Nazario wiped out the Valencias he would be handing them Michoacán. Or so they believed.

Zeta training camps have been uncovered across Mexico. They consist of ranches where recruits learn ambush tactics and practice firing belt-driven machine guns and other heavy weapons. Nazario and his henchmen trained in one of these camps, according to Mexican and American agents.

The Zetas brought their experience from the Mexican military. But it was turned on its head. They were no longer a government army fighting a guerrilla group, but acted more like a guerrilla group themselves. They would hide in the countryside and use dirt roads to launch ambushes on military convoys, opening with a 50-cal and following with grenades and rifle fire. Nazario took these tactics to Michoacán.

Backed by the Zetas, Nazario won a swift victory against the Valencias, leaving a string of corpses around the Hot Land in 2005 and early 2006. But then Nazario made his tactical U-turn. He turned against the same Zetas who had armed and trained him. To rally Michoacán residents to his side, Nazario wrote in his propaganda messages (blankets hung from bridges) that the Zetas were "foreign invaders." He pointed to the fact the Zetas who had come to Michoacán were shaking businesses down and kidnapping. This was true. But Nazario was mum about the fact that he had invited them in. It was classic power games; you create a threat and provide yourself as the solution to it. Read: *The Art of War*.

In this fight with the Zetas in late 2006, Nazario, and his cohorts first called themselves La Familia Michoacana (The Michoacán Family). The name helped rally Michoacán people against an invader. Nazario was also a huge fan of the *Godfather* movies, which were perhaps an inspiration with their talk of mafia families. To announce its arrival, La Familia advertised its "mission" in local newspapers. One appeared in *La Voz de Michoacán*.

"Our sole motive is that we love our state and are no longer willing to see our people's dignity trampled on," said the advertisement, in which they also promised to "eradicate from the state of Michoacán kidnapping, extortion in person and by telephone, paid assassinations, express kidnapping, tractor-trailer and auto theft."[2]

This ad highlights the peculiarities of La Familia compared to other cartels. It immediately created a media face and presented itself as a kind of righteous vigilante group. This position was shaped by Nazario on his narco mission from God, but also reflects idiosyncrasies of Michoacán and its history of armed groups administering justice.

Many residents of the Hot Land seemed to believe the propaganda. Alvarez, the businessmen and contemporary of Nazario, owned a gas station by this time. He said that La Familia called for funds to help drive the Zetas out and he complied.

"People were scared of the Zetas. We were hearing about how the Zetas were carrying out massacres and kidnapping like crazy. There was a lot of fear. And La Famila presented itself as the answer, a way to protect us. We thought it would. But we fell into a trap. Nazario and his mob were just as bad as the Zetas. And the payments we made would turn into extortion."

The fight between La Familia and the Zetas was bloody. Anyone accused of giving information to the other side was murdered. La Familia stuck bodies on public display with threatening messages. And they began decapitating.

The technique of head-chopping may seem ancient, but it only began in a big way in the Mexican drug war in 2006. The inspiration for the technique is hard to pin down exactly. Genaro García Luna, the federal security chief under Calderón, said it was a copy of Al Qaeda in Iraq. Others have pointed to former Guatemalan special forces in the Zetas, who used the technique in the civil war. Whatever the inspiration, it was effective at spreading terror.

La Familia hiked the stakes. They rolled five heads onto a disco dance floor while it was packed with revelers. A cameraman filmed the atrocity and sold the video to a news agency, but the editors decided not to release it because it was too disturbing. In the film, you see the view of the cameraman walking into the Sol y Sombra club in the town of Uruapan soon after the heads have been thrown. He first fixes on the faces, which look spookily peaceful, the tension drained away with their lives. But as the image opens out you see the necks are severed and bleeding onto the white tiled floor. A message is written on a large white piece of paper and dumped by the heads.

"LA FAMILIA DOESN'T KILL FOR MONEY. IT DOESN'T

KILL WOMEN. IT DOESN'T KILL INNOCENT PEOPLE. THOSE
DIE WHO HAVE TO DIE." It then ends with the uncanny phrase that
left journalists wondering who this new cartel was: "LET THE PEOPLE
KNOW, THIS IS DIVINE JUSTICE."

This claim to be looking after people's security was a constant feature of
Nazario's rule. He installed an alternative justice system, in which local
bosses judged and punished those who carried out "anti-social" crimes
such as robbing or raping. This was the same street justice that takes place
in the favelas of Brazil and garrisons of Jamaica. But the Maddest One
added his loco twist. He pronounced in the name of the lord and punishments were in the style of Old Testament justice. Alleged criminals were
flogged, like in Roman times, or even crucified.

In the town of Zamora, the mob made a line of alleged criminals
march through the main street in the evening. They had no shirts, showing
deep whip marks on their backs, and carried signs admitting their crimes.
Mexicans refer to petty criminals as rats and they were named as such. "I
am a rat and for this La Familia punishes me," said one sign.[3]

Hot Land residents also described to me how the cartel offered a debt-
collecting service. If people were owed money, they could go to La Familia,
who made sure they got paid—and kept a third themselves for the service.
If people didn't cough up, the cartel would take their houses and force
them into exile.

This alternative justice system won support. Mexico's poor rural areas
have always been on the edge of the law and crime increased with the
opening of Mexico's political system. This comes back to the central
problem that Mexico's democratic transition focused on elections and
markets, but not on the justice system. While Mexico became more
democratic and opened its borders, it had not become safer, allowing
gangsters such as Nazario to step into this void.

Nazario had likely been dreaming of his quasi-religious rule before he
established it. For a start, he had to have had the time to write his
Pensamientos, or "Thoughts." He distributed this to his followers from late
2006 once he controlled the Hot Land.

Pensamientos reflects the hodgepodge of Nazario's ideas. Some phrases
sound like the evangelical preachers he followed.

"I ask God for strength and he gives me challenges that make me strong; I ask him for wisdom and he gives me problems to resolve," reads one entry.

Others are reminiscent of revolutionary Zapata.

"It is better to be a master of one peso than a slave of two."

And others, still, sound like they come from his beloved Kaliman.

"He who has fear and confronts it is valiant. He who has fear and runs from it is a coward."

I want to find out how much the cartel troops believed in this narco religion. So in the town of Antunez, I talk to Hilario, a former gunman for Nazario's army, who served with a mob lieutenant called Toucan (named after the tropical bird found in southern Mexico). A wiry thirty-four-year-old with tattoos on his neck, Hilario was jailed for cooking meth in California before being deported to Mexico and joining the Maddest One's militia.

Hilario describes how he was made to attend a course to study Nazario's writings. I had heard of these courses before, but he gives me fascinating details.

"A bus came to the town and picked us up. It took us to Morelia for the course, which lasted all week. We studied *Pensamientos* and all we ate was rice and beans. On the last day, Nazario came out to talk to us. He was wearing all white like Jesus."

When he describes this, I think of Colonel Kurtz in *The Heart of Darkness*. Nazario took over his tribe, got a God complex, and went off the rails.

Nazario also spread his message in evangelical temples and Christian drug rehab centers he funded. This came at a time when many Mexicans turned to Protestant groups amid a historic decline of Catholicism. In 1950, more than 98 percent of Mexicans professed to be Catholics. By 2010, the number had dropped to 82 percent. Many in poor criminalized communities felt the staid Catholic Church didn't speak to them like the new sects. Some turned to religious deviations such as the Santa Muerte, or Holy Death, a female grim reaper figure.

Hilario says that he was going through a tough patch when he first came back from the United States and Nazario's religion helped him. But as he got closer to Nazario, guarding meetings when he met with Toucan, he saw the Maddest One as a hypocrite. He said Nazario could switch between his alter egos of righteous preacher and cold killer.

"He would suddenly flip. One second he was talking about religion and the next he was ordering a hit on somebody."

However hypocritical he was, Nazario's faith served a purpose. His rules kept troops in line and gave the movement a semblance of purpose, a mission. His narco hit men weren't just carrying out wanton murder. They were waging holy war.

CHAPTER 38

While Nazario delivered his unholy justice, two thousand miles away in Washington, lawmakers grappled with America's latest drug craze: methamphetamines. Their efforts would inadvertently hand the Maddest One a billion-dollar business opportunity.

Like with cocaine, German scientists discovered amphetamines in the nineteenth century. They are cheap and effective stimulants that give you energy to move fast, work fast, and speak fast, hence the nickname: speed. Japanese scientists improved the formula to make the stronger methamphetamine. Meth gives a rush of energy that can last more than four hours, along with the ability to have sex for a generous chunk of that. (It has an inhibitory effect on ejaculation.) Several sides in the Second World War used meth to keep soldiers alert during grueling campaigns; German pilots took it in a pill form called Pervitin before their blitzkrieg airstrikes and there are claims that Japanese kamikazes were on it during suicide missions.[1]

In postwar America, some people used meth for work, especially truck drivers on long hauls. Pharmacists also sold a meth diet pill called Obetrol. An old newspaper advertisement for it shows a fat skier unable to move. "Either lose 45 pounds or wait for six more inches of snow," says his slim skiing buddy.[2] The answer: take Obetrol and shake like a speed freak until the pounds burn off.

In 1970, Congress banned meth under the Controlled Substances Act—a cornerstone of Nixon's War on Drugs. Enterprising crooks realized it was easy to make your own from ingredients such as pseudoephedrine, which is found in cold medicine. The chefs walked out of pharmacies with box loads of meds and cooked the meth in bathtubs. Biker gangs dominated this industry, not only serving truck drivers but also a growing number of partiers wanting a boost. It became a poor man's cocaine, used in rural America. It was also a hit in the gay scene in San Francisco.

By the turn of the millennium, American meth use had rocketed, especially in small towns in the American heartland. In his beautiful book *Methland*, Nick Reding explores the causes, focusing on Oelwein, Iowa, population 6,126. He paints a portrait of the industrialization of agriculture and the loss of community leaving a depressed and soul-searching town turning to crank. Meth also gained popularity among workers sweating long hours in meatpacking factories, many of whom were undocumented Mexicans.

As meth use spiraled, doctors saw its horrific side effects. It wasn't all speeded up fun and marathon sex. Tweakers, as users are known, came with meth mouths of rotted teeth and black gums. They also suffered insomnia, hallucinations, and paranoia. Some scientists argue the drug causes brain damage, irreversibly changing the pleasure, learning, and motor systems.

Amid a furor, Congress approved the Combat Methamphetamine Epidemic Act of 2005, restricting sales of meds with pseudoephedrine. People can now only buy small amounts with prescriptions and their names and addresses are registered.

The measures were impressive at smashing the American meth industry. The number of labs busted on U.S. soil went down from a peak of almost 24,000 in 2004 to less than half that, or 11,573, by 2013. But the industry migrated to Mexico. Meth seized on the southern border climbed steadily, from 2.3 metric tons in 2004 to 5.2 tons in 2009 to 15.8 tons in 2014.[3] Such movement of drug production is known as the balloon effect; you pressure the balloon in one spot and the air moves to another.

Several Mexican cartels moved into the meth trade. But Nazario and his Familia had distinct advantages. Many members had spent time in small U.S. towns and knew how to cook. I talk to one chef who first learned to make meth in San Bernardino, California, in the nineties—before he served seven years in U.S. prison and was deported. Nazario himself was indicted for meth in Texas in 2003—before the 2005 law.

An even bigger advantage is that Michoacán is home to Lázaro Cárdenas, the busiest freight port in Mexico. Cartel contacts bought precursors in countries including China, India, Syria, Iran, and Egypt and smuggled them in titanic loads through the porous Pacific harbor. Once they had the ingredients, La Familia cooked it on an industrial scale; they ditched the biker bathtubs for "super labs" hidden in the mountains. Soldiers found water cisterns big enough to irrigate major food farms, along with dozens of barrels and generators. Instead of churning out meth by the pound, they made it by the ton.

Mexican gangsters developed a stronger product than the bikers ever had. They favored a crystal form that comes out in white, blue, or pink colors. DEA agents said it was the cleanest meth they had seen, some close to 100 percent pure.

With such immense production, many cooks themselves liked to tweak and sell it locally. In the Hot Land, they call it *hielo*, or "ice," because of its transparent crystalline appearance. Gangsters in Apatzingán became bad speed freaks just like the meatpackers in Oelwein, Iowa.

Nazario responded by banning the sale of his meth in Michoacán. He describes this in his writings, and residents that I talk to in Michoacán villages confirm it is true. The Maddest One did seem to have principles after all. As he had suffered from substance abuse himself, he didn't want those around him suffering. Or maybe he knew that if his troops were meth heads, they would be too paranoid. Some ignored it and took ice anyway.

But Nazario had no qualms about selling meth to the gringos. La Familia pumped it through their U.S. network, often among Michoacán émigrés. It established its biggest operations in California, Texas, and Georgia. But its tentacles reached many other states, including New York, Missouri, Mississippi, Oklahoma, Colorado, both Carolinas, and Washington.

Narco economics are notoriously hard to calculate because of their clandestine nature. But DEA agents have said that Mexican meth now accounts for 80 to 90 percent of the drug used by Americans.[4] A 2012 White House study called "What America's Users Spend on Illegal Drugs" estimated there were 1.3 million chronic meth users and another half million occasional tweakers. It estimated that together they spent between six and twenty-two billion dollars on meth every year.[5]

Mexican gangsters don't take all of that. Cartels generally sell wholesale, only serving up multiple kilos. Unlike the Jamaican posses, they don't want to expose themselves on street corners, where police can easily detain them. The meth dealers on the street include people of all races and social classes, often with no knowledge of which cartel might have handled their drugs.

But wholesale meth is massively profitable because it is so cheap to make. To get cocaine you have to buy it from Colombians or Peruvians and ship it through Central America. But Mexican gangsters make meth themselves from precursors at industrial prices.

"These guys get ingredients worth sixty-five dollars and turn them into drugs worth eighteen thousand dollars or more," says Vigil, the DEA's former head of international operations. "That wealth turns into power. It allows the cartels to buy sophisticated weapons. It gives them an opportunity to expand their distribution tentacles. It allows them to buy political favors through corruption and it allows them to buy the necessary equipment, boats, and aircraft to transport those drugs."

The drug business is funny money that makes millionaires and billionaires stupidly fast. Nazario, the man who grew up drinking river water, handled tens of millions of dollars. This made him an increasing megalomaniac. But he was also calculating, investing in the political protection and muscle to keep hold of his business.

Nazario paid and armed foot soldiers, creating an army of thousands that moved into the entire 113 municipalities in Michoacán, and spilled into the surrounding states of Guerrero, Guanajuato, Jalisco, and Mexico State. Growing so fast, La Familia became a sprawling organization that Nazario would struggle to control. It also gained the attention of Mexican and U.S. agents. Michoacán traffickers were no longer scattered and weak but had become one of Mexico's biggest cartels. When President Calderón took power in 2006 and declared a national offensive on drug cartels, he pointed to La Familia as the first mob he wanted to destroy.

CHAPTER 39

Soldiers force suspects to their knees and line them up along the side of the road into the Michoacán mountain town of Aguililla. Two helicopters buzz overheard, flying low over the curving street while a convoy of Humvees rumbles into the central plaza. Seeing the troops and their prisoners, many residents rush to their homes. Others stare at the soldiers like they are from a strange foreign army come to occupy their town.

It was December 13, 2006, two days after President Calderón declared his offensive on drug cartels and I had rushed with other reporters to see it in action. Under orders to hit La Familia, the army swept through the Hot Land. By Christmas, the soldiers had arrested dozens of suspects, seized mountains of guns, marijuana, and meth, and shot dead several alleged cartel thugs in firefights.

Calderón launched his offensive in Michoacán for several reasons. He was born in the capital, Morelia, so it was personal to him, his friends in business lobbies moaning about the shoot-outs and dumped bodies. Some owned holiday homes or hotels in the Hot Land. La Familia was also the newest cartel on the block and looked like a gang that the government could take down. If they decimated one cartel, security chiefs figured, then others should fall into line. Nazario may also have offended Calderón's religious sensibilities. Calderón was a strict Roman Catholic and his father had supported the Cristero uprising back in the 1920s. Nazario was a blasphemer as well as a narco.

Throughout Calderón's six-year reign, Michoacán was a key and personal part of his offensive. He flew to the military base in Apatzingán and saluted troops while dressed in an olive green army jacket and floppy camouflage cap. This broke a tradition of Mexican presidents who have emphasized a clear separation from the military since the end of the

Mexican Revolution.[1] Later, when federal police claimed they had killed Nazario, Calderón spoke on national radio to personally celebrate the takedown.

> In Michoacán, the civil elected authority has to govern. Criminals cannot govern, however friendly or generous they might be. The law of the cartel cannot reign in a state. The government has to rule and that is what we are doing there.

And in one of his last acts as president, Calderón returned to Michoacán to inaugurate a road and sang a popular ranchero song called "El Perro Negro," or "The Black Dog," along with a brass band. The song composed by José Alfredo Jiménez is fittingly about a tough from Apatzingán who is shot dead (read: Nazario?). It was written before the days of drug ballads but follows a similar tradition. The Apatzingán tough is referred to as a *valiente* or a brave one, which became a term for drug trafficker.

> *On the other side of the bridge,*
> *From Piedad Michoacán,*
> *Lives Gilberto, the valiente,*
> *Born in Apatzingán.*

Calderón said his military offensive aimed to reestablish the rule of law in spaces where it had been lost, impose the power of government over the power of gangsters. His language moved into the gray area between crime and war. He never legally declared a war. But he spoke to his troops in martial terms, calling traffickers "the enemies of Mexico" and talking of "recovering territory." He also relied overwhelmingly on the army. At the peak of the campaign, he had ninety-six thousand soldiers and sixteen thousand marines fighting cartels in a dozen states.[2] Mexican governments had used the army against gangsters before, but never on this scale.

But rather than being emblematic of victory, Michoacán highlighted the problems that Mexican security forces faced against cartels. In May 2007, a convoy of soldiers traversed the hills near a town called Carácuaro, when about thirty gunmen ambushed them. Five soldiers died, the biggest loss for Mexico's army since the 1994 Zapatista uprising.

Calderón called the soldiers "national heroes" and ordered in more troops. They came under more fire. While soldiers shot dead and arrested hundreds of La Familia operatives, they lost a steady stream of their own men. In Apatzingán, a group of gunmen holed up in a house and held off soldiers for two hours in a prolonged firefight in broad daylight. The shooting caused children to flee their kindergarten and panic rippled across the city. A colleague, Mauricio Estrada, took video of the firefight on a camcorder. It looks like footage from Iraq, soldiers crouching behind their Humvees and trees as bullets hit the dirt street, tearing up dust.

La Familia thugs had training from the Zetas and meth money to buy a huge stockpile of guns. They got these largely from U.S. gun shops, smuggling them back in the same trap cars that they took their meth north with.[3] And they fought like a guerrilla group, ambushing and hiding inside their communities—like Mao's fish in the sea.

Robert Bunker, the external researcher for the U.S. War College, describes how the cartel battle tactics mirror those of insurgents.

"These guys use the fifty cals and burning vehicles to create avenues of approach, and they create kill zones. These are all very military-like behaviors. If we look in the United States, criminals don't tend to stand and fight. They tend to run. And criminals don't tend to set up ambushes."

Narcos often fight with platoon-size units, like the thirty gunmen who ambushed soldiers in Carácuaro. Other times, they are as large as companies with more than a hundred gunmen. In the biggest battles, the cartel thugs have reached battalion level, with more three hundred men-at-arms.

President Calderón faced the old problem of fighting against guerrilla tactics: You cannot control the territory simply with military bases and patrols. The enemy hides and then comes out when the troops are out of sight. You need to control every inch of ground.

The U.S Army Field Manual says that in counter-insurgency you need a ratio of one soldier for every fifty residents.[4] The Mexican troops never had close to these odds. During Calderón's presidency, there were rarely more than ten thousand troops in Michoacán, giving them one soldier for every four hundred. The troop levels were low because the army was spread out fighting cartels in eleven other states. This was another of Calderón's problems: he couldn't fight cartels on so many fronts at once.

Meanwhile, El Tio claimed in a 2006 interview with the Mexican magazine *Proceso* that La Familia had four thousand gunmen. Later La Tuta would claim they had ten thousand. These spokesmen could be exaggerating their strength. But even if they were tripling it, La Familia had an immense force by guerrilla standards.

In some cases, La Familia gunmen would ambush soldiers and lose, suffering heavy casualties. The soldiers were better trained and disciplined than the gangsters, some of who would be stoned or high on meth. I long wondered why cartels waged such suicidal tactics. A lieutenant colonel who fought in Michoacán offers me an answer. He says it was a way to put constant pressure on the army. And the cartel had plenty of young triggermen who it treated like cannon fodder.

"The cartel wants to show the population that it is powerful and can attack the army. They want people to lose respect for us. And soldiers suffer from bad morale because they are being shot at all the time. Another problem is that they pin us down with gunfire, while they could be moving drugs somewhere else."

The Mexican army hit back hard. But those it hit were often innocent civilians. Within six months, Mexico's human rights commissioner had received more than fifty complaints from Michoacán residents of soldiers beating them with rifle butts or torturing them. In one horrific incident, four teenage girls described soldiers taking them to a base and beating and raping them over several days. A medical examiner confirmed the assaults. The attack happened shortly after the ambush that killed the five soldiers. Maybe this was the soldiers' revenge.

On the other side, La Familia targeted anyone accused of giving information to the army. "See. Hear. Shut Up. If you want to stay alive," said a note in the town of Tepalcatepec. Next to it was a severed head. Residents were caught between two brutal sides.

While Nazario battled the army, he carried on fighting the Zetas, pushing them out of the state. The Zetas hit back. They were furious that Nazario had double-crossed them. Their revenge, it appears, was a heinous attack on Michoacán civilians.

On September 15, 2008, revelers in Morelia celebrated Mexico's Independence Day in the central plaza. Per tradition, people ate, drank, and sprayed each other with foam. At eleven P.M., the governor made his cry of "Viva Michoacán, Viva Mexico," and rang a bell. On the third ring, people heard two thundering bangs. For a moment, they thought they were fireworks. Then bloody victims fell onto the ground. Panic surged through the crowd. The assailants had thrown two grenades into the packed square of revelers.

A cell phone video shows the instant. People are still cheering the Viva

Mexico when the bangs go off, and applauses turn to screams. Many run, terror on their faces. Dozens crouch in pain. The Mexican national anthem booms in the background. Eight people died and more than a hundred were injured, some crippled.

A week later, security forces arrested three men for the attack. They confessed on camera to being Zetas and throwing the grenades. La Familia also blamed the Zetas, in messages written on blankets. "We unite ourselves to the pain of our countrymen, innocent people that do not need to live with the terrorism of the Zetas," said one of the narco mantas.

A raging President Calderon also called it a terrorist attack. The term can be tricky to define. But in this case, I agree with him. I think slaughtering civilians in a public celebration for some ulterior gain is terrorism.

But whatever you call it, shocked Mexicans asked the underlying question: Why? Why were gangsters hurting civilians if their fight was with a rival cartel?

The answer could be that the Zetas wanted to hurt La Familia by doing what they call *calentar la plaza*, or "heating up territory." By causing such violence, they would force Calderón to launch further operations into Michoacán, which would disrupt La Familia's operations.

But as always in the fog of the Mexican drug war, clouds of doubt exist. Rumors spread that Nazario himself might have been behind the attack. He was responding to the military offensive with terror that would hurt the government—but he blamed it on the Zetas to keep the support of his people. In 2015, more doubt was added when a judge released the three suspects, ruling that they had been tortured into making their confessions.

I still think Zetas the most likely culprits. But people spending their lives suffering from shrapnel wounds may never be sure.

Following the Morelia attack, Calderón pushed harder into Michoacán. If the Zetas had wanted to heat up the plaza, it had worked. The lead was now taken by the rapidly expanding federal police.

The federales are built on paramilitary lines, wearing black armor and often hiding their faces with ski masks. They pack a level of firepower akin to the soldiers but boast a higher level of education. While army recruits are mostly from Mexico's poor south, many federales hail from Mexico City.

When Calderón took power, the federales only had six thousand officers for the whole of Mexico. But raising the security budget—with the help of three hundred million dollars a year from Washington under the Merida Initiative—the president expanded the force exponentially. When Calderon left office, the force would boast thirty-seven thousand officers. They operated inside Mexico's Security Ministry, under Genaro García Luna, a square-jawed former intelligence agent. García Luna was a key architect in the offensive on cartels and close to the president, in many ways, the real number two in Calderón's administration.

I talk to Elias Alvarez, a tall beefy commissioner, who headed the federal operation in Michoacán for several years. Alvarez gives me the official line that federales played by the rules and respected human rights. But I also want to get a more candid perspective from the rank and file. For this, I find an officer called Ramon. Meeting Ramon through a mutual friend, I get his detailed and frank revelations of what the feds really did.

Raised in the working-class Iztapalapa borough of Mexico City, Ramon had begun a law degree at the National University but dropped out after his girlfriend got pregnant. The federal police was a decent career option, with a starting salary of more than a thousand dollars a month, way above the $180 minimum wage. Ramon signed up in 2006 and rose a couple of ranks, before going to Michoacán in 2009.

Like many federales, the first thing that grabbed Ramon's attention was the lure of women while away from home.

"There are amazing-looking women in Michoacán, tall girls with brown skin and green eyes. And they love the federal uniform. Everyone is calling you *comandante*, whatever your rank is. We were like an elite and the girls recognized that. We would sneak women back into the hotels or take turns in the patrol cars."

It wasn't all fun, however. The government pressured the federales to bring in Nazario. But it was hard to find the kingpin as Nazario moved in the hills, protected by spies and residents who loved and feared him. So instead they went after his lieutenants. The idea, Ramon explains, was that if they smashed the midlevel of the cartel pyramid, the top would come tumbling down.

The feds sniffed out the gangsters' weak spot: parties. The Hot Land villains loved a wedding, a girl's fifteenth birthday, or any other excuse to dance to a brass band and get plastered. Most of these parties were family related, so the key was to follow the gangsters' loved ones, especially their children and girlfriends. The technique soon scored results.

In April 2009, four hundred federales stormed the baptism of a baby born to a La Familia member. They nabbed forty-four gangsters (not including the baby). Among them was a Familia lieutenant called Rafael Cedeño, a close confidant to Nazario. Cedeño had been posing as a state human rights commissioner as he executed people.

Ramon describes how they squeezed Familia prisoners with the Mexican police's tried and tested technique: torture.

"I didn't want to get involved at first. But everyone was doing it and I just went along. After a while, it became normal. We did what we had to do to get the information. We smacked them, starved them. We put plastic bags on their heads and watched them spit blood. And they all talked in the end. They gave us more addresses and phone numbers and we arrested more of them."

The federal tactics of storming family gatherings infuriated Nazario, and he counterattacked in July 2009. He struck as an immediate reaction to the arrest of one of his top men, Arnoldo Rueda, alias La Minsa. But the scale of attacks indicates that La Familia had been planning an offensive for some time, gathering intelligence on where and how to hit the feds hard.

The federales nabbed Rueda in a safe house on the edge of Morelia in a predawn raid on a Saturday. Minutes after they pulled him from his bed and shoved him into a car, gunmen stormed out of a nearby house, shooting and hurling grenades in a wild attempt to free him. The feds repelled them.

La Familia rapidly called its men to arms across Michoacán and in neighboring Guanajuato. They drove in convoys to police bases and sprayed them with grenades and gunfire; they ambushed police cars on patrol; and they stormed into hotels where police were staying.

Ramon himself came under fire in one of the assaults. He was in a federal convoy heading toward a base in New Italy when their vehicles got rattled by gunshots.

"They had high ground from a ridge above us and we were trapped in our vehicles. It was a bad fucking situation. As officers tried to get a line of fire they were hit. It is one thing when you are firing at people. I can even enjoy that. But when you come under fire it is really not very nice."

One officer was killed and three were injured before the federales managed to return fire and their assailants fled. They had got off lightly. In their deadliest hit, La Familia gunmen kidnapped twelve federal police off duty in the municipality of Arteaga. The gunmen tortured them and dumped their bodies along the road. "So that you'll come back for another one of us," read a message by the corpses.

Within three days, La Familia had launched twenty-three attacks, killing sixteen feds and injuring many more. Mexican columnist Ciro Gómez Leyva called it La Familia's "Tet Offensive."

Then right after the wave of attacks, La Familia raised an olive branch. Spokesman La Tuta delivered the message by brazenly phoning a Michoacán news show as it broadcast live. The startled anchor gave a worried frown and then cautiously asked La Tuta a question.

"The attacks on the police. Are they by you? After the arrest of Arnold Rueda, La Mensa?" The anchor's voice was shaky.

La Tuta launched into his answer as the newscast aired.

With all respect for the president of the republic. We respect the army and the navy. We have nothing against them. We know it is their work but we are asking that they watch how they behave ... Show respect for our families. That is all we are asking. If you respect us, then we will respect you ... The only thing we want is peace and tranquility. We know that (drugs) are a necessary evil ... It is not going to finish. We want to arrive at a consensus. We want to arrive at a national pact.

La Tuta's underlying message is that the gangsters will back off if the government backs off. Going back to Ben Lessing's theories on the logic of crime wars, it is a classic case of violent lobbying. La Familia murdered police to pressure them to stop arresting their operatives and busting their meth labs.

La Familia used techniques similar to those of insurgents around the world. But the logic driving the violence, as defined by Lessing, is what differentiates them. The Taliban ambush troops to topple the Afghan government. La Familia simply wanted the Mexican government to leave them alone.

But there is another dimension to this fighting: the role of corrupt police. Nazario had been digging his claws deeper into the Michoacán state apparatus. Some of this corruption has now been exposed. But the officials proven to be on the cartel payroll are likely the tip of iceberg. First La Familia controlled many mayors and their police forces in the

Hot Land. The small-town rulers had often grown up with the gangsters, and if they didn't cooperate then they were extremely vulnerable. Next, La Familia got state police commanders, judges and deputies on its payroll.

Federal agents arrested a state police commander called Miguel Ortiz who worked for La Familia, and he described how the corruption functioned. As always, these confession videos need to be scrutinized carefully, but Ortiz's testimony is convincing—if terrifying. The confession was particularly chilling as local journalists in Morelia say Ortiz had been a friendly cop who liked to chat and joke with them; until they saw him on the ten-thirty news describing how he chopped people's heads off.

Known as Tyson because of a thick neck and bulldog face, Ortiz began working with Michoacán gangsters as a twenty-one-year-old cop in 2001, becoming a fully fledged member of La Familia when it took to the scene in 2006. If La Familia wanted someone taken prisoner they would call Tyson and he would arrest them and hand them over. Tyson also began to execute the victims himself. While Mexican cops used to just turn a blind eye on drug traffickers, they had become full-on mob assassins.

Tyson's murders got him promoted within La Familia. He was given his new rank of head of the Morelia plaza at a ceremony in the countryside. He traveled on the road from Apatazingan to Aguillilla and then left the car and walked two hours into the hills. Nazario himself arrived to bless the promotion.

Tyson then officially left the police. But he still wore his badge, drove around in cop cars, and commanded officers as well as hit men. In 2009, Tyson participated in the attacks on federal police. He describes getting a call in the morning at five A.M., very shortly after La Minsa had been arrested, and told to get as many state police cars as he could. Cartel gunmen swept in from the countryside to fire on the feds. Some of the La Familia hit men were traveling in a Mitsubishi van, which got a flat tire. So Tyson transferred them to patrol cars and drove them to a Walmart where they got into taxis and fled the scene.

His confession that state police worked with gangsters to attack federal officers gets back to one of Calderón's key problems: the security forces themselves had fragmented.

Not every official in Michoacán worked for the cartel. But those who didn't risked death. Ben Lessing also has a term for this type of violence.

He calls it "violent corruption," bloodshed to pressure officials to work for the gangsters. In Mexico, it has long been known as *plata o plomo*, the choice of the silver of a coin or lead of a bullet.

Lessing believes this source of cartel violence against the state is more common than the "violent lobbying" terror attacks, but less visible. Whereas violent lobbying often targets random police officers as a form of pressure, violent corruption hits specific officers who refuse to fall into line.

In 2010, gunmen assassinated the state undersecretary of public security. In his confession, Tyson said it was because the victim was interfering with police who were on the cartel payroll. Then they went after his boss, Michoacán Security Secretary Minerva Bautista.

I talk to Bautista about the attack. She is a modest and down-to-earth woman with a history of activism that led her to the state security job. It strikes me how the Mexican drug war throws such ordinary government workers into the line of fire.

"We had been at a state fair. I was worried so I was in a bulletproof car with bodyguards. We drove down the road when we saw this big truck trailer blocking our path. I didn't realize what was happening at first. Then bullets hit our car.

"I can't really say if I was scared or not. I didn't have time to think. I just lay down between the seats and listened to the bullets rattling against the side of the vehicle. They went on and on. I thought for a minute, 'This is it. I'm dead.' But somehow, I made it through."

The gunmen fired an astounding twenty-seven hundred bullets at Minerva's car. Two of her bodyguards died. But she only suffered light injuries.

The attack shows that while some Familia gunmen were trained, others were amateurs. A soldier would have known how to create a line of fire at a fixed point, until the caps sliced through the armor. The assailants just sprayed and sprayed. But still, twenty-seven hundred bullets would make any guardian angel work overtime.

CHAPTER 40

In October 2009, residents of Jester Avenue, a leafy street in Oak Cliff, suburban Dallas, were awakened by the sound of a police squad smashing down the door of a wooden one-story home. The owner was a quiet thirty-six-year-old Mexican national who rarely showed up to the street of middle-class families with kiddies' bicycles and plastic pools in the gardens. He was also the regional operative for La Familia Michoacana, distributing its crystal meth and cocaine across Texas. The home contained piles of Tupperware boxes with gleaming white crystal besides stacks of dollar bills.

Other officers were simultaneously making raids across not only Texas, but the entire United States. They kicked down doors in California, New York, Mississippi, Massachusetts, Missouri, Georgia, Nevada, and Washington. Over forty-eight hours, a total of three thousand police nabbed 303 suspects—all alleged to be Familia operatives.

When Attorney General Eric Holder announced what he called "Project Coronado," he described it as the largest ever U.S. operation against a Mexican drug cartel. The officers seized $3.4 million in cash, 730 pounds of meth, and four hundred weapons, including a homemade grenade. The op, he said, shows how the U.S. stands shoulder to shoulder with the Mexican police officers being dumped on roadsides.

The sheer level and depravity of violence that this cartel has exhibited far exceeds what we have, unfortunately, become accustomed to from other cartels. La Familia operates primarily from the state of Michoacán, Mexico. However, as we've shown today, their operations stretch far into the United States. Indeed, while this cartel may operate from Mexico, the toxic reach of its operations extends to nearly every state in the country.

That's why we are hitting them where it hurts the most—their revenue stream. By seizing their drugs and upending their supply chains, we have disrupted their 'business as usual' state of operations. As I have said before, this is not a one-country problem and solving it will take more than a one-country solution.

The busts followed several years of investigations and hundreds of other arrests, Holder revealed. In 2010, the U.S. Treasury named Nazario as a designated kingpin. This meant that any American company or person doing business with him could be fined a million dollars. This was followed by more busts and intelligence packaged into so-called Project Delirium. This name, an agent tells me, was a dig at the delirium of the Maddest One.

The first question that jumps out from Coronado is why the feds targeted La Familia for their biggest ever operation. The Sinaloa and Gulf cartels have been around longer and trafficked more drugs. Holder calls out La Familia as being more violent. But the Zetas have probably killed more people in Mexico, and some in Texas.

However, American agents give me two explanations for going after La Familia on such a scale. The first was that their Mexican colleagues were forthcoming about passing the Americans information on the Michoacán mob. Calderón and García Luna were determined to smash La Familia and show at least one emblematic victory. But they were frustrated by grappling with a machine that was pumped with billions of dollars. They needed the Americans to cut off the oxygen of greenbacks.

Secondly, American agents bumped into La Familia wherever they went. With so many operatives in immigrant communities, La Familia built a distribution network in a few years that rivaled older cartels, carving out cells into the heart of small-town America.

The network grew so fast that it became exposed. Seasoned Sinaloan hoods used communication that was harder to trace, such as encrypted cells and Skype calls. But the Michoacán gangsters discussed deals on phones, which the feds tapped. Among them was Jose Gonzalez, alias the Panda, who worked out of Chicago. He made daily calls to a boss in Michoacán. Ricardo Hernandez in Dallas also chatted about meth deals on his phone. Both pleaded guilty and were given multi-decade sentences.

Their court files reveal telling details about the mob's modus operandi. Unlike the eleven million undocumented migrants in the U.S., the ranking Familia operators came in with papers. They lived in middle-class neighborhoods, often with their families, and bought houses in cash.

In Dallas, Hernandez would oversee meth shipments coming from the border to safe houses across the metropolitan area. Dallas acts as a hub for the cartel, a wholesale warehouse where dealers from other cities and states can collect their supply. Hernandez took in mountains of cash, which his hoods hid in trap cars, and drove south to Michoacán, the court documents say.

Hernandez and Gonzalez admitted to being midlevel La Familia operatives. But many others swept up in Coronado were on the bottom rung. They were often young, some only teenagers, and undocumented; the cartel paid them peanuts to sit in stash houses, eat pizza, and keep their eyes on the towers of crystal. If they got nabbed, they often got multi-decade sentences. But most knew nothing about the cartel; some didn't even know who they were working for.

While Coronado sounds impressive, the seizures also had a limited impact on La Familia. Three million dollars is a fortune to most of us. But the meth industry makes billions. The 790 pounds of meth seized was also a piss in the ocean of the forty metric tons that Americans could have smoked or snorted that year. La Familia was hurt, but it could gradually replace its people and reestablish operations.

Furthermore, the U.S. agents struggled to flip their detainees and get intel that could nail Nazario and his court in Mexico. The men were too scared that their loved ones back home would be cut up or boiled in acid. Mexican police were left with their own sources to nail Nazario.

In December 2010, the federales finally got their break. They got intelligence that Nazario would be going to an early Christmas party in a village called El Alcalde. It's a ramshackle settlement right next to the ranch where the Maddest One grew up, full of his friends and family. In his seasonal generosity, Nazario would be handing out Christmas presents, including fridges and cars, to his loyal supporters.

The feds claim they got the information from an anonymous tip-off. But I find that hard to believe. To mobilize thousands of troops, they would need secure intelligence, either from a phone tap or an informant who the feds were sure was good. The Mexican government was offering a thirty-million-peso reward for Nazario, so there was incentive for someone to snitch.

Alvarez, the commissioner who led the operation, described to me how they assembled two thousand officers to sweep on El Alcalde. But straight away, he saw problems with the logistics. They wanted to move forces quietly without tipping off the target, but that was hard with such numbers. It was also challenging to surround El Alcalde and cut off escape routes as it was in hilly country. Forces were spread out in difficult terrain.

On December 8, the federales got word that Nazario had arrived. Vast convoys of federal police rolled down the roads. Black Hawk helicopters (provided by Washington) buzzed over the hills. Cornered, Nazario ordered a counterattack. The feds had expected this. But they had not expected its ferocity.

"They had a wall of more than forty trucks at the entrance to El Alcalde," Alvarez says. "There was about five hundred *sicarios* [hit men]. They opened fire and it was a long and hard battle."

The battle turned out to be one of the most ferocious in the Mexican drug war, and indeed in the nation's recent history. Police fired from helicopters, but came under attack from Browning machine guns that almost brought a chopper down.

The firefights erupted throughout the entire night and into the next day. Like in the "Tet Offensive," La Familia hit other police positions and shoot-outs erupted in twelve municipalities in Michoacán, including the state capital, Morelia, New Italy, and Uruapan. This time the federales had prepared not to leave easy targets.

The cartel thugs also hijacked dozens of trucks and buses and torched them on the main highways, blocking the movement of police. This tactic is borrowed from radical protesters, and has been used by cartels across Mexico, winning its own term: *narcobloqueos.*

During this fighting, Nazario fled El Alcalde with a contingent of gunmen to a nearby village called Holanda. The feds caught him halfway there, leading to another blazing firefight. In this maelstrom, the officers claimed they shot dead Nazario, but said his gunmen dragged his body into the hills.

Overall, the feds shot dead more than fifty cartel members, Alvarez claims. Five federal police officers were killed and others were injured, he says. At least three civilians including an eight-month-old-baby died in the crossfire.

The police officer Ramon had been drafted back to Mexico City after suffering an automobile injury. He was in the federal police headquarters in Mexico City during the battle, but was communicating with officers on the ground. He tells me a different story.

As the firefights raged, he says, federal police lost more than fifty officers.

"They got ambushed and couldn't hold them. It was a total disaster."

If the claim is true, it would be the worst single loss for the Mexican security forces in recent history.

When I visit El Alcalde in 2014, I find a veteran who fought with La Familia. Like many others he later flipped sides to join the vigilantes, and I talk to him at a barricade on the edge of the village. He describes how they ambushed a convoy of federal trucks on the road from Apatzingán, an account that fits in with Ramon's version. I travel the route and it has several points that would favor ambushes, high ground over a narrow road.

"We blocked the road on both sides and they were trapped. We had a good position and we just kept shooting. We fired thousands of bullets and grenades. It was a massacre."

I went to the Federal Police public relations department and described the testimonies I heard. Officials said they stuck to the number of five casualties.

However, it makes sense that high casualty levels could have been hidden. Such a loss would have been devastating for the police, the Calderón administration, and the morale of Mexico generally. The losses could have been shifted to other stats. During the administration of Calderón, the security ministry conceded that 384 federal police officers were killed. They also admitted that at least forty-one disappeared.

When Calderón first launched the offensive, the federales held ceremonies for the fallen troops. But they abandoned these at the end of 2010, precisely around the time of the battle of El Alcalde.

Such losses would also be an incentive to the federales to make the claim they killed Nazario. The alleged death of the Maddest One took the spotlight off the police casualties. It made a mission that caused so much death appear worthwhile.

Claiming a kill with no body was audacious. But the government went for it anyway. Security spokesman Alejandro Poiré made the declaration publicly at a press conference on December 10. He said they killed Nazario on December 9, into the second day of the battle. Four days later, President Calderón spoke of the death in an interview on Mexico's W Radio.

"Everyone knew about the fiesta, the meeting, the summit, and the principal leader fell," the president said. "What happened was the severest hit to La Familia."

Four years later, he would eat his words.

CHAPTER 41

On a dirt road by the village of Holanda, amid wild bushes and twisted trees, are thirty-seven iron crosses painted white. The largest, over six feet tall, is for the Maddest One. "Nazario Moreno González, The Maddest One," is painted on the horizontal bar. "Born March 8, 1970. Died December 9, 2010."

This site, deep into bandit country, is where Nazario and his henchmen fled the federal police but got trapped. Journalist Francisco Castellanos discovered it, visiting under the guard of the cartel itself. I come later when vigilantes are reclaiming the area. It is still a difficult place. As photographer Ross McDonnell and I take pictures, vigilantes watch nervously for cartel thugs.

In front of the crosses is a shrine lit up by a lantern. At its center is a San Nazario statuette, like that in the Mexican army museum. For the narco cult of Saint Nazario, this was the holiest temple, their Mecca.

When police first discovered the crosses, they said it was evidence that Nazario was dead, and believed his body was somewhere underneath them. Now we know he wasn't, the crosses take a different light; they were part of an elaborate hoax to make us believe Nazario was dead.

One giveaway could be the writing on the crucifixes. While some are adorned with typical narco nicknames, others have Muslim names including Muhammed, Abdul Azim, and Sulaiman. In some messages, a rival cartel had mocked La Familia, calling them Islamic fundamentalists on meth. Were La Familia hitting back at that joke? Or did Nazario, in his flirting with holy war, like making a link to Jihadists?

* * *

Other signs also pointed to Nazario's death. One was a recording of right-hand man La Tuta addressing a crowd of supporters. The audio was leaked to Mexico's biggest TV station.

"God is with [Nazario] in his holy glory," La Tuta says. "He is with you all, and he knows that he can count on you . . . Everyone get ready with their guns."

To this an old woman cackles out, "What lovely words, *profe*. This encourages me. *Arriba La Familia Michoacana*."

Decoding this audio gets into the crazed triple bluff of narco political espionage. The police might have leaked the recording, wanting to confirm the kill. But now we know that it was a hoax, it looks like Nazario was pulling the strings all along.

The appearance of the Saint Nazario statuettes is also tricky to decode. When I reported on them at the time, I emphasized how traffickers had turned their fallen drug lord into a saint after his combat death. Now we know that Nazario had survived, the process of his "canonization" reads differently; he encouraged his own veneration, his megalomania reaching dizzy heights.

It seems unlikely Nazario actually planned to fake his death. He wouldn't have wanted the attack on his village, which almost killed him. But he took advantage of the government's blunder, putting up the crosses and the Tuta ruse.

Many would view a fake death as an opportunity to escape. Nazario was a multimillionaire from the meth trade; he could have run to the Caribbean and spent his life on a beach sipping daiquiris now that nobody would be after him. But Nazario didn't see it like that. Most cartel bosses can't walk away; however much money they have, their horizons are limited. They don't want to sit in a villa in Italy or a ranch in Australia. They prefer to wallow in the hills of the Sierra Madre, romancing young village girls and being saluted by farmers, a king in a gangster kingdom. Nazario didn't see his fake death as a chance to escape. He saw it as a chance to turn himself into a deity.

The first action the ghostly Nazario took was to rename his mob the Knights Templar after the Jerusalem-based crusaders. The name shows how delusional the Maddest One was by this stage. (Operation Delirium . . .) But it also served a purpose. The concept of the Knights could create a tighter cult. The gunslingers became Templars, sacred soldiers. The red Templar cross became an identifiable graphic in safe houses and on guns, a brand symbol. The Maddest One even made up a coat of arms. Its shield has the face of Saint Nazario in the top left corner, Jesus on the right, a Templar cross on the bottom left, and an ax and mace on the bottom right.

He also introduced a pocket-size Templar book of codes, listing fifty-three commandments the Knights had to obey. I am reminded of the manuals of the Brazilian commandoes. Like those, the orders were a mixed bag. Some stressed the lifelong commitment of being a Templar.

"Every officer who has accepted being part of the group the Knights Templar of Michoacán is in it for life and cannot abandon the cause," says order number four.

Others play up the pretense of the cartel fighting for a righteous cause.

"The Knights Templar will establish an ideological battle and defend the values of a society based on ethics," says order number twelve.

And others underline how the member's loved ones were at risk if they messed up.

"Any knight who betrays the Templars will receive the maximum punishment, their properties will be taken and the same fate will befall their family," says number fifty-two.

The Templar concept also allowed the Maddest One to expand his religious-warrior fantasy. He introduced ceremonies with the crusader theme, in which gangsters dressed up like knights to initiate new members or promote operatives. A federal police raid netted 120 plastic helmets used for these rites. It wasn't all fun and fancy dress though. Initiates were made to cut up victims. And in some cases, they were made to eat the victim's flesh.

Naturally, this cannibalism has caused revulsion, even making headlines in British tabloids that hardly touch foreign issues. It is sad to sensationalize such depraved behavior. But it was a tragic fact, confirmed by federal police.

People are often stumped in explaining how the gangsters got so sadistic. It perhaps helps to understand how the violence was institutional. It was not just individuals suddenly acting in evil ways all over Mexico. The cartels armed people and gave them the mission of carrying out terror, which brought out their most devilish behavior. It's the same way that armies all round the world commit atrocities. But it can be worse when you don't have a government to install some limits. It is like how African warlord Joseph Kony made child soldiers eat the flesh of their victims.

The name Knights Templar confuses many observers who wonder why flesh-eating meth traffickers would call themselves after warrior monks. It is also odd as Nazario was evangelical. To add to the confusion, the Knights Templar put up banners welcoming Pope Benedict XVI in 2012 when he visited the Mexican state of Guanajuato, which borders Michoacán.

"We want peace in Guanajuato. Don't think about starting violence with the arrival of his Holiness Benedict XVI. You've been warned," said one banner hanging from a bridge. The pontiff could rest assured that Nazario and his mob guaranteed his security.

However, it is not worth getting too caught up in trying to decipher the contradictions of Nazario's religion. Even he regards himself as nuts, the Maddest One. But however confused, his unholy ideology helped in controlling his cartel.

The myth of Saint Nazario and his Knights Templar spread through song. Mexico's trafficking heartlands feed an industry of bands that cheer on gangsters. Unlike many musicians who struggle to make their living, the drug balladeers have an effective business model. They charge traffickers per ballad and can make big money playing their private parties (which can mean putting up with days of drug-induced debauchery).

Bands wrote dozens of songs about Nazario, La Tuta, Kike Plancarte, and their head-chopping henchmen. But the real anthem of the Knights Templar was performed by a California-based band called the BuKnas de Culiacan. Like all narco songs it was banned on Mexican radio. But it went viral on YouTube, alongside photos of the Templar coat of arms and dead policemen. The song salutes the mix of modern and ancient in the cartel.[1]

They combine horses with new trucks,
Swords and shields with Kalashnikovs and bulletproof jackets,
The men are sturdy,
They are from Michoacán,
They were La Familia,
But now they are called,
The Knights Templar,
Their fights are like crusades,

From catapults and grenade launchers,
From the little boars (50 caliber bullets),
Trucks that are 4 by 4 and armored,
They say they were like monks,
And today they are guerrillas,
They have their temples and their camps,
They are brave bastards,
But if you betray them,
Or do stupid things,
They are like the inquisition.

(Chorus)

They are under the command
Of the most wanted,
The one that they say was murdered,
The story is another legend,
The legacy of the macho goes on
The madman that was converted
To a Knight Templar.

The Templars' musical connections also gained media attention when it was exposed that a local diva was in fact the daughter of Templar boss Kike Plancarte. Melissa Plancarte was known as the Barbie as she resembles a Barbie doll. She doesn't sing drug ballads, but croons a style called *grupera*—a Mexican poppy country music dominated by glamorous women. Melissa scored a moderate hit with a song called "*Yo soy así*" ("I'm Like This"), in which she rides a horse dressed in slinky clothes and argues with a boyfriend besides a waterfall.

When local newspapers outed her for having a cartel father, they showed a photo of her dressed in Templar colors. In the picture, she wears a super-tight dress with a red cross covering her breasts while brushing her hair back and pouting her lips. For people who had lost family members and suffered kidnappings at the hands of the Templars it was too much to bear. Comments splattered social media calling for her head.

"A career built on the suffering and pain of working and innocent people," said a Facebook message.

"You are pretty but it is shame you have no brain. He who lives by the gun dies by the gun and you are as guilty as your father to allow the abuse and do nothing," said another

Children of drug traffickers have long moaned that they get punished for the sins of the fathers. Perhaps they have a point. You don't choose for your dad to be a mass-murdering capo. But in any case, in show business, no publicity hurts too much. The Barbie Grupera was invited to speak on top Spanish language TV shows from Univision to CNN Español about her tribulations, boosting her online video views from thousands to millions.

The rebranding of his cartel as the Knights Templar gave Nazario a chance to kick out those he hated. Only his most loyal followers were allowed to join the new gang. The rest stayed in La Familia, which the Knights Templar declared war on and drove out of Michoacán.

This creates confusion and some reports have mistakenly said that the Knights Templar were a splinter from La Familia. Really, the Templars were the core of the cartel, and those who stayed with the name Familia were the splinter. Among them was Nazario's old rival Monkey Mendez.

In his later testimony, Mendez claims he broke with Nazario because the Maddest One's thugs were extorting and kidnapping. Arrested Templars claimed the opposite and said they forced the Monkey out because his men were out of control. It's most likely that both sides committed atrocities, but Nazario was jealous about sharing power and wanted an excuse to turn on his old comrade.

The Templar gunmen rapidly exterminated the Monkey's henchmen, leaving a pile of bodies outside Morelia. The Monkey fled Michoacán, only to be arrested by federal police in the quiet city of Aguas Calientes in June 2011.

The remnants of La Familia were pushed into the neighboring Guerrero and the State of Mexico next to the capital. They continue to cause trouble there to this day, burrowing deeper into North America's biggest metropolis.

CHAPTER 42

The lumps of iron ore lie abandoned in such titanic piles that they look like a metallic lunar landscape in the green hills. Soldiers shut down the mine here outside Aguililla as it belonged to the Knights Templar. But once they had confiscated the hundreds of tons of raw metal nobody knew what to do with it so they have left it to reflect the scorching sunlight.

Next to the heaps of ore, I find a disgruntled mine contractor. Rolando Chavarria normally rents his truck to haul iron from the mine to the city, but he has been out of work since the soldiers put up *clausurado* signs. He squats under a tarp, cooking beans and tortillas.

"It is good the government fights crime but what about us?" Chavarria asks over his boiling pots. "We need some income. I am going to starve to death if they don't get this mine open again soon."

He is not alone. When they government finally cracked down on Templar mining in 2014, they shuttered more than a hundred pits in Michoacán. This took away six thousand direct jobs, according to the miners' union. In total, security forces confiscated a mind-numbing seven hundred thousand tons of minerals, leaving heaps like the one in Aguillila throughout these mountains.

The amount of ore shows the Templars moved into the iron industry on an immense scale. But it was only one of various businesses they diversified into. They also hacked their way into limes, avocadoes, cattle, construction, and real estate. In fact, it became hard to run any business in the Hot Land without the Templars wanting a piece.

While Nazario always had his hands in different rackets, evidence indicates that the Knights Templar really took over the Michoacán economy from 2011 onward. American drug agents like to say that cartel diversification proves the war on drugs is working. As the feds hit

Nazario's network in the U.S., including operations Coronado, Delirium, and another called Knight Stalker (versus the Knights Templar), they bit into the cartel's finances. Calderón's military crackdown also put the cartel on costly war footing. The gangsters could have been forced to look for extra funds.

But other evidence challenges this assertion. The Justice Department's 2013 "National Drug Threat Assessment" concludes Mexican meth was more abundant than ever. "Price and purity data and increased methamphetamine flow across the Southwest Border indicate rising domestic availability, most of which is the result of high levels of methamphetamine production in Mexico," it said. This glut had caused prices to drop, it said, but only because Mexican cartels were so productive; if anything they were victims of their own success.

Nazario could have expanded his business portfolio because of pure greed. Like in legal corporations, the drive is to get bigger and bigger, swallowing smaller entities and breaking into new markets. Nazario and his lieutenants kept on wanting bigger mansions and more cars and recruited more people who had to be paid. The Knights Templar diversified because it could, and the government seemed incapable of stopping it.

The Knights Templar's first step into its new businesses was extortion. This had begun several years back when Nazario rallied residents to help them fight the Zetas. Many people began paying voluntarily, as the Apatzingán businessmen Alvarez describes; they believed that they should pay Nazario because the Zetas were worse. The mass graves the Zetas left in northeast Mexico were good propaganda to make this case.

This is a classic way that organized crime gets its teeth into communities. Oxford University's Diego Gambetta is one of the top specialists on the mafia. He describes how businesses in Sicily will often voluntarily pay mobsters to look after them, creating what he calls "The Business of Private Protection."

"The mafia's 'consumers' are quite cynical about it and know that the mafia protection is often not good but a lesser evil," Gambetta writes.[1]

According to Gambetta, when people pay voluntarily, it is not extortion but classic protection. People are complicit in organized crime and don't go to the police, allowing the mob to grow. But in many cases, the payments soon become involuntarily. This is what happened in Michoacán.

"They asked for more and more money," Alvarez says. "They wanted more than a million pesos from my businesses. It got to a point that they were going to bankrupt me."

The victims began as those typical of shakedowns: taxi drivers, restaurants, hotels, junkyards, discos all had to pay their monthly quota or face the consequences. These businesses move a lot of cash and it is easy to find the owners and force them to pay.

In Latin America's crime wars small businesses are usually more vulnerable than big companies. A gang of men with guns can walk into a restaurant and tell the owner to pay up or his family will suffer. But if they arrive at corporate offices, it can be harder to get through the door.

However, the Knights Templar became so powerful, they also preyed on multinationals. I talk to executives at mining and agricultural companies that concede they made payoffs in Michoacán. In return, the Knights Templar would guarantee them security through the area. Many preferred to give the quota than take the risks, slipping into Gambetta's business of private protection.

The risks that multinationals faced came to international attention in 2012, when Templar gunmen hit a local unit of PepsiCo in one of the biggest attacks on a foreign company in Mexico in recent years. The PepsiCo unit Sabritas sells potato chips so its trucks have to travel extensively. However remote the villages in Mexico, Sabritas potato chips always seem to make it there. "You can never only eat one chip," says their slogan, painted on their yellow trucks beside a smiley face.

At dawn on Friday, May 25, a Sabritas worker drove a truck into Apatzingán to make his delivery to a supermarket when gunmen ordered him out. While he watched from the sidewalk with a gun to his head, they doused the truck with gasoline and set it ablaze. Attacks followed across Michoacán and into Guanajuato. By the end of the weekend, gunmen had destroyed more than thirty trucks and two warehouses belonging to PepsiCo.

There was immediate speculation the attacks backed up an extortion threat. However, the Knights Templar said otherwise. In their narco mantas, they said they were "punishing" PepsiCo for working with police; federal agents had hidden in Sabritas trucks to nab a Templar operative, they claimed.

"The companies are sources of employment for Michoacán society and we respect their labor," read a manta. "But they must limit themselves exclusively to their business or they will be punished."

PepsiCo officials denied police using their vehicles and said they didn't know why they were targeted. Either way, the attack served to back up the Templars' extortion bids. The pictures of the Sabritas' smiley-faced trucks twisting in flames splashed across newspapers, passing the threat to every corporation working in the state.

Michoacán agriculture was an especially lucrative business for the Templars. The avocadoes are known as green gold as they are shipped north in such vast quantities, especially when it's the Super Bowl and Americans munch on guacamole. The Templars taxed farmers for every kilo of avocadoes they grew. Like all good taxers, they also sucked money from other links in the production chain, including the wholesalers, veg shops, and exporters.

After they had been extorting the industry for a while, the Knights Templar realized they didn't have to shake down a small percentage, but could take over businesses directly. Corn growers in various Michoacán villages describe the process to me. They were all forced to sell their crops to the Knights Templar at a price the mob fixed at three pesos per kilo. The Templars then sold on this corn to the tortilla makers for six pesos a kilo. They doubled their money for doing next to nothing. The Templars did the same with beef. A rancher in the town of Tepalcatepec tells me how the Templars forced him to sell his cows for twenty-two pesos per kilo; and they sold them on for thirty-eight pesos.

Alongside avocadoes, limes are the big moneymaker in Hot Land farming; the citrus fruit features strong in Mexican cuisine, from flavoring tacos to easing down tequila. Many are traded in the regional market on the edge of Apatzingán, where I take a closer look at how the business is run. On designated days, the wholesalers and producers go to the market to set up deals. Lots of men in cowboy hats wander around with plastic crates full of limes. When they make a deal, they write it on paper; the wholesaler agreeing to buy x amount of kilos.

The business involves a lot of cash as many farmers won't take checks. I hang out with some lime wholesalers, twin brothers, who set up deals to buy forty tons at twenty pesos a kilo that day. They promise eighty thousand pesos or about sixty-five hundred dollars, which they will pay in cash.

To put order in this market, a group called the Citrus Growers Association sets the daily price. The Templars saw the best way to skim from the business was simply to take over this association. They could set the price that included their cut.

Unsurprisingly, head-chopping meth cooks are not the best people to responsibly set lime prices. They pushed it up to take more for themselves, doubling the price between 2013 and 2014. This created a ripple effect of people feeling the pinch of high lime prices across the economy. Bars from Mexico City to New York looking for limes to ease shots complained of costs. At salons in Mexico City specializing in kiddies' parties, lime juice got clipped from the menu. Canadian supermarkets charged a dollar for a lime. Drug cartel power had reached an area that nobody would have imagined.

The Templars' foray into mining was also a gradual process. Chavarria, who carries ore in his truck, explains how the cartel got steadily more involved.

"First they charged quotas to everybody who worked here as well the owners. We carried on as normal, just having to pay them. But then they took over the mine for themselves."

The Templars increased productivity by ignoring environmental regulations and government permits. Hills that hadn't been exploited were soon churning out iron. This is the magic of gangster capitalism: the cartel can muscle whoever it works with and ignore laws. While this causes a lot of harm, it made many people money, including contractors such as Chavarria.

"I had work all the time so I can't complain. And so did everybody else. The industry creates a lot of secondary jobs, from the people bringing food to the workers to those selling us gas. To be honest, I have never seen the mining industry so productive."

The Templars took over mining as the Chinese economy was on fire, its factories hungry for metal. The port Lázaro Cárdenas has boats sailing directly to Shanghai. In the first six months of 2013, ships carried a record 5.5 million tons of iron from Lázaro.[2] A considerable amount of this would have been Templar rock, with the cartel controlling over a hundred mines.

Seeing no bounds, the Knights Templar waded into another money-maker: local politics. The gangsters had long paid bribes to officials. But as they became so strong, they flipped this deal. Instead, mayors had to pay the cartel.

These shakedowns were exposed when videos later emerged of mayors sitting with La Tuta and discussing terms. Other mayors went on record describing how they had to pay the Templars. To defend themselves, they claimed they were victims of extortion rather than themselves corrupt.

The mayors said they paid 10 percent of their annual budget to the Knights. In small towns such as Tepalcatepec, the budget was only about four hundred thousand dollars a year. But the big cities of Lázaro Cárdenas and Morelia moved tens of millions of dollars. The federal government provides much of mayors' budgets, so the gangsters were effectively skimming the federal pot.

Shaking down officials is an immense display of power that has not been given sufficient attention. For decades, it was the state extorting gangsters. When Nazario flipped this, he altered the nature of narco politics.

The Michoacán town of Antunez, population nine thousand, was a physical testament to this gangster warlord power. When you first drove in, it looked like another parochial Mexican town, with dusty roads, brightly painted homes, and a quaint church. But the first clue that things weren't right was a shrine to Saint Nazario by the entrance sign. The Templars placed these throughout their empire, marking the rule of the Maddest One. Continuing into the central plaza was the mansion of the local Templar boss, Toucan. The mansion even shared a wall with the main church.

I later went into the mansion when the vigilantes stormed it. It had swimming pools served by a bar and vast bedrooms with en-suite bathrooms, showing the amount of money that the Templars were moving. All is built in the ostentatious style of "narco-tecture," with garish colors and Greek pillars alongside pictures of cowboys. Toucan boasted two other huge properties in Antunez, including a ranch with stables full of fine breeds. In gangster style, the horses were named "The Lover," "The Gladiator," "The General," "The Dandy," and "The Prophet."

The Templars built similar mansions across Michoacán. Even in a hamlet called La Huerta, I find a mini-mansion for a local boss called "El Monstruo"—The Monster. In the city of New Italy, the capo Enrique Plancarte had a mansion with an indoor pool.

Nazario himself had flamboyant hideaways. Among them was a sprawling ranch known as the Fortress of Anunnaki, with horse stables, a ring for cockfights, and a casino. When I visit the area where Nazario was born, vigilantes show me more of the Maddest One's properties. He had acquired vast stretches of land, forcing residents to sell or give him their homes.

It is rough hilly terrain covered by woodland so it is hard to get a sense of the entire size of the Maddest One's estate. But we get to a big plain that runs toward a river, and a resident signals that all of this belonged to Nazario. It reminds me of the aristocrats of England owning chunks of the countryside; Nazario had become a feudal lord.

But while the government could not restrain him, Nazario's predatory behavior finally woke a monster. And a time came when dishwashers, lime pickers, and doctors had the chance to prove themselves in the face of gunfire and terror.

CHAPTER 43

Clad in sombreros and baseball caps and clutching assault rifles, shot-guns, and machetes, the men take defensive positions on the hillside neighborhood of Tierra Colorada. Their envoys knock on doors to call the residents from their homes. As the sun lowers over the hills, two hundred residents wander out cautiously and gather in a clearing. A middle-aged man with a protruding belly and a rifle hanging from his shoulder struts in front of them. He addresses the crowd in a steady, confident voice.

"You have suffered too much at the hands of kidnappers, extortionists, and drug cartels," says Esteban Ramos, a taxi driver turned militia leader. "It is time to fight back. If you are in favor of our community police and want to join or support us, then step forward."

The crowd is silent. Nobody moves. Finally, a middle-aged man in a baggy red T-shirt stands up and walks forward. He is followed by a youth, barely out of his teens. Eventually, nine men stand in front of their brethren and raise their hands. The crowd cheers. A new vigilante squad has been born.

Watching this moment, I can't help but feel moved. It reminds me of the scene in the movie *The Patriot* when Mel Gibson's son is recruiting a militia to fight the Brits. It might be a world away from the American Revolutionary War. But these men also face a brutal enemy that plunders their land, and risk their lives taking a stand.

Covering Mexico's vigilante movement was like watching an action movie in many ways. It was full of larger than life characters, took dramatic twists, and had high-intensity action scenes. Like good movies, there were inspiring heroes on a moral mission and despicable baddies, such as Nazario, a big enough villain for any Hollywood set. But like the best movies, it became morally hazy by the end, the heroes showing cracks, and finished leaving you with a mix of fear and hope of what might come next.

The vigilantes had a rock star appeal. The left saw the pictures of ragged men with AKs as a revival of Latin America's guerrilla movement. But the right also sympathized with farm owners and businessmen bearing arms to defend their livelihood. And immigrants in the United States were delighted to see people rising up in their homeland in a narrative that dovetailed with the American spirit of frontier vigilantism.

The self-defense squads had articulate leaders who won massive public sympathy when they appeared on TV. There was Hipólito Mora, the humble lime farmer in his bulletproof vest; José Mireles, the gallant tall doctor with the Kalashnikov easing off his shoulder; and Estanislao Beltrán, known as Daddy Smurf because of his zany long beard. They provided fresh relief compared to the crooked politicians people were used to watching.

After covering Mexican gangsters for a decade, I was also swept up. Cartel thugs had decapitated, burned, kidnapped, extorted, raped, savaged, and ravaged. Police, soldiers, judges, mayors, lawmakers, and governors had betrayed their people. When the vigilantes rose against this, it put some confidence back in the human spirit, and the strength at the core of the *pueblo mexicano.*

Yet, after two years, the problems of vigilantism were too big to deny. One thing is holding up the ideal of armed struggle. The other is seeing it in action. It's ugly. As vigilantes drove out the cartel, they tortured and murdered. In 2013 and 2014, police tallies count 1,894 people killed in Michoacán, the victims of both sides.[1] The vigilante ranks also filled with the gangsters they were supposed to be fighting against. And you wondered how much better off anyone had become.

To understand how militias of cow farmers, cab drivers, and clinicians took on narcos, you have to look at the long history of vigilantism—and community policing—in Mexico. This idea on how to fight Mexico's post-modern problem of narcos came from its most ancient indigenous communities.

Since the Spanish conquest, certain forms of alternative policing have existed alongside the mainstream justice system. The viceroys of the Castilian crown controlled cities and silver mines while they allowed indigenous villages a level of self-rule. After independence from Spain, the central government struggled with civil war in which vigilantes were active in swathes of the country.[2] Following the 1910 revolution, competing armies also held sway, and their ragtag militias administered rough justice; iconic photos show irregular troops hanging bandits from trees.[3]

The PRI government that ruled from 1929 until 2000 forged a more powerful central state. Mexico escaped the civil wars and coups that plagued much of Latin America. But some armed groups claiming the right to administer justice did appear. Among them was the Party of the Poor led by teacher Lucio Cabañas, who named its militia "The Peasant Justice Brigade." Cabañas was inspired by revolutionary Zapata and became an icon for the Mexican left, especially in Guerrero, where current vigilantes hail him as a hero.

"These historical anecdotes go on influencing many political actors from various parties," Cuauhtémoc Salgado, president of the Guerrero section of the PRI, tells me. "Guerrero has been characterized as a bellicose state."

When the Zapatistas rose in 1994, they adopted an unorthodox leftist position, combining anarchistic elements with a revival of indigenous Mayan customs and a touch of Catholic liberation theology. Their armed challenge lasted only twelve days before a bishop brokered a cease-fire. But in the decades since, the Zapatistas ran "Boards of Good Government" over as many as 150,000 people.

The Zapatista councils claim "autonomy" and enforce their own justice, including crackdowns against drug and human smugglers. Alcohol is banned in many communities. However, most Zapatistas do not use prisons; punishment often consists of community work, such as chopping wood.

The Zapatista rebellion inspired indigenous groups across the country. Mexico is home to more than fifteen million indigenous people, more than any other nation in the Americas.[4] Often living on the margins of the system, they organized themselves to fight rising crime.

The biggest community police movement emerged in Guerrero with the founding of the Regional Coordinator of Community Authorities (CRAC) in 1995, a year after the Zapatista uprising. The CRAC officers are volunteers who serve between one and three years, during which time the community provides them with food. When cartel crime ravaged Guerrero in the 2000s, the community police movement grew to fifteen hundred officers. I speak to one of their leaders, Eliseo Villar, a stocky indigenous man in the force's olive green color, and he explains why they took up guns.

"Our project of a community system imparts security, justice, and education by bearing arms. Clearly, we have a right to do this, because the government has not attended to our needs. For this we saw the need to organize ourselves, to have our internal rules and identify ourselves with a uniform."

The CRAC is a more moderate group. But it also uses controversial tactics, not only detaining suspects but also imprisoning them in makeshift jails. Suspects are tried by elected commissars and assemblies voting in public plazas. While the CRAC emphasizes rehabilitation, they also lock up some prisoners for years.

The CRAC cites the United Nations declaration on indigenous people as giving them the right to impart justice. However, the issue of how indigenous justice systems should co-exist with mainstream laws is a subject of deep debate.

Influenced by the Guerrero community police, Purépechas over in Cheran, Michoacán rose up against the Knights Templar in 2011. Fed up with Templar gunmen illegally logging in their woods, they took up rifles and blocked their roads with defensive barricades made from sacks of sand and stone. These barricades would define the new type of trench warfare seen across Michoacán.

Robert Bunker, the national security scholar, looks at these developments using the disease metaphor.

"It is almost like the community has created its own antibodies. What has happened is the federal government is not providing security to the people. So the people have a choice. They can accept the abuses of the cartels and the gangs or they can arm themselves. This is a survival instinct."

Following these indigenous community police, the self-defense squads emerged in 2013 and spread to a dozen narco-ravaged states. The squads first rose in the Costa Chica area of Guerrero in January. In response to the kidnapping of a village spokesman in the town of Ayutla, vigilantes with shotguns and machetes went house to house until they found him tied up. The militias then spread like wildfire into nearby towns where people suffered from extortion and kidnapping.

The new movement was spearheaded by activist Bruno Placido. While Placido had been in an indigenous community police force, his militias morphed into something different. They spread from indigenous villages to Spanish-speaking towns. And rather than just guarding their own streets, they would mass hundreds of vigilantes to go after cartel targets. Once they occupied towns, they would call people into squares and enlist residents into ten-man cells. (A similar number forms a squad in formal military units.)

When vigilantes rose up in the Michoacán Hot Land the following month, they used identical tactics.

The vigilantes who fought Nazario and his Knights began plotting in hushed voices and darkened rooms. Ranchers, builders, and teachers complained quietly to each other about the Templars, but it seemed too risky to take a public stand. However, as vigilantes rose against gangsters in neighboring Guerrero, the bravest decided it was time to fight.

By 2013, the level of Templar abuse was off the chart. The thugs kept extending their extortion demands. They didn't just limit shakedowns to businesses. They charged people for the right to hold private parties. They taxed people for buying new cars or plasma TVs. They charged them for the number of square meters of their homes. In response, thousands of residents fled to the United States and were among the rising claimants for political asylum.

But the vigilantes say the real breaking point—or, as the Mexican saying goes, the drop that spilled the glass—was when the Templars used rape as a weapon of terror. As Templar thugs collected extortion payments they would abduct the wives or daughters of residents. They would also hang around outside schools, checking out the girls they wanted to rape, the vigilantes say.

Vigilante leader Doctor Mireles discussed this terror in widely broadcast statements. He claimed that in his small-town clinic in the last quarter of 2012, he dealt with forty girls who were raped. The youngest was just eleven years old. It is hard to verify these numbers. But some level of rape was almost certainly taking place.

The bastion of the Michoacán vigilante movement was in the farming towns of Tepalcatepec, Buenavista, and La Ruana. While they were Hot Land towns, many residents considered the Templars outsiders, from Apatzingán. Templar thugs also treated the towns as conquered territory they could loot. This is a common pattern across Mexico; cartels are more benevolent in their hometowns and more predatory in turf they take over.

The first uprisings took place in La Ruana and Tepalcatepec. Only a few dozen were there on day one. The lime farmer Hipólitio was one. Another was Juventino Cisneros, a cattle rancher known as El Tilín.

Cisneros is a wiry man who was fifty-two when the vigilantes rose. Like many in the movement he had been in the United States, spending eight years in Bakersfield, California. He returned to run his cattle business, only to find his town ravaged by the cartel. As well as paying Templar extortion, he suffered a deep personal loss when his son was murdered. He was sure the cartel did it, but no one was brought to justice.

"You feel so impotent with all the odds stacked against you. The police were corrupt. Mayors were on the cartel payroll. The government had failed us. It had left us by ourselves. But finally our moment came."

Cisneros joined with the plotters. They had a few guns stashed and got relatives to bring others from the United States. They planned their action for February 24, 2013, which was symbolic as it is Mexico's flag day.

They used the word "uprising," to describe their stand against the Templars. They would be in revolt, but against the cartel, not the federal government. This reflects the weirdness of narco politics in Mexico, and what it means to have chunks of the state captured by cartels.

La Ruana rose first under Hipólito, with Tepalcatepec following several hours after. Just fourteen of them launched the revolt in Tepalcatepec, marching with their guns to the cattle market where Templars would come to extort them.

"Of course, we were scared. We thought we might all be killed. But we knew it was now or never. And people joined us. Within an hour, there were fifty of us. By the end of the day we were hundreds strong. The people were ready."

The Templar gunmen did not come that day, giving the self-defense squads the chance to build barricades. The Templars finally attacked some weeks later, killing a vigilante, but the squads shot dead several cartel gunmen.

"Many of us were in rifle clubs and knew how to shoot. A lot of these cartel assassins were young and drugged up," Cisneros says. "We showed them they were not invincible."

The war was on.

CHAPTER 44

When the Michoacán self-defense squads won their first victories, new members flocked to their ranks. Some were well-meaning. Others were paid to fight. Many ranch owners got their workers to take up guns for the cause. They often paid the same two hundred pesos, or about sixteen dollars, a day they gave them working on the farm. Instead of picking limes or milking cows, they bore rifles and slept in the trenches.

I find a paid vigilante at the barricades who had just been deported from the United States for drunk driving. Coming home jobless, he joined the militias, going within a few weeks from $150 a day working construction in San Jose, California, to $16 a day risking his life. But he said he was happy to fight the tyrannical Templars.

Some dubious characters with gangster connections also joined the movement. The vigilante leaders made the call to let anyone join if they were against the Templars. This was perhaps their biggest error. However, at the time they faced a powerful enemy and wanted all the help they could get. Some recruits had criminal records for guns or fighting. Others had drug trafficking and cartel connections. Some of these hustlers wanted to topple Nazario because of the Templars' predatory behavior; they might grow marijuana but be against kidnapping. Others wanted to take over Nazario's trafficking routes, and worked for rival gangs such as the Jalisco New Generation Cartel.

I don't believe (as some people have claimed) that the Jalisco Cartel ever orchestrated the entire self-defense movement. But they controlled certain players within it, supplying them with guns and money, which made their factions some of the strongest. Mexico's federal attorney general also cited evidence of these links.[1]

War costs. Vigilantes needed to buy food, gas, and bullets. As they liberated areas from Templar extortion, some businessmen were happy to contribute. Michoacán émigrés also sent money to help their brethren, with the vigilantes setting up Facebook pages. And players with cartel connections brought in suitcases of cash.

The self-defense squads created a paramilitary structure. They formed squad-sized units of ten to twenty men, each with a point man. These reported to midlevel commanders, who in turn reported to regional commanders, natural leaders like Doctor Mireles and Mora. About thirty of the regional commanders formed a ruling council. However, there was never a single supreme leader and the commanders jockeyed among themselves, later bickering and acting like petty warlords in their own turfs.

Some vigilantes had served in the army, and they trained others in battle techniques such as how to advance into gunfire. They got many guns from the United States; the vast majority of cars entering Mexico are not searched so it is easy to drive south with trucks of rifles, as the cartels do. As they gained territory, vigilantes also ransacked Templar safe houses and seized their rifles, cars, and bulletproof jackets.

To increase their odds against the Templars, the vigilantes built their own homemade armored vehicles. The Zetas had built such road machines, so the vigilantes followed their designs. The media joyfully calls these fighting machines "monsters" or "narco tanks." They don't actually have treads or cannons like tanks, but they look plenty nuts enough, resembling the souped-up trucks of *Mad Max*.

I check out the fleet of trucks at the vigilante HQ in Tepalcatepec (in a cattle stables). Each machine looks more crazy than the next. Francisco Espinoza, a twenty-six-year-old cowboy turned vigilante, explains how they built them.

"We were going into heavy gunfire and we needed protection. So we made these monsters of our own, based on the vehicles that the Zetas had built. There were people in the town with metal workshops and they helped us put them together. As we learned what worked in the field we improved the designs."

The trucks have armor up to four inches and even mobile sand trenches to soak up bullets. They have swiveling gun turrets and shooting galleries to fire from inside, with slits that remind me of the arrow holes at English castles. And they have battering rams to smash enemy cars or even plow into buildings.

* * *

The self-defense movement erupted shortly after Calderón finished his term and President Peña Nieto took over. Calderón left office after his military offensive had turned into a humanitarian disaster, with sixty-six thousand cartel-related deaths, twenty thousand disappearances, and widespread cases of soldiers torturing and killing. Peña Nieto brought the PRI back to power after twelve years in the wilderness, partly because many voters felt it had been safer in the old days.

Taking office, Peña Nieto's team launched a campaign dubbed in political circles "changing the narrative." In laymen's terms, this meant changing the conversation. They steered officials away from talking about crime and got them to talk about reform and investment. Captured gangsters were no longer paraded in perp walks. Peña Nieto stuck to suits and business talk rather than flak jackets and warmongering. In his first days in power, the tactic was blissfully successful. Magazines ran stories about "Mexico's Moment," a time when the Aztec tiger was finding its place in the sun.

When the vigilante movement erupted a month into Peña Nieto's term, some thought this could also be a presidential plot. The conspiracy theorists found ammunition when Peña Nieto hired Colombia's former top cop Oscar Naranjo as an adviser. In Colombia, paramilitaries also called themselves self-defense squads as they fought FARC guerrillas and carried out massacres. Mexico was copying the Colombian tactic of using militias to do the dirty work, they mused.

Personally, I prefer the cock-up theory to the conspiracy theory. I think Peña Nieto was as surprised as everyone else by the vigilantes. His handling of them over the following years shows a stumbling change of positions rather any clear strategy. He switched from attacking them to ignoring them to working with them to attacking them again.

The federal government first clamped down on Michoacán vigilantes in March, two weeks after they had risen. Soldiers stormed the town of Buenavista and nabbed thirty-four from a self-defense squad, accusing them of links to the Jalisco cartel. They also seized forty-nine Kalashnikovs and Uzis, bulletproof vests, and three ounces of marijuana. (Many vigilantes smoked weed.)

However, the arrests had no deterrent effect, and the vigilante movement kept growing. Within months, clamping down would mean arresting thousands, so the Peña Nieto government switched tack to ignoring it. It accompanied this with denial. Vigilantes were not a real problem, officials said. There were hardly operating anywhere.

The reality was that self-defense squads had become a formidable force that was transforming the Mexican drug war.

Principal battlefield commanders emerged among the vigilantes. These included a former Texas car salesmen known as Simon the Americano and a rancher called Alberto Gutierrez, who went by the nom de guerre Comandante Cinco. Along with leaders such as Doctor Mireles, these commanders moved from sporadic gun battles to a strategy of conquest.

I followed Cinco on his operations. Until a few months before, the forty-year-old had led the life of a wealthy farmer. Now he led convoys of vigilantes to seize towns. He always carried an AR-15 and sidearm and sported a bulletproof vest and baseball cap with "Cinco" stitched on it.

"Did I ever I think I would be in a war? No way," he tells me, between shouting orders on a chain of cell phones and radios. "I never imagined this happening in a million years. But this shit can just come to you. I couldn't let the Templars hurt us anymore."

Cinco seems a natural leader, charismatic and respected by the troops. He is also seen as a good fighter, a keen marksman in shooting clubs who went from firing at bull's-eyes to firing at narcos. As vigilantes advanced, he got into fierce gunfights with Templars. He was at a barricade one night when more than twenty Templars attacked. He fought them off, killing several and avoiding casualties, he says.

"They like to intimidate people. To kidnap. To rape. But now we are intimidating them. Violence is all they understand."

I ask about what they do with prisoners. Does he really believe the vigilantes have a right to take life?

He gives me a hard look.

"If they captured me, do you think they would let me live?"

It was a grueling campaign. Templars ambushed vigilante barricades and disappeared people who sympathized with them. A frontline emerged on the road from Buenavista to Apatzingán. The vigilantes built a network of five barricades on it to repel the Templar attacks. At night, they put flaming torches on the road to warn people of their checkpoints. But it was still tricky for motorists to drive through with both sides having itchy fingers on the triggers.

As a result, the frontline became a wall that people avoided crossing.

The vigilantes were also scared about venturing into Templar territory in case gangsters recognized and murdered them. For months, they were cut off from Apatzingán where they bought supplies, and instead traveled long distances into neighboring Jalisco for goods.

The vigilantes broke this deadlock by working their way through the mountains around Apatzingán, taking key towns such as the narco stronghold of Aguililla. The self-defense squads developed a tactic for taking communities. First, they contacted locals who would help fight the cartel. Then they stormed in using overwhelming force, with hundreds of gunmen and dozens of trucks. When they occupied the town they would gather residents in the square and declare the community liberated. The locals would then build their own barricades, extending the territory of the movement.

By October, seven months after the uprising, the vigilantes were reaching far across the mountains. The Templars realized this movement was a challenge to their very existence. They hit back, provoking shoot-outs that left twenty-three dead on a single day.

Then the lights went out.

In the early morning of October 27, half a million people in Michoacán were jolted by their TV sets, fridges, and lamps switching off. Electric pumps also shut down, leaving houses without water. Power cuts are common in Mexico, normally in limited areas for short times. But this blackout covered town after town across the Hot Land and lasted most of the day.

It was no accident. Gunmen had stormed eighteen electricity substations. When workers fled, the gunmen opened fire on the generators and hurled Molotov cocktails. For extra impact, they set six gas stations ablaze. Politicians claimed it was an act of "terrorism." It definitely made people terrified.

While the Templars did not claim responsibility, they were almost certainly behind the blackout. However, their motives differed from previous attacks. Before they had pressured police to back off. Now it seemed they wanted security forces to come. If the army swept into the Hot Land, they hoped, it would stop the vigilante advance. It was a twist on "violent lobbying."

The attack was backed by a propaganda campaign. The Templars displayed narco mantas saying the vigilantes were hit men from the Jalisco cartel. Spokesman La Tuta also released a video. In the footage, he was filmed in a woodland in front of a dozen masked gunmen with military grade weapons.

"Those from Jalisco bring the vigilantes to Michoacán. They are behind them. The proof? The arsenal of arms they have. From Jalisco, they come, they come," La Tuta says, waving his arms in the air. "Why don't the police and soldiers uphold the rule of law, and arrest them and hand them over to be prosecuted? Why are the vigilantes hiding their faces? I am categorized a criminal and I know I'm wanted. But it is not my intention to hurt people."

The video got millions of hits on YouTube, partly because people are just damn curious to see a gangster boss speaking on film.

Peña Nieto still lacked any strategy for dealing with the Michoacán crisis. His mind was elsewhere. His government was at a key moment in passing reforms to overhaul Mexico's fiscal, education, and energy laws. After tough negotiations, Congress approved the biggest change to oil laws in seventy years, allowing foreign companies a piece of Mexican petroleum. Peña Nieto signed it on December 21 and went into his Christmas holidays with a political victory. As he celebrated the New Year, Michoacán reached a boiling point.

CHAPTER 45

As 2014 dawned, vigilantes poured from the hills to surround Apatzingán. Their first target was Parácuaro, which they stormed on January 4. The Templars could not give up a base so close to their heartland without a fight. They hijacked buses and left them burning on the highway to try and stop the vigilante convoys. The vigilantes drove around them, using dirt roads. Templar bosses knew they were outnumbered and fled, but ordered their gunmen to take a stand.

Pitched battles ensued, with vigilantes fighting their way in street by street. A Templar stormed out of a building carrying a bazooka. A vigilante reacted fast, spraying bullets before the Templar could fire his load. The narco fell to the ground, his dead finger lying limp on the bazooka trigger.[1]

The remaining Templars realized they were outgunned and ran, fell, or surrendered. As the vigilantes secured the town, they stormed the police station and disarmed local officers, who they accused of being in league with the cartel. (They probably were.)

Vigilantes then smashed up the shrines to the Maddest One, toppling the symbols of the narco saint. In one place, they took a bulldozer to rip up a statue of Saint Nazario. They were vanquishing his ghost.

I find Comandante Cinco sitting at a table in the center of Parácuaro days after the vigilantes have taken it. He waves his hand to show a peaceful plaza.

"We have driven the Templars out," he says. "In a few hours, we did what the police and soldiers couldn't do in years."

He has a pertinent point. You have to look at how the security forces failed to get rid of the Templars, despite their blatant narco mansions. The vigilantes made the difference as they come from the same communities, knew who the thugs were and where they were hiding. And they could take the gloves off to fight them.

Later, as the vigilantes call people to the Parácuaro square, an older resident approaches me and uses a metaphor to explain the success of the self-defense squads. He clasps his hands together, interlocking his fingers.

"When the police and army attack, the community does this," he says, and pushes his fingers closer together.

"But when the self-defense squads come and work with the community, it does this," he says, and pulls his hands apart, showing the Templars being broken.

Towns fell daily. Within a week, vigilantes stormed the city of New Italy. The attack provoked another fierce battle. Mexico's nightly newscast led with scenes of crouching vigilantes exchanging gunfire and bleeding bullet victims. For Peña Nieto, denial was no longer an option.

The president sent in the cavalry. As he got plugged into the issue, he finally realized that Michoacán would be a defining battleground in his administration, and sent in even more troops than Calderón had. By late January, twelve thousand soldiers and federal police swarmed on the Hot Land. To lead the operation, he appointed his friend Alfredo Castillo as a federal viceroy to Michoacán.

At first, it wasn't clear how the incoming troops would treat vigilantes. The self-defense militias were breaking a dozen laws; they had illegal guns, they detained suspects, and they murdered. But with their articulate leaders on TV, the public sympathized with them. There is also a strong case that the rule of law had long vanished in Michoacán and in these conditions, the vigilantes were vindicated.

At first, Peña Nieto and his envoy Castillo didn't make their position clear. Amid the ambiguity, soldiers arrived in the recently liberated Antunez (home to the mansions of Toucan), and disarmed vigilantes. But within an hour, hundreds of residents surrounded the troops and demanded they give the vigilantes their guns back. They had saved them from the tyranny of the Templars, something the soldiers had never done.

Residents pushed and the soldiers opened fire, killing three, including an eleven-year-old girl. The TV images of her small coffin angered many Mexicans. Not only did the security forces fail to protect people from cartels, they also killed children.

Sensing the mood, the Peña Nieto administration switched its position. It decided that the vigilantes were clearly winning and the security forces would work with them to go after the gangsters.

The federal police had suffered heavy losses at the hands of the Templars, so their officers were happy to coordinate with the self-defense squads. In the new bizarre landscape, you would go through a checkpoint of federal police, drive a hundred yards, and go through a checkpoint of vigilantes.

The Hot Land is always a strange place, but it was especially surreal in the first months of 2014. Barricades zigzagged through the valley and over the border into Guerrero. Teenage kids with machetes and potbellied middle-aged men with Kalashnikovs would ask you for ID. The sight of armed groups became normalized. You presumed they were vigilantes. But then they could be Templars. Or Jalisco New Generation.

Men (and occasional women) stood at barricades day and night watching for enemy snipers. When they came, the bullets would often rain down without them knowing where they were firing from and they would shoot back wildly into the bush.

Despite the bloodshed, the toppling of the Templars unleashed a euphoric atmosphere. Residents who had long lived in fear could talk openly about the rule of the cartel; how they extorted, abused, raped. The vigilantes ransacked narco mansions, drinking at gangsters' bars and diving into their pools. At the barricades, they would joke and sing, share bottles of beer, and cook dishes in big pots. A favorite was the delicious *carne apache*—beef marinated in lime juice. And they smoked heinous amounts of weed.

The self-defense movement edged closer to Apatzingán, with villages such as La Huerta on the edge of the city rising up. The deeper vigilantes got into Templar territory, the more Templar gunmen they captured. While they killed or exiled the top Templars, they gave most captured gangsters the option of joining them. They described this action of changing sides from the Templars to the self-defense squads as "flipping."

At a barricade in La Huerta, the vigilantes show me three Templars who have flipped. They make them do extra work such as hauling sacks of sand to pay for their crimes. But they say they will forgive them once they have redeemed themselves.

I interview one of these "reformed" Templars who describes how he cooked meth, who his boss was, how much he was paid. As he reveals the details, he is nervous at the vigilantes sitting close by fiddling with their rifles. He gives abrupt answers, his eyes flicking around. I realize I am playing a part similar to the interrogators in narco videos, in which hit men will make a captured gangster confess how he worked for a cartel, and what crimes he did. On the videos, this normally ends with a bullet in the brain.

In other towns, I see flipped Templars who are armed and moving freely. In Parácuaro, I meet Manuel, a bulky thirty-two-year-old who cooked meth and sometimes worked as a gunman for the cartel. I interview him at a vigilante barricade on the edge of the city. While he speaks, he is cocking his rifle and eyeing over the trench for the enemy.

Manuel spent most of his life in the United States, and speaks perfect English (he says "fuck" a lot). He is more candid than most. It is not only a few of the vigilantes from Parácuaro who were former Templars, he reveals, but almost all of them.

Manuel went to the U.S. as a small child and grew up in the suburbs of Portland, Oregon. While Portland is largely peaceful, it has a gang problem, which Manuel found his way into, joining the Barrio 18 and doing drive-by shootings. However, he survived his wayward youth and became a construction worker, laying drywall for two hundred dollars a day and fathering four children.

"I had a life like any other American. I lived the American dream. But I didn't realize it could fucking end like that." Manuel clicks his fingers.

In 2012, he was arrested for hitting his girlfriend. He claims she made it up because he cheated on her. The crime got him deported. Returning to the town of his birth, he found Parácuaro under the bloody rule of the Templars. The local boss was keen to recruit Manuel as he had experience with guns from his gang days.

"Almost everybody here worked for the Templars," he says. "You were either with them or they could kill you."

Manuel cooked meth in labs in the nearby countryside for about a thousand dollars a barrel. He also accompanied narcos to collect debts, which got violent. However, when I asked whether he considered himself a member of the Knights Templar, he shakes his head and smiles incredulously. He says he has no time for the Templars' bizarre beliefs.

"It's all bullshit," he says. "Nazario's balls went to his brains. Dressing like Jesus and shit. La Tuta is one of those educated violent people who loves to fuck with you."

When the self-defense squads invaded Parácuaro, Manuel joined them.

"I flipped. I had no choice. Now I'm scared the Knights Templar are going to kill this whole fucking town for turning against them."

However, Manuel hasn't done too badly out of the uprising. He has a brand-new truck that he "decommissioned" from a Knights Templar boss who fled town. "It's mine now," says Manuel, who stands a head taller than his dozen comrades in the trench.

Still, Manuel says he dreams of escaping Michoacán to return to the United States and his former life. He wonders why I, as a Brit, would want to spend any time here.

"I'd love to get out of here and go home. Why would anyone choose to live in a place like this?"

CHAPTER 46

The big prize was Apatzingan. It was the heart of the Templar empire, the controlling town of the Hot Land. If self-defense squads took it, it would be a virtual knockout blow. At the barricades everyone spoke of the inevitable siege on Apatzingan. They all feared (or hoped) it would be a bloodbath.

The problem was that vigilantes struggled to find allies in the city. In most towns, they could find enough residents who wanted vengeance on the Templars. But Apatzingan was where the cartel was born and residents were more loyal. And gangster control had been so strong in Apatzingan for so long that many people could not imagine them leaving and didn't want to risk speaking out.

Vigilantes eventually found their ally in the unlikeliest of places: the Church.

Father Gregorio Lopez, known as Padre Goyo, met with the vigilante leaders and agreed to support them taking the city. To sway the public mood, he gave sermons calling the Templars sinners and urging people to stand against them. The Templars were furious and threatened to kill him. But Padre Goyo refused to back down. He went on preaching against the cartel from the pulpit, wearing a bulletproof vest as he poured the wine and gave the holy bread. I go to one of his masses in the Apatzingán cathedral and am surprised how sharp his words are.

"I am not scared. I don't know fear. Fear is for the Templars and the devil," he tells his flock.

I interview him after mass, trying to find what drives him to take such risks. He is a stocky forty-six-year-old, friendly if with a slightly crazed look. When he describes his life story, I can't help but see the parallels with that of the Maddest One. Padre Goyo was of a similar generation, born in

1968, also in a rural village with a large family, having ten brothers and sisters. Like the Maddest One, he came to Apatzingán as a teenager, arriving when he was sixteen. While Nazario chose the life of crime, Padre Goyo chose the cloth, finally qualifying as a priest at age twenty-six.

Like the Maddest One, Padre Goyo sees visions. After his mother passed away he says he spoke to her spirit. She told him he had to fight the Templars.

"I saw how they were killing my friends, my brothers, my sheep, and as the pastor I have the obligation to be speaking out. If I do nothing for my sheep I am not a pastor. If a dog bites your children, and you do nothing then you are worse than the dog."

I ask him what he thinks about Nazario's faith and he shakes his head. He looks more regretful than angry.

"[Nazario] messes with the Biblical question to gain fame and cohesion. He utilizes God like a weapon, like a lever, like a trampoline. He believes in saints, he believes in God. But it is in a strategic way."

I ask the padre if he supports the vigilantes' right to take lives. Surely, the Bible says "thou shalt not kill." He says there are exceptions.

"In legitimate defense it is valid [to kill]. But first you have to exhaust all the resources, the law, dialogue. The last resort is self-defense."

He doesn't carry a gun himself, sticking to words and wearing his bulletproof vest. He also carries a GPS and has contacts in military intelligence following him, he tells me. The Templars call constantly threatening to murder him.

Padre Goyo is inspired by liberation theology, the leftist strain of Catholic teaching. He follows martyrs such as Salvadoran Archbishop Oscar Romero, who a gunman shot dead during mass, sparking the civil war. Goyo is writing a book called *The Hopes of the Hopeless*, inspired by Romero's *The Voice of the Voiceless*.

Senior Catholic bishops do not openly support Padre Goyo's stance. But they do not condemn it, which he sees as a tacit nod in his favor. Padre Goyo is actually one of several priests in Mexico who have stood up to cartels. In San Fernando, Tamaulipas, I find a priest who spoke out against gangsters and went with a parishioner to resolve a kidnapping; when the gangsters saw him they beat him with a wooden stick on the lower back as punishment. The most famous of all the gangster-fighting clerics is Padre Alejandro Solalinde, who supports migrants against mass kidnappings by the Zetas. Solalinde has become a national figure and fervent critic of the Mexican government.

It strikes me how these priests—unelected religious representatives—
have been better at standing up for their people than politicians, the secular
elected democrats. It's a paradox of Mexico's malfunctioning democracy.

Padre Goyo's masses became rallies to overthrow the Templars. Even
attending them was risky. But as the gatherings got larger and self-defense
squads drew closer, people lost their fear. The padre created a group
called CCRISTOS, a Spanish acronym that referred to followers of
Christ. He gave them white T-shirts, similar to those of the self-defense
squads. But Padre Goyo insisted it was a peaceful movement.

"I don't have a pact with any cartel or even the self-defense squads," he
tells me. "My only pact is with Christ."

Nevertheless, he was openly close to leaders such as Hipólito. To test
the water, Hipólito and others vigilantes drove into Apatzingán to attend
a mass. The vigilantes stood in the church wearing their bulletproof vests
and then spoke to the citizens in the square. When vigilantes had tried
marching in Apatzingán back in October, Templar gunmen opened fire
on them. But on this Sunday, police and soldiers stood by and the air was
free of gunshots. The vigilantes saw the moment was right to strike.

The self-defense squads hit Apatzingán at dawn on Saturday, February 8,
2014. They moved simultaneously in five convoys and set up bases around
the perimeter of the city. The largest was in the lime market, which
became a headquarters of the new power arriving; soon city officials and
businessmen would go there to hold quarter with the vigilante leaders.

I sped down from Mexico City with colleagues. As we drove into
Apatzingán, we saw the Templars had put narco mantas across bridges
threatening the vigilantes. They also made threats on the radio waves of
walkie-talkies.

"Self-defense squads. If you keep on advancing we are going to fuck
you up (partir su madre)," said a voice, identified as Templar boss Pantera.
"We'll be throwing bombs all over the place . . . We are not responsible if
innocent people die."

However, when we got to the vigilante bases, we saw they had overwhelming numbers, with some two thousand around the city. In contrast,
the Templar army had been rapidly dissolving as their men were killed,
ran, or flipped.

The vigilantes held the perimeter through the day, without taking the center of Apatzingán. By nightfall, the Templars had not attacked them and the atmosphere was jubilant. Under the moon, I watched stoned vigilantes clasping their rifles and spontaneously performing a reenactment of the fight against the cartel to guffaws of laughter.

The following morning, the vigilantes made a triumphant drive through the center in a convoy of 120 trucks, all overflowing with gunmen. Soldiers and police stood by. It was a bizarre sight. The security forces seemed more like United Nations peacekeepers than the government.

As the vigilantes consolidated their control, they worked more systematically with the security forces. Vigilantes had ground intelligence the police lacked. When they got addresses of Templars they passed them to federales who went in blasting.

The vigilante information gathering got ugly. I watched them take a terrified teenage girl for interrogation. They questioned some suspects in the Apatzingán cathedral patio. They held others in makeshift prisons in cattle ranches or warehouses. Suspects complained of being tortured. Residents searched for missing family members who had last been seen at the hands of self-defense squads. Maybe these victims were Templars. Maybe they weren't.

As the Peña Nieto administration worked with vigilantes it was complicit in the torture and disappearances. The vigilantes had effectively become a paramilitary doing the government's dirty work. Yet it is a tough question as to what Peña Nieto should have done in this extraordinary situation. It would have been madness to move against the vigilantes at this point. Any course was problematic.

While ugly, this combination of security forces and vigilantes hammered the Templars. And they zeroed in on Nazario himself.

The undead narco saint retreated into the highlands of his birth, moving around a triangle of mountains between Apatzingán, Aguililla, and Arteaga. People there still sheltered him, and Nazario loved the wilderness. He moved in hills only mules can travail and switched houses by day or night.

The vigilantes led search parties and "liberated" villages to gradually close the noose. I trek with a squad searching homes.

We get to a Templar safe house in the hills. It's a one-story home of white wood, better than many shacks here. The vigilantes storm in taking combat positions but the enemy has fled. They curse, wanting someone to fight.

There is a hot pot of stew on the stove showing the gangsters have only just gone. Their spies must have seen us coming so they ran. The vigilantes rip up the floorboards and walls searching for anything they left: bullets, drugs, money. They settle for ransacking an electric fan.

My colleague Ross McDonnell went with another group of vigilantes into a house that Nazario himself had just been in. Some of his books were on the shelves, including *The Art of War,* along with a DVD box set of Hitler documentaries. There was also a teenage girl, who had apparently been Nazario's latest love interest. The vigilantes spared her, but made her cook for them.

One of the vigilantes that I trek with is a corn farmer called Elias. He took up arms as the Templars had tortured him for not paying his extortion quota. The thugs beat Elias on the lower back with a stick giving him injuries that he still suffers from when he stands up or lies in bed at night.

"They showed no mercy when they beat me." He grabs my arm hard, shaking with anger as he describes it. "The pain drives me. It drives me to look for justice."

I wonder if what he wants is more revenge. Or is there a real difference between these concepts?

CHAPTER 47

When we get to the final scene in the life of Nazario, there are two versions. They are both dramatic. But I think the second sounds most realistic.

Version one is the government's. In this reel, Nazario meets his death in the early morning of March 9 after he celebrates his forty-fourth birthday. The marines say they found him high in the hills near a town called Tumbiscatío; when they ordered him to surrender he fired and they shot him dead.

They offered few other details. One official told a Mexican newspaper Nazario had been traveling alone on a mule. Another said he had just visited a girlfriend. To prove he was gone they released pictures of his fingerprints and the video, in which you see his corpse with a blackened beaten face.

There are good reasons to doubt the government's account. Even though he had lost much support, it is odd that he would be alone. It would be an immense stroke of luck for security forces to simply run into him. And the government offered no explanation for the facial bruising.

I hear the alternate version from several sources inside the self-defense movement, including from Adalberto Fructuoso Comparán, head of the vigilantes in Aguililla. They say vigilantes had plotted with Nazario's bodyguards to take him down. The bodyguards realized their boss was finished and were tired of his increasingly loco ways. While Nazario celebrated his birthday, they turned on him and held him until vigilantes arrived. The vigilantes and bodyguards then beat Nazario into the next world. They handed his corpse to the marines; it made the government look good and saved the vigilantes having to deal with murder charges.

A message offering a similar account was posted on a vigilante Facebook page. But the Mexican government stuck to their version. Mystery surrounds Nazario in death as it did in life. Some conspiracy theorists even say he never died at all. When the government has got it wrong (or lied) once, it's easy to believe it could do it again.

I am personally convinced the narco saint died that day. This time, they had a body. They also had a wake, a week later in the city of Morelia, and I sped down there to arrive outside the funeral home.

Nazario's wake is in a luxury locale with gleaming white pillars and spacious rooms. The screen announces his name simply as "El Más Loco"—The Maddest One—and guests arrive all in white, the color of his beloved Kaliman. A band plays drug ballads to a gathering of mostly women and children. Many of his gangster friends stay away, as soldiers are close by watching.

A man in a suit with a scar across his face tells us to leave or there will be trouble. We loiter outside, and he tells us to leave again in an angrier voice. We leave.

Later that night, a convoy of vehicles takes Nazario's body into the hills of his birth. No journalists have yet discovered if he was buried or cremated or where his remains might lie. His family could be hiding his final resting place for fear it would be defaced.

In the weeks after Nazario's death, his Templar empire collapsed like a deflating bouncy castle. The remaining towns fell and Templar money collectors stopped coming, liberating businesses from extortion. Almost all the cartel bosses were killed or arrested.

But one Templar evaded everyone: the joker in the deck, La Tuta. Despite the fact that he released his propaganda videos, and even gave interviews to two TV stations, the security forces couldn't find him. I follow troops on an operation to hunt him. With intelligence that he is wandering on a mule, they get every force involved, state police, soldiers, marines, federal detectives, and thousands of vigilantes. They make a net around the mountains and close in over days. But they find nothing.

To add insult to injury, a stream of new videos appeared showing La Tuta with various mayors and even the governor's son. In response, federal police handcuffed a long line of politicians. The Michoacán governor resigned after his son was carted off to jail. The rotten Michoacán apparatus crumbled with the Templars.

I wondered if La Tuta had done what other Mexican narcos could never manage and fled to the Caribbean where he was laughing from a beach. But finally, soldiers busted him in a house in Morelia. Before then, he had been hiding in the mountains in a dank bat-infested cave, where he used to keep prisoners.

Peña Nieto now faced the problem of what to do with the thousands of ragged vigilantes, teeming with ex-Templars. He decided to give them badges. Under his viceroy Castillo, a new State Rural Force was created of vigilantes in uniforms.

Some self-defense leaders resisted. Doctor Mireles said there were too many gangsters and spoke against the government in increasingly revolutionary language. The government arrested him on gun charges and shipped him to federal prison.

Other vigilante bosses joined the new police. The Rural Force ended the images of gunmen in jeans and baseball caps embarrassing Peña Nieto. But it was a time bomb waiting to go off. Many former Templars and Jalisco cartel affiliates now had badges. It is at this time I find the "Dirty Dozen," some in Rural uniforms, showing off their G3s and grenade launchers. A documentary filmed at this time, Cartel Land, even showed a man in a Rural uniform describing how he cooked meth. It also went inside a base where Rurales were questioning people and screams of torture could be heard.[1]

Residents of Hot Land towns filed dozens of complaints that the Rural Forces were shaking people down and trafficking drugs. At the close of 2014, rival Rural Force groups had a shoot-out that left eleven dead, including Hipólito Mora's son. In 2015, the envoy Castillo was replaced by a general and the government said it would review disbanding the force.

Michoacán seemed to have traded one set of gangsters for another.

The collapse of the Templars was also a big boost to their rivals in the Jalisco New Generation Cartel. The Jalisco mob took over Templar meth routes, adding them to its empire that now stretched from the Pacific to the Gulf of Mexico. They copied the Templar guerrilla tactics, and even turned them up a notch.

When the Peña Nieto government tried to take down Jalisco leaders in 2015, its gunmen assassinated dozens of police. In a single ambush, they shot dead fifteen state and federal troopers. In another attack, Jalisco thugs fired a rocket-propelled grenade at an army helicopter, making it crash and killing eight soldiers and a police officer. The image of Mujahedeen bringing down Soviet choppers with stinger rockets sprung to mind. That same day, a May first public holiday, the Jalisco mob blocked roads with burning trucks at thirty-nine points. Police also raided a farmhouse to discover that the cartel even had its own gun factory, assembling untraceable AR-15 rifles from component parts.

Peña Nieto may have an even bigger problem than the Templars.

To add to the president's woes, the July 2015 escape of Chapo Guzmán from prison shook public confidence that he could control drug traffickers any better than Calderon or Fox had. Guzmán fled what was supposed to be the nation's top security prison—its Supermax—through a mile-long tunnel with electric lights and air vents.

The brazen jailbreak raised hard questions about corruption in the prison or even higher up in the administration. It also infuriated U.S. DEA agents, who had helped Mexican marines capture Guzmán in 2014 in the resort of Mazatlan. That arrest of Guzmán, which came two weeks before the death of Nazario, should have been Peña Nieto's great success. Instead, the escape became his great failure.

Vigilantism is likely to be a significant feature of Latin American crime wars in the coming years. Unless governments can drastically reduce crime, some will take justice into their own hands. In Honduras in 2015, the journalist Orlin interviewed members of a vigilante death squad killing Maras. Vigilante militias are also expanding across the favelas of Rio.

In some situations, I can sympathize with victims turning to the gun. The indigenous community police can certainly be worked with, especially as traditional village councils keep a leash on them. But I don't see how vigilantes can provide a long-term solution to organized crime. There is always the danger they will carry out atrocities or themselves become a mafia.

Nazario's form of gangster capitalism is also likely to be a recurring theme. In northeast Mexico, the Zetas got involved in coal mining. In Colombia, I reported on illegal gold mining, in which drug traffickers took over wildcat pits, often getting children to crawl down the perilous holes. The gold ended up in exchanges from Amsterdam to New York at insanely high prices. It is almost as profitable as cocaine.

And we will likely see the Maddest One's use of narco religion again. In São Paulo, Brazil, I find an academic studying how evangelical churches and the First Commando of the Capital mix together. They use the same rhetoric, calling affiliates "brothers," talking of "baptism" (whether into the Commando or the church) and of an "enemy" (the devil or the system). Back in Mexico, some of the followers of Zeta boss Heriberto Lazcano, "The Executioner," also venerate him like a saint.

Perhaps this battle for souls takes place as we are at a historic crossroads of both political and spiritual beliefs.

After Nazario's death, I go back to El Alcalde, close to the ranch where he was born. At the entrance to the village is a shrine to Saint Nazario, with a figurine of the holy narco. The vigilantes half smashed it up, leaving it cracked and torn. But they didn't bother taking a bulldozer to it and its ruins survive covered in dust and weeds. More recently, someone sprayed graffiti on it.

"*Chayo Loco. Chinga tu madre,*" the paint says. "Chayo, you madman. Fuck your mother."

Even after death, the hate goes on.

PART VI

Peace?

CHAPTER 48

The American area code flashes up on my cell phone as I ride on a bus back through Michoacán to Mexico City. It's a desperate call for help from a mother in pain.

Ann Devert of Westchester County, New York, can hardly sleep or eat because her son Harry has disappeared crossing from Michoacán to Guerrero. A free-spirited thirty-two-year-old, Harry was fulfilling a dream, riding a motorcycle across the Americas to reach Brazil for the World Cup. It was the latest leg on Harry's journeys far and wide that he wrote about on his blog, *A New Yorker Travels*.

> I'm the owner of a big smile and a broad taste for adventure. I haven't always (or barely ever) walked the beaten path, and I try and live by my ever-evolving set of rules and values as well as I know how. I try to be a good human being. I am a life observer, a world traveler and a resident, light and dark, good and bad, a thinker, an admirer and a critic, a lover and a fighter. I'm passionate about life and I LOVE living. I'm not sure what the purpose of this life is, but I love to talk and debate about it endlessly.[1]

Crossing Mexico on a green Kawasaki, Harry cruised into Michoacán and toward the Pacific Ocean. He was last seen at a gas station in a town called Huetamo. He sent a message that soldiers had just escorted him along a stretch of road. Then . . . nothing.

The pain in Ann's voice cuts through me. She is sure Harry is alive. Could he have hit his head and lost his memory? Is he being held somewhere, even though nobody has called to ask for a ransom? "Somebody is feeding my son and knows where he is," she says with force.

She is reaching out for information and asks what I think as a journalist.

I pause and swallow. I have to tell her that Huetamo is on a frontline between gangsters in Michoacán and rivals in Guerrero, and both sides eye the highways. I have to say that what you think are soldiers can be cartel gunmen in disguise. I have to say the gangsters in the area are brutal murderers, and there is a real chance that her son is dead.

Ann is perseverant. She is sure Harry is alive. She wants to come down to Mexico to search for him.

When the call finishes, I stare out the bus window at the beautiful lakes of Michoacán. Covering such slaughter, it is easy to become jaded. The piles of corpses, the murder statistics, the confessions of killers, lose their human meaning. As journalists on this beat, we try to keep our cool covering a story of global importance, even while politicians try their best to ignore it. Sometimes, we're too cut off.

But Ann's pain reaches me. And tears well up in my eyes and pour down my cheeks.

I guess it's because I hear the voice of my own mother in hers. Her love and determination shine through; as does the way she is entering a world so alien to her, one that scars her as it has scarred so many.

Ann does come down to Mexico, braving dangerous areas and even reaching out to those inside cartels who may have information. I talk to her several more times, hearing how the search develops, trying to give any advice I can. Other journalists who cover Mexico's violence try their sources for information. A private detective comes on board.

Ann has moments of hope, finding clues that appear to show her son is alive. "Major help to find Harry is right here, right now. Que Viva Mexico! Que Viva Harry!" she writes in an e-mail.

But the road turns dark. A group of vigilantes put out banners saying a regional cartel boss has murdered Harry. A message stuck next to a corpse also blames a gangster for Harry's death.

Ann returns home without finding him. From New York, she continues to pursue all avenues.

Four and a half months after his disappearance, police and soldiers find Harry. He is in a field just over the state border into Guerrero. His body is cut into pieces, decomposing and stuffed inside a garbage bag. His motorcycle is next to him, battered and covered in earth.

The motive for the murder is still unclear. Did gunmen mistake Harry for a rival trafficker? Or an American drug agent? Or was it a robbery? Or was he just too slow to stop at a cartel "checkpoint"?

DNA samples confirm his identity. Ann writes a message on a Facebook page on which friends have supported her struggle.

> There is no doubt this is Harry, my beloved son ... Harry carried each of us in his vast heart. And because there is a place for Harry in each of our own hearts ... Harry is alive because YOU are alive.
> "ALIVE!, Ma!!!" he would say to me. "How great is that?!!"
> I ache from missing my son who was Life's great gift to me.

Three months later, the police and cartel hit men abduct the forty-three students, also in Guerrero. Ann writes to me again.

"The fact of the students' murders does make me feel as if Harry's murder were not merely something he brought on himself," Ann says. "No one is safe in Guerrero. The authorities who are supposed to protect citizens are not the bedrock of society, they are quicksand. Perhaps this event will be the tipping point that initiates the total overhaul of the corruption and violence that have a stranglehold not just on development but on normal people's lives."

Like other grieving parents of the thousands of innocent victims of Latin America's crime wars, Ann searches for some meaning to her son's death. When soldiers die in battle, families have the satisfaction that their loved one perished for a cause. But when gunmen kill someone for just being in the wrong place, it is hard to make sense of it.

Ann rightly points out the bloodshed should make us "overhaul" the system. A million murders over a decade is unacceptable. If there is a meaning to these murders, it is perhaps that they should force us to search for peace.

When thousands took to the streets to protest the disappearances in Guerrero, they called for the students to be returned alive.

"*Vivos se los llevaron, vivos los queremos,*" became the slogan—"Alive, they took them. Alive, we want them."

They were likely asking for a miracle. If gangsters or police had not burned the students on the garbage dump, as Mexico's attorney general said, they had probably killed them somewhere else. There was no ransom demand or any other sign they had kept them alive. The government faced a demand that was likely impossible to fulfill.

Handling the crime wars across Latin America and the Caribbean can often seem an impossible task. Brazilians fear that favelas will always be on the edge of society. Jamaicans moan that politicians will always turn back to gangsters to secure their ballots. Hondurans say resignedly their society is doomed to be violent.

But history shows that human beings are capable of changing societies. Failed policies can be corrected. Corruption is not genetic. If one nation can make an effective justice system, another can too.

The Mexican government cannot bring back the forty-three students alive to their grieving families. But it can stop others from suffering the same fate.

Protesters have called for the resignation of presidents over the crime wars. Governments need to be overthrown for change to happen, they say. The demand harks back to the protest movements of the Cold War. Dictators Pinochet, Galtieri, Baby Doc, and Trujillo killed to maintain power. The people had to topple them to move forward.

There are valid reasons to change many leaders today. There are certainly some corrupt politicians who should not be in power. But in the crime wars, the solution is not as simple as toppling a president. After they are gone, you will still be left with billions of drug dollars, corrupt police, and ineffective courts. It's not just necessary to overturn an oppressive government, but to mend a corrupt system. And this corrupt system is not even in one country. It is a collective problem that Mexico, Brazil, Honduras, El Salvador, Jamaica, the United States, Britain, Spain, Italy, and others face together; and recent history shows how bad the world is at dealing with international challenges.

In searching for a solution, it helps to come to terms with what the problem really is. Governments find it uncomfortable to admit that cartels and commandos clearly challenge the nature of the state and its monopoly on waging war and administering justice. The fact that gangsters have won genuine support in some marginalized communities is also a painful truth.

The twenty-first century has thrown up a world where irregular forces with scattered cells of combatants provide an immense challenge for democratic governments. Light infantry weapons are everywhere, and it is easy for criminal gunmen to communicate and move money. Governments find their tanks, warships, and bombers are useless against these ragtag criminal militias. They often choose stalemates as the best option.

Yet while gangster warlords show frightening firepower, I do not believe their rule constitutes an actual alternate state. They care about selected aspects of domination in their territory. Cartels secure roads, control police, take over economic assets, and strong-arm politicians. But they let the government run schools, provide water, and collect garbage. They are a shadow power rather than a shadow government. They want a weak and corrupt government, which they can live off, like a tapeworm feeds off a host.

This differentiates the crime militias of the Americas with Islamist militants or old-school communist guerrillas. In Peru, the Shining Path used guerrilla warfare to create "liberated zones," where the government could not enter, and tried to build an alternative Maoist state there. Likewise, the logic of Islamic radicalism has led to the so-called Islamic State and its caliphate. When it took Mosul in Iraq, one of its first actions was to take over schools and radically change the curriculum. They care about what is inside people's minds, not just making money.

Gangster warlords nurture their culture, their pseudo religion, and their rhetoric of fighting for the poor. But this doesn't constitute an ideology. The cartel massacres cannot be justified in religious scripture from the seventh century or revolutionary manifestoes. We don't have to call on moderates in their communities to argue over the interpretation of their faith. But we need to change conditions in communities to stop the cartel life being more appealing than a legitimate job.

We journalists often disparage governments for what they do. That is a key part of our work. Yet it is easier to criticize than to offer solutions, and we need to search for real proposals. Are we just hearing the testimonies of killers and crying mothers out of interest, or can they help find working policies?

I base these following conclusions on fourteen years of reporting, and talking to thousands of people involved. Yet they are still simply ideas up for debate. Some may agree with certain points and not others. The important thing is to work out how to tackle this problem now, not after a million more murders.

I divide the conclusions into three areas: reforming drug policy, building justice systems, and transforming ghettos. I see these as the three pillars in confronting the region's crime wars.

CHAPTER 49

DRUG POLICY REFORM

On November 6, 2012, as Obama made his reelection victory speech in Chicago, voters in Colorado and Washington State jumped up and down over a different win: the legalization of marijuana. Amid the discussion of Obama's second term, many missed the seismic implications of the cannabis votes. This was the first time anywhere on the planet that marijuana was legalized since modern drug prohibition began a century ago. Even Holland had only kept its famous coffee shops open through legal ambiguity. Colorado and Washington directly confronted the U.S. federal government and the United Nations. It looked like the laws might be rapidly struck down.

Yet legalization not only survived but spread. In 2013, Uruguay became the first entire country to legalize, and in 2014, Oregon, Alaska, and Washington, D.C., said yes to ganja. This wave of reform confirmed there was a real turning point in drug policy. It followed several countries decriminalizing drug possession and a major shift in the tone of the debate, especially in the bloodstained nations of Latin America.

Modern drug prohibition began with the 1914 Harrison Act that banned most opium and cocaine in the United States. But it was Nixon who escalated this to the "War on Drugs" in his 1969 to 1974 presidency. This takes us right back to the Cold War, hippie festivals, and Robert smuggling weed over from Juárez again. Nixon's strategy—to browbeat foreign governments, militarize antidrug efforts, and create the DEA, a multi-billion-dollar agency fighting the offensive in over sixty countries—defined U.S. policy for the next four decades.

Nixon had absolutist objectives; he believed that with the right pressure, governments could obliterate drugs. "Our goal is the total banishment of drug abuse from American life," he said in his 1972 campaign. The U.N. took these same goals on board. Even as late as 1998, the United Nations Office on Drugs and Crime (UNODC) held a meeting in New York under the slogan, "A drug free world. We can do it."

Four decades after Nixon, this goal has obviously not been met. The United Nations itself estimates the global drug trade is worth four hundred billion dollars a year. Both the U.S. drug czar and UNODC have finally given up hope of a drug-free world and talk of containment. Drug warriors concede that military raids, crop burning, multinational stings, and prisons packed with drug offenders, which together cost the U.S. upward of forty billion dollars a year, will not end the drug trade. They now argue they are just stopping it getting bigger.

This has created an ominous experience: the war on drugs failed to end the narcotics trade while it created an enormous global black market that has funded cartels with catastrophic consequences. This realization is at the heart of the renewed debate. Drug policy reformists are winning ground fast, while drug warriors struggle to be heard. In the U.S. states that legalized marijuana, opposition from social conservatives was scattered and muted. We live through a paradigm shift in thinking.

Drug policy reform does not mean legalizing every drug, and certainly isn't to say that drugs are good. But it is a fundamental change in approach. The key to the new reasoning is that problematic drug use cannot be stopped by "war" but is a health issue. Societies need to offer as much help as they can to reduce the harmful effects of drugs, while also drastically reducing the size of the black market.

The decades of experience show that harder drug policies do not necessarily mean fewer drug users. Holland, with its more liberal approach, has always boasted fewer users than the United States. Since Portugal decriminalized the use of all major drugs in 2001, narcotics use has been relatively stable, while HIV infections from needles and drug-related deaths have gone down.[1] It achieved this by switching to treatment programs.

Just a decade ago, politicians across the Americas saw questioning the war on drugs as political suicide. But first former and then current presidents began to challenge it. Among them are Colombians César Gaviria and Juan Manuel Santos, Brazilians Fernando Cardoso and Lula, Guatemalan Otto Pérez Molina, Argentina's Cristina Kirchner, Uruguay's José Mujica, and Mexicans Ernesto Zedillo and Vicente Fox. Even Calderón, who waged his bloody offensive on cartels in Mexico, has questioned whether prohibition works.

Surveys in the United States now show that more than half of respondents support marijuana legalization.[2] Hundreds of celebrities, from newscasters to billionaires to movie stars, have come out in favor. Legalizing weed in the four U.S. states and D.C. has created a paradox. While the United States invented the war on drugs, parts of it have become a global vanguard of progressive laws.

Despite the pendulum swing, key institutions perpetrate the war approach. These include the U.S. Drug Czar's office and DEA as well as global agencies in dusty offices that you may never have heard of such as the International Narcotics Control Board. Drug policy reform means confronting these entrenched bureaucracies. A big battle will take place at the United Nations General Assembly Special Session on Drugs in April 2016. Prepare for fireworks.

Reforming drug policy will impact the whole world, but will make an especially big splash in the Americas. As the trail in this book shows, the region has suffered history's bloodiest wars financed by the narcotics trade, from Mexico to Jamaica to Brazil to Honduras. Drug money is not the entire problem. But it is a big part of it. And drug policy is an area that we can make a difference in. What we do in the United States, Britain, Spain, Italy, and other countries will directly affect lives on the streets of Latin America and the Caribbean.

The most urgent objective is to reduce the size of the narco black market in the region. Neither the Shower Posse nor the Red Commando nor the Knights Templar could have become such deadly forces without drug profits. If these crime families earn fewer narco dollars they will have less money to buy guns, bribe police, and train kids to be assassins.

Critics argue that drug policy reform in itself will not destroy these mafias. They are right. But it can reduce their power substantially so they don't overwhelm nations. They could become more like criminals in the United States and Europe and not gangster warlords devastating communities.

Marijuana is the first drug on the table. Uruguay and the legalizing U.S. states have taken a lunar-size step. But the process needs to move much further. If societies are ready to accept it, and I think they are, it is time to legalize marijuana across the region and push organized crime completely out of the business.

Nobody can claim they know the exact percentage of cartel money made from cannabis. The very nature of a black market means we can't count it accurately. But evidence based on seizures and user surveys all points to billions of dollars. (Estimates on what Mexican cartels alone make from cannabis vary from one billion dollars to twenty billion dollars.)[3] Despite the pace of marijuana reform, the Zetas and Knights Templar are still making profits from smuggling cannabis into the United States. The strength of marijuana-funded gangsters in Mexico or Jamaica also has a knock-on effect into Central America and other nations in the chain of crime wars.

If marijuana becomes legal across the hemisphere then these billions would move from the hands of gangsters into those of legal businessmen and tax coffers. Ganja is an industry that is heavy on workers; many take their first step into a crime family by growing marijuana, selling it on a corner, or smuggling it. That link would be severed, and legal jobs created.

While legalizing weed garners mass support, most people cannot envision lifting the ban on hard drugs—cocaine, heroin, and crystal meth. Perhaps policy reform needs to move forward with cannabis regulation before a discussion on these can take place. After marijuana, the priority is to confront the cocaine market, as it generates so much money. White dollars fund the Zetas in northeast Mexico, the Maras in Honduras, the Red Commando in Brazil, and dozens of other mafias. Heroin and meth are particularly heinous, but are cheaper and less widely used.

However, there is a first step on hard drugs that people can find a consensus on: addiction treatment needs to be stepped up. Rehab workers now have decades of experience treating people with problematic drug use and have developed effective ways of helping junkies confront their demons. These treatments need to be more widely available. Addicts use big quantities, with some spending more than a hundred thousand dollars a year on smack, crack, or meth, so everyone that kicks it is a big hit to traffickers. Money currently spent on marijuana prohibition, or even that generated by the legal business, could be switched to rehab. If treatment campaigns could reduce users by a third, that would be a substantial whack on finances of meth traffickers in Michoacán or heroin producers in Guerrero.

There is a common counterargument to drug policy reform. If gangsters made less money selling drugs, it goes, they would turn to other crimes, such as kidnapping, which really hurt people. By this logic, legalizing drugs could actually lead to more violence. Some police officers, business lobbies, and even gangsters themselves claim this. Prosecutors have shown me cases of criminals who got cut off from drug trafficking (for example, when a supplier was arrested) and turned to kidnapping to make quick cash.

But on further investigation, this argument falls apart. When gangsters make billions of dollars smuggling drugs they become more powerful, overwhelming law enforcement and turning to other crimes. When they make less from drugs, police have a better chance of dealing with them. Therefore, countries with big trafficking networks such as Mexico and Colombia have suffered from the world's highest kidnapping rates.

You can also see this logic within countries. Tamaulipas is one of Mexico's biggest drug trafficking states, sharing a border with Texas. It also suffers from the highest kidnapping rate in the nation. Yucatán State is rarely used by traffickers, and has one of the lowest kidnapping rates as well as Mexico's lowest homicide rate—about the same as Belgium.[4]

Even if drug money does shrink from a tidal wave to a stream, however, Latin American nations need to confront militias of violent criminals. They cannot allow gangsters like the Maddest One Moreno or Dudus Coke to claim territory and challenge the state. They have to battle crimes such as extortion and murder, whatever happens with narco markets. And this involves a huge overhaul in the police and justice systems.

CHAPTER 50

HOW DO YOU POLICE CRIME WARS?

It is easy to criticize how Latin American leaders confront cartel blood-shed. But from a government's point of view, there aren't easy answers. If gangsters wreak havoc in a city, critics scream the government is too passive. If it sends in troops, they shout it is being repressive. Rulers are damned if they do and damned if they don't. Even when they catch king-pins, critics say they are scoring media points and it won't change things. Of course, officials often have their pockets stuffed with drug dollars. But even politicians who aren't in league with narcos struggle to find a working policy.

However, the years of crime wars have taught at least one lesson: large parts of the region's security forces are fundamentally flawed and need to be reformed from the bottom up. When the U.S. and other nations lend support, it has be in building new institutions—not just bankrolling rotten ones.

After the Cold War, international organizations focused on building electoral systems and markets in the emerging democracies of Latin America. The U.N., European Union, and Organization of American States sent election monitors and helped young political parties hammer out voting rules. Likewise, the World Trade Organization and World Bank oversaw deregulation carried out by the region's Harvard-educated techno-crats. If people had the freedoms to choose their leaders and make money, it was assumed the rest would follow. But they missed a vital element in viable democracies: the rule of law. Latin America shows that you can have elections and markets hand in hand with dysfunctional justice systems.

Through the twentieth century, order in much of the continent was kept by dictatorships, whether they were military, as in Brazil and Honduras, or virtual, as in Mexico. They kept control with curfews, imprisonment without trial, and police and soldiers killing with impunity.

When democracy dawned, these same security forces didn't know how to operate. Many police officers across the continent understood how to torture and disappear people but not how to gather evidence. As they stumbled into the new era, they have carried on making cases by forcing confessions, sparking outrage from human rights groups. This has created a sorry status quo. The security forces often don't act, creating lawlessness, and when they do, they torture and kill.

Impunity rates are off the charts. In Europe, about 80 percent of murders lead to a conviction. In Latin America as a whole, it is close to 20 percent.[1] In Honduras, the conviction rate hit less than 4 percent— similar to that in Juárez when it was the world's murder capital.[2] At the same time, jails hold many innocent people who were tortured into confessing. It's a double tragedy.

Going back to dictatorships is off the table. While it is not impossible to see generals or politicians trying it in some places, the people would never accept it. Societies have to build police and courts that function under democracy.

Some academics say that violence has a function in human societies. The world wars forced nations to form international organizations, such as the United Nations and European Union. In Latin America, violence should force nations to build working justice systems.[3]

Governments and civil society groups have to view the building of these justice systems as a generational project. Presidents can lay bricks but they need their successors to add cement and paint, a tough challenge in the short-term point scoring of electoral politics.

But what kind of security forces do societies want to build? The balancing act is to limit the capacity of gangster militias while not hurting the population.

All nations in the region need to set a long-term goal of getting soldiers off the streets. While some extreme circumstances can warrant sending out the troops, a lasting solution has to be based on police forces. Soldiers are trained to kill. That is the whole point of soldiery. When they are used instead of police, they will kill, and some of those victims will be innocent. This was shown when the army stormed Tivoli Gardens in Jamaica.

In Mexico, Calderón unleashed the army to fight drug cartels in 2006, in what was supposed to be a temporary measure. Almost a decade later, they are still there. Agents arrested soldiers for "executing" prisoners, during the massacre of twenty-two people in the town of Tlatlaya in 2014. This is likely the tip of the iceberg. According to the Mexican army's own numbers, soldiers killed more than two thousand alleged criminals under Calderón. Most cases were never investigated, so it is impossible to know how often lethal force was justified.

Yet, police forces have to fit the conditions. If you sent an unarmed bobby of an English village into Tivoli, he would be lucky to come back with his head on his shoulders. Unfortunately, you need police who are well armed and combat trained. Latin American countries also need to invest more than European countries. This is tough as they are poorer. But if you are dealing with a hundred times the murders you need more officers to solve them. Colombia has reduced its murder rate by spending 5 percent of its entire budget on security.

In Monterrey, Mexico, I watch young recruits of the Fuerza Civil force training in a black room with a video simulator. They are practicing getting ambushed by cartel gunmen and responding in milliseconds to avoid getting their heads blown off. They train in five man (and woman) units, covering each other. However, their training is different from the military in that they are prepped to only fire when their lives are threatened and arrest, not kill, their enemy.

Nuevo León State formed the Fuerza Civil in 2011 when violence hit record levels there. They brought in academics and local businesses to design something outside the box. Their first requirement was that recruits could not have been police officers anywhere in Mexico, so they weren't dirty from the job.

To fight the inevitable corruption, the Fuerza Civil also created a large internal affairs department. This is a crucial element needed in forces across the continent as a constant check and balance.

When internal affairs punishes officers it causes bad headlines. The Nuevo León force found three officers slept with some female detainees, causing a stink. Yet it is better to suffer the short-term bad publicity than let the rot grow. The Nuevo León force also makes most officers stay in a barracks, leaving them less exposed to bribery and less vulnerable to attack. This is a difficult tactic to sustain in the long term, but housing estates for officers could be viable.

The Fuerza Civil oversaw the reduction of murders by three quarters—

from more than two thousand in 2011 to some five hundred by 2014. It is a potential that could be followed across Mexico.

One challenge is that that the country still has more than two thousand town and city police forces, many rotten to the core. City police in Iguala worked with the Warriors United to disappear the students. Both Mexican presidents Calderón and Peña Nieto called for all local police to be abolished and replaced by thirty-one state forces.

The proposal has met resistance, especially from some local mayors who want to keep their budgets. Critics also point out that it doesn't matter how many forces you have if they are corrupt and that Mexican state and federal police also moonlight for cartels. This is true, but to begin to build new forces it is easier with a state model, where you can create effective internal affairs departments. Eradicating the hundreds of corrupt municipal forces would be a step forward.

Other examples of more effective police forces in the region include those of Nicaragua, created by the Sandinistas, Chile, and Colombia. All have flaws. But they also have elements that can be incorporated into working models.

To monitor the success or failure of police, society needs good data. Governments have to hand out homicide numbers and allow them to be checked independently. The Violence Observatory in Honduras was advanced in this, but unfortunately the government took it over in 2014, eliminating its autonomy.

A Latin America tradition of aggressive crime reporting helps by trailing the streets to find corpses. If the government claims there are fifty murders and reporters have found a hundred bodies, they know something is up. Overall homicide numbers are better than trying to guess exactly how many killings cartels carried out; the problem with the latter is the data is too ambiguous so it is easy to manipulate the figures.

Alongside better police, a mammoth challenge is creating effective prosecutors and courts. Mexico is carrying out the biggest judicial reforms in centuries, moving from a closed-door to an open model with juries, which is supposed to be ready in 2016. This change is good but needs much more work. A side effect of a more open judicial system is that some villains could be freed because the evidence isn't there. The media needs to adjust to covering this. If the evidence is full of holes you cannot blame a judge for throwing out the case.

Fighting impunity starts at the top. Gangbangers in Central America often pointed out to me how their politicians get away with stealing hundreds of millions. Why should they be honest, they asked, if their leaders are filthy? The Shower Posse or Knights Templar would never have grown so powerful without their political alliances.

Trying to stop corruption in Latin America can seem like trying to count grains of sand on a beach—impossible. But battles over corruption are raging in a big way now, and victories are happening. Anti-graft activists have created online tools to try and force political candidates to show their wealth and conflicts of interests.[4] Aggressive journalists and campaigners have caught out powerful politicians in Mexico, Jamaica, Brazil, Honduras, Salvador. In September 2015, Guatemalan President Otto Perez Molina was even forced to resign over corruption allegations. It is not pretty. But the scandals mean the poison is coming to the surface where it can be drawn out.

CHAPTER 51

HEARTS AND MINDS

Boys Town football club lies in the heart of the West Kingston ghettos, a bone-dry field across the road from Trench Town. I sit in the shade of the stands talking to coach Carl Brown on a baking afternoon. Carl grew up in Trench Town, went on to play professional soccer, and coached the Jamaica national team. Now he is back home, using his love for the game to battle for the hearts and minds of the next generation.

It is not easy. Carl competes with dons who turn youths into murderers. He can offer a kid a stipend and the adrenaline of scoring a goal in Jamaica's semi-professional league. Perhaps he can nourish their dream of one day playing in the English premiership, like Raheem Sterling or John Barnes. But dons offer cash and cheap fame right now.

"Boys Town loses some of them to criminality." Carl speaks slowly, sits with a straight back, the discipline of a sportsman. "But if I save one life, just one life from the path of destruction, then I have achieved something."

Despite the struggle, Carl feels a magic every time the team plays. When the youths are on the field, they are escaping from the ghetto and guns, the hunger and hustle. They are safe at that instant.

"This takes them away from an environment where the police or bad men can shoot them. Here they can express themselves and they are free. It gives some hope. And hopelessness is very cruel."

Carl is part of an army of community workers fighting the real battle in Kingston, San Pedro Sula, San Salvador, Ciudad Juárez, Apatzingán, Antares, and countless other hot spots across the continent. Most are involved in independent projects that take sport, art, music, and love to transform lives. Like many who make this effort, Carl says the struggle is uphill because criminals offer more than the authorities.

"We have been let down by the government. Nobody cares about these people. Education has been a failure. So when the don comes along and provides some basic needs, they see him as a messiah."

This fight for hearts and minds is often labeled as crime prevention. It is more than that. It is a struggle for a just and functioning society. It is the search for an environment where a thirteen-year-old mass murderer, a decapitated head in the street, would be unthinkable.

Hearts and minds is the label applied by forces fighting insurgency. The Americans lost in Vietnam, they realized, because the population was against these foreign invaders. But this comparison holds strong in crime wars of the Americas. One reason people will join a cartel and fire on police is because they don't recognize the legitimacy of the state, or at least don't see it as offering anything.

As crime wars rage, there has been a growing recognition of how important this battle is. After Ciudad Juárez became the most murderous city in the world, national and foreign aid flooded to social schemes in the city, helping to drastically reduce the homicide rate. Following this, Peña Nieto took office and launched a national crime-prevention program.

However, the thinking on effective social work needs to be developed much more. Peña Nieto's prevention scheme lacks direction. In its opening booklet, not only did it talk about keeping kids out of gangs, it discussed chasing things as banal as vendors selling cigarettes in singles. One problem is that many in both government and media don't take these schemes as seriously as military strikes. Unlike gun battles, it doesn't make for sexy copy. (Believe me, I've tried.)

Prevention can also be an ambiguous term, covering anything from building a road to opening a school. When Peña Nieto launched his prevention campaign he said they were backing it with nine billion dollars. It sounded incredible. That kind of money could really turn things around. But on closer inspection, it turned out he was just relabeling $8.75 billion that was already going to education, infrastructure, etc. He only earmarked $250 million of new money.

In contrast, community workers on the ground have succinct ideas on how to stop youths from joining the crime armies. Among them is Gustavo de la Rosa, a human rights defender in Ciudad Juárez.

"You can identify exactly who the ten kids are on the corner who are being drawn into gangs. You have to work with them one on one, help them to stay in schools, offer them options. You may not save every life. But you can save many."

De la Rosa points out the government cannot only launch these schemes when a city becomes the most homicidal on the planet. It needs to operate them constantly, make them institutional, part of the structures of the state.

It is important to get to kids when they are young. Once they have been initiated into a gang or a cartel, committed murder, *become addicted to killing,* they are beyond redemption in many ways. Thousands of children and teenagers are on the streets right now at this crucial turning point. We have to stop them becoming the next generation kill.

As well as the focused youth programs, wider schemes to regenerate communities make a difference. City mayors such as Leoluca Orlando in Palermo, Sicily, and Andres Fajardo in Medellín, Colombia, transformed slums, which successfully reduced crime. Such techniques could also overhaul San Pedro Sula, the slums of San Salvador, the favelas of Rio. If residents see paved streets, parks, and monuments they can feel a sense of belonging; if they see dirt roads, blackouts, and garbage, it is easy to believe the system is against them.

People often point to cultural elements to explain how sweet children transform into gun-toting assassins. You don't need to be a social conservative to recognize that many gang members grow up in broken families immersed in addiction and violence.

Carl Brown at the football ground sees the problem as a change from a collective spirit he knew growing up in the ghetto to rampant individualism. He uses the example that Trench Town residents used to share big pots of stew, putting in what they could and all taking a bowl. Now everyone buys their own bag of food, or goes hungry.

"People have become self-centered. They think, 'If I am full then the world is fine,'" Carl says. "They have stopped caring about others."

Priests, preachers, and teachers all try to improve values, with limited success. Politicians have also tried to clamp down on gangster culture. Mexican censors have fined producers for putting on shows of narco ballad artists. Brazil's gangster beats are called *funk proibidão* because they are just that—prohibited.

I think the effects of culture are real. But they are also limited and tough to change. Middle-class kids in London or New York also grow up in single-parent families, listen to gangster music, and take drugs, yet almost never get pulled into such ultraviolent gangs.

Perhaps it is a combination of factors. When you mix broken families and gangster culture with poverty, cartels, and impunity, it is a lethal cocktail.

In communities scarred by violence, many don't know what peace looks like. Teenagers in Brazilian favelas, Jamaican garrisons, and Honduran slums see these crime wars as a natural state of affairs. It's normal to have men on the corner with Kalashnikovs, shots ringing out at night, corpses hanging from bridges.

How will they know when peace has arrived? Will it be when soldiers no longer storm the ghetto? When they no longer see gangster militias? When they are no longer scared? Is it when the murder rate has dropped from a hundred and fifty per hundred thousand to fifty? Or not until it reaches twenty?

Back in Kingston, Jamaica, I visit Rose Town, a ghetto sliced in two by warring posses. Next to the frontline, activists used charity money to build a library. I go there at dusk. A few hours earlier, I drove through a murder scene on the edge of Rose Town. But now it looks peaceful. Teenagers, young men, old women sit in the library reading.

I wouldn't go so far as to say the library has transformed the community. It is still a homicidal ghetto. The frontline is a no-man's-land of burned out houses. Many youths still wield guns. Amid this, the library stands out like an odd appendage. But it does provide an oasis. And perhaps it is a seed.

One of the librarians, Calvin Gibbs, is a sixty-year-old who has lived in Rose Town all his life. Calvin talks eagerly about the history of the slum and goes to a desk in the library to pull out newspaper cuttings about political violence as far back as the 1960s, and even earlier.

We take the conversation outside, sitting on the sidewalk. It is getting dark, and the street buzzes, dance hall music banging from speakers, a dozen people moseying at a crossroads, sipping rum, smoking. Calvin describes how the violence developed over the years. He recalls the battles in 1980 at the height of the Cold War when the posses would fight in the name of Manley and his socialism against the shock troops of conservative Seaga.

"They came down that street there with pickax, sticks and guns." He points his finger up the road. "Them shoot a woman right there."

He chats on about drug trafficking and the rise of Dudus, the President. Like others, he explains how people turn to the don because he provides a degree of order. He names dozens of young men from the community who have died by the gun. We talk about the youth killed that day, apparently at the hands of a ranking posse member.

Reflecting on this bloody history, I feel that despair that the killing is somehow inevitable.

"There has been decades of violence," I say. "Can you envision it any other way? Can this really change?"

He glances at a group of youngsters boogying on the corner outside the rum shop and answers slowly. I write his reply in big uppercase letters in my notebook. Months later, when I pick up the pad and read it back, I stare long at the six words of his answer, soaking them in.

I THINK THERE IS ALWAYS HOPE.

Acknowledgments

Dudley Althaus was my boss and mentor covering Mexico for the *Houston Chronicle* from 2003 to 2005. He had discussed the idea of a regional project on the new crime groups of the Americas back then. Who were these gangsters that had become a strange and impending threat, he asked; how did they wield power; how did they challenge governments? He was always ahead of the curve. The *Chronicle* never did it and eventually shut down its foreign operation amid the meltdown of international newspaper coverage. Later, that seed helped me form the thesis for this book; I hope it does service to Dudley's notion.

Dudley taught me countless things about being a journalist. But the best advice was in three words: "Maybe I'm wrong." You get into a story. You think you have it figured out. But wait, "Maybe I'm the fuck wrong." Then you get deeper into it and discover things you had never thought of. *Saludos al padrino de la cantina.*

Reporting on this book from 2011 to 2015, I conducted interviews with hundreds of people, as well as drawing on thousands of interviews from covering Latin America since 2001. Some are cited. Many aren't, but their words shaped it and helped me understand this phenomenon better. Thanks to every one of you, from academics to fellow journos, police to politicians and priests, mothers, fathers, brothers and daughters, drug addicts to drug growers, social workers to sociopaths, coyotes to killers. I know some of you literally risked your life telling those things. Some of you are already in the next world.

Special thanks to those who helped me in the field, the Brazil commando, Joe Carter, Wellington Magalhaes, Florian Pfeiffer, Ali Rocha, Paxton Winters, Andre Fernandes, Camila Nunes Dias, Flora Charner, Vagner Marques, Sylvia Colombo, the Jamaica and Caribbean posse,

Colin Smikle, Nick Davis, Karyl Walker, Horace Levy, Anthony Harriott, Daurius Figueira, Roslyn Ellison at the Trench Town Reading Center, Gavin Judd, Sandy, Chez and Maru, the Central America gang, Orlin Castro (and Fresa, Mango, and the rest of his crew), Iris Amador, Freddy Pineda, Eddie Murillo, Juan Carlos Llosa (RIP), Karla Ramos, El Sueco, Elio Garcia, the Martinez brothers, Juan, Carlos, and Oscar and the rest of the *El Faro* crew especially Jose Luis Sanz, the Mexico media mafia, Juan Alberto Cedillo, Alejandra Chombo, Fernando Brito, Diego Enrique Osorno, Alejandro Almazan, Alejandro Sanchez, Jose Gil Omos, Sanjuana Martinez, Brett Gundlock, James Frederick, Mike O'Boyle, Marcela Turati, Luciano Campos, Frankie Castellanos, Frankie Contreras, Dalia Martinez, Jesus Lemus, Leo Gonzalez, Daniel Fernandez, Daniel Hernandez, Daniel Becerrill, Kieran Murray, Dave Graham, Frank Jack and all the Reuters team, Sayda Chinas, Rodrigo Soberanes, Emilio Lugo, Cynthia Ramirez and all at Letras Libres, Tomas Bravo, Javier Verdin, Sergio Ocampo, the Nuevo Leon crew, Alfredo Corchado, Jose de Cordoba, Keith Dannemiller, Jonathan Roeder, Jo Tuckman, Elizabeth Malkin, Marion Lloyd, Dave Agren, Eduardo Castillo, Hans Maximo, Erik and Liz Vance, Nathaniel Parish, Nara Gonzalez, the esteemed, Enrique Krauze, Lorenzo Meyer, Edgardo Buscaglia, Cristobal Pera, Enrique Calderon, Alejandro Hope, Jorge Chabat, Raul Benitez, all the professors that used my book, James Creechan, Ben Lessing, Chris White, and globe-trotters, Adam Saytanides, Myles Estey, Ross McDonnell, Mike Kirsch, Debs Bonello and Ulises, Kirsten Luce, Bernardo Ruiz, Alex Leff, Lizzy Tomei, David Case and the GlobalPost team, George Grayson (RIP), Sam Logan, Steven Dudley and the Insight Crime team, Robert Bunker, John Sullivan, Oscar, Nancy, Luigi, and my compadre Rob Winder.

As always my agent Katherine Fausset for believing in my work from blastoff and editor Anton Mueller for leaping into this project, supporting my vision and giving me the time to make it happen, along with the rest of the team at Curtis Brown and Bloomsbury, including Kerry D'Agostino, Sara Kitchen, and Rachel Mannheimer. My dad, for all the brainstorming, and my mum, who helped with days of translation work. *Y como siempre mi esposa Myri, aguantando los viajes y presion de este trabajo. Te amo.*

Bibliography

General

Bowden, Mark. *Killing Pablo: The Hunt for the World's Greatest Outlaw*. New York: Penguin, 2001.

Felbab-Brown, Vanda. *Shooting Up: Counterinsurgency and the War on Drugs*. Washington: Brookings Institution Press, 2010.

Glenny, Misha. *McMafia: Crime Without Frontiers*. London: Bodley Head, 2008.

Hari, Johann. *Chasing the Scream: The First and Last Days of the War on Drugs*. New York: Bloomsbury, 2015.

Reding, Nick. *Methland: The Death and Life of an American Small Town*. New York: Bloomsbury, 2009.

Reno, William. *Warlord Politics and African States*. Boulder: Lynne Rienner Publishers, 1998.

Streatfeild, Dominic. *Cocaine: An Unauthorized Biography*. New York: Picador, 2001.

Van Creveld, Martin. *The Transformation of War*. New York: Simon & Schuster, 1991.

Williamson, Edwin. *The Penguin History of Latin America*. London: Allen Lane, 1992. New Edition, London: Penguin, 2009.

Brazil

Amorim, Carlos. *CV _ PCC: A Irmandade Do Crime*. Rio de Janeiro: Editora Record, 2003.

Barcellos, Caco. *Abusado: O Dono do Morro Dona Marta*. Rio de Janeiro: Editora Record, 2003.

Bellos, Alex. *Futebol: The Brazilian Way of Life*. London: Bloomsbury, 2002.

Dowdney, Luke. *Children of the Drug Trade: A Case Study of Children in Organized Armed Violence in Rio de Janeiro*. Rio de Janeiro: 7 Letras, 2003.

Fernandes, Andre. *Perseguindo um sonho: A história de fundação da primeira agência de notícias de favelas do mundo.* Rio de Janeiro, ANF Produções, 2014.

Da Silva Lima, William. *Quatrocentos Contra Um: Uma História Do Comando Vermelho.* Rio de Janeiro, Vozes, 2001. New edition *400 Contre 1: La Véridique Histoire du Comando Vermelho.* Montreal: L'Insomniaque, 2014.

Rohter, Larry. *Brazil on the Rise: The Story of a Country Transformed.* New York: Palgrave Macmillan, 2010.

Jamaica

Gunst, Laurie. *Born Fi' Dead: A Journey Through the Jamaican Posse Underworld.* New York: Holt, 1995.

Levy, Horace. *Killing Streets & Community Revival: Community Stories (70's–80's).* Kingston: Arawak, 2009.

Samuels, K.C. *Jamaica's First President: Dudus 1992–2013, His Rise, His Reign, His Demise.* Kingston: Page Turner Publishing House, 2011.

Sives, Amanda. *Elections, Violence and the Democratic Process in Jamaica.* Kingston: Ian Randle Publishers, 2010.

Thomson, Ian. *The Dead Yard: A Story of Modern Jamaica.* London: Faber and Faber, 2009.

Central America (and its L.A. gang connections)

Henry, O. *Cabbages and Kings.* New York: McClure, Phillips & Co, 1904.

Logan, Samuel. *This is for the Mara Salvatrucha: Inside the MS-13, America's Most Violent Gang.* New York: HarperCollins, 2009.

Martinez, Oscar. *The Beast: Riding the Rails and Dodging Narcos on the Migrant Trail.* New York: Verso, 2013.

Rafael, Tony. *The Mexican Mafia.* New York: Encounter Books, 2007.

Schlesinger, Stephen and Kinzer, Stephen. *Bitter Fruit: The Untold Story of the American Coup in Guatemala.* New York: Anchor, 1983.

Ward, T. W. *Gangsters Without Borders: An Ethnography of a Salvadoran Street Gang.* Oxford: Oxford University Press, 2012.

Mexico

Blancornelas, Jesús. *El Cártel: Los Arellano Félix: la mafia más poderosa en la historia de América Latina.* Mexico City: Plaza & Janes, 2002.

Bowden, Charles. *Down by the River: Drugs, Money, Murder, and Family.* New York: Simon & Schuster, 2004.

Corchado, Alfredo. *Midnight in Mexico: A Reporter's Journey Through a Country's Descent Into Darkness.* New York: Penguin, 2013.

Campbell, Howard. *Drug War Zone: Frontline Dispatches from the Streets of El Paso and Juarez.* Austin: University of Texas Press, 2009.

Grant, Richard. *Bandit Roads: Into the Lawless Heart of Mexico.* London: Little, Brown, 2008.

Grayson, George and Logan, Samuel. *The Executioner's Men: Los Zetas, Rogue Soldiers, Criminal Entrepreneurs, and the Shadow State They Created.* New Brunswick: Transaction Publishers, 2012.

Hernández, Anabel. *Los Señores Del Narco.* Mexico City: Grijalbo, 2010.

Illades, Esteban. *La Noche mas Triste: La Desaparicion de los 43 estudiantes de Ayotzinapa.* Mexico City: Grijalbo, 2015.

Krauze, Enrique. *Biografía del Poder: Caudillos de la Revólucion Mexicana (1910–1940).* Madrid: Andanzas, 1997.

McLynn, Frank. *Villa and Zapata: A History of the Mexican Revolution.* New York: Caroll & Graf, 2000.

Osorno, Diego Enrique. *El Cártel de Sinaloa: Una Historia del Uso Político del Narco.* Mexico City: Grijalbo, 2009.

Poppa, Terrence. *Drug Lord: The Life and Death of a Mexican Kingpin.* New York: Pharos, 1990.

Ravelo, Ricardo. *Osiel: Vida y Tragedia de un Capo.* Mexico City: Grijalbo, 2009.

Shannon, Elaine. *Desperados: Latin Drug Lords, U.S. Lawmen, and the War America Can't Win.* New York: Viking, 1988.

Tuckman, Jo. *Mexico: Democracy Interrupted.* New Haven: Yale University Press, 2012.

Turati, Marcela. *Fuego Cruzado: Las Víctimas Atrapadas en la Guerra del Narco.* Mexico City: Grijalbo, 2010.

Vulliamy, Ed. *Amexica: War Along the Borderline.* London: Bodley Head, 2010.

Womack, John. *Zapata and the Mexican Revolution.* New York: Vintage, 1970.

Notes

Part I: War?

Chapter 1

1. Both former Iguala Mayor Jose Luis Abarca and his wife were prosecuted on organized crime charges. As of mid 2015, the cases had not been resolved. The case garnered widespread coverage including Eyder Peralta, "Mexico Charges Former Iguala Mayor in Missing Students Case," NPR, Jan. 14, 2015.

2. Federal Attorney General Jesus Murillo Karam first publicly announced his conclusion that the cartel had murdered the students at the Cocula dump at a news conference on November 14, 2014, seven weeks after the attack.

3. The following are Mexican federal government figures on cartel murders and total intentional homicides.

	Cartel Murders	Intentional Homicides
2007	2,819	10,253
2008	6,824	13,155
2009	9,612	16,118
2010	15,259	20,680
2011	16,990	22,852
2012	14,857	21,736
2013	10,076	18,331
2014	6,797	15,649
(Total cartel murders 83,234)		

The total homicide numbers are compiled by the Sistema Nacional de Seguridad Publica, taken from state police departments, and published on its website. The estimates of cartel murders are made by a unit in the intelligence agency CISEN and provided to federal officials. These same figures are also published in Benito Jimenez,

"Bajan con Peña narcoejecuciones," *Reforma*, Jan. 3, 2015. Some analysts and media outlets have accused the Mexican government of underreporting the number of cartel murders. For example, the newspaper *Zeta* of Tijuana claimed there were eighty-three thousand such killings during the 2006 to 2012 presidency of Felipe Calderón alone, about a quarter more than the government reported. One clear inconsistency is that Mexico's autonomous national statistics institute, known by the acronym INEGI, has counted death certificates and found higher total homicide figures than the police departments reported during several years. For example, in 2011, the INEGI recorded 27,199 total intentional homicides—or 19 percent more than the police departments reported.

4. Some earlier estimates had put the Tlatelolco death toll much higher, but the most thoroughly documented count is from a collaboration of the National Security Archive and *Proceso* magazine, published in Kate Doyle, "The Dead of Tlatelolco," *Proceso*, Oct. 1, 2006.

5. Nobel Prize-winning Peruvian writer Mario Vargas Llosa coined the phrase "Perfect Dictatorship" in 1990 in a debate organized by *Vuelta* magazine.

6. Federal prosecutors say in their reports and statements that soldiers and federal police were active in the Iguala area during the night of September 26 to September 27 when the students were abducted. This is widely reported as in Juan Pablo Becerra, "El Ejercito en la noche de Iguala," *Milenio*, Jan. 26, 2015. Family members protested outside military bases calling for a further investigation into the soldiers' activities, while some journalists accused the federal forces of taking part in the violence. Federal prosecutors responded that they had found no evidence that soldiers or federal police were involved in the attack on students. See "Ejercito y PF no participan en aggresion a normalistas de Ayotzinapa: PGR," CNN, Dec. 16, 2014. As of mid 2015, the issue continued to be hotly debated.

7. This is described in interview with Rio CORE commander Rodrigo Olveira in chapter 12. Also see "Naval Special Warfare Personnel Train with Elite Brazilian Unit," Naval Special Warfare Group 4 Public Affairs, May 20, 2010.

8. "Citizen Security with a Human Face, Evidence and Proposals for Latin America," Executive Summary, 3, United Nations Development Program, November 2013.

9. Report, "The 50 most violent cities in the world 2014," by the Mexican non-governmental organization Citizens Council for Public Security and Criminal Justice (Spanish acronym CCSP-JP).

10. "Citizen Security . . ." Executive summary, 3.

11. This alleged massacre is covered in detail in chapter 14. Also detailed in *Movimiento Mães de Maio, A Periferia Grita: Mães de Maio Mães do Cárcere,* (São Paulo: Fondo Brasil De Direitos Humanos, 2012).

Chapter 2

1. Juan Alberto Cedillo covered these death ranches in a series of stories including "Suman 500 los restos humanos hallados en narcofosas en Coahuila," *Proceso*, Feb. 8, 2014. Diego Enrique Osorno also wrote a detailed report on the killings in "How a Mexican Cartel Demolished a Town, Incinerated Hundreds of Victims, and Got Away With It," *Vice*, Dec. 31, 2014.

2. I am referring to mother Irma Hidalgo, whose son Roy Rivera Hidalgo was abducted in 2011.

3. The allegations of gladiatorial fights were uncovered by Dane Schiller in "Mexican Crook: Gangsters arrange fights to death for entertainment," *Houston Chronicle*, June 11, 2011.

4. Villa is said to have ordered the killing of eighty-four victims in San Pedro de la Cueva, Sonora, in December 1915. The comparison of the San Fernando massacre being the biggest since San Pedro de la Cueva is also made in Gary Moore, "Unraveling Mysteries of Mexico's San Fernando Massacre," *InSight Crime*, Sept. 19, 2011.

5. This mark of more than one thousand battlefield deaths is used by various analysts including Michael Doyle and Nicholas Sambinis, "International Peacebuilding: A Theoretical and Quantitative Analysis," *American Political Science Review* (December) 94: 4, 2000.

6. Ben Lessing, "Logics of Violence in Criminal War," *Journal of Conflict Resolution*, forthcoming.

7. Bunker is also former Minerva Chair at the U.S. Army War College, a research associate of the Terrorism Research Center, and author of over two hundred publications on the issue.

Chapter 3

1. Martin van Creveld, *The Transformation of War* (New York: Simon & Schuster, 1991), 2.

2. While it is extremely difficult to calculate the size of the illegal drug industry, the most thorough estimates are made by the United Nations Office on Drugs and Crime, as in its 2012 report, "Transnational organized crime: Let's put them out of business," in which it says that the illegal drug industry is worth $320 billion a year.

Part II: The Red

Chapter 4

1. The Comando Vermelho has almost always been translated as Red Command. However, I prefer to use commando as I think it is a better reflection of the spirit of the term as used by gang members. The Comando

Vermelho invokes the image of an elite force inside the favela. Gangs also use names that sound good to them and they identify with. In English, the noun "command" is awkward to refer to a gang or group.

2. This splinter is known in Brazil as the Terceiro Comando. Brazilian prosecutors say in their description of the gang on the website http://www.procurados .org.br that it was formed in 1994. Other sources say the traffickers who formed it were already drifting away in the 1980s. Later, the Third itself splintered, creating the Pure Third Commando.

3. More than 2.5 million people live in favelas in Rio State. In Rio city, where the presence of illegal armed groups has been most closely counted, a 2013 study at Rio State University by Alba Zaluar found armed groups in 82 percent of favelas, with 37 percent being controlled by drug traffickers and 45 percent by the militias.

4. William Mangin, "Squatter Settlements," *Scientific American*, Oct. 1967.

5. Alex Bellos, *Futebol: The Brazilian Way of Life* (London: Bloomsbury, 2002) 33–36.

6. The *Trans-Atlantic Slave Trade Database* is online at www.slavevoyages .org. The number of slaves arriving on U.S. plantations includes those shipped directly from Africa and those who arrived via the Caribbean.

7. Brazil's census information is published by the *Instituto Brasileiro de Geografia y Estatística*. Information on favelas is summarized in press release "2010 Census: 11.4 million Brazilians (6.0 percent) live in subnormal agglomerates," Dec. 21, 2011.

8. Interview with author, May 16, 2014.

Chapter 5

1. Carlos Amorim, *CV_PCC, A Irmandade Do Crime* (Rio de Janeiro: Record, 2003), refers to William as "the brain" of Red Commando.

Chapter 6

1. William da Silva Lima, *Quatrocentos Contra Um: Uma História Do Comando Vemelho,* (Rio de Janeiro: Vozes, 2001). Republished in 2014.

2. Film directed by Caco Souza, *400 Contra 1: Uma História do Crime Organizado,* 2010 (Brazil).

Chapter 7

1. Da Silva, 21.

2. I am using jail and prison interchangeably as in common British usage, rather than the technical U.S. distinction of jail as temporary holding institution.

3. Da Silva, 25.

Chapter 8

1. CIA dispatch, "Castro's Subversive Capabilities in Latin America," Nov. 9, 1962, declassified Mar. 18, 2004.

2. Maria Rost Rublee in *Slaying the Nuclear Dragon: Disarmament Dynamics in the Twenty-first Century*, 152, edited by Tanya Ogilvie-White and David Santoro (Athens: University of Georgia Press, 2012).

3. "Brazil Marks 40th Anniversary of Military Coup: Declassified Documents Shed Light on U.S. Role," The National Security Archive, Mar. 31, 2004.

4. "White House Audio Tape, President Lyndon B. Johnson discussing the impending coup in Brazil with Undersecretary of State George Ball, Mar. 31, 1964," The National Security Archive.

5. Da Silva, 37.

6. Interview with Elvira Elbrick as part of The Association for Diplomatic Studies and Training, Foreign Affairs Oral History Project, Spouse Oral History Series, interviewed by Jewell Fenzi, Oct. 24, 1986.

7. Department of State Intelligence Cable, "Widespread Arrests and Psychophysical Interrogation of Suspected Subversives," Apr. 18, 1973, sent by U.S. Consul General in Rio de Janeiro, declassified June 5, 2014. In National Security Archive. Secretary of State John Kerry gave a copy to Brazilian President Dilma Rousseff on a trip to Brazil.

8. "Rousseff reveals how she was tortured as student by the Brazilian military regime," MercoPress, June 20, 2012. Also cited in Brazilian media.

Chapter 9

1. This quote is taken from documentary film *Senhora Liberadade* (Freedom), Caco Souza, 2005.

2. Da Silva, 45.

3. Ibid., 67.

4. Ibid., 74.

Chapter 10

1. Amorim, 166.

2. Ibid., 166–167.

3. Da Silva, 17.

4. Ibid., 87.

Chapter 11

1. Theresa Bradley, "Brazil now consumes 18 percent of the world's cocaine," *Quartz*, Sept. 24, 2012, uses estimates provided by the UNODC. There are

several other estimates of Brazilian cocaine use, including the II Brazilian national alcohol and drugs survey. These other estimates also put Brazil as the world's second biggest cocaine consumer in total quantities.

2. The crack survey, entitled *Estimativa do número de usuários de crack e/ou similares nas capitais do país*, was carried out by the Oswaldo Cruz Foundation (Fiocruz), which is part of the Brazilian health ministry. It was released September 2013, following groundwork in 2012.

3. *Forbes* put Escobar on its billionaire list from 1987, when the list was launched, until his death in 1993.

4. The casualties of Avianca Airlines Flight 203 included 101 passengers, six crew members, and three people on the ground.

5. Felbab-Brown, Vanda, *Shooting Up: Counterinsurgency and the War on Drugs*, (Washington, DC: Brookings Institution Press, 2010) 19. The FARC Seventh Guerrilla Conference took place in 1982.

6. Peruvian President Fernando Belaúnde Terry discussed the idea of narco-terrorism in an interview with *El Tiempo* newspaper, published on Sept. 18, 1983.

7. Cited in indictment March 3, 2003, *United States v. Luis Fernando Da Costa*, Criminal No. 02-122 (RCL).

Chapter 12

1. *Elite Squad: The Enemy Within* grossed more than $63 million, almost all of it in Brazil, according to the Internet Movie Database.

Chapter 13

1. Luke Dowdney, *Children of the Drug Trade: A Case Study of Children in Organized Armed Violence in Rio de Janeiro* (Rio de Janeiro: 7 Letras, 2003).

Chapter 14

1. Marco Antonio Coelho, "From pickpocket to bank robber," *Estudos Avancados*, 21 (67), 2007, translated by Rodrigo Sardenberg.

2. Amorim, 390.

Chapter 15

1. "Obama: Lula Is 'Most Popular Politician On Earth,'" *Associated Press*, May 3, 2009.

Part III: The President

Chapter 16

1. Daraine Luton, "Dogs ate my sister," *Jamaica Gleaner*, May 28, 2010.

2. HG Helps, "Dudus ran like a 'puss,'" *Jamaica Observer*, June 14, 2010.

3. Gary Spaulding, "Sacrifice: Souls Lost For the Cause," *Jamaica Gleaner*, May 30, 2010.

4. Robert Mackey, "Jamaicans Ponder Cross-Dressing Gangsters," June 25, 2010, cites Miller. Miller's full post was also on facebook.com/notes/kei-miller/bad-man-nuh-dress-like-girl.

5. Interview with author, Oct. 27, 2014.

Chapter 17

1. *Report of the National Committee on Political Tribalism*, also known as the Kerr Report, July 23, 1997, 5.

2. *Di Jamiekan Nyuu Testiment* (Kingston: The Bible Society of the West Indies, 2012), Luuk 11.2–4.

Chapter 18

1. Andrea Downer, "Valerie Jackson-Daley: An Unsung Hero," *Jamaica Gleaner*, Oct. 17, 2005.

Chapter 19

1. For Jamaica murder stats, I refer to reports by the United Nations Office on Drugs and Crime, which themselves take them from the Jamaica Constabulary Force. This comparison of homicide stats is also made in Horace Levy, *Killing Streets and Community Revival* (Kingston: Arawak publications, 2009).

2. Desmond Allen, "The continuing rise and rise of Desmond McKenzie," *Jamaica Observer*, Jan. 15, 2012.

3. Office of the Public Defender, *Interim Report to Parliament*, 6, Apr. 29, 2013.

4. Ian Thomson, *The Dead Yard: A Story of Modern Jamaica* (London: Faber and Faber, 2009), 153.

5. Phrase coined by Jamaican army head Rear Admiral Hardley Lewin in 2005, see "Army chief says . . . Tivoli mother of all garrisons," *Jamaica Observer*, Oct. 8, 2005.

6. The "blood for blood" comment is widely quoted including in Laurie Gunst, *Born Fi' Dead: A Journey Through the Jamaican Posse Underworld* (New York: Holt, 1995), 84.

7. Manley interview with Gil Noble, originally aired WABC-TV, Nov. 6, 1977.

8. Rally quote reproduced in BBC documentary *Blood and Fire: Jamaica's Political History*, originally aired on BBC, Aug. 4, 2002.

9. Ibid.

10. Ibid.

11. Ibid.

12. Interview on Alternative Views, hosted by Douglas Kellner, aired 1982 on PBS.

13. Thomson, 201.

14. Gunst recounted interview with Green Bay survivor in Gunst, 100–103.

15. One colorful account of One Love Peace Concert is Robin Denselow, "Bob Marley Presides Over the Peace Concert," *Guardian*, June 16, 2011.

16. Quotes taken from audio of Peter Tosh speech at One Love Peace Concert, 1978.

Chapter 20

1. Dominic Streatfeild, *Cocaine: An Unauthorized Biography* (London: Virgin, 2001), 271–272.

2. *Report of the National Committee on Political Tribalism*, also known as the Kerr Report, July 23, 1997, 8.

3. Among references, the story of this gun seizure is told by author Laurie Gunst in documentary episode on Lester Lloyd Coke of *Lords of the Mafia*, Associated Television International, 2000.

4. The 1,400 figure for the posse murders is widely cited, including in Liz Robbins, "Vivian Blake, 54, Founder of Jamaica Drug Gang, Dies," *New York Times*, Mar. 25, 2010.

5. "Jim Brown Is Still Dead, Isn't He?" *Newsweek*, Apr. 5, 1992.

Chapter 21

1. K. C. Samuels, *Jamaica's First President: Dudus 1992–2010* (Kingston: Page Turner, 2011), 90.

2. All court quotes from Dudus trial come from documents from *The United States of America v. Christopher Michael Coke*, in the United States District Court, Southern District of New York, CR0971.

3. Sinkinson made the comments on BBC Radio 4. Also cited in "Jamaica Battles UK Drug Mules," on BBC website, Jan. 4, 2002.

4. The *Independent* newspaper cites the report in a letter published on its website as part of documents related to the Mark Duggan inquest. It is dated Sept. 26, 2012.

Chapter 22

1. Bunny Wailer, "Don't Touch the President," 2009.

Chapter 23

1. *The Essential Writings of Ralph Waldo Emerson* (New York: Modern Library, 2000), 551.

2. Aidan Hartley, *The Zanzibar Chest: A Memoir of Love and War* (London: HarperCollins, 2003), 175.

3. Records of Jamaican government contracts are released by the Office of the Contractor General. An example of a contract listed for Incomparable Enterprises is on June 24, 2009, when the Minister of Water and Housing gave 10 million Jamaican dollars for repairs to Bustamente Highway.

4. Samuels, 142.

5. Gary Spaulding, "'Dudus Typically A Don,' Says PM," *Jamaica Gleaner*, Mar. 18, 2011.

Chapter 24

1. Quote from video of campaign rally used in Golding campaign commercial, aired July 2007.

2. Taken from video of Jamaican parliamentary session, Dec. 8, 2009.

3. Dan Murphy, "Jamaica's Bruce Golding denies link to drug lord Dudus Coke," *Christian Science Monitor*, May 26, 2010.

Chapter 25

1. Mattathias Schwartz released the results of the Freedom of Information Act request on his website www.mattathiasschwartz.com.

2. Office of the Public Defender, *Interim Report to Parliament*, 34, Apr. 29, 2013.

3. Ibid., 243.

4. Paul Henry, "To Mom with love, your son Dudus," *Jamaica Observer*, Sept. 25, 2011.

Part IV: He Who Holds the Word

Chapter 26

1. The Customs and Border Patrol provides statistics on its website, www.cbp.gov, under the headline "Southwest Border Unaccompanied Alien Children."

2. Paul Vale, "Protests in Arizona Over Immigrant Children Show the Ugly Side of American Populism," *Huffington Post*, July 16, 2014.

3. Elisha Fieldstadt and Phil Helsel, "Murrieta Protesters and Supporters Clash, With No Buses in Sight," NBCNews, July 4, 2014.

4. "Children on the Run," United Nations High Commissioner for Refugees, Mar. 2014.

5. Ibid.

6. In January and February 2015, Mexico deported 25,069 Central Americans, double the number compared to the same months in 2014, according to figures published by Mexico's Instituto Nacional de Migración.

7. O. Henry, *Cabbages and Kings*, 147–148. New York: McClure, Phillips & Co, 1904.

Chapter 27

1. "Honduras: Internal Displacement in Brief," Internal Displacement Monitoring Center, Dec. 31, 2013.

2. Homicide figures from the Honduran Violence Observatory at the Instituto Universitario en Democracia, Paz y Seguridad. New Orleans figure from FBI Uniform Crime Report.

3. Ibid.

Chapter 28

1. Stephen Braun and Paul Feldman, "Killings Related to Street Gangs Hit Record in '87," *Los Angeles Times*, Jan. 8, 1988.

2. Carlos Martinez and Jose Luis Sanz, "El Origen del Odio," *El Faro*, Aug. 6, 2012.

3. These origins of the Mara are also covered in Samuel Logan, *This is for the Mara Salvatrucha: Inside the MS13, America's Most Violent Gang* (New York: HarperCollins, 2009).

4. Tony Rafael, *The Mexican Mafia*, (New York: Encounter Books, 2007), 32.

5. The fight is recounted in Carlos Martinez and Jose Luis Sanz, "El Origen del Odio," *El Faro*, Aug. 6, 2012.

6. Figures from the L.A. County Sheriff Department.

Chapter 29

1. Figures from the L.A. County Sheriff Department.

Chapter 30

1. There are also some smaller additional sections in the prison, such as for inmates who have left the gangs and inmates who have to be separated, such as sex offenders.

2. Stories on that prison riot include, "Motín en centro penal deja tres muertos y 41 heridos," *La Tribuna* (Honduras), Mar. 12, 2015.

3. Among robberies of heavy weapons from the Honduras army was the theft of 22 RPG launchers cited in, "Reportan robo de 22 lanzacohetes de unidad militar en Honduras," *Notimex*, Feb. 7, 2012.

4. I covered this mass killing working in Nuevo Laredo for the *Houston Chronicle*. It happened on Oct. 8, 2004.

Chapter 32

1. The Salvadoran homicide figures are taken from the United Nations Office on Drugs and Crime, which are themselves taken from Policía Nacional Civil of El Salvador.

2. This anecdote is told in detail in Carlos Martinez and José Luis Sanz, "La nueva verdad sobre la tregua entre pandillas," *El Faro*, September 11, 2012.

3. Ibid.

4. This point is made succinctly in "Why El Salvador has a pact with its gangsters," *The Economist*, Feb. 2, 2014.

5. Oscar Martinez, "Making a Deal With Murderers," *New York Times*, Oct. 5, 2013.

Part V: The Saint

Chapter 34

1. Widely quoted, including in Rocio Hernandez, "Territorio Sonoro," *El Universal*, Feb. 21, 2009.

Chapter 35

1. Douglas Massey, Jacob Rugh, Karen Pren, *The Geography of Undocumented Mexican Migration* (Oakland: The University of California Press, 2010).

2. These two guerrillas are profiled in Luis Ramirez Sevilla, "Voces y memorias desde abajo: comunistas y guerrilleros en la historia official y presente del PRD," *Relaciones*, June 18, 2006.

3. John Eldredge, "Wild at Heart: Discovering the Secret of a Man's Soul" (Nashville: Thomas Nelson, 2001.)

4. Ibid.

5. Mark Barna, "Mexican drug cartel co-opts 'Wild at Heart' message of local Christian author," *Colorado Springs Gazette*, June 25, 2010.

Chapter 36

1. This case is detailed in my first book, *El Narco: Inside Mexico's Criminal Insurgency* (New York: Bloomsbury, 2011), 29–31.

2. See note [War, 1, note 2].

Chapter 37

1. Confession of Mendez was on a video released by Mexico's Federal Police in June 2011.

2. Published in *La Voz de Michoacán*, Nov. 22, 2006.

3. Rafael Rivera, "La Familia castiga y exhibe ladrones," *El Universal*, Jan. 30, 2010.

Chapter 38

1. Megan Garber, "'Pilot's Salt': The Third Reich Kept Its Soldiers Alert With Meth," *The Atlantic*, May 31, 2013.

2. Advertisement depicted from *California Medicine*, in February 1970, reproduced in Nicholas Rasmussen, 2008 book *On Speed: The Many Lives of Amphetamine* (New York: New York University Press).

3. Seizure figures provided by U.S. Customs and Border Protection.

4. Sari Horowitz, "U.S. Cities Become Hubs of Mexican Drug Cartels," *Washington Post*, Nov. 3, 2012.

5. "What America's Users Spend on Illegal Drugs," Executive Office of the President of the United States, Office of National Drug Control Policy, June 2012.

Chapter 39

1. The last president who was a member of the Mexican military was Lázaro Cárdenas, a revolutionary general who ruled from 1934 to 1940. I am using the Mexican Revolution in the broader term, lasting until the return to civilian presidents in 1940.

2. Mexican Army records show the biggest deployment of troops was in 2011, with the 96,000 across the country. Also cited in "Calderón devolvió a 50% de la tropa a los cuarteles," *Milenio*, Dec. 16, 2012.

3. Between 2009 and 2014, the Bureau of Alcohol, Tobacco, Firearms and Explosives (ATF) traced 73,684 guns seized from Mexican criminals to U.S. gun sellers, according to data published by ATF.

4. The 1 to 50, or 20 to 1000, ratio is stated in the US Army Field Manual, and widely cited, including in Steven M. Goode, "A Historical Basis for Force Requirements in Counterinsurgency," *Parameters*, Winter 2009–10.

Chapter 41

1. Lyrics reproduced courtesy of Twins Music Group.

Chapter 42

1. Diego Gambetta, *The Sicilian Mafia: The Business of Private Protection* (Cambridge: Harvard University Press, 1996), 3.

2. Rafael Rivera Millan, "Cae más del 50 por ciento exportación de mineral en LC," *Cambio de Michoacán*, Jul. 4, 2014.

Chapter 43

1. International homicides in Michoacán are counted by the state police department and published by the Sistema Nacional de Seguridad Pública (SNSP).

2. Paul J. Vanderwood, *Disorder and Progress: Bandits, Police, and Mexican Development* (Lanham: Rowman & Littlefield Publishers, 1992), 32. There was also much vigilantism across the border in the U.S. during this period; see Richard Maxwell, *Strain of Violence: Historical Studies of American Violence and Vigilantism* (Oxford: Oxford University Press, 1975).

3. "Executing Bandits in Mexico 854" and "Un Bandido colgado en el ed de Nay, Mex," archive photos reproduced in "¡Vámonos a la Bola!", *Proceso*, Edición Especial no. 31, Nov. 2010.

4. The Mexican 2010 census found 15.7 million indigenous people, based on the definition of one adult member of the household speaking an indigenous language or self-identifying as indigenous.

Chapter 44

1. Rosa Santana, "Cártel de Jaliscó armó a autodefensas: Murillo Karam," *Proceso*, Jan. 30, 2014.

Chapter 45

1. Colleague Francisco Castellanos took a photo of the fallen man with the bazooka.

Chapter 47

1. *Cartel Land* was released at Sundance in 2015, directed by Matthew Heineman, with coproducer Myles Estey.

Chapter 48

1. From website www. anewyorkertravels.com in section "About Me."

Part VI: Peace?

Chapter 49

1. There is still debate about the impact of Portugal's reform, but the most convincing evidence suggests that the law has not had a major impact on the amount of drug use. A good overview of the debate and evidence is provided in Caitlin Hughes and Alex Stevens, "A resounding success or a disastrous

failure: Re-examining the interpretation of evidence on the Portuguese decriminalization of illicit drugs," *Drug and Alcohol Review*, vol. 31, Jan. 2012.

2. An annual Gallup poll shows a steady rise in support for marijuana legalization, with more than 50 percent in favor since 2014. Some other polls find more than 60 percent in favor.

3. I give a breakdown of these numbers and sources in my first book, *El Narco: Inside Mexico's Criminal Insurgency* (New York: Bloomsbury, 2011), 282–283 and 137–146.

4. Kidnapping and homicide rates published by Mexico's Sistema Nacional de Seguridad Pública.

Chapter 50

1. "Crime in Latin America: A Broken System," *The Economist*, July 12, 2014.

2. "Impunity in Honduras Highest in Central America at 96," Telesur, Dec. 2, 2014.

3. This point is made articulately by Joaquín Villalobos in "Bandidos, Estado y Ciudadanía," *Nexos*, Jan. 1, 2015.

4. Among these projects is Transparent Candidate, by the Mexican chapter of Transparency International.

Index

A Note on the Author

Ioan Grillo has reported on Latin America since 2001 for international media including *Time* magazine, *Reuters*, CNN, the *Associated Press*, PBS *NewsHour*, *GlobalPost*, the *Houston Chronicle*, CBC, the BBC World Service and the *Sunday Telegraph*. His first book, *El Narco: Inside Mexico's Criminal Insurgency*, was translated into five languages and was a finalist for the Los Angeles Times Book Prize and the Orwell Prize. A native of Britain, Grillo lives in Mexico City.